Hinsdale County, CO – A Magical Place!

Hinsdale County is located high in the San Juan Mountains of southwestern Colorado. The Continental Divide crosses Hinsdale County twice and the headwaters of the Rio Grande River and the Lake Fork of the Gunnison River, a tributary of the Colorado River, are located within the county. Geologically, seventy million years ago volcanic mountains formed in the western part of the county and the debris they spewed became the mesas formed in the eastern part of the county. About 1300 A.D. one of those mesas, Mesa Seco, broke apart and the resulting Slumgullion Earthflow formed a dam across the Lake Fork River forming Lake San Cristobal, the second largest natural lake in Colorado. Lake San Cristobal is the namesake lake for Lake City, the only incorporated town in Hinsdale County.

With a population of 800 in an area of 1,123 square miles, Hinsdale County is the most remote county in Colorado measured by population density. With only forty-five miles of paved roads over that area, it lays claim to being the most remote county in the lower forty-eight states.

Over 96% of Hinsdale County is public land. There are four National Forests and four Wilderness Areas within its borders. There are five peaks exceeding 14,000 feet and over twenty peaks exceeding 13,000 feet of elevation.

Given its natural attributes and remoteness, Hinsdale County has drawn outdoor enthusiasts of all stripes. It is a popular destination for hunters, fishermen, off-road vehicle enthusiasts, mountain bikers, runners, ice climbers, campers, and of course hikers.

I hope this guidebook helps you better enjoy Hinsdale County.

THE TRAILHEADS OF
HINSDALE COUNTY

David M. Dayvault

WESTERN REFLECTIONS PUBLISHING COMPANY®

Lake City, Colorado

ISBN 978-1-937851-68-2

First Edition
Printed in the United States

Cover, Text, and Maps Design by Laurie Casselberry
Laurie Goralka Design

Cover photo Uncompahgre Sunrise © Michael Underwood

Western Reflections Publishing Company
P. O. Box 1149
951 N. Highway 149
Lake City, Colorado 81235
www.westernreflectionspublishing.com
(970) 944-0110

Dedicated to the memory of Brian Landeck

1958-2005

CONTENTS

Forward and Dedication

One might ask what drives a Certified Public Accountant (CPA) in his sixties from Wichita, Kansas, who never aspired to be a writer, to undertake an effort such as this. While I've often thought that hiking provided a nice counterpoint to the activities which have consumed my career, the story begins much earlier.

Like many boys of my age, I joined the Boy Scouts upon turning eleven. I was fortunate to find a troop with many involved fathers and we had an active camping program. I embraced all that scouting had to offer, achieving my Eagle Scout rank and serving as a Scoutcraft Aide one summer at the local council wilderness camp, Quivira Scout Ranch. Over the course of my scouting career and continuing into adulthood, I've spent more than 365 nights inside a tent. However, the high point of my time as a Boy Scout came in the form of my three trips to Philmont Scout Ranch, a backpacker's delight containing over 214 square miles in the Sangre de Cristo Mountains of northern New Mexico. This high adventure experience involved ten days of backpacking in small groups. I was fourteen, fifteen and twenty at the time of each of my treks, the latter two led by our troop's Assistant Scoutmaster, Ken Landeck.

Ken had two sons in the troop, Don who was a year younger than I was and Brian who was four years my junior. As each of us aged out of scouting we wanted to continue backpacking. Some combination of the three of us went on twelve backpacking trips in the American West from 1975 to 1986. Don, having pursued degrees in civil and environmental engineering, was the organizer of most of them. When Don couldn't make the trip, those duties fell to me.

I lived in St. Louis for several years after college, returning to Wichita in 1978. Don's career took him between Houston and California. Brian also became a CPA, but after a period in public accounting, he found a more comfortable fit as an international taxation auditor for the Internal Revenue Service. His career with the IRS took him between Washington DC and Seattle. Thus, our trips required some coordination.

Each trip lasted about a week and took us primarily to national parks. Grand Canyon National Park, Rocky Mountain National Park, Zion National Park, and Grand Teton National Park all rated multiple visits. In 1984 Don planned a trip to the San Juan Mountains and I visited Lake City for the first time as the three of us climbed Uncompahgre Peak. Little did any of us know it at the time, but it was to be the final hike that the three of us were to take together.

Meanwhile, my hiking and camping experiences continued down another track. Shortly after returning to Wichita from St. Louis, I received a call from a friend of my father, Lee Phillips III, who was Scoutmaster of a small troop in Wichita. He was looking for an assistant with experience in the outdoor activities so crucial to a successful scouting experience. Lee was the grandson of one of the co-founders of Phillips 66 and the aforementioned Philmont Scout Ranch was previously owned by an uncle. After working with the troop for under a year, Lee asked me to succeed him as Scoutmaster, a position I held for the next seven years. Even before my tenure, the troop had a history of annual trips to Colorado and camping away from a formal scout camp setting. I continued this tradition for six years where we camped on land in Park County, south of Breckenridge. After several days we would move on to Buena Vista for a shower and then backpack for the remainder of the week. Brian Landeck accompanied me on the first of those trips.

After two more trips with Brian, I married in 1986 and the trips with the Landeck brothers ceased to be an annual event. While Amy was a good sport and we took several camping trips together, she was more of a beach person. As two sons arrived in 1989 and 1991, the prospects for more hiking and backpacking were put on hold. However, we still came to Colorado with some frequency and would rent a cabin in one place or another and take hikes appropriate for a family with small children.

When our marriage ended in 1996 and I had shared custody of the two boys, then aged seven and four, the prospects for backpacking diminished further. However, I saw that a successful vacation with my children needed to include mountains, a beach, an amusement park, or a lake. Lake City offered two of those. After several years of trips elsewhere in Colorado we came to Lake City in 2001 and never looked back. I purchased a lot in 2006 and built a house that was completed in 2012.

Meanwhile, Brian and I took one more trip together. In 2002, he and I signed up for an REI sponsored trek which included nine days of backpacking in Sequoia National Park, culminating in a climb of Mt. Whitney—the tallest mountain in the lower forty-eight. Brian had battled a weight problem throughout his life and he undertook a great deal of preparation for this trip, including climbing Mt. Elbert and Mt. Massive. By the time we began our trek, he was in better shape than I was. At the conclusion of the trip we both admitted it was the hardest thing that either of us had ever done. Two days after reaching the summit of Mt. Whitney, I said goodbye to him for what was to be the last time at the Fresno airport.

Brian Landeck died in a climbing accident in Washington in March 2005. Six months later Don Landeck and I scattered his ashes at the summit of Angel's Landing in Zion National Park. This book is dedicated to Brian's memory.

Once I completed my house in Lake City my hiking excursions began again, on steroids. As I strove to reach the higher altitudes with the better views, I got into better physical condition which in turn allowed me to go further, higher, and faster. I believe that is called a virtuous circle. I joined a group that hikes the Lake City area trails on Thursdays hoping to learn new trails and to teach others what I had learned. I also met some wonderful people.

In July 2017, Lake City Arts held a book signing and reading hosted by Kay Rock, who had recently published a book relating to retirement. Kay's husband, Steve, hiked with the Thursday group and he and I had become friends. The following morning, I led the group on a hike that had navigational challenges. At the end of the hike, Steve suggested that I write a hiking guide.

While I felt I could compose a passable business letter and I had written a column for the newsletters of two industry organizations that I had chaired, I never have been an aspiring writer. Perhaps though, I have been an aspiring teacher. Early in my career I felt I wanted to continue working as long as I was either learning or teaching others that which I had learned. I've since discovered that I never have stopped learning, and that I have enjoyed those instances where I've been able to pass on what I know.

That, in a roundabout way, has led me to write this book. I want to teach others what I have discovered about hiking in the Lake City area.

You may have noticed the similarity between the title of this book and that of the novel by Robert James Waller, *The Bridges of Madison County*, which was made into a 1995 movie starring Clint Eastwood and Meryl Streep. In addition to the similarity of the titles, this book shares another thing with the Waller novel. It too is a romance.

Brian Landeck

Brian Landeck

Introduction

In writing this book my purpose was to create something that would be useful over a number of years for anyone wanting to hike in the Lake City, Colorado area. I'm trying to serve the day hiker, not necessarily the mountain climber or the backpacker. There are any number of climbing guides that serve the former and most of the backpackers I've seen in the area are on the Colorado Trail. Their needs are well served by Colorado Trail Foundation's Official Guidebook.

This is not the first guidebook covering trails in the Lake City area. I've read, used, and admired the book *Lake City Hiking* by Lyn Lampert. It is a compilation of eighteen articles that appeared in a magazine published by Lyn promoting the Lake City area that appeared in the late 1980s. As discussed later, trails are constantly evolving as trails are created, re-routed, or reclaimed by nature. This book covers more territory and should serve as a useful update and supplement to Lyn's guidebook.

Maps of the area are another resource for the hiker, although each has its strengths and limitations. I have an extensive set of Quadrangle maps produced by the U. S. Geological Survey. These will show in the greatest detail those features which were present based upon aerial surveys. However, most of those surveys occurred decades ago. There are several *Trails Illustrated* maps produced by National Geographic which indicate many trails in the area, some of which I've never been able to locate. The scale of the *Trails Illustrated* map is much smaller and the contour lines can be hard to read. Finally, the U. S. Forest Service produced maps of the area covered by National Forests and other public lands. These maps have a still smaller scale and do not show any contours. All of these maps show trails that are no longer present and omit other trails that are.

Trails are created by man in an area ruled by nature. What man creates nature can take away. Without regular use trails begin to disappear, particularly in open grassy areas. While posts and cairns have been placed to designate the pathway in many open grassy areas, those posts, cairns, and other trail signs can and will fall under the forces unleashed by nature. There are trails created by wild game or stock animals that have nothing to do with the trail you are seeking. There are trails created by hunters and their horses that will lead you only to their campsites. However, there are several general rules. Many of these trails had their genesis as mining trails or roads. The excavation work done by the early pioneers has generally withstood the ravages of nature. Where water runoff has created streams, the streambeds will be present even if the waterflow is intermittent. Elevations and contour lines can be relied upon. While the boundaries between wooded and open areas can change slightly, they are still pretty good indicators of what type of terrain to expect. Trails hold up better in wooded areas than in open areas. If you lose a trail in an open area, you may be able to find it again as it enters the woods. Rock cairns remain good trail indicators. If it seems unclear why a rock cairn was placed in a particular spot, it may be clearer when you are going in the opposite direction. In other areas, ask yourself what the most likely path is to take if you were making the trail. This requires a clear understanding of the ultimate destination of the trail. When in doubt, go back to where you were last certain of being on the correct trail and return to your starting point if necessary. In writing this guide, I am trying to create something that will be useful over a period of many years. However, the tension between man and nature will render any hikers guide useful only so long as the trails remain active enough to overcome the efforts of nature to reclaim its own. Nature will always have the last word. This guide was written between 2017 and 2022, and each section reflects the conditions on the day that I last hiked the trail. This includes the effects of the severe winter of 2018-2019 and the resulting avalanche activity.

This guide is organized by geographical area and then by trailheads. Where trails fork and several options present themselves, I'll discuss these in sequence under the listing of each trailhead. This approach has its limitations as many of our trail systems interconnect in such a way that you can enter at one trailhead and exit at another. When this occurs, I'll refer you to the section discussing the appropriate extension of the trail. As this guide is designed for the day hiker, those breaks may seem to occur at an arbitrary point and not necessarily at a campsite or trail intersection. Despite the title of this book, some of the trailheads are located in adjacent counties where the trail leads into Hinsdale County. The focus is to serve the hiker who is using Lake City as a base.

The individual trailheads are organized by area: those in close proximity of town, those north of town accessible from Colorado State Highway 149, those west of town accessible from County Road 20 following Henson Creek, those southwest of town accessible from County Road 30 following the Lake Fork of the Gunnison River, those south and east of town accessible from Colorado State Highway 149, those south and east of town accessible from the Cebolla Creek Road (also known as the Deer Lakes Road, County Road 50 and Forest Service Road 788), and those south of Spring Creek Pass accessible from Colorado State Highway 149. A hike is only as good as the hiker's ability to reach the trailhead and each trailhead begins with a description of how to locate it. The names of the trailheads given in this guide come from different sources. Some come from the designations of the Forest Service, others from local usage, and a few I've designated myself. When a trailhead has multiple names in common use, I've tried to include them.

I've included fifty-one trailheads in this guide, which form the bulk of the narrative. At the end of the book, I've included a postscript containing my opinions as to which hikes are particularly suited to each season of the year as well as which have seasonal challenges. I've also provided lists of hikes that are particularly popular, those where you are likely to enjoy the trail by yourself, and those that seem hardly worth the effort. Also included in the postscript are lists of hikes that are particularly suited to beginners and shorter hikes. Finally, I've included alternatives to going and returning by the same route.

All trails vary in difficulty. Depending on the hiker, a difficult hike might be based upon the length, the elevation gain, the terrain, or navigation issues. I've discussed each of these for each trail and I will let the reader use his or her own judgment. Having said that, I've indicated which hikes are suitable for beginning, intermediate, or experienced hikers. Also, some trails are better suited to different times of the year depending on snow melt, the prevalence of mosquitos, seasonal wildflowers, stream flow, and other factors.

In a further effort to make this guide useful, I've indicated where water crossing shoes are helpful at certain times of the year. Having said that, there are certain streams where the waterflow is such that the support of boots is best. Having overcome the hesitancy to hike in wet boots, I prefer at times to plow on through rather than take the time to change into water crossing shoes which may not provide the support needed to cross a swift flowing stream with a rocky bottom. I keep an old pair of boots for this purpose and will indicate those water crossings where I have found this practice helpful.

I've indicated the trailhead elevation and the total elevation gain for each hike. This is a net number, and most hikes will have their share of ascents and descents. Still, I usually find climbing 3,000 feet more challenging than climbing 300 feet ten times. The return trip is another matter, and I will note those hikes that have significant climbs on their return. A climb late in the return trip can be demoralizing.

All distances are approximate and distances driven are expressed in decimal form (i.e. 1.5 miles) based upon odometer readings and are more precise than distances hiked. Distances hiked are generally rounded to the nearest .25 miles.

While over 96% of Hinsdale County is public land, you should be respectful of the rights of private property owners. I've tried to indicate where trails cross private land. Not all of the boundaries are marked. While there are some fences on public land, the existence of fencing is a good indicator that you are adjacent to private land. The existence of mining relics is also a good indicator that the land may be private as Hinsdale County has many patented mining claims.

I think that you will find that the trails included in the guide contain some of the best hiking that the San Juans and Colorado have to offer. I hope that this guide can enhance your experience.

Happy hiking.

A Word of Caution

While the back country of Hinsdale County is beautiful, it is also unforgiving. Having hiked the area over many years I've learned to respect what nature has given us. I've made my share of mistakes while hiking and by following the news reports I've seen many mistakes made by others.

"A man's got to know his limitations." This was said by Harry Callahan, played by Clint Eastwood in the 1973 film *Magnum Force*. That holds true with hiking. Each hiker needs to be aware of his or her own health conditions and limit his or her activities accordingly. We've had several deaths in Hinsdale County in recent years from visitors in the back country who succumbed to coronary and pulmonary disease. If you have a health event while in the back country, it can take a long time to receive medical attention.

Be aware of the upcoming weather conditions. While hiking early in the day can reduce the chances of being caught in a thunderstorm, storms occur in the morning as well. In addition to lightning, the storm dangers include hypothermia due to high winds and falling temperatures.

Be aware of the road conditions. The risks associated with hiking don't begin at the trailhead. Many of our trailheads involve driving over roads that are challenging in the best of times. Following a heavy rain, some places along these roads remain too slick to hold a vehicle should it lose traction.

Even the most careful of hikers are likely to suffer a fall from time to time. Some of the trails contain loose, pebbly rock which is treacherous when the slope is more than modest. These sections are more dangerous while descending. I've tried to identify these places in the narrative. Trekking poles can help you regain your balance at times, but don't eliminate the risk of falling.

You should carry water, rain gear, and extra clothing at all times. Conditions change throughout the day and you'll want to be able to shed or add a layer of clothing as circumstances change.

In my years of hiking, I've been fortunate to have not encountered a situation that I or my hiking mates have not been able to handle without outside assistance. I recognize that may not always be the case. I carry a Colorado Search and Rescue (COSAR) card and I encourage all hikers to obtain and carry such a card which are available online or through several sources in town. The cost is quite modest. The proceeds from these sales go to support the local and state search and rescue efforts. Each year there are multiple calls for search and rescue operations in the Lake City area and the volunteers of the local team devote countless hours under adverse conditions to help rescue distressed hikers. I salute their efforts.

As I often hike alone, should I get into trouble I carry a satellite beacon which can be activated in the event that rescue efforts are needed. Once purchased, these devices must be registered with the National Oceanic and Atmospheric Administration (NOAA) giving the user's identity and emergency contact information. Once activated, a signal is given via satellite to NOAA which in turn contacts the local authorities giving them the name and GPS coordinates of the distressed hiker. Mine is a basic model and other models are available with additional features. Your cellphone will be out of range during most of the hikes contained in this guide.

I hope that by using the suggestions above, you can have a safer hike with less anxiety. Enjoy.

Tips For Using This Guidebook

In preparing this guidebook, I've tried to include most of the trailheads and trails that appear on commonly used maps and trails that are in common usage. Many of our trailheads serve multiple trails and many of these trail systems are interconnected. As a result, there are challenges in constructing this narrative as I wanted to include quite a bit of information but still make that information understandable to the reader. Many of the trailheads contain trails that branch off at some point while the narrative continues along a main trail, only to return to the side trail later. This can be confusing. In an effort to avoid confusion, I've adopted the following organizational devise:

Each trailhead is assigned a number, from one to fifty-one. The trail beginning at the trailhead is assigned that number, plus the letter A. Various points along the trail are assigned that number plus a letter (B, C and so on). When a trail beginning at one trailhead connects with a trail beginning at another trailhead, that point is marked by the number and a letter of the originating trail while the name of the connecting trail is designated on the map. These numbers and letters appear in the narrative when discussing the trail intersections and are also designated on the maps accompanying the narrative for each trailhead. The narrative and the maps are meant to be used together.

For example: *Waterdog Lake – From Town* has been designated trailhead 3. The main trail leading to Waterdog Lake has been designated trail 3A and the Waterdog Lake trailhead has been marked 3A on the map. There is a side trail leading to Station Eleven and the intersection point of these two trails has been marked 3B on the map. Later the main trail is joined by the trail called *Waterdog Lake – From CO SH 149*. That point is designated 3E and the intersecting trail is indicated as "Waterdog Lake – From CO SH 149" on the map. The destinations are marked as well. Waterdog Lake is designated 3C and Station Eleven is designated 3D.

Hinsdale County contains much wild and rugged country. Many of the trails included in this guidebook should not be attempted by the casual hiker. I've included a rating system indicating which trails are best suited for beginning, intermediate, or experienced hikers and those descriptions are listed at the conclusion of each section of the narrative. In an attempt to help the casual hiker select a suitable hike, I've also listed the trails designated by trailhead number, including the letter designating the trail's beginning and ending points, beginning elevation, elevation gain, mileage, and the rating in the appendix.

Trail guides are not meant to be read cover to cover. In using this guide, after reading the opening segments, you may wish to jump to the postscript. In that I've included some recommendations as to which trails you might enjoy and those that you might wish to avoid.

In selecting a hike, give due consideration to weather and likely trail conditions as well as to your own abilities. Many hikers select a hike based upon the recommendations of others or familiarity with the trail. Other hikers are looking for something new and welcome the adventure. You'll find both in *The Trailheads of Hinsdale County*.

ABBREVIATIONS USED –
CO SH – Colorado State Highway
FSR – Forest Service Road
CR – County Road
MP – Milepost
4WD – Four Wheel Drive
ATV – All Terrain Vehicle
BLM – Bureau of Land Management
USGS – United States Geological Survey
Quad – Quadrangle map produced by the United States Geological Survey
GPS – Global Positioning System

The Colorado Trail and the Continental Divide Trail both cross Hinsdale County and they overlap for much of the territory covered by this guide. For convenience I refer to the sections where they overlap as the Colorado Trail, unless there is a reason to do otherwise.

When referring to *Trails Illustrated* maps, there are three which cover the trails discussed in this book. Unless otherwise noted, when I refer to the *Trails Illustrated* map, I'm referring to the "Telluride, Silverton, Ouray, Lake City" map. The other maps covering the area are labeled "La Garita, Cochetopa Hills," and "Weminuche Wilderness."

American Basin

Katherine Heidt

Upper Vickers Ranch below Station Eleven

Glenn Heumann

Trailheads Located in Greater Lake City

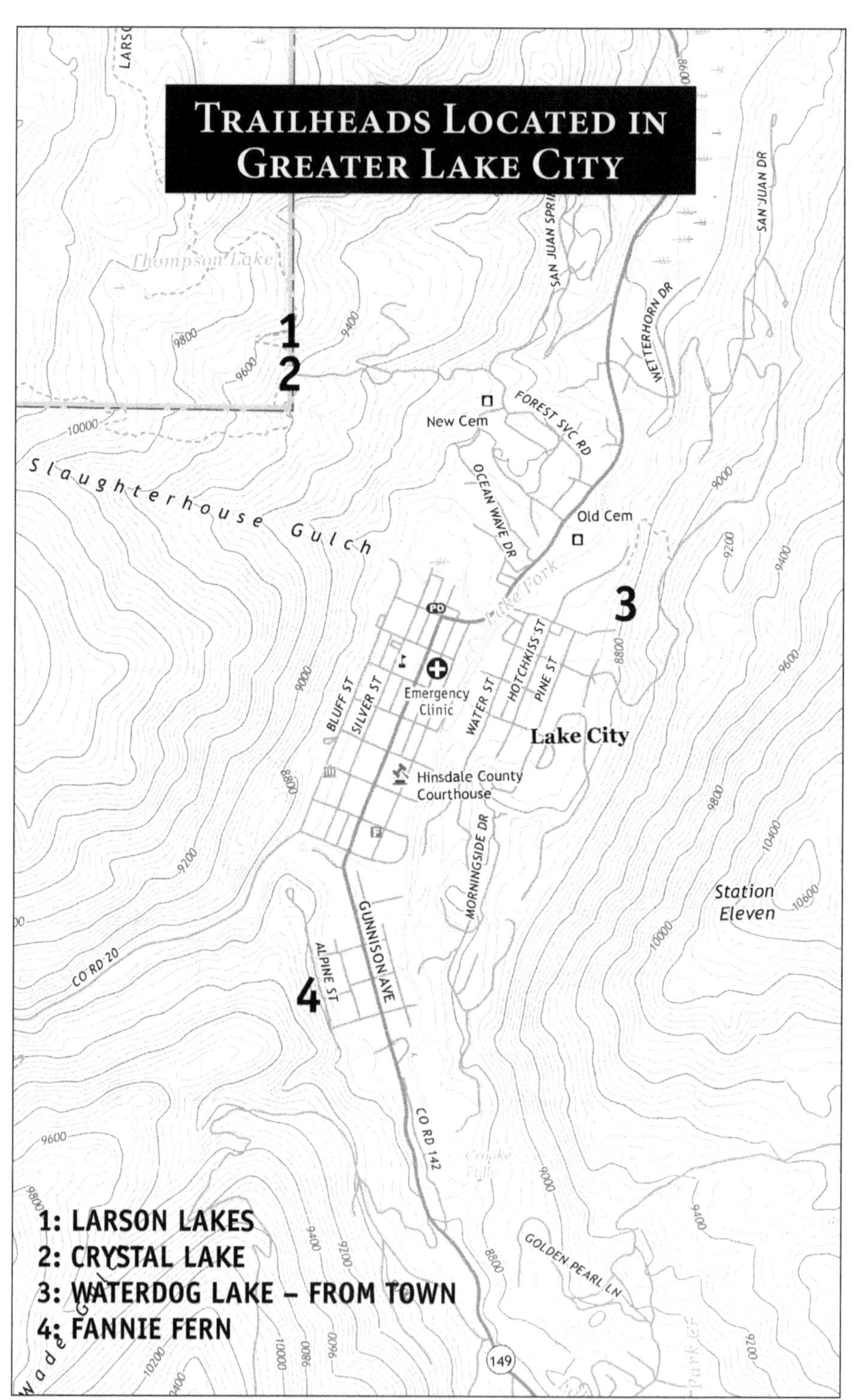

1: LARSON LAKES
2: CRYSTAL LAKE
3: WATERDOG LAKE – FROM TOWN
4: FANNIE FERN

LARSON LAKES

Quad: Lake City

DRIVING INSTRUCTIONS: From town drive north on CO SH 149. After passing the city limits, look to your left for a sign indicating the way to the Crystal Lake and Larson Lake trailheads and the IOOF Cemetery. Drive west on Balsam Rd. to the cemetery parking area. If you are 4WD equipped, you may want to go the additional .7 miles to the trailheads for both Crystal Lake and Larson Lakes. Parking is limited to about five vehicles at this trailhead. Trailhead elevation - 9,400 feet. If you park at the IOOF Cemetery add .7 miles (each way) and 500 feet to the distances and elevations referred to below.

THE HIKE: The Larson Lakes Trail continues beyond Larson Lakes to connect with the Independence Gulch Trail system and the trail leading to Crystal Lake. Either of those hikes would be longer than most hikers would want to undertake in a single day, but are worthwhile nonetheless. The trail leading to Larson Lakes is well marked and much of it follows an old logging road. For some reason, this trail is popular with mosquitos, and you may wish to avoid it during June and early July. This trail appears on both the *Trails Illustrated* map, and the portion to Larson Lakes appears on the quad.

From the Larson Lakes trailhead (**1A**) you begin a moderate ascent almost immediately in terrain which alternates between open areas and mixed forest. As you head north, there are several good views of the town of Lake City below. After .5 miles the trail veers to the left and you are in mixed forest for most of the rest of the way. At the 1-mile mark you will encounter a trail sign showing the cutoff to Thompson Lake, to your left (**1B**). Thompson Lake (**1D**) is a good destination early in the season or if you only have time for a short hike. Continuing to the right toward Larson Lakes you continue to climb gradually during the next mile through forest that is primarily aspen. Remember this hike for mid-September. At the 2-mile mark, the trail flattens for almost a mile as you are heading west utilizing an old logging road. As you turn right to leave this road, you will descend to the first of many water crossings. None of these is particularly wide and after the spring runoff you should not need water crossing shoes. During this next mile you will be ascending generally, although descents prior to several of the water crossings are present. The ascents become more frequent as you approach the 4-mile point, and you will alternate between forest and clearings. Upon reaching the largest clearing you are almost to the trail cutoff, which is at the far end of the clearing. There the trail sign indicates that Larson Lakes, via the Larson Lakes Cutoff Trail, lie .5 miles to your left (**1C**). The main Larson Lakes Trail continues straight ahead, to the point where it connects with the Little Elk Trail, servicing the Independence Gulch region and the Crystal Lake Trail. If you wish to take the side trip to Larson Lakes, you will be rewarded with a view of the lakes, which are idyllic, but only after a steep 400-foot climb over the last .5 miles. At Larson Lakes (**1E**) you will find several good camping spots as well as views of Crystal Peak and the Clay Pots.

Continuing north from the Larson Lakes (**1C**) turnoff you immediately enter a forest, and your ascent is gradual to moderate gaining 400 feet over the .5 miles that it takes to reach the trail sign indicating the intersection with the Little Elk Trail (**1F**). The sign shows Little Elk Trail and Independence Gulch to the right and the Larson Lakes Trail continuing straight ahead. The rest of the Larson Lakes Trail is discussed under the section for Crystal Lake, as this is part of the return route from the Crystal Lake / Larson Lakes loop.

While the Crystal Lake / Larson Lakes loop can be undertaken from either direction, most hikers will want to start on the Crystal Lake side. Using this direction, you do most of your climbing early, as Crystal Lake is 1,000 feet higher than Larson Lakes. If you were to begin at the Larson Lakes trailhead there is a 1,400-foot climb from the Larson Lakes cutoff to the top of a mesa.

From the trail sign indicating the turnoff to the Little Elk Trail and Independence Gulch (**1F**), you descend 1,400 feet over the course of 2 miles, hiking alongside, but well above Independence Gulch. The trail connects the Larson Lakes/Crystal Lake Trail system with the

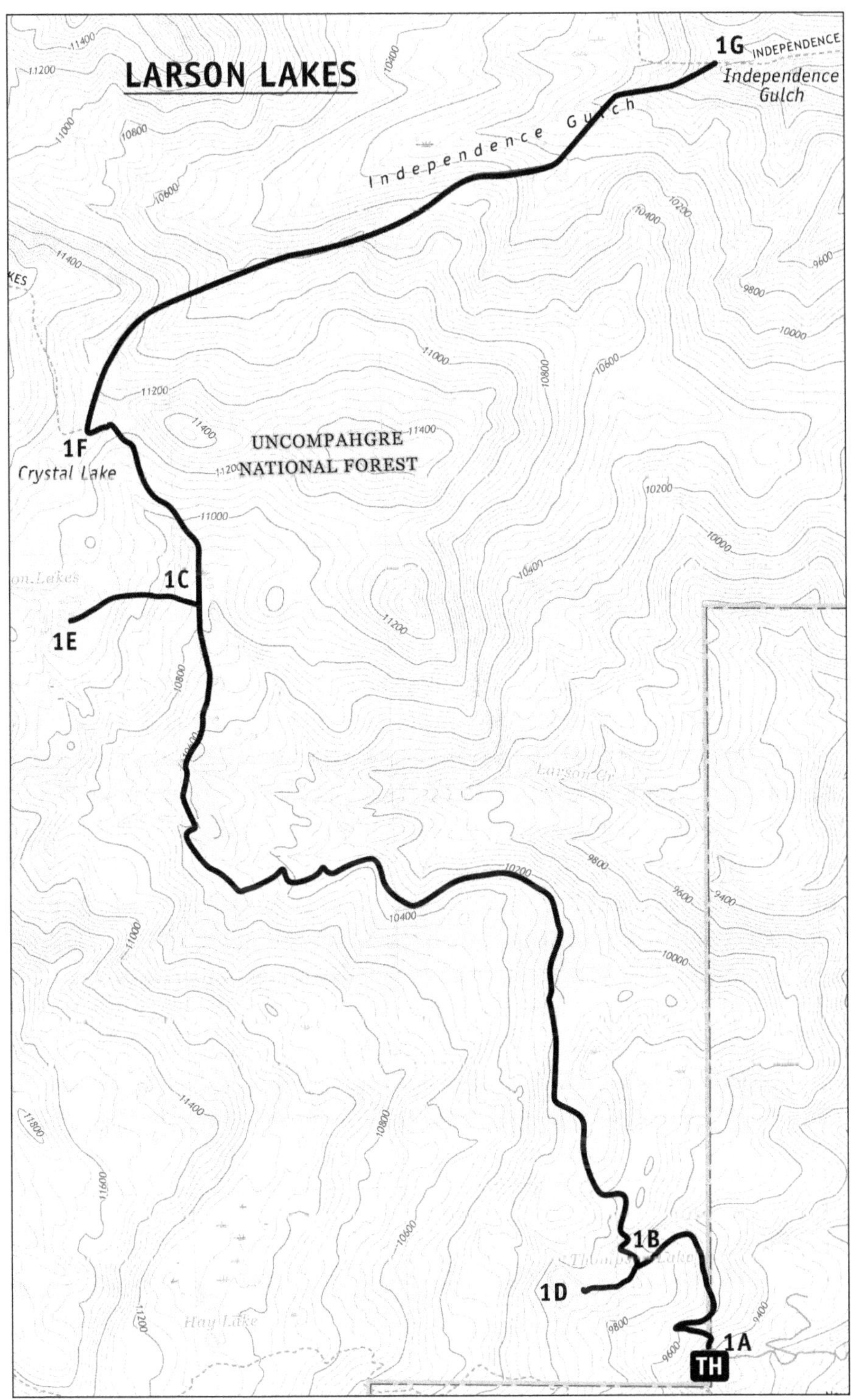
1G
INDEPENDENCE
Independence
Gulch
LARSON LAKES
Independence Gulch
1F
Crystal Lake
UNCOMPAHGRE
NATIONAL FOREST
1C
1E
Larson Cr
1B
1D
1A
TH

Independence Gulch Trail system. It receives little use and can be confusing in spots.

From the trail sign (**1F**), head north toward the woods. The trail may not be fully evident in the open area, but there is a post indicating the point where the trail enters the woods. The trail is better developed in the forest and on the upper portion of the trail. The descent is moderate most of the way with a few steeper sections. You are in forest for most of the way. After 1.5 miles the trail enters a clearing and is well marked along the clearing's edge. After passing through this first clearing and reentering the forest, there is a second clearing shortly afterward. The trail is overgrown in the second clearing, but it redevelops at the base of this second clearing. The trail becomes increasingly difficult to follow as you approach Independence Gulch, which can be crossed without stream crossing shoes for most of the season. After crossing Independence Gulch, the trail is difficult to find on the far side. If you have difficulty finding it, climb toward a clearing on the north side of the stream and the trail will be evident at the lower end of that clearing. You then reenter the woods and descend toward a second stream, a tributary of Independence Gulch. After this second stream crossing and a short ascent, you will encounter the Independence Gulch Trail, on the southern portion of its loop, which has a wooden post indicating the trail you are on leads to Larson Lakes (**1G**). The remainder of the Independence Gulch Trail is discussed in that section.

RATING: The trail to Thompson Lake (**1D**) and return covers 2 miles and gains 1,000 feet. It is within the capabilities of any beginner. The trail to Larson Lakes (**1E**) and back covers 10 miles and gains 1,700 feet. Despite its length, it should be accessible to most intermediate hikers, although the last portion can be challenging. The trail to the Independence Gulch loop intersection (**1G**) and back covers 15 miles and climbs 1,800 feet before descending 1,400 feet. The difficulty of following this trail should limit it to the most experienced hikers.

CRYSTAL LAKE

Quad: Lake City, Uncompahgre Peak

DRIVING INSTRUCTIONS: From town drive north on CO SH 149. After passing the city limits look to your left for a sign indicating the way to the Crystal Lake and Larson Lake trailheads and the IOOF Cemetery. Drive west on Balsam Rd to the cemetery parking area. If you are 4WD equipped, you may want to go the additional .7 miles to the trailheads for both Crystal Lake and Larson Lakes. Parking is limited to about five vehicles at this trailhead. Trailhead elevation - 9,400 feet. If you park at the IOOF Cemetery add .7 miles (each way) and 500 feet to the distances and elevations referred to below.

THE HIKE: The Crystal Lake Trail goes for 4 miles where it forks to turn left to Crystal Lake or right to loop back by Larson Lakes and return to your starting point. This trail system also connects to the Ridge Stock Driveway and there is a separate connection to the Little Elk Trail which accesses the Independence Gulch Trail system and points northward. The trail to Crystal Lake and the loop as far as the Little Elk Trail intersection is discussed in this section. The remaining portion of the Crystal Lake / Larson Lakes loop is discussed in the section for Larson Lakes. The connection with the Independence Gulch Trail system is discussed under the section for Larson Lakes. The connection with the Ridge Stock Driveway is not covered in this book. In addition, Crystal Peak can be climbed from the Crystal Lake side, although that is not the most popular route for climbing Crystal Peak. For some reason, this trail is popular with mosquitos and you may wish to avoid it during June and early July. All of these trail systems appear both on the *Trails Illustrated* map and on the quads.

The trail to Crystal Lake begins behind the retaining gate at the trailhead and is marked with a trail sign (**2A**). After a short distance you cross a creek, which should be passable without water crossing shoes at any time of the year. You then begin a steady moderate climb which doesn't really let up for the whole trip to Crystal Lake. You pass through a wooded area into a large open area which allows views of the town of Lake City below. Later, you enter an aspen grove, then an open area before passing through a second aspen grove. By the time you emerge from the second aspen grove, you have gone over 2 miles, covered over half of the distance to Crystal Lake, and have climbed 1,500 feet. Upon emerging from the second aspen grove, you will find a fairly flat rockslide area on your left and an evergreen forest on your right. Shortly afterward, you will pass quickly through another evergreen forested area and find yourself again with a rockslide on your left and an evergreen forest on your right. Looking to your right you should see Hay Lake, which is surrounded by forest. Hay Lake is rather unremarkable compared to Crystal Lake. You then veer toward the left and climb through another forested area with a rockslide to your right. Even with passing all these rockslides, you never cross much rock and the trail is in good condition to Crystal Lake. You then pass through a series of short, rocky switchbacks which take you by a picture window view of Mesa Seco and Station Eleven before switching back to the left and hiking along a ridge. Along this ridge, you will get views of the mountains on the south side of Henson Creek. The climb lessens somewhat, and this final portion of the trail is the most enjoyable.

You will reach a point where the trail appears to divide. Both forks rejoin after .5 miles. I've generally chosen the trail which goes to the right, above the left fork, however on my most recent trip it was blocked by a large, downed tree that wasn't easy to bypass. The left fork has fewer visual obstructions offering better views to the south. The right fork avoids a steep climb shortly before the trails merge. Your pick. After the trails merge you climb up the Crystal Lake drainage and onto a flat meadow. The trail cuts to the left and a trail sign (**2B**) indicates that by going to the left you will reach Crystal Lake (**2E**), which is 100 yards away.

Crystal Lake is, in my opinion, the prettiest mountain lake in the area. It has wooded areas around much of the lake and contains a small, wooded island. There are several nice campsites and two picnic tables. Should you want to camp at Crystal Lake there are several nice side-hikes, including an ascent of Crystal Peak. The preferred trail to Crystal

Peak comes from the west and is discussed under the Crystal Peak / Clay Pots section. Twice I've attempted to climb Crystal Peak from the south side of Crystal Lake, climbing north toward the saddle separating Crystal Peak and the Clay Pots. Both times I reached rockslides and boulder fields and felt uneasy moving forward as some of this rock was loose. Both times I turned back. While the trail is unmarked, I've spoken with hikers that have climbed Crystal Peak from the south side of Crystal Lake so I know it can be done. I just can't recommend it based upon my experience. If you wish to climb Crystal Peak from Crystal Lake, there is a second way, which leaves the Crystal / Larson loop 2 miles past Crystal Lake which follows grassy areas throughout. This route is discussed below **(2C)**.

For a shorter side hike from the lake, you should go around the southern end of the lake. There is a drainage from the lake which you will need to cross so you should keep some distance and elevation between you and the lake as you begin this side-hike. There is a trail which comes and goes leading south from the lake through an open area, before disappearing into the woods. If you continue south after this trail disappears, there is a saddle which is the low point in the ridge separating the Crystal Lake drainage from the Henson Creek drainage **(2F)**. This ridge has fine views of the Henson Creek drainage, Uncompahgre and Wetterhorn Peaks, and other points south and west.

From the trail marker designating the turnoff to Crystal Lake **(2B)**, should you go to the right you will be on the trail that loops back to Larson Lakes and the trailhead where you parked. You proceed through an open area where the trail may be overgrown in places, but posts are present to assist you. This section gains elevation very modestly and enters a lightly wooded area less than .5 miles from the trail intersection. The trail turns toward the west as it passes through the wooded area, passing a small pond gaining elevation in fits and starts. At one point the trail descends across an open draw with a small pond near the bottom of the draw before ascending the other side and back into forest. After emerging from the forest, nearly 2 miles from Crystal Lake, there is a spot where you appear to have clear passage to a saddle to the north of Crystal Peak and a good view of the peak. While both of these are illusory, this is the route to Crystal Peak referred to above and it will be discussed later in this section **(2C)**.

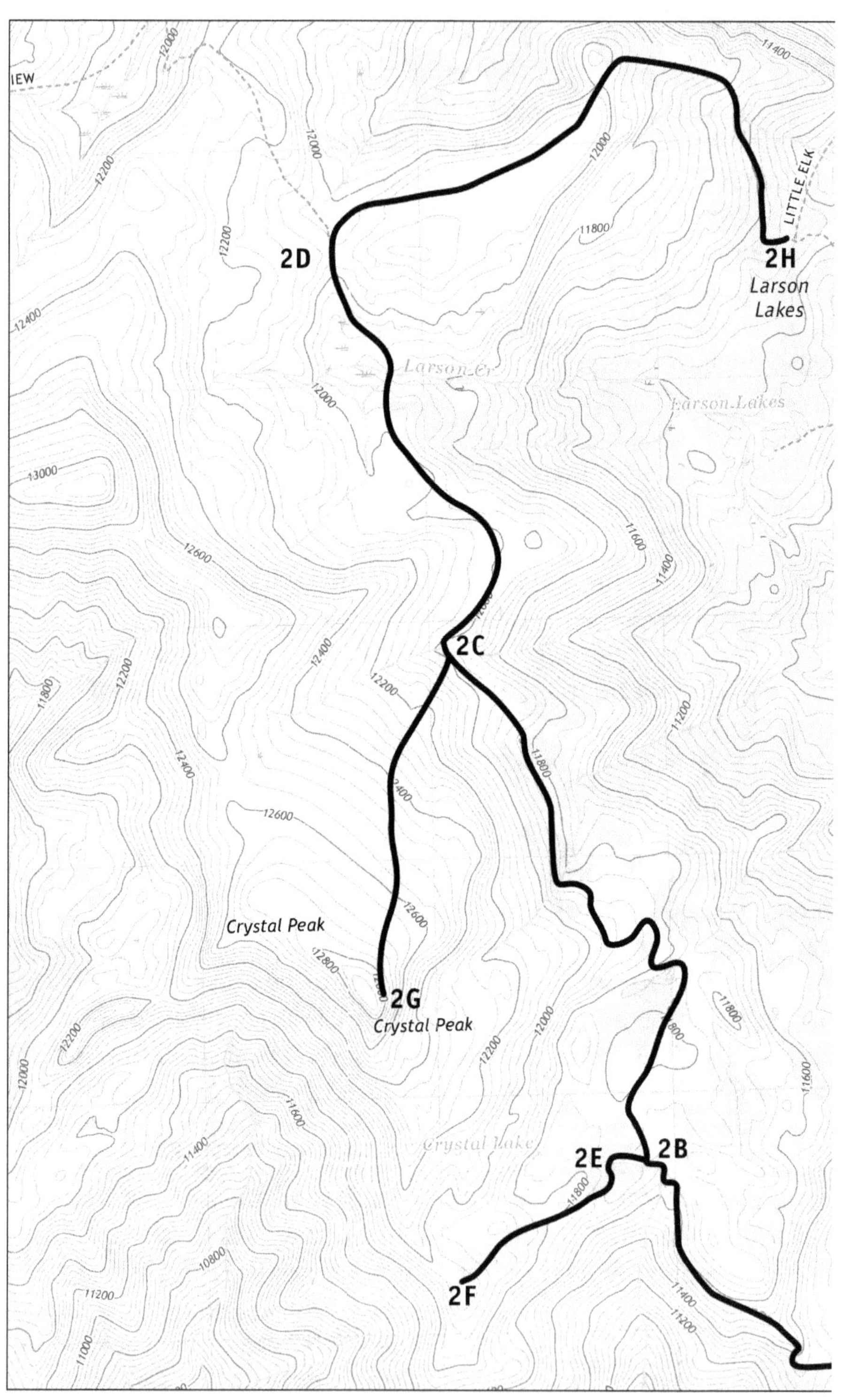
IEW
12000
12200
11400
12000
11800
2D
2H
LITTLE ELK
Larson
Lakes
12400
12200
12000
Larson Cr
Larson Lakes
13000
11600
12600
11400
12400
11800
2C
12200
12200
11200
11800
12400
12600
2400
12600
11800
Crystal Peak
12800
12200
2G
800
11800
Crystal Peak
12200
12000
11600
12000
11600
Crystal Lake
2E
2B
11400
11800
10800
2F
11200
11400
11000
11200

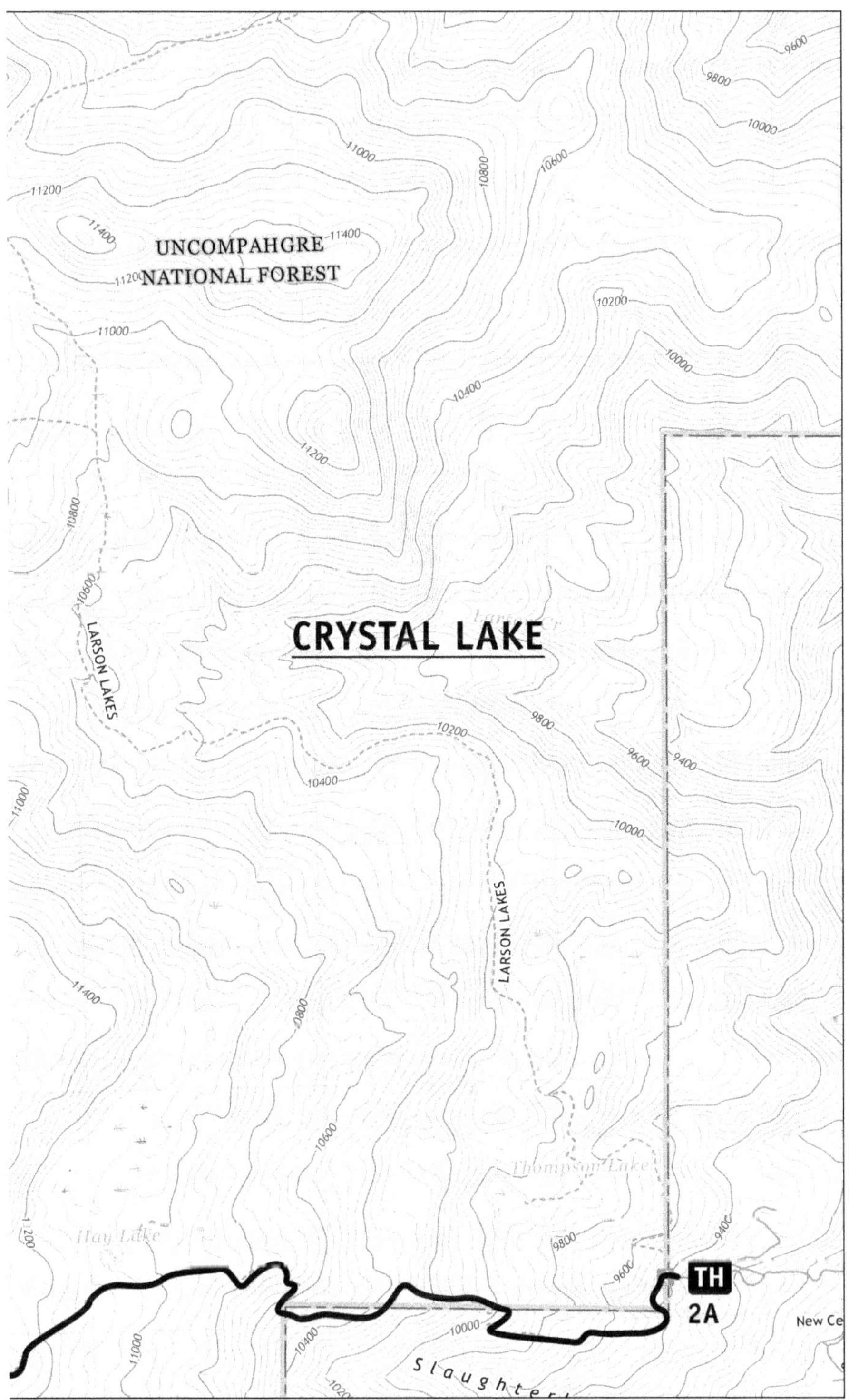

9600
9800
10000
11000
10800
10600
11200
11400
10200
10000
UNCOMPAHGRE
NATIONAL FOREST
11200
11000
11400
10400
11200
10800
10600
LARSON LAKES
CRYSTAL LAKE
10200
9800
9600
9400
10400
11000
10000
LARSON LAKES
11400
10800
10000
10600
Thompson Lake
11200
Hay Lake
9800
9600
9400
TH
2A
New Ce
Slaughter
10000
10400
10200

The terrain begins to change at this point as most of the time you are in the open and there are several semi-flat areas, similar to mesas, with drainage draws between them. You will cross three draws, each larger than the last and ascend to a flat area after each draw. The first two draws only have water seasonally while the third has a stream which flows year-round. By the time you have reached the second draw you can see the geologic formation known as the Clay Pots above and to your left. This formation and directions to reach it are discussed under the Crystal Peak / Clay Pots section. The Clay Pots will remain within sight for quite a while as the area is open and you are traveling in a semi-circular fashion around them. The remaining views from the middle section of this loop trail are quite stunning as there is quite a contrast with the mesas and the surrounding exposed rock.

After ascending from the third draw, containing the stream crossing, you will pass over a saddle and descend toward the intersection with a trail which will connect you with the Ridge Stock Driveway (**2D**). The connecting trail is not covered in this book. The trail sign indicates that the Larson Lakes Trail is to your right and the trail connecting with the Ridge Stock Driveway is straight ahead to the north. You will have traveled 3.5 miles from Crystal Lake to reach this point and will have gained and lost up to 200 feet three times. While the elevation gain from the trailhead to the high point of the trail is 3,200 feet, the gross amount climbed is over 3,500 feet.

At the trail intersection (**2D**) there are also two posts, the taller one being part of a series of posts leading to the top of a mesa along the Larson Lakes Trail. As the short grass on the side of the mesa gives way to tundra on top of the mesa, these posts are your best guides. You will climb 200 feet to the top of the mesa which is the high point on this loop, and you have no noteworthy climbs after reaching the top of the mesa. The mesa is flat for the .75 miles that you are along its top. As you reach the north end of the mesa, there is a post, followed soon afterward by a cairn, which will lead you down a rocky draw to start your descent.

Descending from the mesa, the trail is difficult to follow at times. You are descending a fairly steep draw, using multiple switchbacks. Later the trail enters a wooded area, and the trail becomes a bit easier to follow until you reach an open area covered with sand and gravel and the trail is nowhere to be found. The trail will emerge to your right (south) signified by a small cairn and as you descend 50 yards from this open area the trail will become better defined as you enter the woods. Later, the trail widens as it utilizes a logging road for a distance. Continue through the woods until you see the trail sign connecting the Larson Lakes Trail to the Little Elk Trail, leading to Independence Gulch **(2H)**. This trail is covered under the section for Larson Lakes as is the rest of the Larson Lakes Trail leading you to the trailhead where you started.

While the Crystal Lake / Larson Lakes loop can be undertaken from either direction, most hikers will want to start on the Crystal Lake side. Using this direction, you do most of your climbing early, as Crystal Lake is 1,000 feet higher than Larson Lakes. If you were to begin at the Larson Lakes trailhead there is a 1,400-foot climb from the Larson Lakes cutoff to the top of the mesa.

Returning to the point nearly 2 miles from Crystal Lake where you appear to have a clear view of Crystal Peak and the saddle to the north of the peak **(2C)**, this is your departure point for a good approach to Crystal Peak. What appears to be Crystal Peak is actually a formation below the peak which blocks your view of the peak. What appears to be the saddle north of the peak is actually the first of several false saddles as you approach the peak. Nevertheless, the terrain is tundra for the duration of the approach and there are few rocks as you climb steeply toward this saddle, then another and then another. Crystal Peak will become visible as you climb, and you can make your way across the tundra toward the peak. As peaks go, Crystal Peak is quite accessible from this direction. Once you reach the summit **(2G)**, there are several high points. Crystal Lake is visible from the furthest of these high points and just to the east of that point. The views from Crystal Peak are unparalleled.

RATING: The trail to Crystal Lake **(2E)** and back covers 8 miles and has an elevation gain of 2,400 feet. This can be done by an intermediate hiker but may be a bit challenging. The side hike from Crystal Lake to the Henson Creek divide **(2F)** adds 2 miles and 200 feet of elevation gain. The Crystal Lake / Larson Lakes loop **(2A)** covers 14 miles and has a net elevation gain of 2,800 feet and a gross elevation gain exceeding 3,500 feet. In addition, there are challenges in finding your way as the section of the trail between the lakes is not used a great deal. The loop should be attempted only by experienced hikers. A round trip hike to Crystal Peak (**2G**) leaving the trail 2 miles beyond Crystal Lake covers 15 miles with an elevation gain of 3,500 feet. It too should be limited to experienced hikers.

Crystal Peak and Crystal Lake

Katherine Heidt

WATERDOG LAKE – FROM TOWN

Quad: Lake City

DRIVING INSTRUCTIONS: From the center of town go north on CO SH 149 crossing the Lake Fork of the Gunnison River on the 8½ Street bridge. From the east side of the river drive one block north, then a block east then another block north until you arrive at the town wastewater plant. Parking for the trail is marked at the plant. Trailhead elevation - 8,700 feet.

THE HIKE: This trail takes you from town rather steeply out of the Lake Fork Valley to a gentle park area. From there you can continue on the trail to Waterdog Lake or take a shorter, but unmarked trip, up to a point marked as Station Eleven which offers some of the best views of the town and the surrounding areas. The trail has the advantages of leaving from town and good drainage, making it a good option for a day following a rainstorm. The trail to Waterdog Lake appears on both the *Trails Illustrated* map and the quad while the trail to Station Eleven appears on neither map. Portions of this trail cross or pass adjacent to private land.

From the parking area at the water treatment plant (**3A**) continue north along the road for .25 miles passing a tennis court and arriving at the gate to a private residence. The trail leaves the road adjacent to the residence gate and there is a trail sign so indicating. The trail ascends quickly, and you can soon see the town behind and below you. It continues a fairly steep ascent until you pass under a powerline adjacent to the San Juan Ranch Estates subdivision. The trail cuts to the right after passing under the powerline and begins another steep ascent. This portion of the trail can be hazardous on the way down due to loose scree. After another .25 miles and a switchback, the trail cuts to the right and enters a grove of aspen trees. The trail eventually becomes

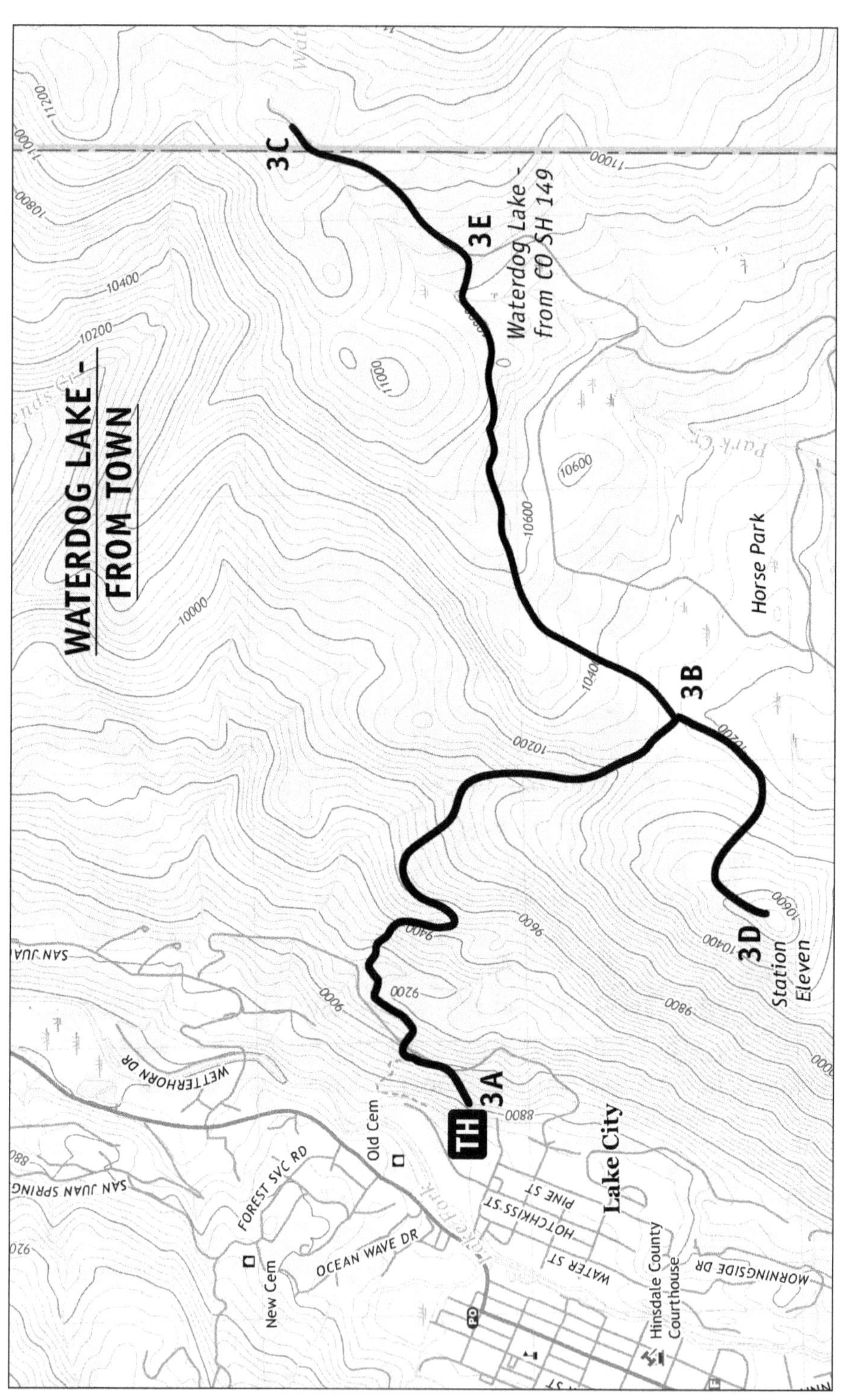

WATERDOG LAKE –
FROM TOWN
3C
3E
Waterdog Lake – from CO SH 149
Horse Park
Park Cr
3B
Station Eleven
3D
San Juan
WETTERHORN DR
SAN JUAN SPRING
FOREST SVC RD
Old Cem
New Cem
OCEAN WAVE DR
TH
3A
Lake City
WATER ST
HOTCHKISS ST
PINE ST
Hinsdale County Courthouse
MORNINGSIDE DR
11200
11000
10800
10400
10200
11000
10600
10600
10400
10200
10000
9400
9200
9600
9800
9000
9800
10400
10600
10000
8800
880
920
PD

more gradual, but never fully flattens out until you break out of the aspen trees into a massive open area known as Horse Park **(3B)**.

If your destination is Waterdog Lake continue on the trail as it cuts left and takes you in a northerly direction. You will be in the trees but still can enjoy the views offered across Horse Park. Shortly afterward, you come into an open area and start climbing again. Once you reach the top of this hill, your worst climbing will be over, but you still will not have reached your highest elevation point. You will go back into the trees, and over the next mile the ascents and descents will be more gradual. You will see a pond to your right. This is not Waterdog Lake. You still have 1.5 miles to go. Not far after passing the pond you will cross a creek and will see the ruins of a pioneer charcoal kiln on your right before breaking into an open area. There is a trail sign ahead **(3E)** which will direct you to the left along a road. This is where you will join the trail leading to Waterdog Lake that leaves from the highway south of town. That trail is discussed under the section named Waterdog Lake – From CO SH 149. Follow this road for a little over 1 mile, climbing gently as you go. As you approach the lake, the drainage from the lake will pass along the road and you will be stepping on rocks within the roadbed to avoid water. Once you've reached the top of the drainage, look to your right and there will be a collapsed miner's cabin next to the lake. You have reached your destination **(3C)**. The road continues along the west side of the lake.

If you're not up for the full trip to Waterdog Lake, an alternate destination is the high point designated as Station Eleven on the quad map. From the point you first reach Horse Park **(3B)** climb up the hill to your right through the short grass staying to the east of the woods. After .25 miles and 300 feet of climbing there is a break in the trees which you can follow a small gulch uphill until you reach an overgrown roadbed. Follow this roadbed southwest until you reach the top of the hill. Even though most of this trail is unmarked, you will reach your destination if you keep climbing. The top of the hill is generally visible whichever way you choose to go. The views in all directions from Station Eleven **(3D)** are tremendous including views of the town, Lake San Cristobal, Crystal Peak along with the mountains behind it, Mesa Seco back across Horse Park, and north toward Crested Butte.

RATING: If you go to Waterdog Lake **(3C)**, the distance covered (9 miles round trip) and the elevation gain (2,500 feet) are significant enough that they are a challenge, but still within the capabilities of intermediate hikers. The terrain is not a problem. If you go to Station Eleven **(3D)**, the distance covered (6 miles round trip) and the elevation gain (2,100 feet) make it a suitable hike for an intermediate hiker.

Waterdog Lake

Katherine Heidt

FANNIE FERN

Quad: Lake City

DRIVING INSTRUCTIONS: Drive south from Lake City on CO SH 149. Shortly after leaving the town limits take a right turn on Vine Street. This road curves back to the north and becomes Alpine Street. The trail begins several hundred yards beyond the gate on your left behind a set of barricades indicating that the road is closed to vehicular traffic. Trailhead elevation - 8,800 feet.

THE HIKE: This trail follows the south side of Henson Creek well above the creek and leads past the Cleveland Mine and ends at the Fannie Fern Mine. It is a short hike suitable for most hikers. It offers occasional views across Henson Creek. There are numerous side trails which can offer a different path on the way down. There is a well-preserved cabin at the Cleveland Mine and a mill at the Fannie Fern Mine. This trail does not appear on the *Trails Illustrated* map, and only the point beyond the Cleveland Mine appears on the quad. Portions of this trail cross or are adjacent to private land.

Leaving the trailhead **(4A)**, you will be on a grass covered double-track road for the first several hundred yards going through an open area near the town's water tower. As you leave the open area the trail converts to a pack trail as it enters the trees. There are several other pack trails that join this main trail. Each of them will take you to Alpine Street but each has a steep spot with loose rocks. You are better off sticking to the main trail on your way down.

Shortly after entering the trees, the trail forks **(4B)**. You should take the right fork. The left fork is discussed later. You will follow this pack trail for over .5 miles mostly through forest, gaining elevation very gradually. When you emerge from the forest there is a flat area, and you spot a well-developed road leading to the right toward Henson Creek

(**4C**). You will want to take the less visible road to the left to reach the mines.

Shortly after the road fork you will reach the Cleveland Mine which has a well-preserved cabin and the ruins of other out-buildings. From this point on you will be on a mining road gaining elevation pretty quickly. The road has two switchbacks before reaching the mill at the Fannie Fern Mine. In the vicinity of the second switchback there are several intersecting mining trails (**4D**). The first intersection takes you to the right and this mining road ends .25 miles away at the base of the Fannie Fern Mill. The route to the left does not lead to the mine but climbs briskly over several switchbacks ending .5 miles from the junction and 300 feet higher atop an open knoll. More on this option later. Continue straight ahead and before long you will reach the Fannie Fern Mine on your left and the top of the mill on your right (**4F**). From this open area, you can look across to the feature known as Sugarloaf Rock. The road continues for .25 miles past the mill, taking one more switchback before ending abruptly, shortly after passing the upper shaft of the mine. The road may have gone further at one time, but there is evidence of an avalanche at the spot where the road ends.

The left fork that you encountered near the trailhead (**4B**) will take you on a higher and slightly more difficult route through the woods before it rejoins the main trail (**4C**) less than a mile from the first junction. This trail is less well marked and at one point it may seem to fade away entirely. When this happens, bear to the left and you will see the trail again before long. There is a second fork shortly before you rejoin the main trail. The left fork is less traveled and disappears within .25 miles. The right fork will lead you downward, and shortly after you emerge from the woods, you will see the main trail just below the road fork that you encounter shortly before you reach the Cleveland Mine (**4C**). This trail junction is hard to spot on the way down, so if you want to take this variation of the hike, you should take it from the bottom initially.

Returning to the fork in the road below the Fannie Fern Mill (**4D**), as stated previously, the road ends at an open knoll .5 miles from and 300 feet above the fork. One hundred yards beyond that point there is a faint single-track trail continuing west and climbing a ridge. I had long wondered to where this trail would lead and had been told that it led to Red Mountain. I was skeptical since this point is some distance

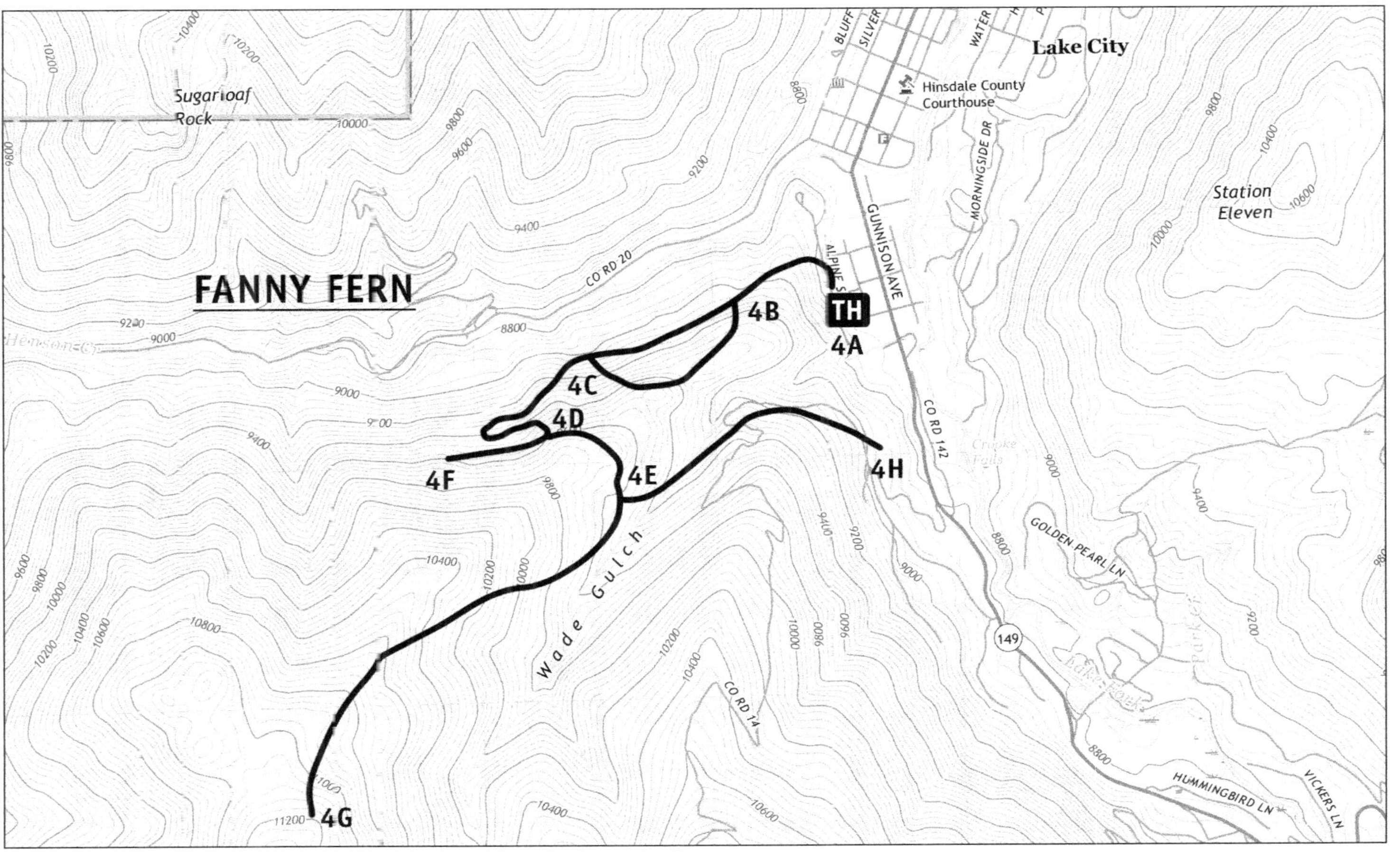

Lake City
Hinsdale County Courthouse
BLUFF
SILVER
WATER H
MORNINGSIDE DR
GUNNISON AVE
ALPINE S
Station Eleven
Sugarloaf Rock
FANNY FERN
CO RD 20
TH
4A
4B
4C
4D
4E
4F
4G
4H
Wade Gulch
CO RD 142
CO RD 14
GOLDEN PEARL LN
HUMMINGBIRD LN
VICKERS LN
149

from Red Mountain but after studying the topo map, I saw this as a possibility. I resolved to follow this trail until I could find its destination or until the trail disappeared. This trail has received little use for many years, but I was able to follow it with only a little difficulty. The area of greatest difficulty is where the trail departs from the mining road at the top of the knoll (4E). Looking up from the top of the knoll there is a mound of earth that may have been left by a mining operation. The trail passes this mound to the south. Keep an eye for that mound on the way down because the trail continues down toward Wade's Gulch. More on that later. The trail climbs moderately to steeply up the ridge alternating between open sage areas and aspen forest. At one point in a sage area the trail was overgrown, but there is a cairn marking the trail before it enters the woods. Two miles after leaving the mining road and gaining 1,000 feet the trail passes the ruins of a mining cabin (4G). As I lost the trail shortly afterward, I concluded that reaching the mining cabin was the purpose for constructing this trail. As the cabin is 2 miles from the summit of Red Mountain, I wouldn't consider this a preferred route for climbing Red Mountain. Having said that, I'm not sure what the preferred route would be for climbing Red Mountain. The views along this route of Red Mountain, Roundtop, and back across the Lake Fork make this difficult hike worthwhile.

On the return trip there is a tricky point I referred to earlier where the trail to the miner's cabin intersects the mining road at the top of the knoll (4E). The trail to the miner's cabin also heads down from this point in an easterly direction. If you want to return to the Fannie Fern trailhead, once you've passed the mound you still have a few trees on the right side of the path. Once you've passed the last dead tree turn to your left and cross the knoll at your current elevation until you see the mining road.

From the intersection of the trail leading to the mining cabin and the mining road (4E), the trail leading to the mining cabin descends to a nice campsite along the stream that fills Wade's Gulch. On the other side of the gulch there is a road which leads downward and ultimately connects with the road leading to the top of Roundtop. As I missed the turnoff point at the top of the knoll, I continued down this route which intersects CO SH 149 near the base of the ski hill (4H). This isn't the first time, nor do I expect it to be the last, where I began a hike at one point and reached civilization at a different point, some distance from my car.

RATING: The distance covered on a hike to the Fannie Fern Mine **(4F)** and mill (4 miles round trip) and the elevation gain (900 feet) are both modest and the terrain is not particularly challenging. This hike should be suitable for well acclimated beginners. The second half of the trail is steeper, and some beginning hikers may prefer to turn back at the Cleveland Mine. A hike to the miner's cabin on the way to Red Mountain **(4G)** would be an 8-mile round trip gaining 2,200 feet of elevation. Due to navigation issues, and the steepness of the trail, this variation of the trail should be limited to experienced hikers. A thru hike from the Fannie Fern trailhead to the base of the ski hill **(4H)** covers 4.5 miles and gains 900 feet. It would be suitable for intermediate hikers.

Fannie Fern Mill

Katherine Heidt

East view from Devil's Creek

Katherine Heidt

Trailheads Located North of Lake City via CO SH 149

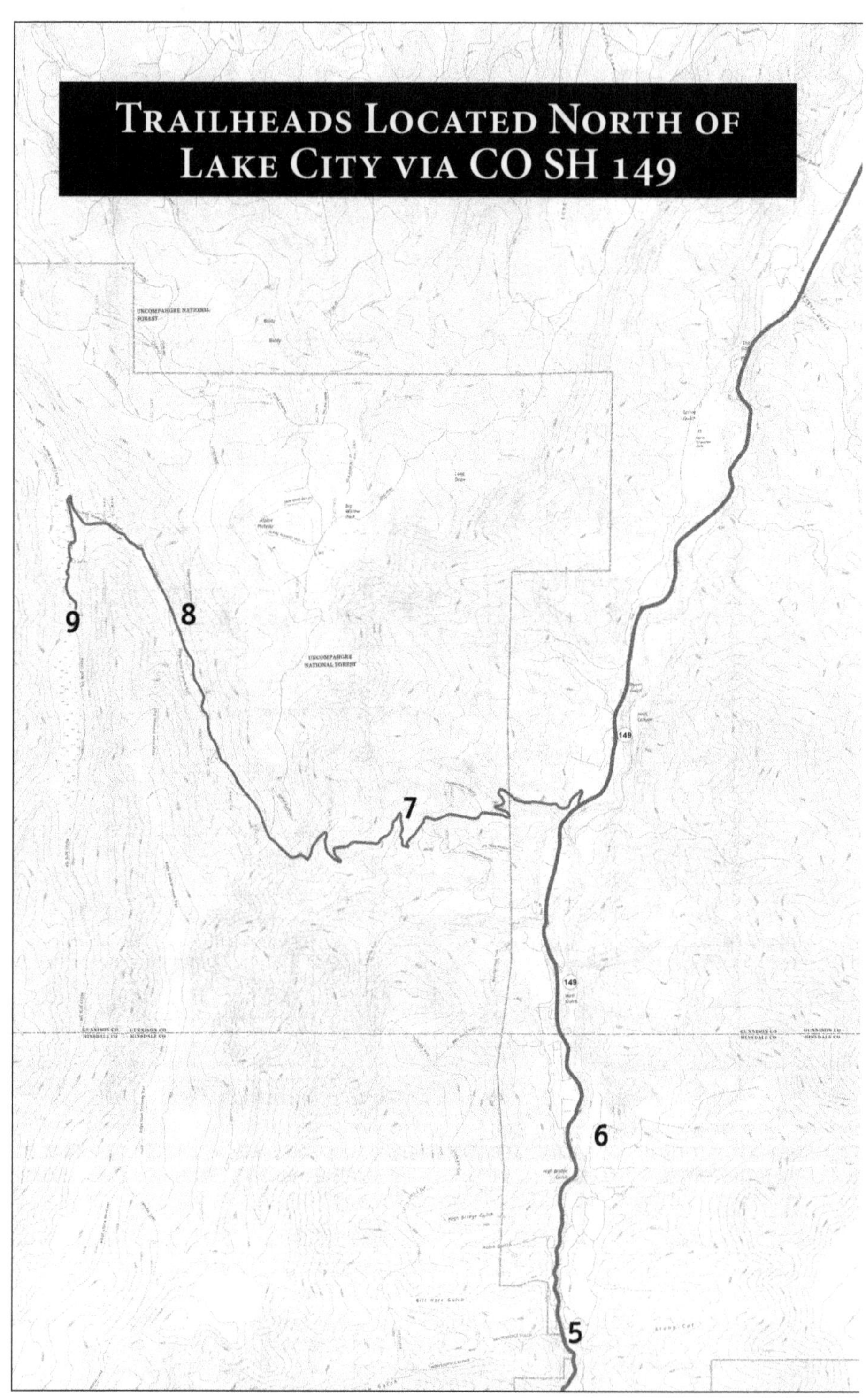

TRAILHEADS LOCATED NORTH OF LAKE CITY VIA CO SH 149
UNCOMPAHGRE NATIONAL FOREST
UNCOMPAHGRE NATIONAL FOREST
149
149
9
8
7
6
5

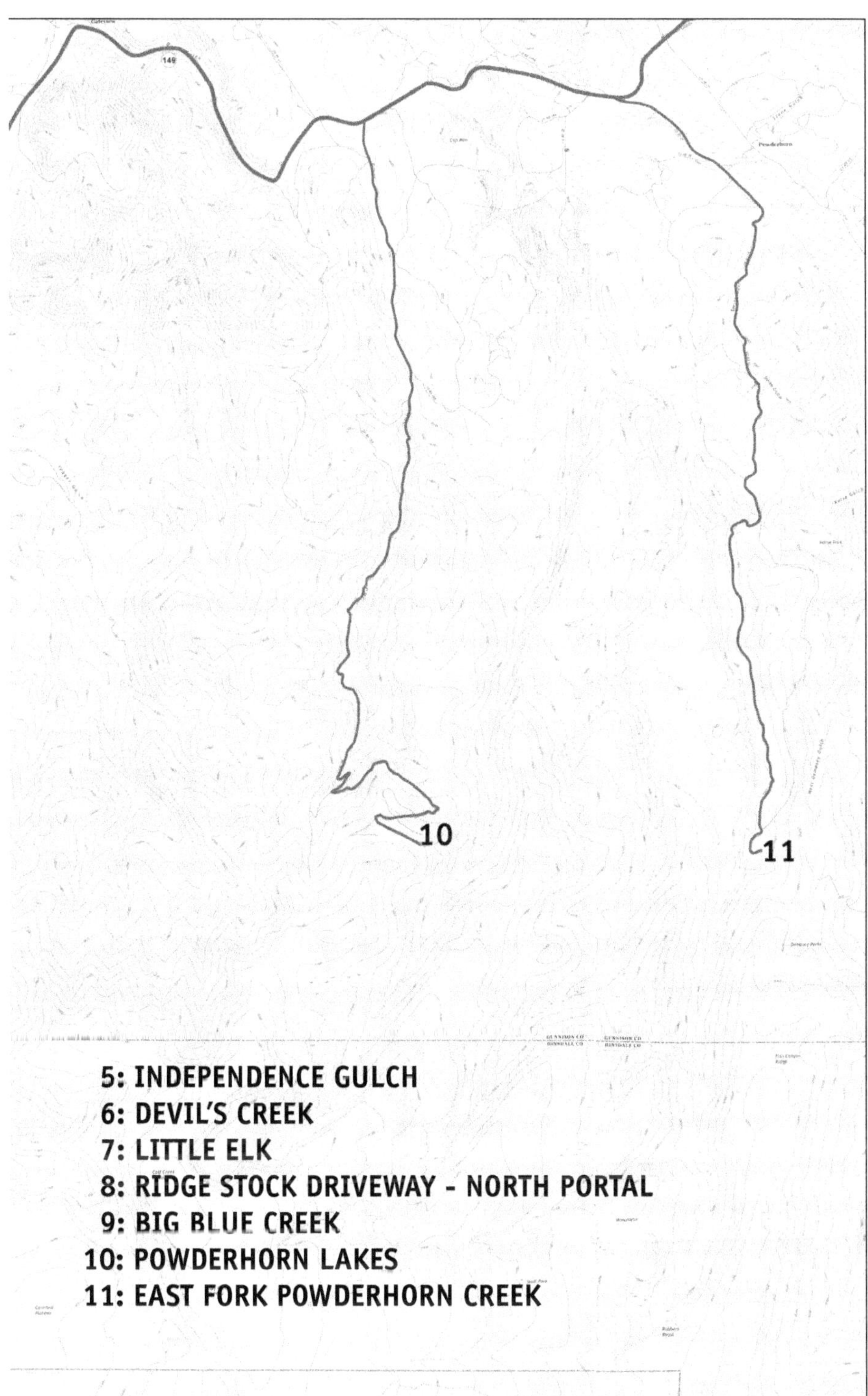

5: INDEPENDENCE GULCH
6: DEVIL'S CREEK
7: LITTLE ELK
8: RIDGE STOCK DRIVEWAY - NORTH PORTAL
9: BIG BLUE CREEK
10: POWDERHORN LAKES
11: EAST FORK POWDERHORN CREEK

INDEPENDENCE GULCH

Quad: Lake City

DRIVING INSTRUCTIONS: Drive north from Lake City on CO SH 149. Almost a mile past MP 77 there is a well-marked trailhead with ample parking on your left. Trailhead elevation - 8,400 feet.

THE HIKE: This hike has several variations and I tend to hike it frequently after rainstorms as you don't have to leave the blacktop with your car and the trail drains well leaving few muddy areas. The trail is more open than wooded and offers wonderful views back to the east side of the Lake Fork Valley in the direction of Cannibal Plateau. While the initial climb is challenging, the overall elevation gain is moderate. This trail is clear of snow in most places any time after Memorial Day, so the trail enjoys a long season. This trail appears on the *Trails Illustrated* map but not on the quad.

All of the variations of this trail begin **(5A)** with a 3-mile ascent to the intersection of the Independence Gulch Trail and the Little Elk Trail **(5C)**. The climb out of the parking area is quite steep at first. There are several spots where it levels out for a bit and then resumes climbing. While the rest of the first 1.5 miles is not any steeper than the initial climb, it's not a lot flatter either. You are in the woods for much of this first segment, although in several places the trees are well spaced, and you have a decent view in all directions.

As you emerge from the woods after 1.5 miles look ahead and to your left. You will see a trail approaching that also serves as the right of way for a water pipeline **(5B)**. You want to continue on the main trail on the right. If you take the second variation of this hike you will return to this point via that water pipeline trail.

Once you make it out of the woods, the climb will be more moderate. You will climb an open hill via a series of five switchbacks and enter a wooded area for a short while. Coming out of the woods you will have a series of seven switchbacks. The distance between switchbacks will shorten as you ascend. Coming off this second set of switchbacks you pass a rock cairn and enter an open flat area 30 yards wide. At the end of this flat area, you will see a rocky ridge which resembles saw teeth. There is a notch through which the trail passes. At this point you will have reached the maximum elevation (10,200 feet) for most of the hike variations. You have gained 1,800 feet to this point.

On the other side of the ridge the trail descends gently through an open area. Once you enter an aspen grove you should start looking for the trail marker indicating the intersection with the Little Elk Trail (**5C**). This intersection is less than .5 miles from the notch. As the trail marker is not directly on either of these trails, it can be hard to spot. Also, I've seen it knocked down more than once or been nailed to a tree. In the first variation of this hike, you will use this as your turn-around point.

The second variation of this hike takes you south along the Little Elk Trail and loops back to the point we mentioned earlier (**5B**). You will descend through the aspen grove for .5 miles and then emerge into a large open area. Continue descending along the trail until it flattens out somewhat. From this point, you will want to leave the trail and move to the southeastern most point of the open area, which is also the lowest point. The trail you are leaving has been kept up by regular horse usage and will take you to a campsite used during hunting season. The original Little Elk Trail has been overgrown by grass but will emerge when you enter the woods. The point you are looking for at the southeast end of the clearing is slightly above a creek and when you go along the creek the trail should be evident, although this trail receives little use. One hundred yards after entering the woods, the Little Elk Trail takes a fork (**5E**) to the right where it leads you across Independence Gulch and ultimately takes you to the Larson Lakes area. This portion of the Little Elk Trail is discussed under the section for Larson Lakes. The trail sign is not always upright as this trail sign is anchored in loose rocks.

Continue the steep descent along the creek. After less than .5 miles, you will reach the point where the water line system intersects this trail. The water system begins at the creek to your right. You will want to turn left following the waterline through the woods. Later the trail emerges into an open area where you can look down toward Independence Gulch. The creek has descended significantly while the trail's descent

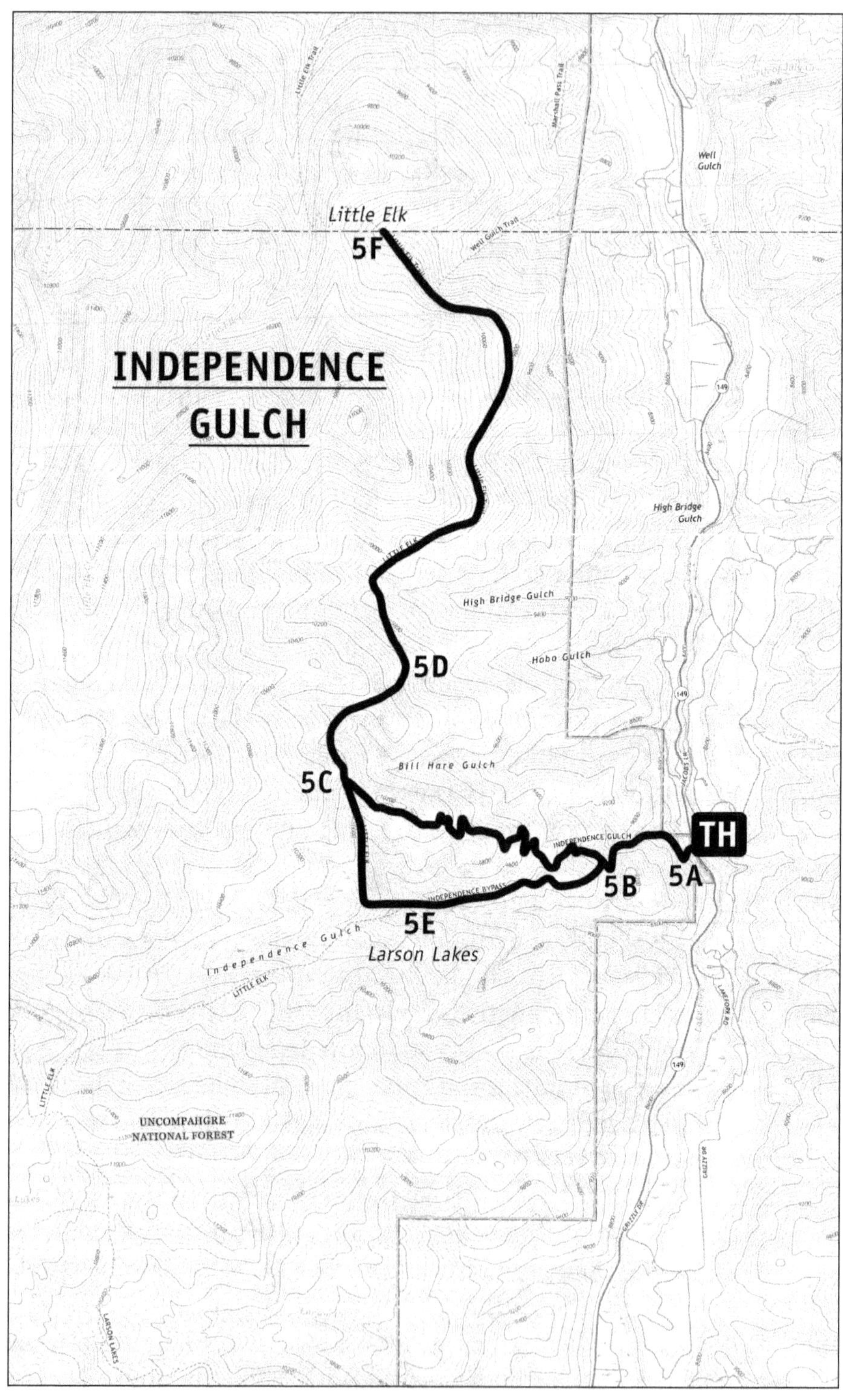

Well Gulch
Little Elk
5F
INDEPENDENCE
GULCH
High Bridge Gulch
High Bridge Gulch
Hobo Gulch
5D
Bill Hare Gulch
5C
INDEPENDENCE GULCH
TH
5B
5A
INDEPENDENCE BYPASS
5E
Independence Gulch
Larson Lakes
LITTLE ELK
UNCOMPAHGRE
NATIONAL FOREST

is quite modest at this point. The trail curves through a rocky area and rejoins the Independence Gulch Trail at the point where it first emerged from the woods (**5B**).

In the third variation of this hike, you will travel north along the Little Elk Trail. This trail is not used a great deal but is not difficult to follow except as noted below. You will emerge from the aspen grove soon after departing the trail intersection (**5C**). As you enter a small open area you will see a ridge on the opposite side of a gulch which has a rocky ridge on the left, another on the right, and a small pass in between. This is your intermediate destination, and it doesn't look too far away. However, you have Bill Hare Gulch between you and this point.

The trail enters a wooded area containing both evergreens and aspen. It passes through this area without gaining or losing much elevation. You will cross one finger of the Bill Hare Gulch which may not contain much water and then cross a small open area before entering the woods again. You will then cross the second finger of the gulch and emerge into a grassy open area where you can see your destination once again.

As you come out into the open area the trail is overgrown with grass in places. The trail goes through this area above where you may think it should. If you lose the trail momentarily, move up the hill. In any event you can see your destination from here.

Climb along the ridge toward the pass and you will probably want to consider this your turnaround point (**5D**). This ridge separates Bill Hare Gulch from High Bridge Gulch. You are at 10,500 feet at this point. If you want to continue north along the Little Elk Trail, be aware that you are about to descend 600 feet which is a pretty steep climb on your return trip.

Continuing north and descending toward High Bridge Gulch you will see the trail is less traveled and there are several places which present navigational challenges for your hike. The trail descends steeply at first through a wooded area, and after reaching a more lightly wooded area the trail becomes more difficult to follow. There is a winter trail sign (a wooden blue diamond suspended from a fir tree branch) at the point where the trail turns to the right and continues into an area sparsely populated with aspen. It then takes a sharp turn to the left, and you enter a wooded area following the first of three fingers of High Bridge Gulch. The descent moderates considerably as you approach the first of the three stream crossings of High Bridge Gulch. None of these should present a problem at any point during the hiking season. After the first stream crossing the trail climbs, then descends a ridge leading to the second stream crossing. Following this second stream crossing the trail ascends and enters an open area, then disappears. Make a mental note of where you entered the open area as it may be difficult to find where the trail leaves the open area on your return trip. Not far into the open area there is a rock cairn. Upon reaching the cairn turn to your right (north) and you will see a second cairn. Follow the direction indicated by the two cairns and look for a spot where downed timber has been cut. This is where the trail leaves the open area. I have lost the trail several times in this area.

Once you've found where the trail leaves the open area, it descends slightly then crosses the third finger of High Bridge Gulch, which may not contain water later in the season. The trail then ascends at a moderate climb along the south side of a significant hill (elevation 10,900) before turning to the north where it passes through open sage for the next mile without gaining or losing much elevation. There are views across the Lake Fork Valley, including a view up Devil's Creek. The trail passes through a small stand of aspen and crosses a dry gulch before turning to the right (east), and then again turns north as it continues on the east side of the hill, through the sage, for another mile. The trail then enters an aspen grove for nearly .5 miles before entering another open area. This area has more grass than sage and the trail is overgrown for much of this meadow. Fortunately, there are several navigational aids. The first is a cairn to your left. Shortly afterward, you will see the first of a number of posts, blonde in color, which are strategically placed to assist you, but are insufficient in number to be foolproof. The first post serves mainly as a guidepost as to where to enter the forest on your return trip. There are three additional posts in the meadow, the first two are in the lower portion of the meadow and can be easily missed if you continue at the elevation at which you entered the meadow. The third post is at the far end of the meadow and indicates the location where the trail enters the aspen forest. There is another post while you are in this brief forest, and another where you enter another meadow. Again, this post will be useful on your return trip to show where the trail enters the forest, because the trail fades once again as you enter this meadow. There is no post on the opposite side of the meadow, but the trail isn't difficult to find as the next forest is a mixture of fir and aspen and the trail is well defined once you are in this forest.

The trail descends moderately and turns to the west at this point as you are about to cross a dry gulch. After over .5 miles in this forest, the trail enters another open area, and you see the first of four friendly posts. Follow the posts, as the trail disappears from time to time through this meadow but cast your eyes on the ridge ahead of and above you. This is the divide between the Lake Fork drainage (where you currently are) and the Little Elk Creek drainage. Once you have passed the fourth post the trail may disappear but climb this ridge as best you are able. Once at the top of the ridge, turn toward your left and work your way toward the trees, and the trail will reappear shortly before you reach the trees. The section on the other side of this ridge is covered under the section for Little Elk (**5F**).

RATING: For the first variation to the intersection of the Little Elk Trail (**5C**), the round-trip distance is 5 miles. and the elevation gain is 1,800 feet. For the second variation looping back by going south on the Little Elk Trail, the distance is 6 miles, and the elevation gain is also 1,800 feet. The third variation going north on the Little Elk Trail to the ridge between Bill Hare Gulch and High Bridge Gulch (**5D**) has a round-trip distance of 8 miles and the elevation gain is 2,100 feet. You have a good trail and good terrain for the entirety of the first variation. The terrain on each of the second and third variations is a little spotty after you leave the Independence Gulch Trail. All three variations should be considered suitable for intermediate hikers. Having said that, if you wish to continue north along the Little Elk Trail beyond the ridge between Bill Hare Gulch and High Bridge Gulch, you are undertaking a hike which should be reserved for experienced hikers. A round trip from the Independence Gulch Trailhead to the point where this narrative refers you to the Little Elk section (**5F**) covers 18 miles with a 2,500-foot (gross) elevation gain on the way out and nearly a 1,000-foot elevation gain on the return trip. A thru-hike from the Independence Gulch Trailhead to the Little Elk Trailhead covers 12.5 miles with a 2,500-foot (gross) elevation gain before descending 1,100 feet to Elk Creek and then gaining 300 feet before reaching the Little Elk trailhead. Either of these hikes is a wilderness adventure but presents navigational challenges at several points and should be reserved for the most experienced of hikers.

DEVIL'S CREEK

Quad: Alpine Plateau, Cannibal Plateau

DRIVING INSTRUCTIONS: Drive north from Lake City on CO SH 149. Past MP 79 there is a road leading to your right down toward the river, which is designated by a BLM sign. Follow this road for .7 miles, crossing the river, and following the BLM signs leading you to the Devil's Creek trailhead, which contains ample parking. Trailhead elevation - 8,400 feet.

THE HIKE: This trail leads to Devil's Lake, which is a hike of great distance and difficulty, but there are several points along the way which make nice destinations in and of themselves. There is quite an elevation gain throughout the hike, but the trail drains well and lends itself to hiking the day after a rain. There are several stands of aspen trees throughout the hike which recommend this trail for autumn hiking. The lower portion of the trail is well traveled, and the trail is not difficult to follow. The upper portion of the trail gets little usage, and the trail is quite difficult to follow in more than a few places. This trail does not appear on the quad; but the trailhead is indicated on the Telluride, Silverton, Ouray, Lake City *Trails Illustrated* map, and the bulk of the trail is on the La Garita, Cochetopa Hills *Trails Illustrated* map.

The trail heads west from a well-marked trailhead **(6A)** and almost immediately turns right (south) climbing moderately over several switchbacks through a lightly wooded area. After the third switchback the trail turns east climbing steadily. You will pass just below a rock edifice and continue east until you meet a jeep road. Take a left turn at this point, which is indicated by a trail sign. The climbing becomes more intense once you are on the jeep road, but after .25 miles, the trail flattens as you enter a sage-covered open area. You will initially be heading north along this arid area, then turning east along a fence line.

After .5 miles hiking through the sage brush, the trail turns to the left, crossing through an opening in the fence.

Shortly after passing through the fence, you will see two carsonite posts indicating you are entering the Powderhorn Wilderness. The trail continues to gain elevation as you pass through the first of several aspen groves. Nearly a mile after passing through the fence, there is a clearing to your left with two buildings and several fences which remain from a cow camp. You have gone nearly 3 miles at this point and have gained 1,400 feet. This may seem like a good turn-around point for a shorter hike, but there is a better destination .5 miles ahead. Looking east up Devil's Creek, you will see a rock edifice with a flat surface. This is easily reached from the trail ahead and it offers wonderful views, but it is not well marked. To reach this, continue along the trail through a grove of aspen until you reach a spot where the trail levels out, and for the first time in a while, there is not a drop-off to your right. One hundred feet from the trail is the flat top of the rock edifice, which makes a fine destination for a shorter hike **(6B)**. You will have covered 3.5 miles to this point.

Continuing along the trail you climb at a lesser rate, and you begin to hear the sounds of Devil's Creek some distance away as you continue through aspen. At one point the trail passes within a few feet of the creek, which is the only reliable water source prior to reaching Devil's Lake. The trail continues to climb, and the trees change from aspen to spruce and fir. There are several points in this section where the trail becomes difficult to follow.

After hiking 1.5 miles beyond the cow camp, the trail emerges from the wooded area and follows along the top of a ridge to the north of the Devil's Creek drainage **(6C)**. This ridge is lightly wooded but offers spectacular views back down the valley toward Uncompahgre Peak and the surrounding peaks. A lush aspen grove offers wonderful views during autumn. The ridge continues east for .5 miles before the trail leaves the ridge and heads south. The plateau to the east of the trail is Calf Creek Plateau and the plateau to the west is Cannibal Plateau. The trail works its way between the two plateaus toward Devil's Lake, which rests between the two plateaus, near their crests.

The trail enters a wooded area and becomes difficult to follow from this point forward. There is a fair amount of downed timber in this area. The trail climbs through the woods and emerges on the Cannibal

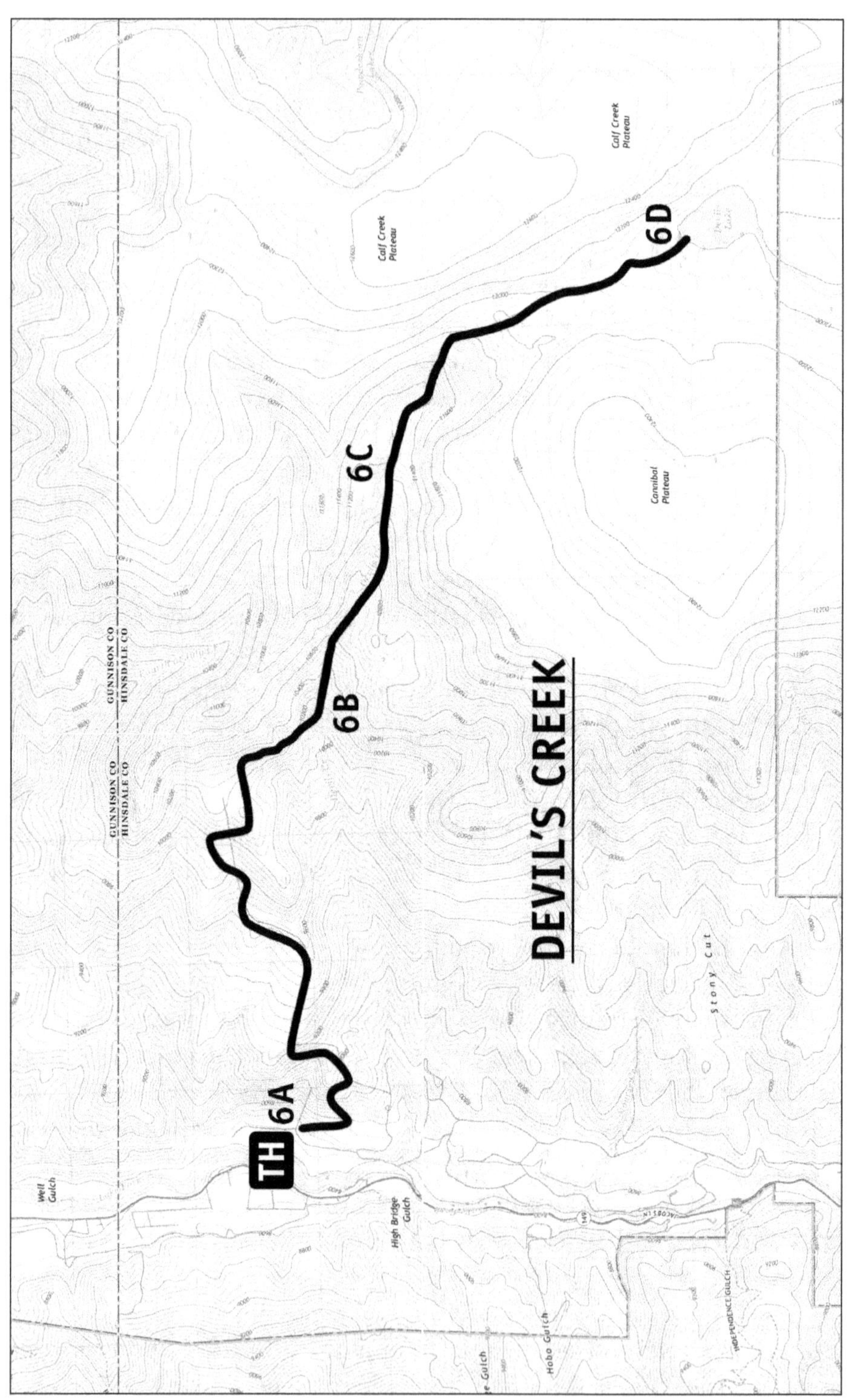

Calf Creek Plateau
Calf Creek Plateau
Cannibal Plateau
6D
6C
6B
6A
TH
DEVIL'S CREEK
GUNNISON CO
HINSDALE CO
GUNNISON CO
HINSDALE CO
GUNNISON CO
HINSDALE CO
Well Gulch
High Bridge Gulch
Hobo Gulch
Stony Cut
INDEPENDENCE GULCH

Plateau side after a steep incline toward the end. You will then pass through a fairly flat meadow, which has overgrown the trail. Two posts lead you through the meadow and into a smaller wooded area. Emerging from this final wooded area, you now have rocks everywhere for the rest of the way to Devil's Lake. There are cairns leading you through the rocks for the last 2 miles to Devil's Lake. The trail continues to gain elevation during this final stretch crossing several ridges before Devil's Lake enters your view. At this point you are still over .5 miles away from the lake and you will descend 300 feet before reaching the lake **(6D)**. Devil's Lake is like no other in the area. This large lake is surrounded by the two plateaus, and you think you may be on the moon, as there is little vegetation.

RATING: The hike to the overlook beyond the cow camp **(6B)** is a 7-mile round trip, climbing 1,600 feet. It is well within the capabilities of any intermediate hiker. A hike to the headwaters of Devil's Creek where the trail emerges from the trees **(6C)** is a 9-mile round trip, climbing 2,600 feet. This should also be achievable by an intermediate hiker. A hike to Devil's Lake **(6D)** is a 14-mile round trip climbing 3,400 feet and should only be attempted by experienced hikers due to distance, elevation, and navigation issues.

LITTLE ELK

Quad: Alpine Plateau

DRIVING INSTRUCTIONS: Drive north from Lake City on CO SH 149. Once in Gunnison County, shortly after passing MP 83, there is a brown Forest Service access sign indicating the road (FSR 868) to the Big Blue area. This is also known as the Alpine Road. Turn left (west) onto this road and shortly after passing the 3-mile marker there is a well-marked trailhead with a parking area on your left. The trail leads south from the parking lot and there is a trail sign indicating the distance to the Uncompahgre Wilderness boundary and to the Larson Lakes Trail. Trailhead elevation - 9,300 feet.

THE HIKE: This is a seldom used trail which leads you into an untamed wilderness. Much of the attraction of the Little Elk Trail is that it connects the Alpine Road to the Independence Gulch Trail, the Larson Lakes and Crystal Lake area, and into the town. I've taken this trail on several occasions and have had navigation issues. There are several places where the trail is difficult to follow and others where nature has reclaimed the trail through new growth. Even with those limitations, it has much to offer the hiker that wants to cover some new and wild territory. This trail appears on the *Trails Illustrated* map, but not on the quad. Portions of this trail are adjacent to private land.

Heading south from the trailhead (**7A**) you soon enter a wooded area for a short time and emerge onto an open hill heading generally downward for the first mile. At the base of the hill the trail disappears in the grassy terrain. Look for two posts to guide you into the second wooded area where the trail emerges and is easy to follow. This second wooded area doesn't last much longer than the first and you enter a second open hilly area with a fence separating you from private land. You are still heading downward when you enter the forest

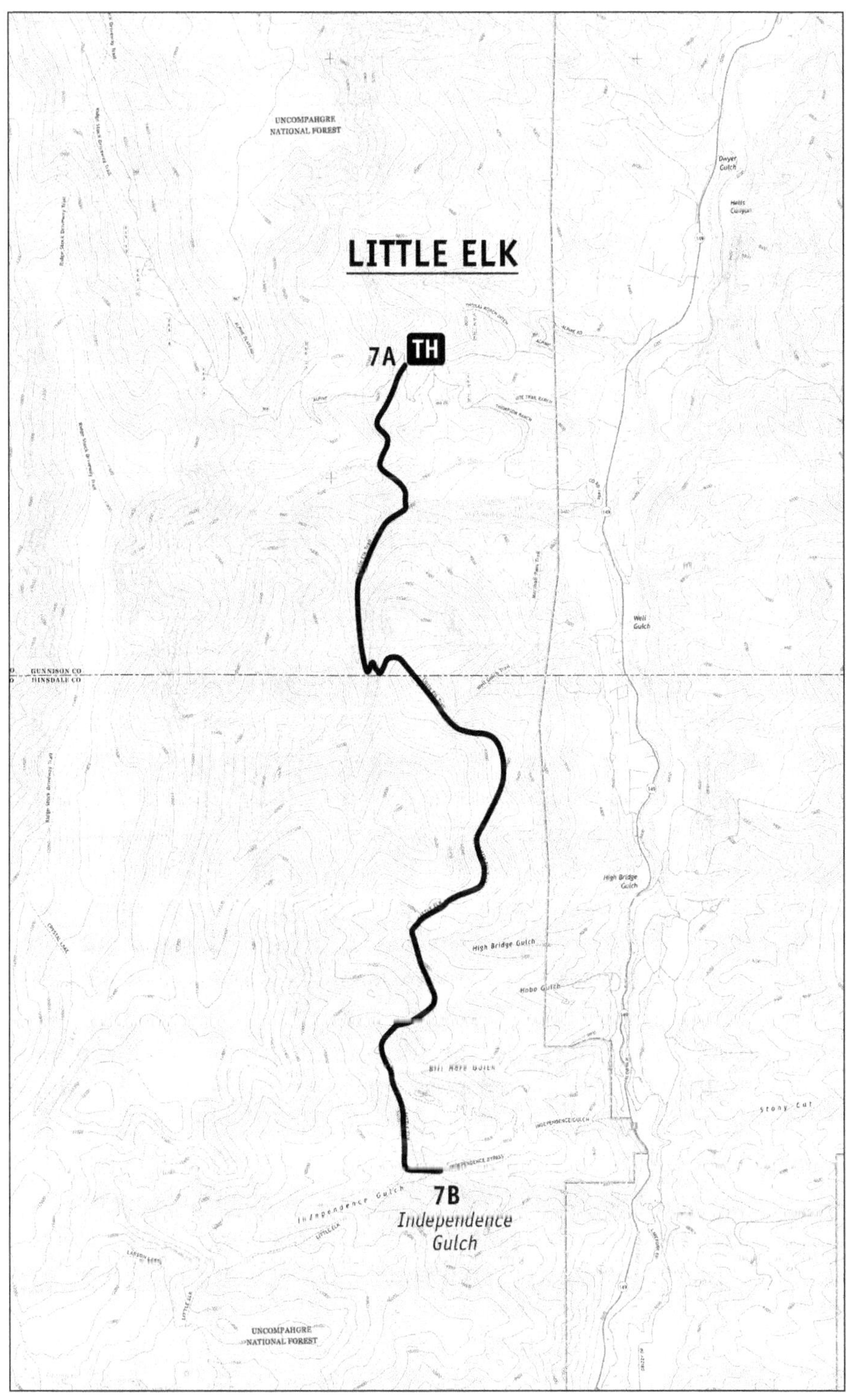
LITTLE ELK
7A TH
7B
Independence
Gulch

once again, where you will remain for quite some time. Soon afterward you encounter a man-made water crossing which is labeled Thompson Ditch on the maps. Depending on the water flow, you may want water crossing shoes to cross Thompson Ditch.

As you continue downward after crossing the ditch you are in a lightly wooded area and the trail takes several switchbacks heading downward at a moderate decline. This area is easy enough to follow on the way in but can be confusing on the way out as there is a second trail below the hiker's trail that is also well developed. On the way down, head toward Elk Creek, which you can hear from some distance away, but on the way back you will need to make sure you are on the upper trail. You may need water crossing shoes to cross Elk Creek early in the season. You have descended 300 feet from the trailhead to the point where you cross Elk Creek.

After crossing Elk Creek, you continue descending for a short distance until you have another water crossing, less taxing than the last. Shortly after that crossing you will see a rock cairn where the trail takes a right-hand turn. Note that spot because you can easily miss the turn on your way back. There is a trail heading to the left which appears as the Little Elk Trail on some maps. This trail has logs across it which indicates that this is not the preferred trail. Taking a right turn at the cairn, the trail heads upstream alongside Little Elk Creek, a tributary of Elk Creek, crossing it and various inlet streams several times. The trail is a steady, but not overly steep, climb for over a mile. During this climb you will pass the Uncompahgre Wilderness boundary sign at the 2.5-mile point. Shortly after the wilderness sign, the trail begins to switchback up a hill to your left and you alternate between forest and open areas as you ascend the hill. You enter the woods as you reach the crest of the hill and the trail divides (7B). The left fork takes you to a nice flat area which can serve as a campsite or lunch spot and goes no further. The right fork descends through an open area with a grove of aspen to your right. This portion of the Little Elk Trail is covered under the section for Independence Gulch. At the crest of the ridge, you are 3.75 miles from the trailhead and have climbed 1,100 feet from the point you crossed Elk Creek.

RATING: The distance covered (7.5 miles round trip) and the elevation gain (1,100 gross, 800 net plus a 300-foot climb on the return trip) suggest a trail for intermediate hikers but the difficulty of following the trail renders this trail appropriate only for experienced hikers.

RIDGE STOCK DRIVEWAY – NORTH PORTAL

Quad: Alpine Plateau

DRIVING INSTRUCTIONS: Drive north from Lake City on CO SH 149. Once in Gunnison County, shortly after passing MP 83, there is a brown Forest Service access sign indicating the road (FSR 868) to the Big Blue area. This is also known as the Alpine Road. Turn left (west) onto this road and proceed 8.0 miles to the west. At that point there is a sheep corral to your right and two posts on either side of the road indicate the point where the Ridge Stock Driveway crosses the Alpine Road. There is parking for several vehicles at the turnouts to the corral as well as ample room along the side of the Alpine Road. Trailhead elevation - 10,000 feet.

THE HIKE: Having covered the Ridge Stock Driveway under the sections for Horsethief Trail, Mary Alice Creek, Matterhorn Creek, and Nellie Creek, it seems logical to follow this trail to the north where it enters Hinsdale County. The trailhead leading into Hinsdale County is in Gunnison County, along the Alpine Road. Finding the trailhead is a bit of a challenge and I did not discover it on my first attempt. The point where the Ridge Stock Driveway crosses the Alpine Road is in a meadow and the trail is overgrown. The posts indicating the crossing can be a bit misleading, as the trail is behind you, to the southeast. There is an older post in the meadow 100 yards from the road, and from that post you can see another. From the second post you can see a trail sign across a small stream known as Soldier Creek. The trail sign that indicates you are on the Ridge Stock Driveway is close to the point where the trail enters the woods **(8A)**. Finding the trailhead is not the only navigational challenge on this trail, but more on that later. This is a dry hike so take extra water. This trail appears on both the *Trails Illustrated* map and on the quad.

The trail enters the forest, begins to climb moderately, and you find seven switchbacks as you climb the northernmost ridge of the Ridge Stock Driveway. The trail is remarkably easy to follow at this point, given what comes later. This may be because there is ample evidence of horse usage as you climb the ridge. After 1.5 miles and 1,000 feet of elevation gain the switchbacks stop and the trail heads south as it continues to climb the ridge. There are several more switchbacks during this section. At this point you begin to alternate between wooded and open areas and the trail becomes more difficult to follow. The terrain in the open areas progresses from short grass to dirt and small rocks to tundra as you continue over the next 2 miles. The trail through the open areas is hard to identify until you reach the tundra. However, if you find yourself off the trail, continue south along the crest of the ridge. As long as you continue to climb, you will re-discover the trail at some point. There is a series of small rock cairns along the northernmost part of the ridge. These aren't spaced well enough to show the way but can provide some confirmation at points where you may have doubts. There is more than one point along the ridge where I have asked myself, "If I were a trail, where would I be?" The trail generally follows a line slightly to the west of the crest of the ridge. If you miss the trail when entering the wooded areas, you may take small comfort in the fact that the wooded areas are small, and you will soon be in the open.

Once you've reached the tundra, the trail becomes easier to follow and as you continue to climb the ridge, you reach the first of several high knobs at the 4-mile point (**8B**). You have wonderful 360-degree views from here including the other side of Big Blue Creek, Uncompahgre Peak, the Clay Pots, Crystal Peak, Cannibal Plateau, and Calf Creek Plateau, moving from right to left. This is the first logical turnaround point. Should you want to proceed further north, take note of a cairn toward the north end of this knob. The trail northward exits the knob at the cairn. You can see the trail northward from the top of the knob and can join it by passing down a rocky incline. The trail exiting alongside the cairn is much easier than descending from the north side of the knob.

For the next mile northward from the knob, the trail is fairly well defined as you cross tundra with a few trees interspersed. You don't gain or lose much elevation from this point onward. As you approach a second knob, there are trees to your left and the knob to your right. The

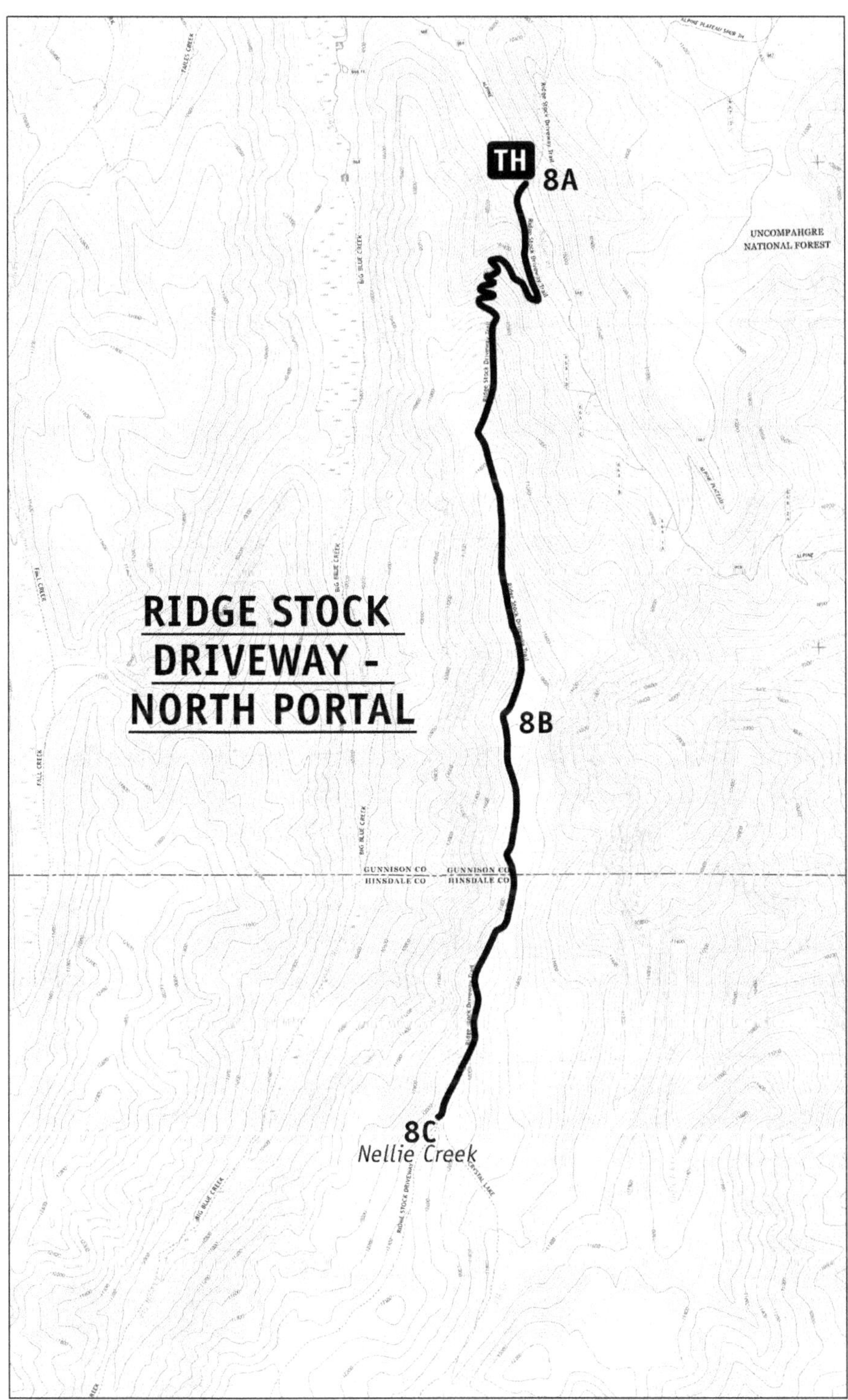

TH 8A
UNCOMPAHGRE
NATIONAL FOREST
RIDGE STOCK
DRIVEWAY -
NORTH PORTAL
8B
GUNNISON CO
HINSDALE CO
GUNNISON CO
HINSDALE CO
8C
Nellie Creek

trail passes between them. There are several other points over the next mile where the trail is hard to follow. In each case go above the trees and below the top of the ridge. You don't pass through trees again until the 6-mile mark where there is a small patch of trees. You don't have the benefit of cairns through this section of the trail but continuing north to the left of the crest of the ridge will lead you in the right direction.

At the 6.5-mile mark you climb to a small ridge and see a meadow on the other side. You have reached the upper end of a water drainage which is usually dry. Beyond the drainage you should be able to see two trail signs, in close proximity, in the middle of the meadow. Cross the drainage and go to the two trail signs (8C). Both of these trail signs are quite old and faded. The first points to the trail leading you to Crystal Lake and to Lake City. The sign designates this as Trail #255. The current designation for this trail is Trail #235. This trail connects to the Crystal / Larson loop. It is not covered in this book. The second trail sign indicates the route to Trail #257. That trail designation is also obsolete as the Ridge Stock Driveway is currently designated Trail #233. The portion of the Ridge Stock Driveway north of this point is covered under the section for Nellie Creek.

On your return trip the navigation issues become more critical because instead of climbing to a single high point, you must find the trail as it enters the trees as it descends toward Soldier Creek. If you lose the trail, you may need to return south by climbing until you find the trail and make a second attempt.

RATING: The hike to the northernmost knob (8B) and return is an 8-mile round trip and climbs 1,900 feet. Although the distance, climb, and terrain would indicate that this should be an intermediate level hike, the navigation issues preclude this. You should not attempt this hike unless there are one or more experienced hikers in your group. The hike to the trail intersection with the Crystal / Larson cutoff (8C) is a 13-mile round trip and climbs 2,200 feet. Again, this should be limited to experienced hikers.

BIG BLUE CREEK

Quad: Sheep Mountain

DRIVING INSTRUCTIONS: Drive north on CO SH 149 from Lake City. Once in Gunnison County, shortly after passing MP 83, there is a brown Forest Service access sign indicating the road (FSR 868) to the Big Blue area. This is also known as the Alpine Road. Turn left (west) onto this road and proceed 12 miles to the west and then to the south. The road passes the Big Blue Campground at the 11-mile point then continues south an additional mile where it terminates at the Big Blue Creek trailhead, which has ample parking. Trailhead elevation - 9,700 feet.

THE HIKE: Despite its distance from the highway, this trail gets a fair amount of use. Big Blue Creek is a popular fishing area, and the trail parallels the creek for much of its distance. Although it begins in Gunnison County, the trail crosses into Hinsdale County near the first creek crossing and continues to its termination at the Nellie Creek trailhead and can be completed as a thru-hike in one day. The northern end, covered by this discussion, is one of the easiest hikes in the area, while the southern end, covered in the Nellie Creek trailhead section, is much more difficult. The preferred way of hiking this as a thru hike would be from south to north, as you would begin at a much higher elevation. This trail appears on both the *Trails Illustrated* map and on the quad.

Leaving the trailhead (**9A**), you enter the woods after a short distance, and will remain in forest for the first several miles, although you are never far from the edge of the forest and can often see to the creek and the bluffs on the other side. The trail rises at a very gradual pace for the first 4.5 miles until you reach the first creek crossing. There are several clearings during the last mile and the creek crossing occurs in

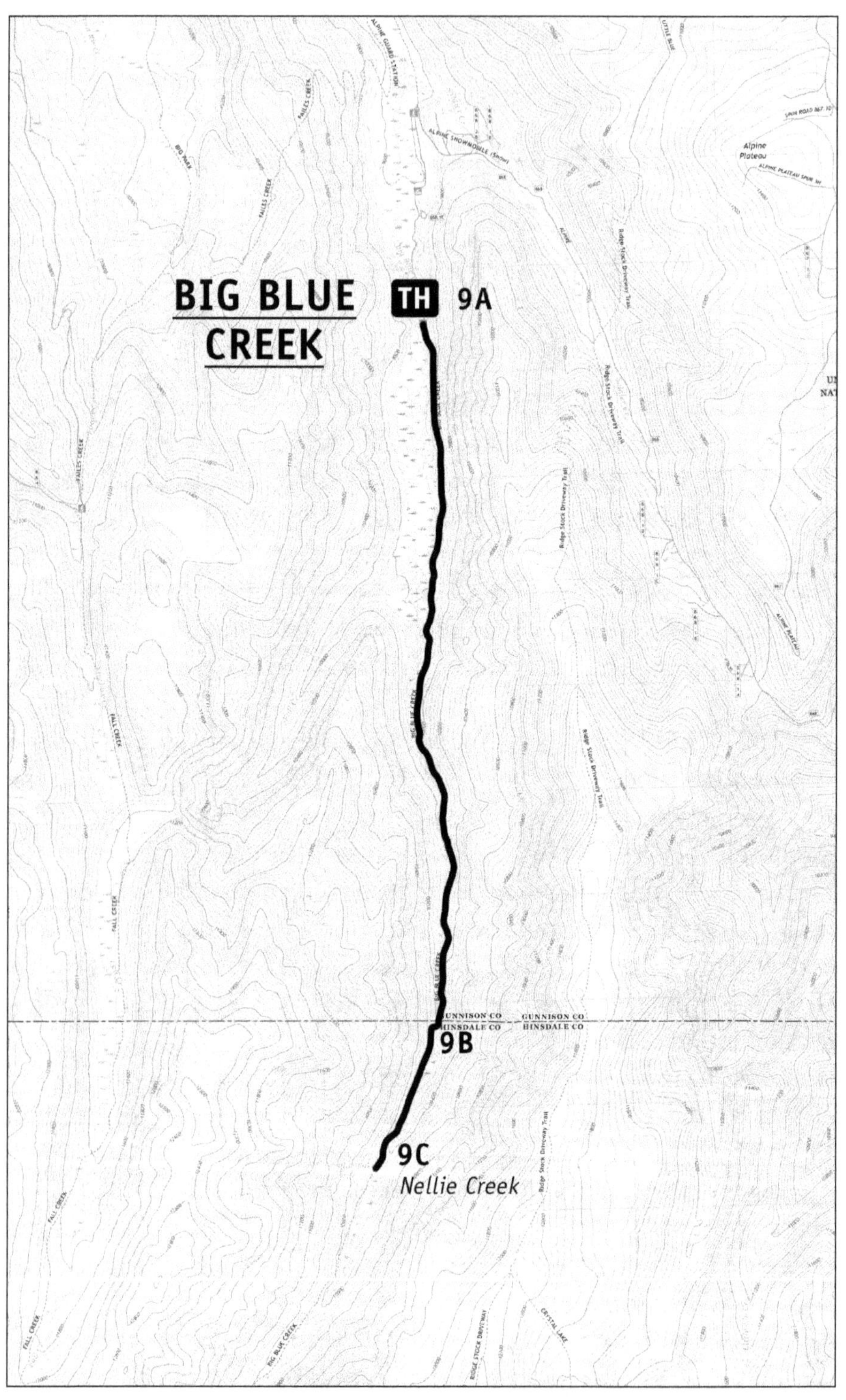

BIG BLUE CREEK
TH 9A
9B
9C
Nellie Creek
GUNNISON CO
HINSDALE CO
GUNNISON CO
HINSDALE CO
Alpine Plateau

one of these clearings. You will need water crossing shoes when crossing Big Blue Creek **(9B)** both here and during the three subsequent water crossings covered in the Nellie Creek trailhead section. There is a campsite in the trees prior to and above the first water crossing, and camping can also occur along the creek.

Beyond the creek crossing, the trail continues for another mile until you reach Slide Lake, a small and unremarkable lake, which serves as the midpoint of the trail to the Nellie Creek trailhead. Campsites are also available at Slide Lake **(9C)**. That portion of the Big Blue Creek Trail south of Slide Lake is covered in the section for Nellie Creek.

Rating: A round trip to the first creek crossing **(9B)** covers 9 miles and has a 500-foot elevation gain. It is an easy hike suitable for beginners. A round trip to Slide Lake **(9C)** covers 11 miles and has a 700-foot elevation gain. Due to the distance and the creek crossing, I would rate this hike as intermediate. A thru-hike to the Nellie Creek trailhead covers 12 miles and should be limited to experienced hikers.

Big Blue Creek

Katherine Heidt

POWDERHORN LAKES

Quad: Powderhorn Lakes

DRIVING INSTRUCTIONS: Drive north from Lake City on CO SH 149 for 22 miles. Past MP 96, Indian Creek Road (FSR 3033), intersects the highway on your right, which is marked by a Forest Service sign. This is less than a mile past the Sapinero Mesa Road. Follow Indian Creek Road for 10.2 miles to the trailhead, which is on your right. There is ample parking at the trailhead. Indian Creek Road does not require 4WD, but a vehicle with high ground clearance is recommended. You should avoid this road after a heavy rain. Trailhead elevation - 11,000 feet.

THE HIKE: This hike leads into the northern section of the Powderhorn Wilderness. While most hikers take the main trail to Powderhorn Lakes, there is a second variation which climbs Calf Creek Plateau and leads to Powderhorn Lakes or to Devil's Lake and points south. There is a third variation which leads to Hidden Lake. There are camping sites at both of the Powderhorn Lakes. This trail does not appear on the quad and only the last portion is indicated on the *Trails Illustrated* map for La Garita, Cochetopa Hills. The trailhead does not lie within Hinsdale County, but the trail leads into the county.

Upon leaving the trailhead (**10A**) you are in a forest for the first 1.5 miles gaining elevation moderately. Shortly before entering a meadow, the elevation drops slightly. The primary trail continues across the meadow. At this point the second variation of this trail (**10B**), discussed below, diverts from the first, although there is no trail sign and no obvious trail. After less than .25 miles the main trail enters the trees once again and begins to descend. For the next several miles the trail alternates between slight ascents and slight descents, all the while remaining in the trees. At the 2.5-mile mark you pass two small ponds on your

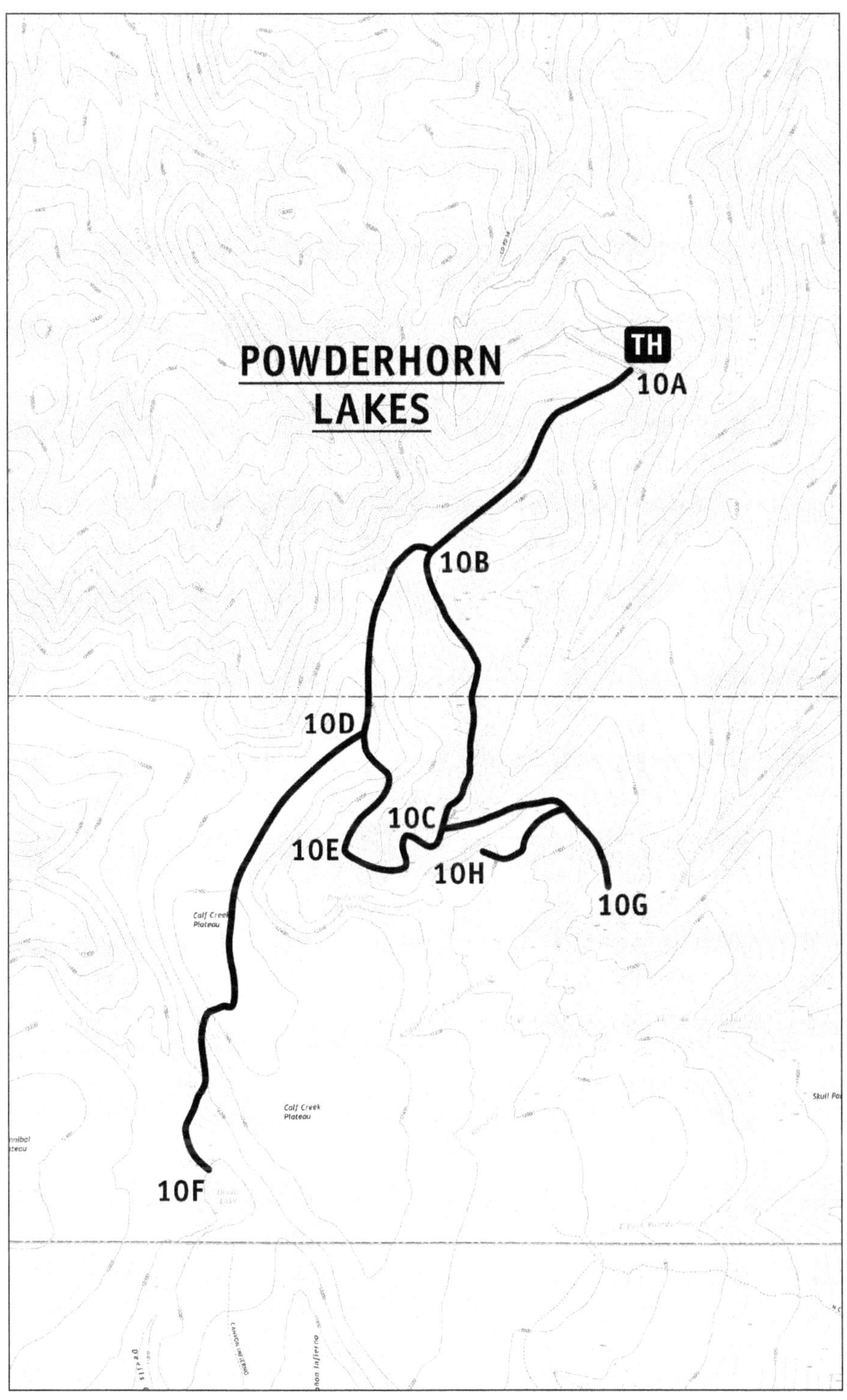

POWDERHORN
LAKES
TH
10A
10B
10D
10C
10E
10H
10G
10F
Calf Creek Plateau
Calf Creek Plateau

right and most of the rest of the trail is a gradual ascent. At the 3.5-mile mark you enter a clearing and encounter a trail sign marking the trail to Hidden Lake (**10C**). Continue straight ahead to Lower Powderhorn Lake which is .25 miles ahead as you encounter that lake's drainage. Lower Powderhorn Lake is a five-acre lake, and you will pass around the west side of the lake before entering the forest again, following the drainage of the upper lake for another .5 miles until you reach Upper Powderhorn Lake (**10E**), which is a ten-acre lake. As you approach the upper lake, pay attention to where you leave the forest, because finding the trail upon your return can be tricky.

Should you want to take the upper trail to the Powderhorn Lakes or continue on to Devil's Lake, upon reaching the meadow (**10B**) cast your eyes above to see the northern face of Calf Creek Plateau. This is your intermediate destination and given the lack of an established trail, keep this destination well in mind. You will take a slight right-hand turn after entering the meadow and will follow the open area around some trees before turning left and beginning your ascent of Calf Creek Plateau. There is no right way or wrong way to climb this plateau. You will be passing through short grass with only a few trees, bushes, or rocks. As you approach the top of the plateau, the climb becomes more gradual, but the top of the plateau is 1,300 feet above the trailhead and 800 feet above the point where you entered the meadow (**10B**).

On the top of the plateau there are two rock cairns which are some distance apart. The easternmost of these resembles a pillar while the westernmost of these resembles a tower. While the need for these is not apparent as you are heading south, they are most useful should you return the way you came. Calf Creek Plateau is massive and these cairns, particularly the tower, are quite useful in navigating your return.

By the time you have reached the top of the plateau, which contains a USGS boundary stake, you have covered 3 miles and you will have an overlook of both of the Powderhorn lakes in another .5 miles. Look for a wooden post to your left (**10D**) as you approach the steep rock cliffs which are adjacent to both lakes on three sides. Should you wish to descend to Upper Powderhorn Lake, there is a trail along a grassy decline which leads to a rockslide before descending to the west end of the upper lake (**10E**). If you wish to return to the trailhead via the lower route, be warned that the point where the lower trail reaches the upper lake is not readily apparent. You may not want to try this unless you have been to the upper lake by the lower route previously and are familiar with the point where the trail reaches the lake.

From the wooden post (**10D**), should you wish to continue along Calf Creek Plateau to Devil's Lake, be aware that the trail is unmarked other than several posts and cairns that you will see intermittently. You will hike 2.5 miles before you will see Devil's Lake, and another mile should you wish to put your toe (or a fishing line) in the water. Despite the lack of trail markings, this is the easiest approach to Devil's Lake from both a distance and elevation standpoint. Devil's Lake is at 12,000 feet. The Powderhorn Lakes trailhead is at 11,000 feet, significantly higher than any other approach. As you cross Calf Creek Plateau, there are some rocky spots, but the terrain is mostly grass. Along the higher points of Calf Creek Plateau there are wonderful views of Uncompahgre Peak and the surrounding mountains. Continue to the south until such time as you can see Cannibal Plateau. Devil's Lake is in a fold between Cannibal Plateau and Calf Creek Plateau. After passing one post trail marker, you will encounter a fence running from east to west which is in remarkably good condition given that it is in a wilderness area. There is an open section of the fence which is near a tall wooden post. The other posts serving this fence are metal.

After crossing through the opening in the fence, you will see a rock cairn ahead and to your left. You will also see a thin metal post with several cross posts ahead and to your right. Head toward the cairn. The thin metal post signifies the highest point on Calf Creek Plateau and isn't really a navigation aid. Upon reaching the cairn, you will join the largely unused trail to Devil's Lake that originates at the Powderhorn Park trailhead. This trail should be followed through the rocky tundra as it leads to the edge of the plateau and descends to Devil's Lake. Small rock cairns assist you in following this primitive trail. You may not wish to go all the way to the lake as this involves a 600-foot descent along a rocky trail. You may see all of the lake by going a short distance down. A further descent will diminish your views of Uncompahgre Peak and the surrounding mountains. Devil's Lake (**10F**) is like no other in the area. This large lake is surrounded by the two plateaus, and you think you may be on the moon, as there is little vegetation.

The third variation of this hike leads to Hidden Lake. This trail is seldom used and is difficult to follow. The trail to Hidden Lake leaves the lower trail to the Powderhorn Lakes at the 4-mile mark and is designated by a trail sign at the edge of a marsh (**10C**). The trail you see across the marsh at the trail sign does not lead to Hidden Lake. This is the trail to the Powderhorn Lakes which loops around and above the marsh, and away from the direction to Powderhorn Lakes designated by the trail sign. The trail to Hidden Lake follows the West Fork of Powderhorn Creek for .5 miles, first close to the creek, and then somewhat above it as the trail enters a forest. The trail is not well defined, but there are posts and cairns spaced to keep you going in the right direction. As the trail descends before crossing the creek, there are the remnants of a trail sign designating the direction to Hidden Lake. As the trail sign is down, it only gives you confirmation that you are still on the right trail. The trail crosses the creek at this point, and you should not need stream crossing shoes.

After crossing the creek, the trail climbs steeply across a rockslide and into a wooded area to the top of a plateau, the northwest side of which forms the backdrop for the two Powderhorn Lakes. There are still a few cairns as you ascend the plateau and two cairns after you reach the top of the plateau, but then it appears that the trail designator laid down his tools. Any evidence of the trail to Hidden Lake has disappeared as nature has reclaimed this trail. There are the remnants of a trail across the top of the plateau heading to the southwest, but this does not lead to Hidden Lake (**10G**). However, it does lead you to the edge of the plateau where you can see down to the trail intersection which you left 2 miles previously, as well as to Calf Creek Plateau on the other side of the lakes (**10H**). The quad map indicates that you would need to enter the wooded area and go .5 miles east to find the lake. As I did not find where the trail leaves the tundra and enters the woods, Hidden Lake remains hidden to this hiker as of this writing.

RATING: For the lower route, the round-trip distance to Upper Powderhorn Lake (**10E**) is 11 miles and the net elevation gain is 700 feet, although the gross elevation gain is more like twice that amount. As all the gains are modest, this is a trail which should be accessible to any intermediate hiker. The upper trail to Upper Powderhorn Lake (**10E via 10D**) is a bit shorter, measuring 7 miles round trip to the overlook, or 10 miles for a loop approaching the lakes by the upper route and returning by the lower route. The elevation gain to the overlook is 1,300 feet. A round trip to Devil's Lake (**10F**) would be 14 miles, or 12 miles if you stop near the top of the overlook. The elevation gain would be 1,600 feet to the top of the overlook. Due to the lack of trail markings, terrain, and distance, either of these two hikes should be limited to experienced hikers. As to a hike in search of Hidden Lake **(10G)**, this would involve a round trip of 11 miles and an elevation gain of 1,000 to the point on the overlook described above **(10H)**. Because of the length of this hike and the navigation issues, this hike should also be limited to experienced hikers.

Upper Powderhorn Lake

Katherine Heidt

EAST FORK POWDERHORN CREEK

Quad: Rudolph Hill

DRIVING INSTRUCTIONS: Drive north from Lake City on CO SH 149 for 25 miles. Past MP 99, Gunnison CR 29 is the second of three county roads leading into the Powderhorn area. Turn to the right and go 1.4 miles to the intersection with Ten Mile Springs Road, which is designated Gunnison CR 59. Turn right and go 8.0 miles to the trailhead. Ten Mile Springs Road does not require 4WD, but a vehicle with high ground clearance is recommended. You should avoid this road after a heavy rain. There is ample parking at the trailhead, which is well marked. Trailhead elevation - 9,500 feet.

THE HIKE: This hike leads into the northern section of the Powderhorn Wilderness to the east of the Powderhorn Lakes trailhead. The *Trails Illustrated* map indicates that the East Fork Trail will take you to Powderhorn Park and the trailhead boasts an impressive list of destinations, including Hidden Lake, Devil's Lake, and the Powderhorn Lakes. Don't believe any of this. Most of the trails in this trail system are overgrown and there is a limited area still served by this trailhead. A portion of this trail does not appear on the quad and only the last portion is indicated on the *Trails Illustrated* map for La Garita, Cochetopa Hills. The trailhead does not lie within Hinsdale County, but the trail leads into the county.

Upon leaving the trailhead (**11A**) you begin a moderate descent of 100 feet to the East Fork of Powderhorn Creek, passing the Powerhorn Wilderness Area boundary along the way. Upon reaching the stream you will soon realize that this is no ordinary stream crossing. You will cross water several times with islands in several places. The stream is not running particularly fast, but places are deep and other places are muddy. You will need stream crossing shoes at all times. As the stream crossing is only .25 miles from the trailhead, you may be tempted to wear your stream crossing shoes from the start, carrying your boots. This will work in some instances but be advised that the trail down to the stream is on the rough side.

After crossing the stream, you hike along the east side of the stream the rest of the way. As there is not a lot of elevation change, the stream doesn't cascade, and is pretty mild compared with most other area streams. There are many ponds where the beavers have had their way with the stream, and much of their handiwork is impressive. With this much standing water, I would think it to be ideal habitat for moose, which I have seen this far north. However inviting this might be, the moose haven't accepted the invitation on any day I've hiked this trail.

You are hiking through wooded and lightly wooded area through-out both variations of this hike, gaining elevation very gradually until you reach the 2-mile point. At that point, there is a detached trail sign leaning against a tree, fortunately pointing in the correct direction (**11B**). To the right is the trail to the Powderhorn Swamp and continu-ing straight the sign designates the East Fork Trail and the route to Robbers Roost.

Continuing along the East Fork Trail, you cross Phelps Cabin Creek shortly after the trail intersection. Stream crossing shoes are not needed. Shortly after the stream crossing the trail enters a meadow, which serves as a campsite. Beyond the campsite the trail enters the willows growing along the East Fork and the trail largely disappears (**11C**). The same thing happens to the southern portion of the trail, as discussed under the section for Powderhorn Park. There is a 3-mile gap where the trail is overgrown.

Should you wish to go to the Powderhorn Swamp, take the right fork at the trail sign (**11B**) and begin a moderate to steep ascent over the next mile. You hike alongside Phelps Cabin Creek for the first por-tion of this climb, crossing it twice in rapid succession. Stream crossing shoes are not necessary. The trail becomes steeper as you continue to climb. After hiking a mile from the fork and climbing 600 feet, you begin to level out and you see a parting of the trees. You are enter-ing the Powderhorn Swamp (**11D**), a grassy and marshy area that is a depression, surrounded on all four sides by higher ground and trees. Upon reaching the entrance to the swamp, there is a cairn with a large post designating the spot to which you must return to find your way

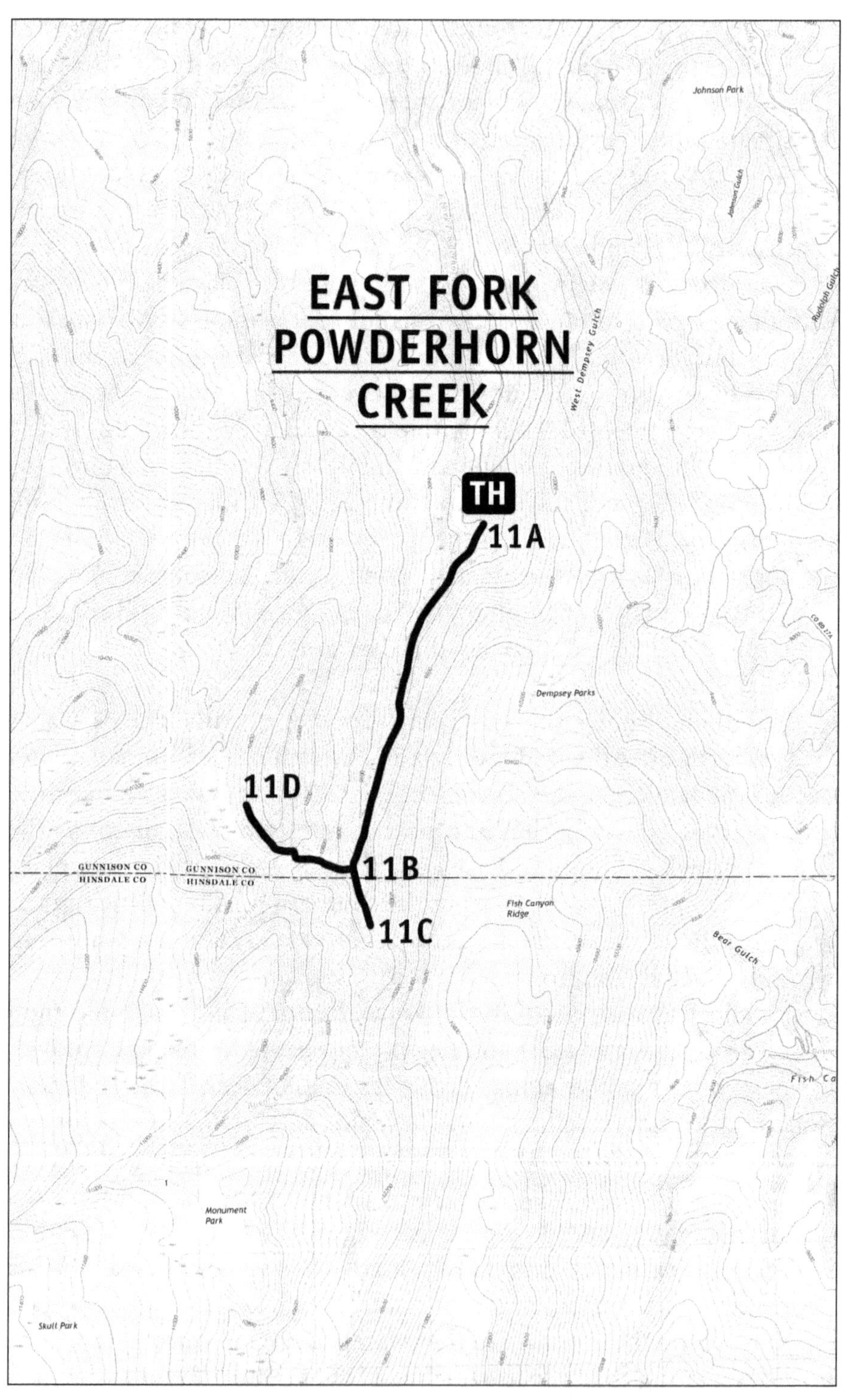

Johnson Park
Johnson Gulch
Rudolph Gulch
West Dempsey Gulch
EAST FORK
POWDERHORN
CREEK
TH
11A
CO RB 27A
Dempsey Parks
11D
11B
GUNNISON CO
HINSDALE CO
GUNNISON CO
HINSDALE CO
11C
Fish Canyon Ridge
Bear Gulch
Fish Ca
Monument Park
Skull Park

back. The trail continues for a short while on the northern edge of the swamp but fades away after reaching several potential campsites.

RATING: A hike along the East Fork Trail to where it effectively ends (**11C**) is a 4.5-mile round trip gaining 300 feet in elevation. It is suitable for a beginning hiker as long as he or she isn't spooked by the first water crossing. A hike to the Powderhorn Swamp (**11D**) is a 6-mile round trip gaining 800 feet. Due to the steepness of the climb to the swamp, it is more suitable for intermediate hikers.

Hiking in the Powderhorn Wilderness

Katherine Heidt

Uncompahgre Peak as seen from the Clay Pots

Glenn Heumann

Trailheads Located West of Lake City via CR 20

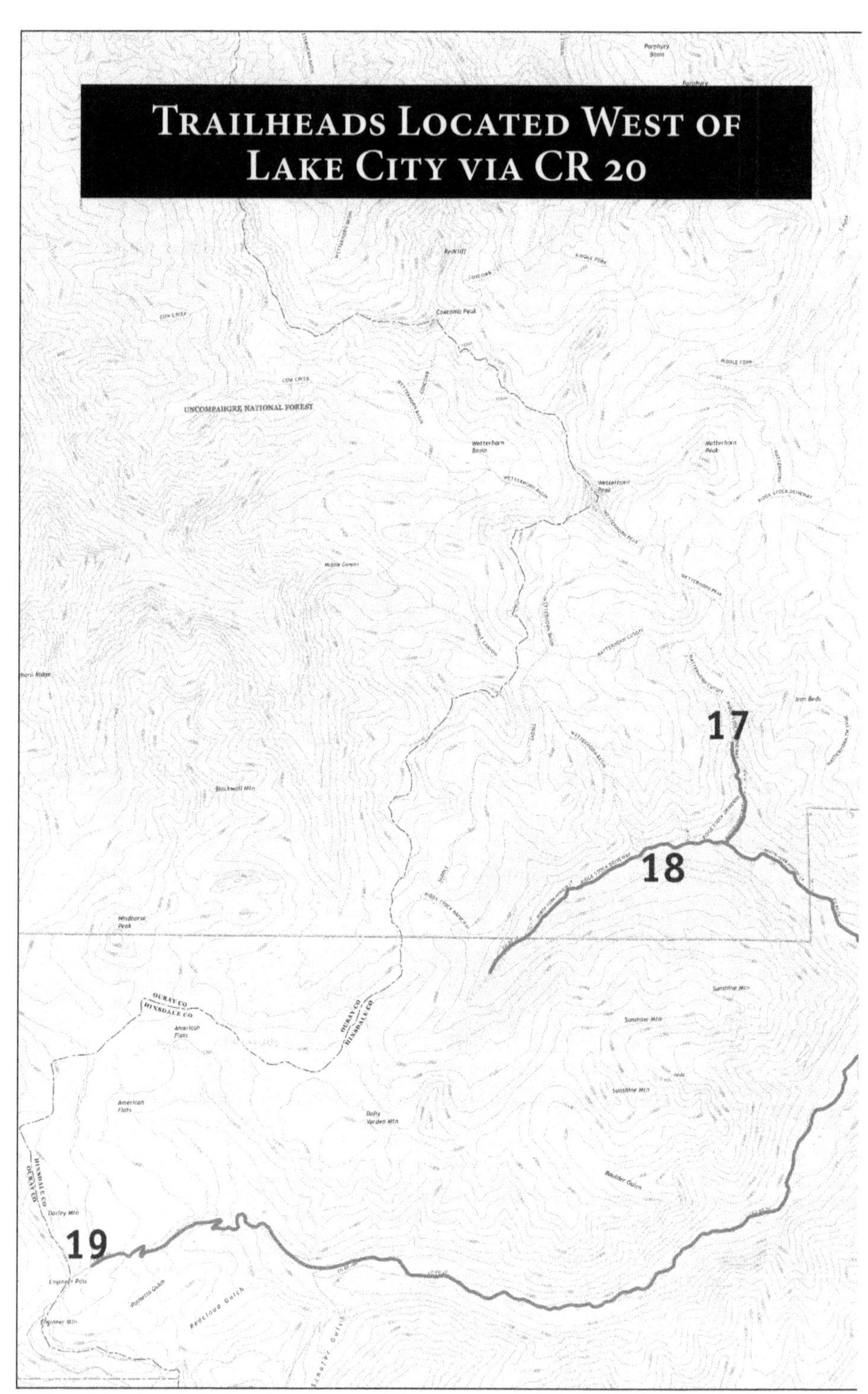

TRAILHEADS LOCATED WEST OF
LAKE CITY VIA CR 20
17
18
19

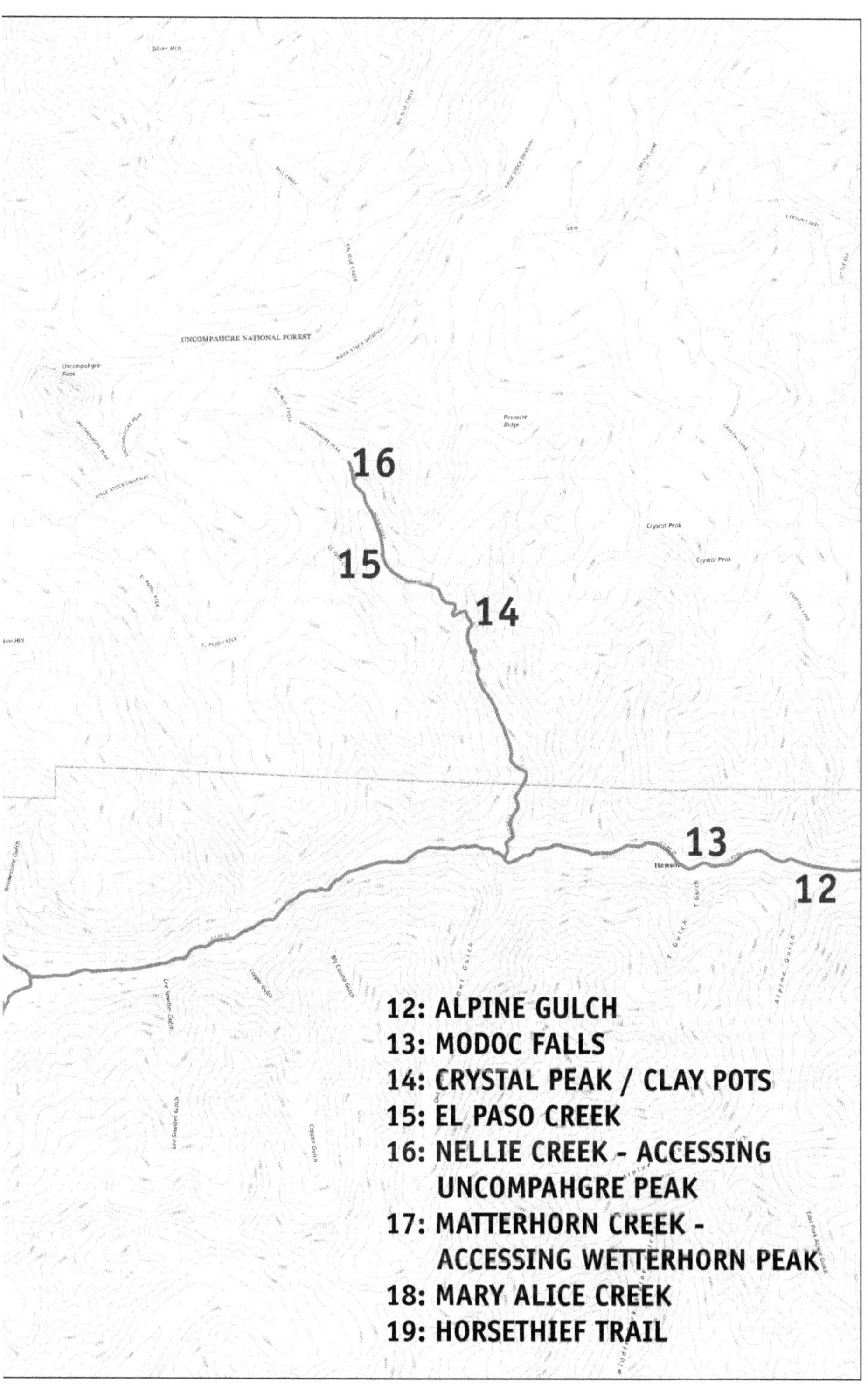

12: ALPINE GULCH
13: MODOC FALLS
14: CRYSTAL PEAK / CLAY POTS
15: EL PASO CREEK
16: NELLIE CREEK - ACCESSING UNCOMPAHGRE PEAK
17: MATTERHORN CREEK - ACCESSING WETTERHORN PEAK
18: MARY ALICE CREEK
19: HORSETHIEF TRAIL

ALPINE GULCH

Quad: Lake City, Lake San Cristobal, Redcloud Peak

DRIVING INSTRUCTIONS: Drive west from Lake City on CR 20 for 2.4 miles. The trailhead is on your left and there is ample parking on the right side of the road with limited parking next to the trailhead. Trailhead elevation - 9,000 feet.

THE HIKE: If you're looking for a hike which will be accompanied by the sound of rushing water, this is the trail for you. There are four variations of this hike, but all follow Alpine Gulch for over 2 miles and involve seven significant stream crossings. You can't count on logs bridging these crossings although they may be present from time to time. The gulch has significant stream flow early in the season and following significant rains. You should expect to get your feet wet on this hike. Because of the rapid stream flow the gulch should be crossed wearing either boots or running shoes. Less sturdy stream crossing shoes should be left behind. I wear an old set of boots for this hike. The first two versions of this hike appear on the *Trails Illustrated* map, while the first three appear on the quads.

The trail follows the west side of the stream for most of the first 2 miles, crossing over and back in rapid succession as terrain on the west side becomes temporarily difficult. Although you are constantly climbing, the ascent is gentle. The first set of two crossings is soon after leaving the trailhead (**12A**). The second set is much further along after the trail climbs significantly above the stream, and the third set not long afterward. It is possible to avoid the second set of crossings by following a trail along the bottom of the rock face adjacent to the stream as long as you don't mind hugging the rocks as you pass. You may prefer to just take the plunge and hike across the stream. If it's early in the season, you won't be able to keep your feet dry for much longer anyway.

At the seventh stream crossing you pass to the east side of the stream where you will stay for a distance. About .25 miles after the seventh stream crossing there is a trail sign designating the division of the trail (**12B**). The most popular option is to continue along the east fork of the gulch which is also the route to Grassy Mountain. The second option is to take the west fork of the gulch which will result in a much shorter hike. A third option leaves the main trail shortly before the trail sign and climbs along an old mining road to a mine. The fourth option is an assent of Grassy Mountain.

Taking the first option, along the east fork of Alpine Gulch, you will remain in the trees for the next 1.5 miles, crossing the stream at least seven times, depending on what you are calling a stream crossing. These become progressively easier as you gain elevation and the stream narrows. The climb during this section is moderate and the trail is well defined. After leaving the trees, you see the expanse of the east fork drainage and encounter two areas which contain downed timber from the 2019 avalanches. As of this writing, the first downed timber section has had a path cut through it and presents no problem. The second section is a different story. Historically, the trail has followed the creek closely as it ascends the east fork drainage. This route is all but impassible at this point but determined hikers have forged an alternate route. There is a faint trail going above and to the left (east) of the creek that avoids most, but not all, of the downed timber. After .25 miles this trail descends to the point where it rejoins the original trail and you can continue up the drainage.

Not long after the blockage the trail turns to the left and enters a wooded area. The trail steepens and contains many switchbacks. Historically this is the most difficult section of the Alpine Gulch climb but has been superseded by the detour around the avalanche timber. This section is not without its pleasures, as it is seasonally filled with wildflowers. The trail remains easy to follow and provides good footing, despite its steepness. At the top of this climb, you level out to a spot which allows your first views of the Lake Fork drainage. For purposes of this narrative, I call this point the top of the Alpine Gulch Trail (**12H**). There is still climbing ahead should you wish to enter the transition zone connecting the east fork of Alpine Gulch and the Williams Creek Trail, or should you wish to climb Grassy Mountain.

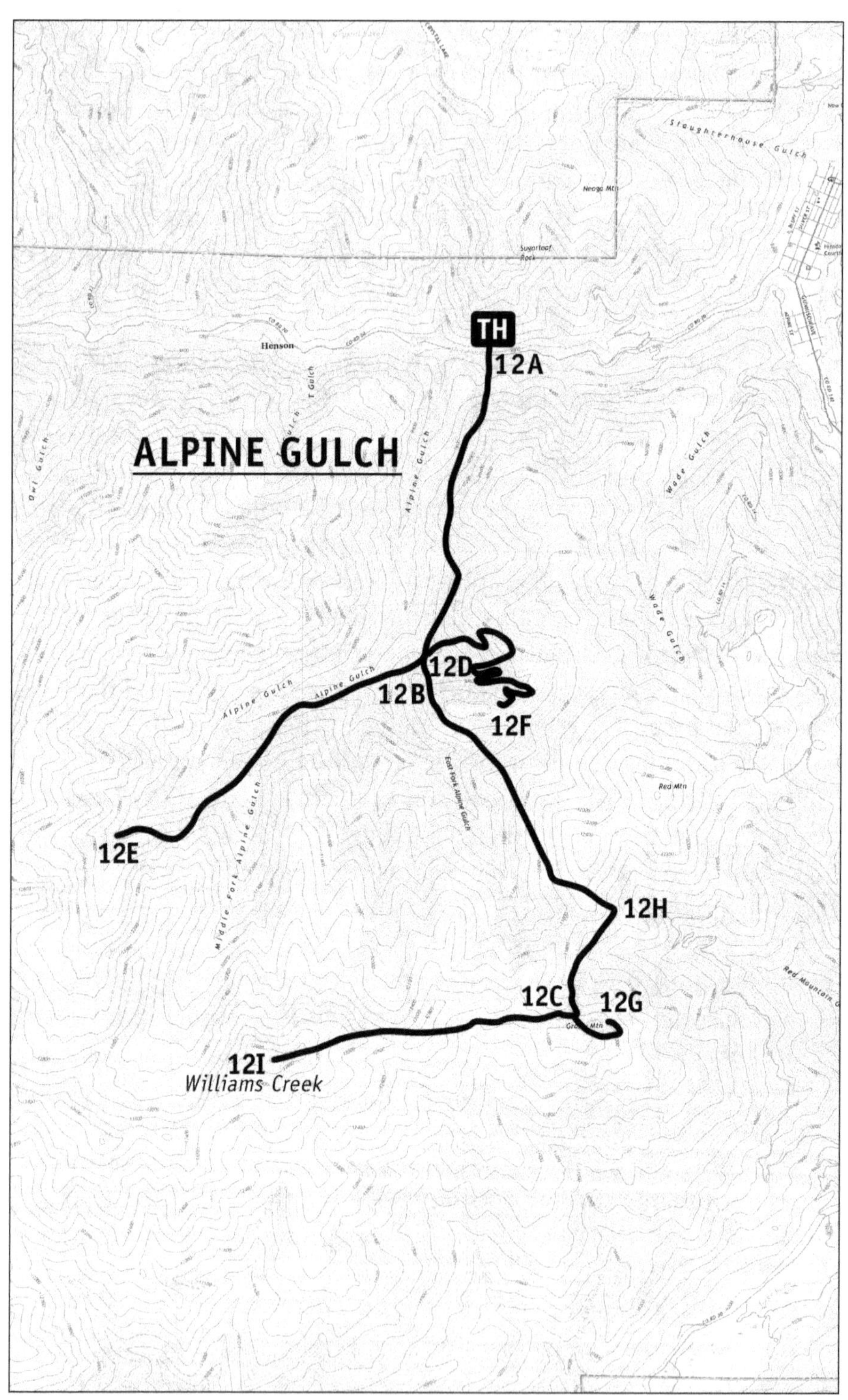
TH
12A
ALPINE GULCH
Henson
12D
12B
12F
12E
12H
12C
12G
12I
Williams Creek

Should you wish to continue into the transition zone, you will turn to the right (west) and climb moderately through a lightly forested area along a ridge. You then reach the first of several switchbacks climbing the ridge, and you begin to lose the trees as you reach the top of the switchbacks. The trail remains easy to follow through this section and there are several cairns along the way. Reaching the top of the ridge, there are adjacent two trails exiting to your right. The first is designated by a large cairn and leads a short distance to an overlook. The main trail continues to the left at this point. Soon afterward there is a second trail leading to the right. This is the original trail connecting the Alpine Gulch and Williams Creek trailheads. It has not been maintained, crosses rockslides, has dangerous spots, and should be avoided. The preferred route continues to the left toward the saddle connecting Grassy Mountain and a ridge to the west of that peak. From that saddle, the trails divide once again (12C). The trail to your left leads in the direction Grassy Mountain, which is 300 feet higher than the saddle and less than .5 miles to the summit. However, that trail does not lead to the summit. Upon reaching a higher saddle, the trail begins to descend. To your left there are two features which are higher in elevation. The further of the two is better defined and appears to be the taller of the two, but the summit is part of the first feature. There is no trail to the summit, so you must choose your own route. There are fine views from the summit (12G). Also, Grassy Mountain isn't grassy.

Back at the saddle separating the trail toward Grassy Mountain and the trail leading through the transition zone to the Williams Creek Trail (12C), the trail to your right leads to the Williams Creek Trail. Continuing toward the Williams Creek trailhead, you climb along a rocky ridge following cairns and a lightly established trail. The trail continues in a westerly direction along the crest of this ridge. A mile from the Grassy Mountain saddle you reach the high point of the ridge, at just above 12,800 feet in elevation. From that point you see where the original rough trail, mentioned in the previous paragraph, rejoins the current trail. This high point is roughly the midway point between the Alpine Gulch and the Williams Creek trailheads. The trail beyond this point (12I) is covered in the section for Williams Creek. For those contemplating a thru-hike between the two trailheads, Williams Creek is the logical starting point for several reasons. The uphill is easier on the Williams Creek side and the trailhead is 200 feet higher in elevation.

More importantly, the Alpine Gulch Trail involves numerous water crossings, and you would probably prefer to have wet boots only at the end of your hike, rather than for almost the whole trek.

Returning to the trail sign after the first seven stream crossings (**12B**), the second option directs you to the west fork of Alpine Gulch where you will cross the stream adjacent to the trail sign for an eighth and final time. Shortly after crossing the stream, you will enter a campground, and the trail leading away from the campground may not be obvious. It will be toward the left side of the campground and will take you back into the trees. From this point on you will be following an old mining road which will steadily ascend for .25 miles and then flatten out for a similar distance. While on the flatter portion you will pass the ruins of a miner's cabin on your left. Throughout this hike, you are passing through an aspen grove which makes this option attractive for a fall hike.

Not too long after passing the ruins of the cabin the trail will be blocked by downed timber likely from an avalanche. While you may wish to turn around at this point or shortly afterward, the trail does continue for another .25 miles. From the trail blockage, work your way down and to the right to an open grassy area with quite a few rocks. This spot gives you your best view of the west fork drainage and may be your likely turnaround spot. If you wish to go on, the mining road crosses the eastern portion of this clearing and continues south, although this part of the trail is rarely used and can be hard to follow. After going a little further, the mining road becomes more of a pack trail, passes through another campground and leads you to the stream where the trail apparently ends (**12E**). The *Trails Illustrated* map shows the trail ending before this point while the Redcloud Peak quad shows the trail crossing the creek and continuing on the other side. There is little evidence of a trail remaining across the creek.

The third option, leading to the mine, leaves the main trail between the seventh stream crossing and the trail sign indicating the junction of the east fork and the west fork of Alpine Gulch (**12B**). After the stream crossing look to your left for the remnants of a mining cabin. You will encounter an old mining road that intersects the main trail 100 yards beyond the cabin (**12D**). The mining road is also 100 yards before you reach the trail sign where the east fork and the west fork routes divide (**12B**). This trail appears on the quad map, but is absent from the *Trails*

Illustrated map. This intersection is unmarked, and the trail is not readily apparent other than the contours of the mining road, which should be your best indicator.

Follow the mining road uphill in a downstream direction, passing a small pond and crossing water a couple of times. These water crossings are nothing like what you have already crossed. The road has six switchbacks over the course of the next 2 miles, the distance between each switchback generally decreasing as you ascend. Because this is a mining road, the grade is gradual although you will gain 1,300 feet in elevation from the time you leave the stream to the time you reach the top. The lower portion of this option is wooded but the trail opens up significantly after the second switchback. As this trail gets little use, there are portions where trees have grown up where the miners' wagons once passed. Continue following the contours of the road. Before reaching the first switchback, the trail is blocked by downed timber caused by the 2019 avalanches. This can be bypassed by climbing above it and rejoining the trail 100 yards later. This is not an easy bypass. Following this blockage, the trail clears once again, and you reach the first switchback. The second switchback can be easy to miss as the road continues straight even after the switchback. There is a small rock cairn marking the switchback. Don't start looking for the cairn too early. There is .5 miles between the first and the second switchbacks.

After the second switchback, the view opens up considerably and you have great views of the other side of Alpine Gulch and down valley. The views only get better as you ascend. The terrain is rocky, but there aren't any places where you are crossing scree. The trail is easy to follow after the second switchback.

After the sixth switchback, you will reach a point where the mining road appears to end as you have reached your highest elevation. The mine is several hundred feet to your right. There is a slight elevation gain to reach the top of a knoll (**12F**) while the mine shaft is to the south of this point. There is a significant amount of discarded mining equipment near the shaft including the pulley which allowed the buckets of ore to be hauled to the surface. The shaft is open, and after tossing a couple of rocks into the shaft I could hear each hit the side wall four or five times before each fell beyond the point where it could be heard. From the top of the knoll above the mine shaft you have a 360-degree view of the surrounding area, including the first two hiking options from this trailhead. At the top of the knoll, you are at 11,100 feet and this is your turnaround point. I consider this option the best hike in the area that you've probably never heard of.

The fourth option from this trailhead is an ascent of Grassy Mountain (**12G**), which was described above.

Rating: For the first option, the roundtrip distance to the top of Alpine Gulch (**12H**) is 10 miles and gains 2,800 feet. A trip to the mid-point between the Alpine Gulch and Williams Creek trailheads (**12I**) covers 14 miles and gains 3,800 feet. A thru-hike to the Williams Creek trailhead also covers 14.5 miles and gains 3,800 feet, before descending 3,600 feet. All of these hikes should be limited to experienced hikers. For the second option, hiking to the end of the West Fork Trail (**12E**), the round-trip distance is 7 miles, and you have 1,200 feet of gradual elevation gain. Aside from the stream crossings, there is nothing challenging about this hike, and it could be hiked by a well acclimated beginner. As to the third option, a hike to the mine on the hilltop (**12F**), the round-trip distance is 10 miles, and all of the 2,100 feet of elevation gain is at a gradual pace. Although this trail is used infrequently, the navigation is not difficult. The downed timber challenges limit this trail to experienced hikers. The fourth option, a trip to the summit of Grassy Mountain (**12G**), is a round trip of 13 miles and gains 3,800 feet. It too should be limited to experienced hikers.

MODOC FALLS

Quad: Uncompahgre Peak

DRIVING INSTRUCTIONS: Drive west from Lake City on CR 20 for 4.1 miles. The trailhead is unmarked, but the trail can be seen heading toward the northeast. There is a primitive pullout section to your left that will accommodate several vehicles. Trailhead elevation - 9,200 feet.

THE HIKE: The trail to Modoc Falls is short and gains little elevation. The falls are well worth seeing and are impressive early in the season. As this trail does not appear on either the *Trails Illustrated* map or on the quad, it does not get a great deal of use and is known primarily to locals. Finding the trailhead may be your greatest challenge. Opposite the trailhead, within a campsite, there are four sets of posts with rails along the top, similar to hitching posts. This may be your best landmark as to where the trail begins. Because this trail is so short, you may want to pair it with something else as you explore Henson Creek.

The trail climbs the embankment above the road (**13A**) before leveling out and ascending gradually through forest for the entirety of this hike. The trail is faint and difficult to follow in one spot. Soon after reaching the top of the embankment the trail appears to divide. The right turn is the more defined trail, but that trail evaporates quickly. The left turn continues to the falls. After .25 miles you reach Modoc Creek and follow it for the rest of the hike, crossing it twice. Soon after the second crossing you arrive at Modoc Falls (**13B**), where the creek drops over 30 feet to trail level. You can walk up to the falls and take a cold shower if you are so inclined. This isn't one of the bigger waterfalls in the area, but you won't find one where you can get closer to the action. The trail effectively ends at the falls, although there is a steep

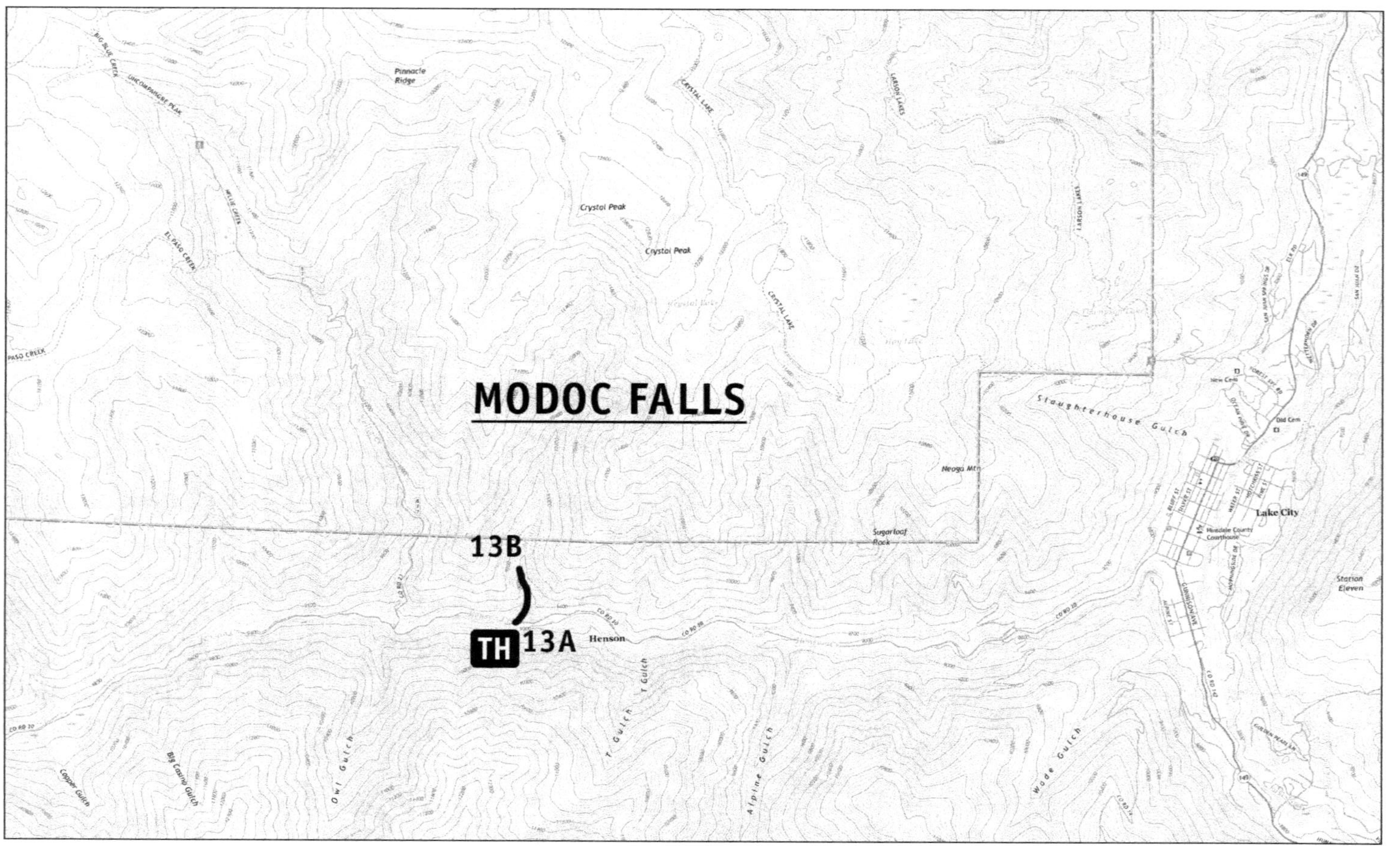
Pinnacle Ridge
Crystal Peak
Crystal Peak
Crystal Lake
Crystal Lake
Larson Lakes
Big Blue Creek
Uncompahgre Peak
Nellie Creek
El Paso Creek
Paso Creek
MODOC FALLS
Neoga Mtn
Slaughterhouse Gulch
New Cem
Old Cem
Lake City
Hinsdale County Courthouse
Station Eleven
Gunnison Ave
Sugarloaf Rock
13B
TH 13A
Henson
Owl Gulch
T Gulch
T Gulch
Alpine Gulch
Wade Gulch
Big Casino Gulch
Copper Gulch

trail to the left of the falls leading you to the top of the falls. It contains loose dirt and rock and is not recommended.

RATING: A round trip hike to Modoc Falls **(13B)** covers less than 1 mile and gains 200 feet. It is suitable for beginners.

Modoc Falls

Glenn Heumann

CRYSTAL PEAK / CLAY POTS

Quad: Lake City, Uncompahgre Peak

DRIVING INSTRUCTIONS: Drive west of Lake City on CR 20 for 4.9 miles. Turn right on the Nellie Creek Road (CR 23, FSR 877) which leads to the Nellie Creek trailhead. The Nellie Creek Road is very rough and 4WD only. After 2.4 miles, which is .5 miles past a ford in Nellie Creek, the main road continues left toward Uncompahgre Peak while a less traveled road turns to the right to the Crystal Peak trailhead, .1 miles ahead, which contains parking for several vehicles adjacent to Nellie Creek. Trailhead elevation - 10,500 feet.

THE HIKE: There are two destinations from this trailhead, Crystal Peak and the Clay Pots which are about the same distance and difficulty. The trail to each is the same until you reach a point 1 mile from each destination. Crystal Peak overlooks Crystal Lake and offers wonderful views in all directions. The Clay Pots are composed of volcanic rock and ash known as the Nelson Mountain Tuff, which remain from an eruption of the San Luis Volcano, over 20 miles to the east. This collapsed volcano, or "caldera" includes Stewart Peak and San Luis Peak. The soft parts of the tuff have eroded leaving the hard, statuesque figures at the end of this hike. There are significant distances and elevation gains involved in reaching both destinations. The lower portion of the trail follows an old mining road which is designated on the quad map while the upper portion of the trail is above timberline, is not well defined, and does not appear on the quads. This trail does not appear on the *Trails Illustrated* map.

From the trailhead (**14A**), you will immediately cross Nellie Creek and find the mining road beginning on the other side. You will want water crossing shoes for this crossing at all times during the season, and early in the season the water flow will probably be too high for you to want to cross at all. If you are hiking this trail late in the season you will probably not need your water crossing shoes for subsequent crossings and you may prefer to leave them along the side of the trail. If the stream flow is particularly high, you will want them for the next two stream crossings.

The trail goes north following a tributary of Nellie Creek through a wooded area, crossing the tributary twice in rapid sequence within 1 mile of the trailhead. The views to the left of aspen groves beneath rock formations are as good as any you will find in the autumn. After 1 mile, the road begins a series of switchbacks as it leaves the stream and climbs moderately toward the east. There will be the ruins of two mining cabins, the first on your left and the second on your right after you have gone almost 2 miles and you will see other evidence of mining operations.

After hiking .5 miles past the cabins, you will reach timberline. Shortly after this you will want to leave the main mining road which continues straight ahead but begins to lose a little elevation. There is a second mining road veering to your left which switches back a couple of times while continuing upward. You will want to continue on this road for .5 miles until you see a saddle on your left which can be reached by climbing through a slight gulch. That saddle is your immediate destination but there is no trail to follow through the tundra. The mining road you are leaving will take you to a higher elevation to the top of a small knob, which offers decent views, but will not lead you to either Crystal Peak or the Clay Pots.

From the top of the saddle, you will have a fine view of Uncompahgre Peak and the surrounding mountains. Looking to the north you will have your first view of the Clay Pots. Turn your back on Uncompahgre and look to the southeast and you will see a saddle to the left which is your next destination. There is a game trail heading toward the Clay Pots that goes nowhere in particular. To the right of this game trail, there is a faint trail which will take you to this saddle, which is where the trails divide (**14B**). There are no trails to either destination from this saddle. You are on your own in short grassy tundra to either destination, both of which are a mile from this saddle. Upon reaching the saddle, you first are able to see Crystal Peak to your right.

To climb Crystal Peak, which is in your view, continue up the ridge, climbing moderately until you reach the summit (**14C**). There are

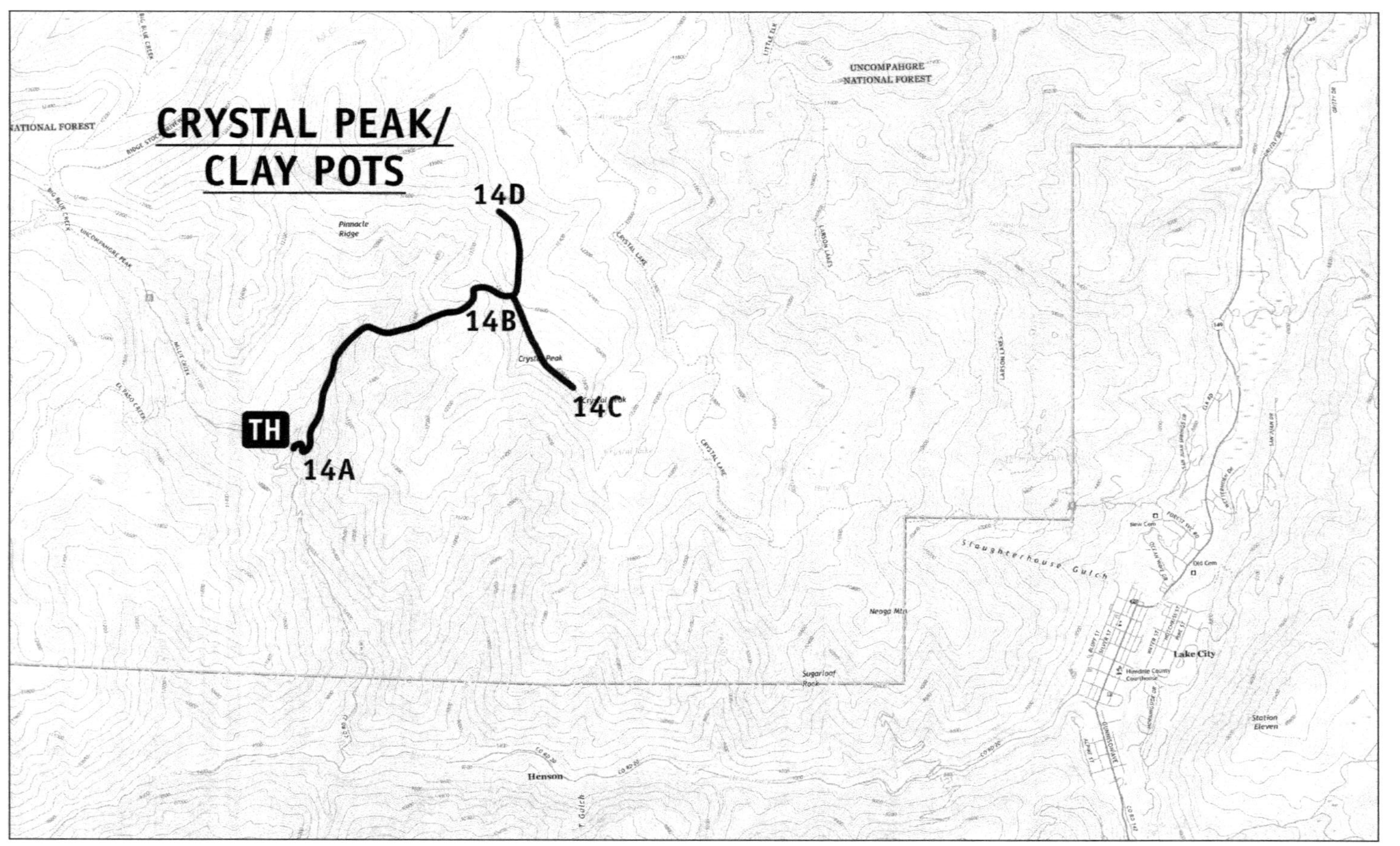

CRYSTAL PEAK/
CLAY POTS
14A
14B
14C
14D
TH
NATIONAL FOREST
UNCOMPAHGRE NATIONAL FOREST
Pinnacle Ridge
Crystal Peak
Crystal Brook
CRYSTAL LAKE
LARSON LAKES
Neoga Mtn
Sugarloaf Rock
Slaughterhouse Gulch
Lake City
Hinsdale County Courthouse
Station Eleven
Henson

several points of similar elevation on top, but you won't be able to look down at Crystal Lake until you reach the furthest point, which isn't necessarily the summit.

To approach the Clay Pots, there is a ridge to your left which contains two bumps. You will need to reach the saddle between those two bumps to get your best view of the Clay Pots. There is a tower-like cairn to the left of the left bump which, while helpful for navigation, isn't your destination. The cairn is further away from the Clay Pots than is the saddle. There is a rocky area between the saddle you are leaving (separating the Clay Pots and Crystal Peak approaches) and the saddle you are approaching. You can either go above or below the rocky area. There are faint remnants of a trail in both places. You will climb until you reach the saddle, and the tower-cairn once again becomes visible to your left. The Clay Pots are visible to your right. Looking at the Clay Pots from the saddle, there is a rockslide between you and the pots. This is not the way. You must go around and below the rock formation to your right. The area below that formation also contains a rocky area and you will want to go below this rocky area. You may see a faint trail toward the lower end of the rocky area and beyond. After passing the rocky area you emerge along tundra and the Clay Pots (**14D**) are once again in view. You can hike to them easily from here. There is a view from one of the further formations that you won't want to miss. Parts of the formation create a quasi-arch and this frames a view of Uncompahgre Peak.

RATING: For either option the round-trip distance is 9 miles. The elevation gain to Crystal Peak (**14C**) is 2,300 feet and to the Clay Pots (**14D**) the gain is 2,100 feet. Both options have no terrain issues until you reach the higher elevations, where you cross over alpine tundra with gentle elevation gains. Navigation can be tricky to either location. Due to the distance, elevation gains, and navigation issues, these hikes should only be taken by experienced hikers.

EL PASO CREEK

Quad: Uncompahgre Peak

DRIVING INSTRUCTIONS: Drive west from Lake City on CR 20 for 4.9 miles to the Nellie Creek turnoff (CR 23, FSR 877). The Nellie Creek Road is very rough and 4WD only. At mile 3.4 along the Nellie Creek Road look for a road across the creek marked with a "Road Closed" sign. This is where you will want to cross the creek on foot but there is no parking at this point. There is ample parking in a clearing 200 yards ahead. After parking, you should return to the "Road Closed" sign, cross the creek and continue along the closed road. There is a second, smaller creek crossing before you reach the edge of the forest. The trailhead for the El Paso Creek Trail is marked at this point **(15A)**. This trail is marked on the *Trails Illustrated* map and on the quad. Trailhead elevation - 11,000 feet.

THE HIKE: For a trail named after a creek, you really don't get very close to the creek. The trail follows mining roads for much of its distance and terminates at the Ridge Stock Driveway which will lead you toward the Matterhorn Creek and Nellie Creek trailheads. There are several stream crossings during the first 2 miles, but stream crossing shoes should not be needed after the spring melt. Once you have entered the wilderness area at just beyond the 2-mile mark there are spectacular views in all directions.

From the trailhead, the trail ascends through forest for the first 1.5 miles. Although this is a mining road, there can be downed timber blocking the road and the trail meanders on well-defined single track in several places, rejoining the mining road afterward. There are several places where you cross water as well. The trail at this point is heavily switch-backed. After 1.5 miles you emerge into an open area and continue to climb via the mining road. After another .25 mile you

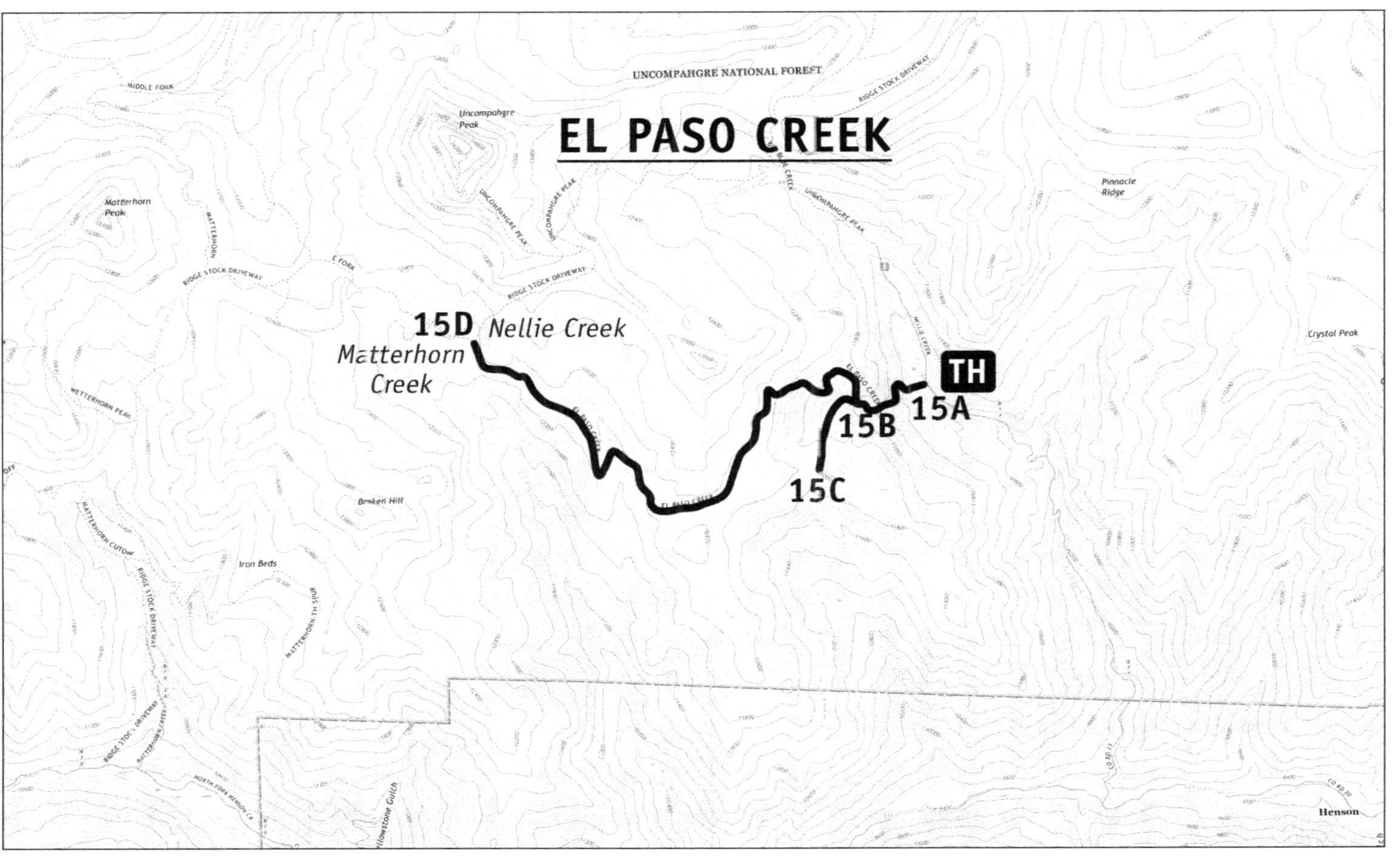
UNCOMPAHGRE NATIONAL FOREST
EL PASO CREEK
Uncompahgre Peak
UNCOMPAHGRE PEAK
UNCOMPAHGRE PEAK
Matterhorn Peak
WETTERHORN PEAK
RIDGE STOCK DRIVEWAY
RIDGE STOCK DRIVEWAY
E FORK
MIDDLE FORK
Pinnacle Ridge
Crystal Peak
15D
Nellie Creek
Matterhorn Creek
TH
15A
15B
15C
EL PASO CREEK
Broken Hill
Iron Beds
MATTERHORN CUTOFF
MATTERHORN TH SPUR
RIDGE STOCK DRIVEWAY
NORTH FORK HENSON CR
Yellowstone Gulch
Henson
CO RD 11

enter the trees. At a bit beyond the 2-mile mark you will encounter a sign designating the boundary of the Uncompahgre Wilderness as you enter into the open basin which will characterize the rest of this hike. El Paso Creek will be to the west, but it is sufficiently below you that you will neither see nor hear the namesake creek during most of this hike.

After passing the wilderness area sign you are in an open area and after a horseshoe turn, you are heading southwest. As you pass a small pond to your left (**15B**), you will see a small grassy hill ahead, called Lunch Mountain by some of the locals. For hikers wanting a shorter hike, this hill is a suitable destination. There are 360-degree views from the top of the hill, including the tops of all five of the Hinsdale County fourteeners. There is not an established trail leading to the top of Lunch Mountain (**15C**).

If you are up for a longer hike, continue along the trail. As you continue west along the tundra, the trail flattens a bit and the rest of the way is characterized by some uphill and some downhill, but mostly uphill. There are a few trees interspersed along the way, but you are largely hiking in the open. As you continue, there are several places where the trail appears to divide. In each case, take the uppermost fork, although these trails will rejoin at some point. After crossing a gulch with loose dirt, you will encounter one of these forks. The map indicates the trail follows the left fork which will descend and curve around a drainage before climbing back to the south. The less defined trail to the right continues to climb but is not difficult to follow. I have taken both routes and each route will rejoin the other route some distance away. The upper route to your right is the more direct route.

As the trail continues to the northwest, there are spots along the tundra where the trail disappears for a while. Continue ahead and you will find it again soon. An advantage of a trail through the tundra is you can see much of what is ahead of you in any direction and the trail will appear at a distance. After you have hiked 5 miles you will see a trail sign which marks the end of this trail (**15D**). You can see the Ridge Stock Driveway to your right as it climbs the ridge south of Uncompahgre Peak. You could return this way to the Nellie Creek trailhead, which is only .7 miles from where you left your car. Less visible as you approach the trail sign is the Ridge Stock Driveway heading west, where it intersects with a number of trails in the Matterhorn Basin and leads you to the Matterhorn Creek trailhead. The portion of the Ridge

Stock Driveway heading west from the trail sign is covered under the section for Matterhorn Creek. The portion of the Ridge Stock Driveway heading east from the trail sign is covered under the section for Nellie Creek.

RATING: Should you follow the trail to the intersection point with the Ridge Stock Driveway **(15D)** and return you will cover 10 miles and gain 1,400 feet. As this trail is difficult to follow, it should be limited to experienced hikers. A hike to Lunch Mountain **(15C)** is a 6-mile round trip and gains 1,300 feet. It would be a more comfortable hike for an intermediate hiker.

The approach to Lunch Mountain

Katherine Heidt

NELLIE CREEK

Quad: Uncompahgre Peak

DRIVING INSTRUCTIONS: Drive west from Lake City on CR 20 for 4.9 miles to the Nellie Creek turnoff (CR 23, FSR 877). The Nellie Creek Road is very rough and 4WD only. At mile 4.1 along the Nellie Creek Road, you will pass an outdoor toilet on your left and the parking area is straight ahead at the road's end. Trailhead elevation - 11,400 feet.

THE HIKE: While the Nellie Creek trailhead is difficult to reach, the trails beginning there are some of the best trails in the area, all offering spectacular views. At 14,308 feet, Uncompahgre Peak is the sixth tallest mountain in Colorado and the tallest in Hinsdale County. As it has a distinctive shape and is visible from many distant points, it is fair to call it the iconic peak for the area. This is the trailhead of choice for those wishing to climb Uncompahgre Peak, but this trailhead offers much more. It intersects the Ridge Stock Driveway, which is a gateway to other trails heading east, west, and north from Uncompahgre Peak. Utilizing this trail system, you can enter at Nellie Creek and exit at several western points, including the Matterhorn Creek trailhead, the Big Blue Creek trailhead to the north, or after intersecting with the Crystal Lake / Larson Lakes loop, the Independence Gulch trailhead, or the Crystal Lake / Larson Lakes trailhead at the edge of Lake City. There are numerous possibilities from this trailhead. This section will discuss four of them. All trails beginning at the Nellie Creek trailhead are marked on the *Trails Illustrated* map and on the quad.

All four variations beginning at the Nellie Creek trailhead (**16A**) cover the same ground for the first mile, until you reach the intersection of the Ridge Stock Driveway (**16B**). This mile gains 500 feet going first through wooded and then open areas that become increasingly rocky as you climb above timberline. The trail intersection is well marked.

From this point you go left if you want to climb Uncompahgre Peak or proceed west along the Ridge Stock Driveway toward the Matterhorn Creek trailhead and beyond. The trail sign indicates that you should turn right if you want to proceed to Big Blue Creek. You should also turn right if you want to proceed along the Ridge Stock Driveway toward the intersection with the Crystal Lake / Larson Lakes loop and north or east to points beyond.

Turning left from this point (**16B**), you are on the Ridge Stock Driveway heading west for the next 1.75 miles, whether you intend to climb Uncompahgre Peak or continue west along the Ridge Stock Driveway. There are a few trees at first, but you are above timberline for the rest of the trail to the ridge that separates the Nellie Creek drainage from the El Paso Creek drainage. The climb is moderate as you gain only 1,000 feet from the previous trail marker to the top of the ridge 1.75 miles later. There is one small water crossing. This is a very gradual climb for the approach to a fourteener. More severe changes in elevation are waiting for you later, whether you are climbing Uncompahgre Peak or whether you are descending into the El Paso Creek Basin.

At the top of the ridge there are several trail signs. The first instructs you to stay on the trail and the second indicates the trail to Uncompahgre Peak is to your right and the trail toward Matterhorn Creek is to your left (**16C**). The Ridge Stock Driveway continues on the trail to your left.

Most hikers departing the Nellie Creek trailhead intend to climb Uncompahgre Peak so we will cover that first. After taking the right turn at the trail sign there is a post ahead and a trail sign instructing you to stay on the trail and little guidance thereafter. Don't worry, this is a well-traveled trail, and it is easy to follow. You climb moderately in a northerly direction along the ridge with great views to your left as you approach Uncompahgre Peak proper. The trail has log check dams offering a staircase effect. Once you reach the end of the ridge and are climbing Uncompahgre Peak the trail steepens and there are several switchbacks as you head toward the west face of the peak. At this point things get interesting. You will be climbing a rockslide at a forty-five-degree angle, some rocks more secure than others. You may want gloves for this portion of the hike as you will be climbing on all fours. Put away your trekking poles as they will only get in the way. Fortunately, this climb only covers 100 vertical feet and you will rejoin a more traditional trail for the home stretch to the summit (**16F**). The

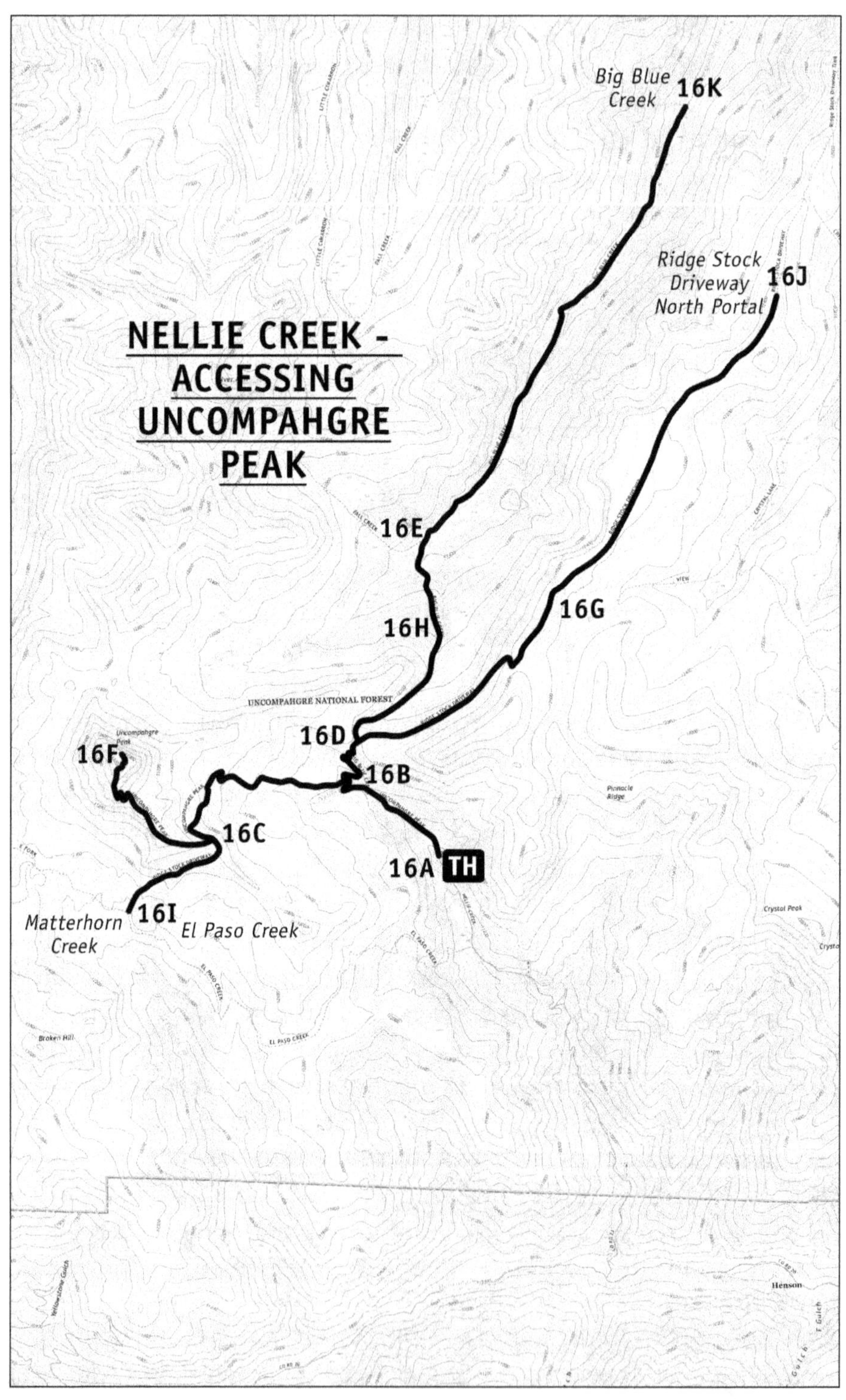

Big Blue Creek 16K
Ridge Stock Driveway North Portal 16J
NELLIE CREEK - ACCESSING UNCOMPAHGRE PEAK
16E
16H
16G
UNCOMPAHGRE NATIONAL FOREST
16D
16F
16B
16C
16A TH
Matterhorn Creek
16I
El Paso Creek
Uncompahgre Peak
Pinnacle Ridge
Crystal Peak
Broken Hill
Henson

home stretch covers over .25 miles and climbs a final 300 vertical feet. There is plenty of room at the summit and the views are unparalleled.

Returning to the fork along the ridge where you had the option to head to Matterhorn Creek as well as Uncompahgre Peak (**16C**), you may wish to take the left fork leading into the El Paso Creek Basin. The descent into the El Paso Creek Basin via the Ridge Stock Driveway has three steep sections, each section more severe than its predecessor. After the initial descent from the ridge, the trail flattens out considerably as you traverse the upper portion of an amphitheater. At the end of this section, there is a wind shelter of rocks and a post with a metal plate containing a message long lost. I can imagine that this was placed by Dante, circa 1317, announcing the first circle of hell. That's the trail ahead, not the scenery, which is heavenly. After the wind shelter, the trail descends steeply over surface that is less than ideal. It flattens for a while before descending again even more steeply over a dirt and gravelly surface. You need to be careful through this section. After this third descent you will flatten out considerably and you will see a trail to your left. This is the El Paso Creek Trail, with which you will intersect .25 miles later after a water crossing. Overall, you descend 800 feet from the top of the ridge to the intersection with the El Paso Creek Trail (**16I**). The trail sign designates the El Paso Creek Trail and the trail toward Uncompahgre Peak, upon which you have been travelling. It does not indicate what lies ahead as you continue west on the Ridge Stock Driveway. This is the way to the Matterhorn Creek drainage and trailhead. That portion of the Ridge Stock Driveway is covered under the section for Matterhorn Creek. As the trailheads for El Paso Creek and Nellie Creek are less than a mile apart, this offers the opportunity for a loop hike can be done in one day, despite its 11-mile length. I would recommend starting this loop at the El Paso Creek trailhead, as the steep areas described above are more safely hiked as uphill climbs than as descents.

Back at the trail sign 1 mile from the trailhead (**16B**), should you turn right, you will climb 500 feet to the top of a saddle along a trail that is well marked and contains several switchbacks. As you climb, the terrain becomes tundra, and the trail becomes more difficult to follow as you reach the top of the saddle. The trail is marked by two posts (the second one was down as of my last visit) and there is a trail marker on the other side of the saddle marking the intersection of the Ridge Stock Driveway and the Big Blue Creek Trail (**16D**).

Should you continue east along the Ridge Stock Driveway, you will gain little elevation over the next mile as you traverse the tundra near the top of a large bowl which serves as the upper Big Blue Creek drainage. The trail steepens and there are a couple of switchbacks as you reach the top of the namesake ridge. The trail stays on the top of the ridge for quite some distance, with little elevation gain or loss during this time, before reaching the trail that will lead you off the ridge and back toward the intersection with the Crystal Lake / Larson Lakes loop **(16J)**. What I've described is likely a multiday hike. For those looking for a day hike, there is a nice spot beyond several cairns .5 miles after reaching the top of the ridge which offers shelter from the wind **(16G)**. This would be an appropriate turnaround point as it is 3.5 miles and 1,400 feet of elevation gain from where you began.

Continuing north along the Ridge Stock Driveway you descend slightly as you continue through the rocks. Emerging from the rocks onto the tundra, the trail disappears for a while. You must continue north near the top of the ridge for the next several miles. The trail will reappear from time to time but there is minimal guidance along the top of this ridge. There is one spot where at a distance there appears to be a pair of cairns, however, when you are closer, these are two large rocks sitting aside each other. Never mind, these rocks are guiding you as correctly as if they were cairns.

There is a large cairn nearly 1.5 miles north of where you saw the last grouping of cairns. From here you can see a high point in the ridge ahead of you. You will pass to the left (west) of this hilltop. As you leave the point where you have found the large cairn you will descend slightly and there are two steel posts to guide you. After passing the second of these posts the trail reappears (barely) as you cross a rocky area. The trail continues north, passing to the west of the tall point referenced earlier and there is a third steel post providing guidance. North of here there are three bumps along the top of the ridge. The first two contain cairns while the third bump, which is the smallest, does not. From this third bump look ahead and to your right below you. There is a grassy meadow which contains the trail intersection for Trail #235, which connects you to the Crystal / Larson loop **(16J)**. You should note that the trail sign is quite old and designates the trail to the Crystal / Larson loop as Trail #255, while the current designation for this trail is #235. That portion of Trail #235 is not covered in this book. That portion of the Ridge Stock Driveway north of this trail junction **(16J)** is covered in the section titled, Ridge Stock Driveway – North Portal.

Returning to the trail sign where the Ridge Stock Driveway and the Big Blue Creek trails divide **(16D)**, should you wish to travel down Big Blue Creek, your trail goes to the left. While it is faint at the top of the pass, the trail gains definition as it descends the bowl along the west side of the drainage. Much of the trail has served as a water channel during snowmelt and is quite eroded. You will descend 500 feet over the next mile through the open bowl before you reach trees. Shortly after reaching the wooded area there is a nice campsite which can serve as a turnaround point for anyone not wanting a long hike **(16H)**.

Should you want to continue north along Big Blue Creek, you will be in forest for the next .5 miles descending moderately, with one short steep stretch. Once you leave the forest the trail divides. Both forks rejoin after a mile. The right-hand fork stays close to the creek, crossing a marshy area and losing definition in the marsh before reappearing along the left (west) side of the lower drainage. The left- hand fork stays higher and dryer as it takes a longer route to the point where the trails rejoin. The left fork is the preferred route. It descends to cross a creek, which will require stream crossing shoes most of the season, before ascending sharply to where you reach a trail sign **(16E)**. The sign indicates that Fall Creek is to your left, Slide Lake is to your right, and the Ridge Stock Driveway is from whence you came. The Fall Creek Trail is not covered in this book.

Continuing along Big Blue Trail toward Slide Lake, the trail is well above the creek as it passes through the edge of a wooded area. A mile from where the Big Blue Creek trails divided, they rejoin as the left-hand fork (the preferred fork) descends before a creek crossing. This crossing will once again require your stream crossing shoes. The trail only stays on the east side of the creek for a short distance before crossing again to the west side and the terrain is pretty tame so you may be able to hike with your stream crossing shoes on during this stretch and save yourself some time and a footwear change.

After this third major creek crossing, the trail remains on the west side of the creek for the remaining 3 miles to Slide Lake. The trail is well defined as it alternates between wooded and open areas - the latter often punctuated by rockslides. There is little of note during this portion of the hike as the creek remains within earshot, but usually out of view. You have little warning before you reach Slide Lake, other than a lessening of the creek noise, as Slide Lake is little more than a wide spot in Big Blue Creek. There is a rockslide on the east side of the creek. For those wanting to camp at Slide Lake, be aware that it is a potent mosquito breeding area. There are plenty of good campsites both above and below Slide Lake along Big Blue Creek. Slide Lake (**16K**) is roughly the mid-point between the Big Blue Creek Trailhead and the Nellie Creek Trailhead. That portion of the Big Blue Creek Trail north of Slide Lake is covered under the section for Big Blue Creek.

RATING: A hike to the summit of Uncompahgre Peak (**16F**) is a 7.5-mile round trip climbing 2,900 feet. It should only be undertaken by experienced hikers. A hike to the junction with the El Paso Creek Trail (**16I**) is a 9-mile round trip with a 1,500-foot elevation gain followed by an 800-foot descent, ascending 800 feet and descending 1,500 feet on the return trip. There are significant terrain issues. It should only be attempted by experienced hikers. Should you follow the Ridge Stock Driveway to the turn-around point described at the top of the ridge (**16G**), you will have a 7-mile round trip with a 1,400-foot elevation gain. This would be a hike suited for an intermediate hiker. A round trip to the point where the Ridge Stock Driveway intersects with Trail #235 (**16J**) covers 14 miles and gains 1,400 feet before descending 600 feet. Due to distance and navigation issues, this hike should only be attempted by experienced hikers. A hike along the Big Blue Creek Trail to the point described at the bottom of the bowl (**16H**) is a 5-mile round trip gaining 1,000 feet of elevation before descending 500 feet into the bowl, then regaining 500 feet before descending 1,000 feet on the return trip. It is suitable for intermediate hikers. A hike from the Nellie Creek trailhead to Slide Lake (**16K**) is a 13-mile round trip gaining 1,000 feet before descending 2,000 feet on the way in and gaining 2,000 feet before descending 1,000 feet on the return trip. Due to the length of this hike and the substantial elevation gain on the return trip, this should be limited to experienced hikers.

MATTERHORN CREEK

Quad: Uncompahgre Peak

DRIVING INSTRUCTIONS: Drive west from Lake City on CR 20 for 8.8 miles to Capitol City. Turn right on the well-marked intersection with North Henson Creek Road (CR 26, FSR 870). The road is 4WD recommended from this point. The turnoff to the Matterhorn Creek trailhead is 2.0 miles from CR 20. The Matterhorn Creek Road is 4WD only and is narrow, steep, and rocky in spots. Many hikers prefer to park along the North Henson Creek Road at the junction with the Matterhorn Creek Road. If you do so, add .7 miles and 400 feet of elevation gain to the distances and elevation gains listed below. Trailhead elevation 10,800 – feet.

THE HIKE: There are several trails that branch off from the Matterhorn Creek Trail, and all lead through spectacular country. I can't say enough about how beautiful this area is. Several of these trails lead out of one basin and into another, then another. You are within the shadows of Wetterhorn, Matterhorn, and Uncompahgre Peaks. One of the trails beginning at this trailhead leads to a fourteener, two lead to the Ridge Stock Driveway (heading in opposite directions), and two lead into a basin north of the Uncompahgre West series of mountains and into the country at the northernmost portion of Hinsdale County. All of these trails appear on the *Trails Illustrated* map, although not all appear on the quad.

Leaving the trailhead (**17A**), you climb moderately through a wooded area parallel to Matterhorn Creek. There are several places throughout the trail where you cross water which feeds into Matterhorn Creek, but all water crossings should present few problems regardless of the season. Crossing Matterhorn Creek early in the season is another matter, but that section of the trail is discussed under the section for

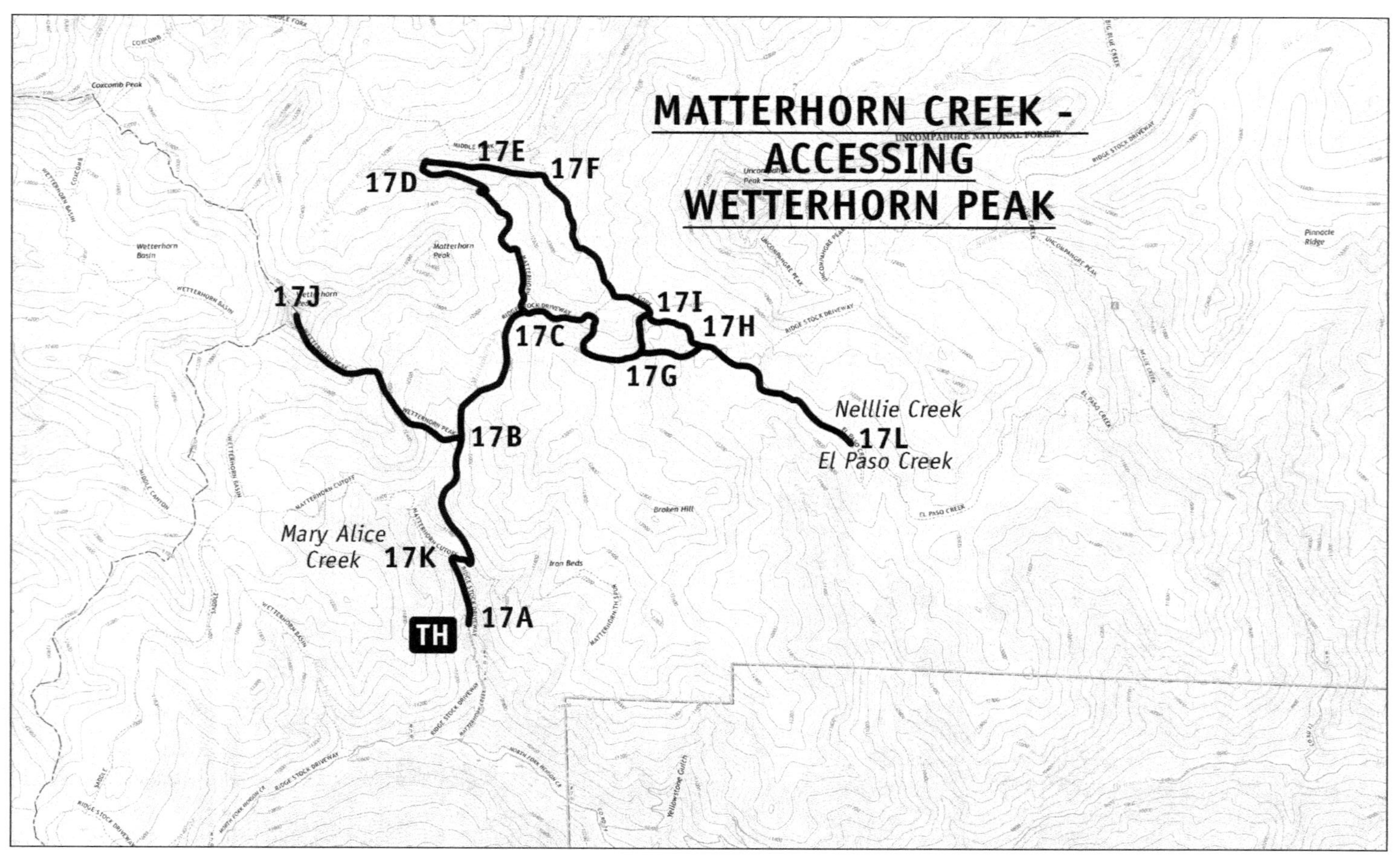
MATTERHORN CREEK -
ACCESSING
WETTERHORN PEAK
17D
17E
17F
17C
17I
17H
17G
17B
Nelllie Creek
17L
El Paso Creek
Mary Alice
Creek
17K
17J
TH
17A

Mary Alice Creek. After a bit more than .5 miles you reach a trail sign **(17K)**. The left fork is the Matterhorn Cutoff Trail, which leads you toward Mary Alice Creek and joins the Ridge Stock Driveway, heading west. Those trails are discussed under the section for Mary Alice Creek.

Taking the right fork from this trail sign **(17K)**, you climb out of the Matterhorn Basin along a trail that has been improved by placing logs across the trail at regular intervals for erosion control, creating something akin to a staircase. The trail climbs moderately, utilizing a pair of switchbacks, before continuing to climb toward the top of Matterhorn Basin. At this point, the trail is mostly open with a sub-alpine grassy terrain, although you pass through several lightly wooded areas as you ascend. After 1 mile you reach the boundary of the Uncompahgre Wilderness. After 1.75 miles you reach the sign **(17B)** designating the trail to Wetterhorn Peak, which is to your left, while the Ridge Stock Driveway continues to the right.

Should you take the left turn at this trail intersection **(17B)**, the trail descends quickly to cross two streams feeding into Matterhorn Creek. You then climb moderately through tundra in a northwesterly direction along a ridge. The peak to the left is Wetterhorn Peak, and the peak to your right is Matterhorn Peak, the lower of the two by 540 feet. The two peaks are separated by a saddle that drops 1,000 feet from Wetterhorn Peak before climbing 500 feet up Matterhorn Peak. If you are so inclined, these two peaks should be climbed separately. After .5 miles from the trail intersection, you leave the tundra and enter rocky areas for the remainder of the hike. The trail is steep as you first enter the rocks, then moderates for the remainder of the hike to a saddle visible to the southwest. Your elevation at this saddle is 13,100 feet and this is the destination of choice for all but experienced climbers **(17J)** The saddle offers views into Wetterhorn Basin and other points west. Wetterhorn Peak is a Class 3 (Yosemite Decimal System – scrambling, a rope might be carried) climb and is the most difficult fourteener to climb in Hinsdale County. The final ascent of 900 feet is narrow, with steep drop offs on either side. As this trail leads to a fourteener, it is well traveled, and the trail is not difficult to follow even through the rocks. Expect company on this trail.

Returning to the trail sign indicating the trail to Wetterhorn Peak **(17B)**, should you continue to your right the trail steepens considerably, and the terrain is dirt and small rocks as you climb along a ridge leading to the top of Matterhorn Basin. Watch your footing on the return trip as this portion of the trail can be slippery. Once you reach the top of the ridge you are climbing along, there is another ridge, perpendicular to the first, which is the point where you exit the Matterhorn Creek drainage area. Along this section you may be confused as there are two, well defined trails running parallel to one another. As the upper trail has spots with significant erosion, the lower trail may have been established as a substitute. Practically speaking, it doesn't make a difference which trail you select as they rejoin after .5 miles. Before reaching the top there is a trail sign (**17C**) indicating that the Matterhorn Trail leads to your left and the Ridge Stock Driveway continues straight ahead.

Should you wish to travel along the Matterhorn Trail, you will see a post above and to the north of you as you stand at the trail marker. The trail is lightly defined as you ascend along the tundra, but you do not climb much further once you pass the trail sign. The trail traverses Matterhorn Peak but does not offer ready access to the top of the peak. As the trail passes to the east of the peak it widens and becomes more defined as it joins a mining road. At one point this mining road divides. Both forks rejoin after a short distance. The left fork is the shorter route but is rougher hiking due to erosion. The mining road descends along the east side of Matterhorn Peak, and you can see a creek well below you. This is the East Fork of the Cimarron River, and you can discern trails on both sides of the creek. At this point the mining road begins a series of switchbacks. The first switchback to the right is genuine, but the next two switchbacks to the right will lead you astray. These lead to a ditch where they end, leaving you with a steep descent to the East Fork. The Matterhorn Trail continues to hug the mountain as it descends at a moderate decline over rocky terrain. As you approach the East Fork you will cross a gulch, but the mining road continues on the other side. Soon you will see a post ahead of you and one to your right. Just past the first post there is a trail sign (**17D**) indicating that the Matterhorn Trail follows the posts and by continuing on the mining road you are now on the Upper East Fork Trail. The Upper East Fork Trail continues for .5 miles then ends.

Continuing along the Matterhorn Trail, follow along the south side of the creek for .5 miles and you will reach a trail sign (**17E**). This trail sign indicates that the Matterhorn Trail continues along the south side of the creek and will intersect with the East Fork Trail. Watch where the arrows point, as there is a semblance of a trail leading down toward the creek and a post on the other side of the creek. Disregard this post if you wish to continue along the Matterhorn Trail toward its intersection with the East Fork Trail. That post across the creek guides hikers along the Middle Fork Trail, which occupies the northern and western bank of the East Fork of the Cimmaron River until it intersects with the East Fork Trail 1.5 miles north of the intersection of the Matterhorn Trail and the East Fork Trail (**17F**). The Middle Fork Trail is not covered in this book. Returning to the previous trail sign (**17E**) indicating the way to the intersection with the East Fork Trail, you will climb slightly and will leave the vicinity of the river as you climb over a small ridge. The intersection with the East Fork Trail is shortly beyond the crest of this ridge and just below a small mining era building (**17F**). From this point you can either return to your starting point via the Matterhorn Trail, or you can loop back via the East Fork Trail, as described below.

Returning to the trail sign where the Matterhorn Trail leaves the Ridge Stock Driveway (**17C**), should you continue east along the Ridge Stock Driveway, you descend, ever so gently, into the basin at the upper end of the East Fork of the Cimarron River drainage. After .25 miles there is a trail sign (**17G**) indicating that the East Fork Trail leads to the left and the Ridge Stock Driveway continues to the right. After another .25 miles there is another trail sign (**17H**) with the same description. There are two ways to reach the East Fork Trail from the Ridge Stock Driveway, the first for eastbound and the second for westbound hikers. These two approaches to the East Fork Trail join after less than .5 miles at a point where there are two posts in close proximity (**17I**). The lower of the two is the junction and this post was once a trail sign, but bare bolts suggest that the sign has been lost.

From the junction of the two approaches to the East Fork Trail (**17I**) the trail descends into the drainage of the East Fork of the Cimmaron River. The descent varies from gradual to steep. The terrain is open tundra near the top of the drainage but gains grass and wildflowers as you descend. The trail is well defined and there are posts placed intermittently. A mile past the junction of the two approaches, the trail crosses from the east side to the west side of the river and you encounter a trail sign (**17F**) marking the junction with the Matterhorn Trail, just below the remains of a small mining era building. This is the same Matterhorn Trail which you passed 1.5 miles back, which allows for a loop hike on your return. That portion of the East Fork Trail north of this junction is not covered in this book.

Returning to the Ridge Stock Driveway, heading east, after passing the second of the signs indicating approaches to the East Fork Trail (**17H**), you will have reached the top of the East Fork drainage and you enter the El Paso Creek drainage and are descending once again. After another .5 mile you reach a trail sign (**17L**) indicating the El Paso Creek trailhead is to your right and that Uncompahgre Peak is to your left. The trail leading to the El Paso Creek trailhead is discussed under the El Paso Creek section. The trail leading to Uncompahgre Peak is the continuation of the Ridge Stock Driveway heading east. That portion of the trail is discussed under the section for Nellie Creek.

RATING: A hike from the Matterhorn trailhead to the saddle below Wetterhorn Peak (**17J**) is a 6.5-mile round trip climbing 2,300 feet. This is within the upper limit of the capabilities of an intermediate hiker. A hike from the Matterhorn Creek Trailhead to that point where the Matterhorn Trail meets the East Fork Trail, via the Matterhorn Trail (**17F**) is a 11-mile roundtrip climbing 1,700 feet before descending 900 feet on the way out, for a total climb of 2,600 feet. This trail has significant navigation issues and should be reserved for experienced hikers. A hike from the Matterhorn Creek Trailhead to that point where the East Fork Trail meets the Matterhorn Trail (**17F**), via the East Fork Trail is a 9-mile round trip climbing 1,700 feet before descending 900 feet on the way out, for a total climb of 2,600 feet. This is just beyond the limits of an intermediate hiker and should be reserved for experienced hikers. A loop hike utilizing the Matterhorn Trail on the way out and the East Fork Trail on the way back (or the reverse) would be a 10-mile round trip gaining 1,700 feet before descending 900 feet on the way out, for a total climb of 2,600 feet. This loop hike should also be reserved for experienced hikers. The trail from Matterhorn trailhead along the Ridge Stock Driveway heading east to the junction with the El Paso Creek Trail (**17L**) is an 8.5-mile round trip climbing 1,400 feet net. This is within the upper limits of the capabilities of an intermediate hiker.

MARY ALICE CREEK

Quad: Wetterhorn Peak

DRIVING INSTRUCTIONS: Drive west from Lake City on CR 20 for 8.8 miles to Capitol City. Turn right on the well-marked intersection with the North Henson Creek Road (CR 26, FSR 870). The road is 4WD recommended from this point. The turnoff to the Mary Alice Creek parking area is 2.7 miles from CR 20 and is immediately after you cross Mary Alice Creek which passes under the road through a culvert. Turn right at this little used turnoff and the parking area is .1 miles ahead. The last section has downed timber from the 2019 avalanches so you may wish to park on the North Henson Creek Road. There is a trail sign at the trailhead, but it is nearly hidden by willows and is of limited help to hikers who are new to this trail. The sign is to the right of the parking area, toward the creek. Trailhead elevation - 11,000 feet.

THE HIKE: I am in a bit of a quandary as I describe these hikes. The trails are not well marked, the terrain rugged, and the ascent steep. Parts remain snow packed until July. I have turned around short of my objective more times than not. I keep going back because these hikes are among the most beautiful in the area and there is a sense of adventure when exploring this part of the Uncompahgre Wilderness. Most hikers will use the Matterhorn Creek or the Nellie Creek trailheads when hiking in this area because they access Wetterhorn and Uncompahgre Peaks. The scenery from the Mary Alice Creek trailhead is every bit as good, but you probably won't see any other hikers.

Most of this trail system is not represented on my quad map, but the *Trails Illustrated* map shows the entire trail system as described below. There are several mining roads and numerous game trails along your route which don't appear on any map. As much of the trail system is above timberline and is not frequently used, there are places where the trail disappears and there are few posts or cairns to guide you. This trail system is as confusing as any in Hinsdale County.

From the trailhead (**18A**) you follow a mining road along the west side of Mary Alice Creek rising quickly in a northerly direction. This trail has loose gravel and is steep enough to be hazardous, especially on the way down. After .5 miles you cross to the east side of Mary Alice Creek and the mining road switches back several times. One quarter of a mile after the creek crossing, the mining road continues straight while intersecting a second mining road which switches back to the left toward the creek. You will want to take the route to the left. After another .5 miles, the same thing happens again, and once again you need to take the route to the left. At least this time the route straight ahead has a number of logs which have been placed there to discourage your passage. As you continue, you will reach timberline and be climbing out of the Mary Alice Creek Basin toward the saddle that separates it from the Matterhorn Creek drainage area. Look for a cairn at this point which is one of several small cairns which will be useful on the way down as the mining trail switches back to the south. You will be following a pack trail from this point on, and the trail disappears from time to time in the tundra. Your objective is to reach the saddle between a big rock formation on your left and another on your right. When in doubt, keep climbing. While there are only two small rock cairns and one post to give you confirmation, the route to the north is the only one that could reasonably lead out of the basin. Upon reaching the saddle, there is a trail sign (**18B**) designating the intersection with Saddle Route #140, better known as the Ridge Stock Driveway. This leads to your left and continues quite a distance to the west. Part of this is discussed below and the remainder is discussed under the section for Horsethief Trail.

Should you turn to the right at the intersection with the Ridge Stock Driveway (**18B**), you will be on a trail with several names. This is the Ridge Stock Driveway as it heads east. It's also called the Wetterhorn Basin Trail and the Matterhorn Cutoff Trail. This continues to climb toward another saddle .25 miles from the previous trail sign where you see two trail signs in close proximity. The trail sign on your left (**18C**) shows the way to the Middle Canyon Trail and the continuation of the Wetterhorn Basin Trail. The trail sign on your right (**18C**) designates the Matterhorn Cutoff Trail and is also the continuation of the Ridge

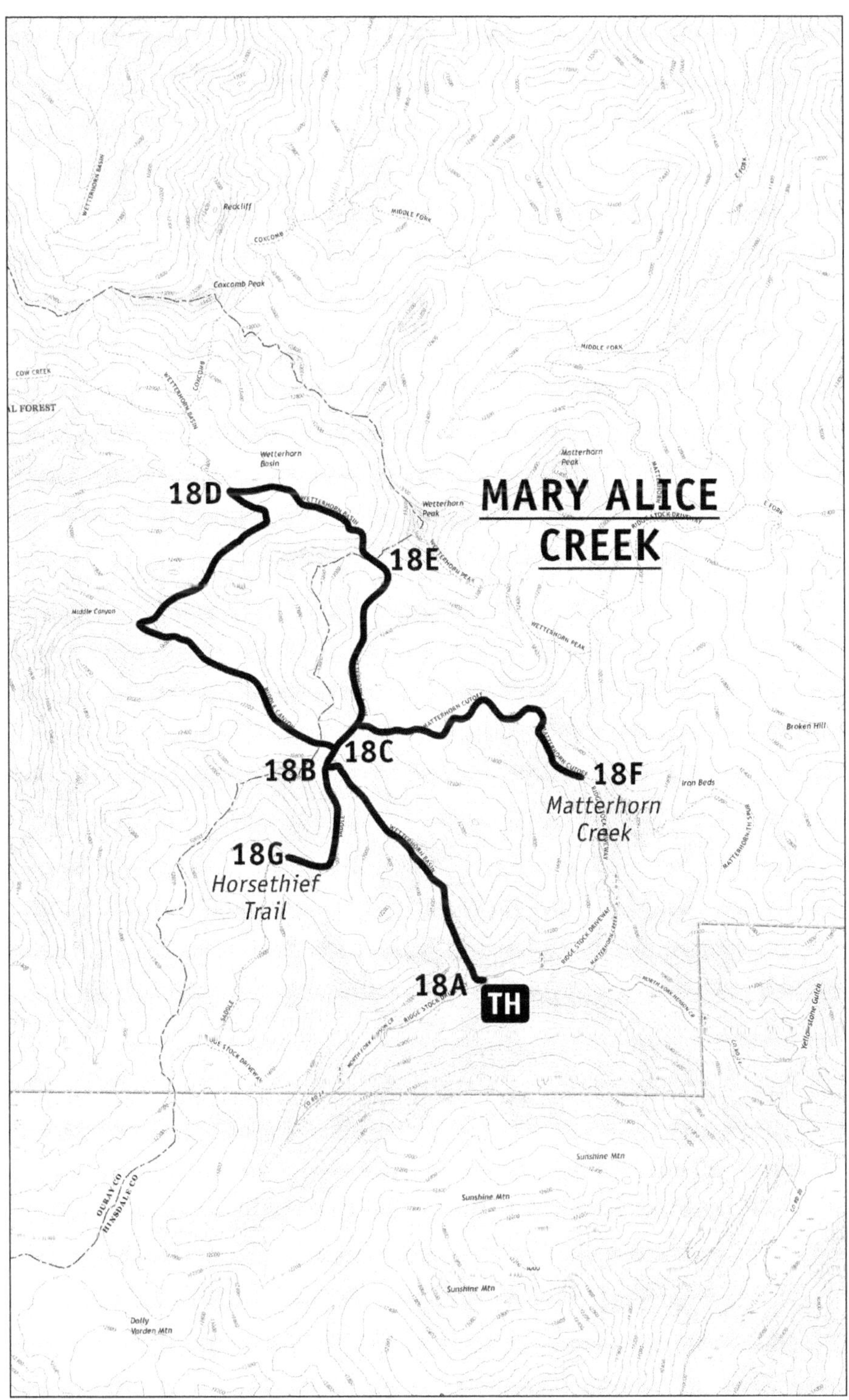

18D
18E
MARY ALICE
CREEK
18B
18C
18F
Matterhorn
Creek
18G
Horsethief
Trail
18A
TH

Stock Driveway. The Matterhorn Cutoff Trail will connect with the trail to Wetterhorn Peak .5 miles above the Matterhorn Creek trailhead. This makes a loop hike possible as the Matterhorn Creek trailhead intersection with the North Henson Creek Road is .7 miles from where you parked at the Mary Alice Creek trailhead. At the point with two trail signs, you are 2.25 miles from the trailhead and have gained 1,400 feet in elevation. Unless you are an advanced hiker you should turn around at this point because there are navigation issues in continuing with the loop returning along Matterhorn Creek and the other two trails leading from this trail sign. I'll discuss the Matterhorn Cutoff Trail first then return to cover the Wetterhorn Basin and Middle Canyon Trails.

If you are in for an adventure, you will be rewarded with magnificent scenery in completing the Mary Alice Creek / Matterhorn Creek loop. The trail comes and goes in the upper tundra area and the direction of travel is far from obvious. In addition, you will cross Matterhorn Creek three times. This creek is wild, but passible during the early part of the season, and pretty mild thereafter. As you descend from the spot with the two trail signs (**18C**), at the first spot where the tundra has overgrown the trail, you will not see the trail reemerge for quite a while. In trying to determine where the trail should go, you have two plausible options. There is a drainage area ahead and to your right that appears to descend to a spot where a creek should form. There is a second drainage area to the left that works its way around and below the first drainage area. You should take the option to the left, as going to the right into the drainage area leads to nowhere in particular.

After descending though the tundra for nearly a mile, you enter some trees for a short while and the trail becomes more apparent. You will cross to the east side of Matterhorn Creek as you enter an open area, and .5 miles thereafter. There is a confirmation trail sign indicating that the Matterhorn Creek trailhead lies ahead. There is a second trail sign indicating that a short cut to the trail to Wetterhorn Peak is closed for regeneration.

Continuing down along the east side of Matterhorn Creek from the trail sign, you will enter a wooded area, cross to the west side of Matterhorn Creek, cross two other feeder streams, then cross back to the east side of Matterhorn Creek, all in rapid-fire order. You will remain on the east side of Matterhorn Creek until you reach the intersection with the trail beginning at the Matterhorn Creek trailhead

(18F). Turning right will take you to the trailhead, while a left turn will continue following the Ridge Stock Driveway and the trail ending at the summit of Wetterhorn Peak. Both of those are discussed under the section for Matterhorn Creek.

Returning to the intersection with the Ridge Stock Driveway heading west **(18B)**, which is marked on the trail sign as "Saddle Trail #140," the sign indicates the trail is to your right and the arrow points toward a boulder field where the trail appears to pass. This is an illusion. Facing the trail sign, the Ridge Stock Driveway is ahead and to your right, across a small stream. A cairn is visible, as is the trail beyond it. The trail passes beneath the boulder field. This portion of the Ridge Stock Driveway gets little use and is difficult to follow. More than once, I asked myself, "If I were the trail, where would I be?"

After passing beneath the boulder field, the trail passes through tundra and gains elevation gently, climbing the bottom portion of a ridge which extends upward to the rock formation above you and to your right. After passing the ridge, you cross a large tundra covered area for over .25 miles. There are several posts in this area. The first one you see to your left is not part of the Ridge Stock Driveway. It denotes the trail to a conical shaped peak that has a feature on top that appears to be a large cairn. The Ridge Stock Driveway continues straight ahead, and after crossing the tundra, begins to descend moderately to steeply as the trail reaches a creek. That portion of the Ridge Stock Driveway west of the creek **(18G)** is covered under the section for Horsethief Trail.

Returning to the spot with the two trail signs **(18C)**, the sign on the left (north) is the junction of the Wetterhorn Basin Trail and the Middle Canyon Trail. The Wetterhorn Basin Trail descends from the trail sign into a basin. Despite the trail's name and the fact that Wetterhorn Peak is ahead and to your right, you are not descending into Wetterhorn Basin. That will come later. You are in Matterhorn Basin which drains to the south while Wetterhorn Basin drains to the north. You will descend slightly before beginning your climb out of Matterhorn Basin, which is taken in two steps. The high point you see ahead of you at the top of the basin is a false pass. The trail is faint, but followable as you ascend. The lowest point above you is your immediate destination. You will pass through an area containing loose rocks and gravel which can be treacherous particularly on the way down just before reaching the false pass. From there you can see the real pass, still more than .5 miles distant and with another 400 feet of elevation to gain, rather steeply I might add. As you climb out of the final portion of Matterhorn Basin, you will pass a small pond to your right, but the trail disappears in the tundra regularly. Don't despair, there is only one possible way out of the basin, as Wetterhorn Peak is to your right and a tall pinnacle is to your left. Once you reach the top of the pass (18E), you will see the trail reappear as it descends steeply into Wetterhorn Basin and Ouray County. I'm designating the top of the pass as your turnaround point and that portion of the Wetterhorn Basin Trail north of this pass is not covered in this book.

Returning to the spot with the two trail signs (18C), the sign on the left (north) is the junction of the Wetterhorn Basin Trail and the Middle Canyon Trail. The Middle Canyon Trail heads to the left toward a cairn, but the trail is not well defined at this point. It continues through rocks as it traverses the rocky hill to the west of the two signs. The trail ascends gradually for 200 feet until you reach a saddle containing a sign designating the boundary of the Uncompahgre Wilderness. As you continue north past this sign, you are entering both the Middle Canyon drainage and Ouray County. The descent into Middle Canyon is guided by posts for the upper portion of the drainage while the trail comes and goes through the tundra. This is a moderate to steep descent for the next .5 miles before the descent moderates as you approach timberline. I can't say enough about how beautiful and wild this area is. There is a great amount of exposed rock along the canyon and on the mountains to the north. The tundra becomes grassy as you descend, and it is filled with wildflowers. As a bonus, the trees you are approaching are primarily spruce which were spared by the pine mountain beetles.

About the time you reach timberline, the trail crosses from the west to the east side of the creek and the guideposts, which have been well spaced up to this point, give way to cairns before you enter the trees. There are two more posts, but navigation becomes more difficult the further you go. After descending 600 feet, the trail turns to the right and begins to ascend out of Middle Canyon toward Wetterhorn Basin. This is not a quick ascent over an obvious pass. There are several false passes, and the trail passes from light forest to tundra to rock during this process. While the trail is faint in spots, it is not difficult to follow, with one exception. At one point there is an unmarked trail to your right, marked by a cairn which takes a higher route into Wetterhorn Basin. Staying on the left trail you will soon top out and be able to see into Wetterhorn Basin. This point, between Middle Canyon and Wetterhorn Basin is a logical stopping point for a day hiker. The Middle Canyon Trail connects with the Wetterhorn Basin Trail (**18D**) less than a mile from this point after a descent of 400 feet. This allows for loop possibilities for a hiker wanting a multi-day hike.

RATING: For the option of turning back at the pair of trail signs at the saddle between the Mary Alice Creek drainage and the Matterhorn Creek drainage (**18C**), the distance (4.5 miles) and the elevation gain of 1,400 feet should be within the ability of most intermediate hikers, although the terrain is rugged. The Mary Alice Creek / Matterhorn Creek loop is a 7-mile hike with the same 1,400-foot elevation gain. The navigation issues, terrain, and stream crossings (if early in the season) make this suitable only for experienced hikers. A round trip along the west bound portion of the Ridge Stock Driveway to the creek (**18G**) covers 7 miles and ascends 1,500 feet before descending 600 feet. Due to terrain and navigation issues this trail should also be limited to experienced hikers. A round trip to the top of the pass separating Matterhorn Basin from Wetterhorn Basin via the Wetterhorn Basin Trail (**18E**) covers 9 miles and gains 2,000 feet. Due to navigation and terrain issues, it should be limited to experienced hikers. A round trip to the pass between Middle Canyon and Wetterhorn Basin (**18D**) covers 11 miles and gains 1,600 feet before descending 600 feet then ascending 300 feet (on the way back). Due to distance, terrain, and navigation issues it should be limited to experienced hikers as well.

HORSETHIEF TRAIL

Quad: Wetterhorn Peak, Handies Peak

DRIVING INSTRUCTIONS: Drive west from Lake City on CR 20 for 17.2 miles. This takes you nearly to the top of Engineer Pass. There is a metal sign on your right to which someone has applied a cutting torch to form the message, Horsethief Pack Trail. There is ample parking along the side of the road just past this sign. The road is 4WD recommended for the last 4 miles. Trailhead elevation - 12,600 feet.

THE HIKE: Most of the elevation to be gained in hiking from this trailhead has been gained by the time you leave your car. The trail leads through an area called American Flats, which while not flat, is at least tamer than most of the surrounding area. There are several ridges to climb and descend from and you will gain and lose up to 300 feet of elevation several times no matter how you approach your hike. The Horsethief Trail intersects the Bear Creek Trail and the Ridge Stock Driveway 2.3 miles from the trailhead. This intersection is on the Hinsdale / Ouray County line. The northern portion of the Horsethief Trail and all of the Bear Creek Trail are in Ouray County, leading toward the town of Ouray. Those trails are not covered in this book. This trail intersection is the westernmost point of the Ridge Stock Driveway, which passes in front of the mountains in the Uncompahgre West series and terminates in Gunnison County. The Ridge Stock Driveway is discussed in the sections for Mary Alice Creek, Matterhorn Creek, Nellie Creek, and Ridge Stock Driveway – North Portal, in addition to the discussion in this section. This hike is fully exposed and at high altitude. It should not be attempted should thunderstorms be in the forecast. Because of the high elevation, there is considerable snowpack early in the season. The snow melt can make things somewhat messy, but water crossings are not really an issue.

The trails discussed in this section appear on both the *Trails Illustrated* map and on the quads.

Soon after leaving the road at the metal trailhead sign (**19A**), you encounter a new wooden sign setting out the distances to various points along the trail. The relevant item is that it is 2.3 miles to the intersection of the Horsethief Trail with the Bear Creek Trail and the Ridge Stock Driveway (**19B**). You will climb gently through alpine tundra following posts as your primary guide. The trail is wide enough for vehicles, but it is not easy to follow. After a mile there is a ridge ahead. The trail will go to the right, around the ridge. Should you be interested in a short side hike, follow a gully up the ridge to the northwest; at the west end of the ridge there is a window between two mountains which allows views to the west side of Engineer Pass toward Ouray. You can rejoin the main trail by heading east along the top of the ridge. Posts and cairns are there to guide you.

Having rejoined the main trail, you will continue following the posts for another mile as you descend the ridge until you see two trail signs in close proximity (**19B**). The first directs you to the Bear Creek Trail to the west. The second contains quite a bit of information as to distances along the Horsethief Trail and directs you to the east should you wish to hike along the Ridge Stock Driveway. A mile from the trail intersection and slightly lower in elevation you see American Lake (**19C**), a small alpine lake which would make a worthy destination.

For those wanting to continue along the Ridge Stock Driveway, you are in for a visual treat. You look across the Fall Creek drainage below you to the Uncompahgre West series of mountains and to some mountains to the north. You pass through tundra with some rocky areas for the next several miles with little elevation gain or loss. You have to traverse a series of gulches which drain into Fall Creek, but other than that this is not a difficult section of the trail. While the trail receives little use, it is not difficult to follow, despite the lack of trail markings. Two miles after passing American Lake, you climb out of the Fall Creek drainage, which is to the north of the trail, cross a saddle and enter the North Henson Creek drainage, which is to the south of the trail.

You encounter a trail sign .5 miles past the saddle, which, while necessary to mark a trail intersection, can create a great deal of confusion (**19D**). The sign indicates that if you continue the way you are going, you will remain on the Ridge Stock Driveway. This is contrary to the

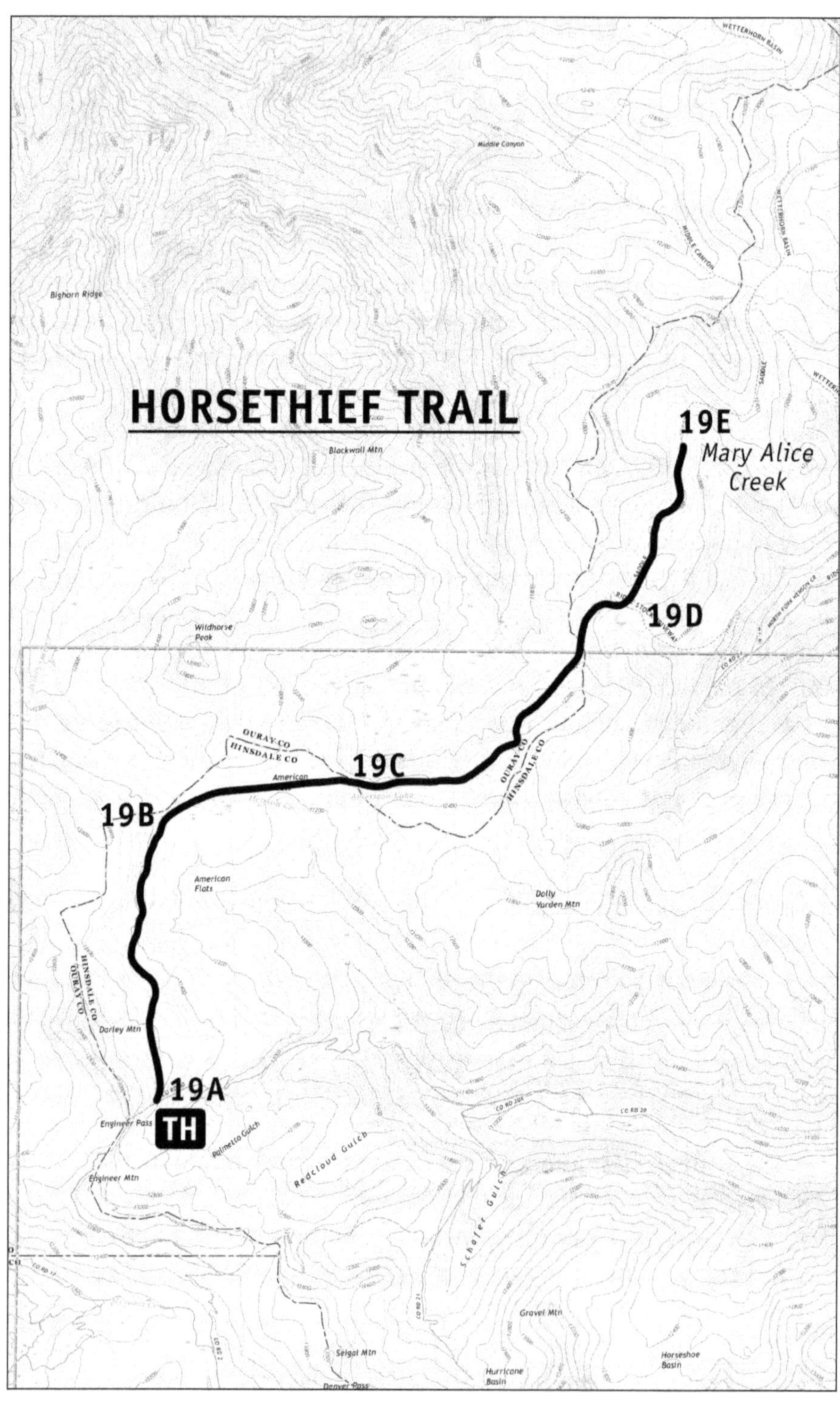

HORSETHIEF TRAIL
19E
Mary Alice Creek
19D
19C
19B
19A
TH

local understanding of what constitutes the Ridge Stock Driveway. By continuing ahead, you will connect with the North Henson Creek Road within a mile, however you will have left what is commonly known as the Ridge Stock Driveway. To continue along the Ridge Stock Driveway, you should take a left turn at the trail sign, which indicates that you will be following Saddle Trail #140 which will connect you with the Wetterhorn Basin Trail in 2.25 miles **(19E)**. While the trail to the right (designated by the trail sign as the Ridge Stock Driveway) connects with the North Henson Creek Road, the connecting trail crosses private land, and the North Henson Creek Road should not be considered an access point to the Ridge Stock Driveway.

Taking the left turn to continue along what is commonly known as the Ridge Stock Driveway, you will see that the trail is now difficult to follow. The trail follows a gulch which climbs steeply to a saddle several hundred feet above you. Once you have crossed the saddle, you are entering a different section of the North Henson Creek drainage and you descend toward the first of two creeks. The trail is overgrown in the grassy terrain, but if you cast your eyes across the drainage, you will clearly see the continuation of the trail as it climbs out of the drainage, above and to the left of a wooded area. Descend toward the first creek, cross it and climb a short distance toward a mostly level grassy area. The trail reappears for a while after the first creek crossing. The trail is mostly overgrown through this grassy area, but you should keep heading to where you see the trail as it climbs out of the drainage. Continuing along the grassy area, the trail will reappear below a rockslide to your left and above a small spruce forest ahead. Once you have passed that spruce forest, you will descend through another grassy area to the second creek crossing before climbing out of the North Henson Creek drainage. That portion of the Ridge Stock Driveway beyond the second creek crossing is covered in the section for Mary Alice Creek **(19E)**.

RATING: A hike to American Lake **(19C)** without the side-hike to view the area toward Ouray is a 7-mile round trip with a 300-foot net elevation loss. Taking the side-hike adds an additional mile. Both should be considered intermediate hikes. A hike along the Ridge Stock Driveway to the point discussed in the paragraph above **(19E)** is a 15-mile round trip descending a net amount of 800 feet, but with several climbs of 200-300 feet both on the way in and the way out. Due to the distance and navigation issues, this should be reserved for experienced hikers.

American Basin in winter

Glenn Heumann

Trailheads Located South and West of Lake City via CR 30

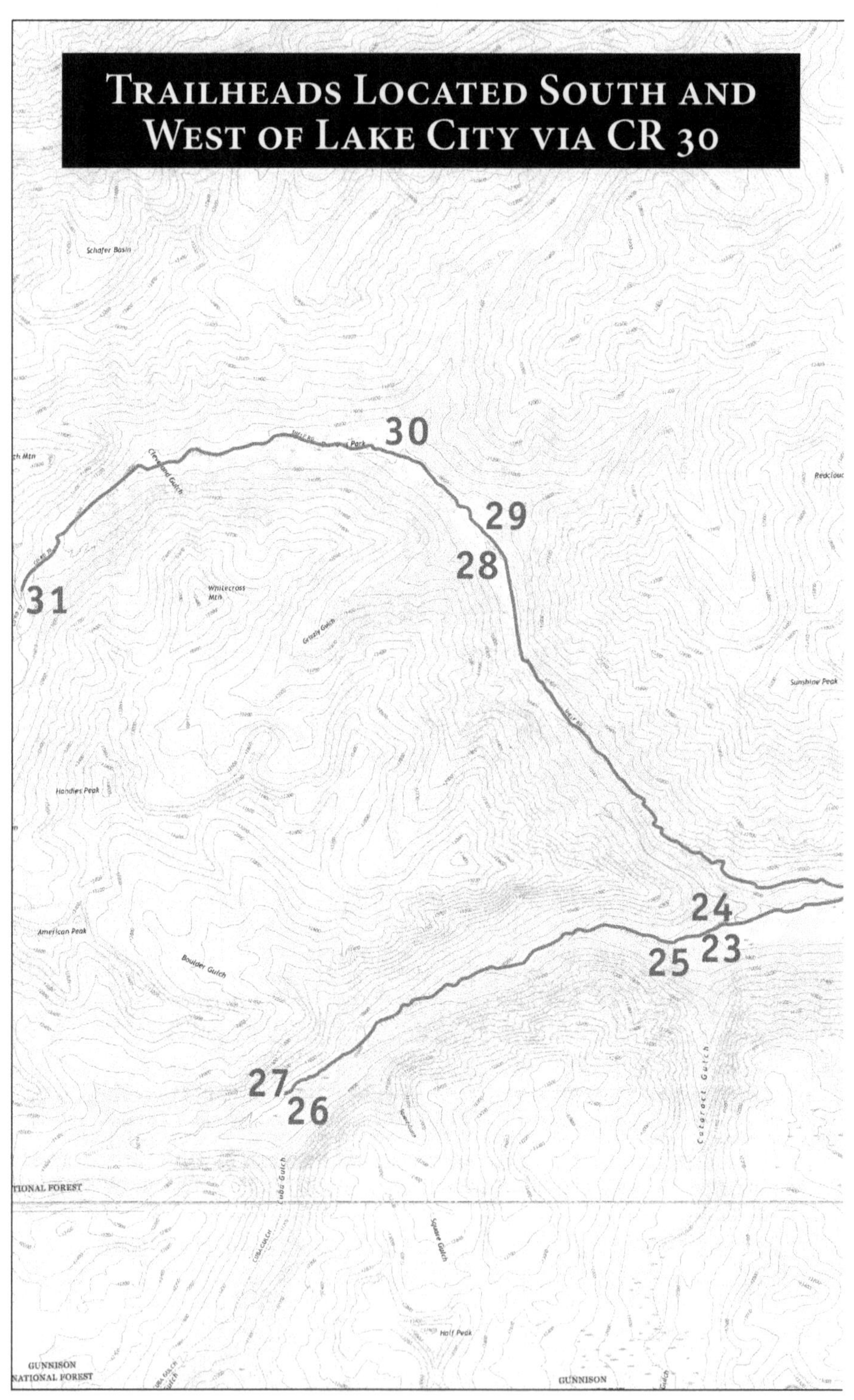

TRAILHEADS LOCATED SOUTH AND WEST OF LAKE CITY VIA CR 30
Schafer Basin
30
29
28
31
Redcloud
Whitecross Mtn
Grizzly Gulch
Sunshine Peak
Handies Peak
24
25 23
American Peak
Boulder Gulch
27
26
Cataract Gulch
NATIONAL FOREST
Half Peak
GUNNISON NATIONAL FOREST
GUNNISON

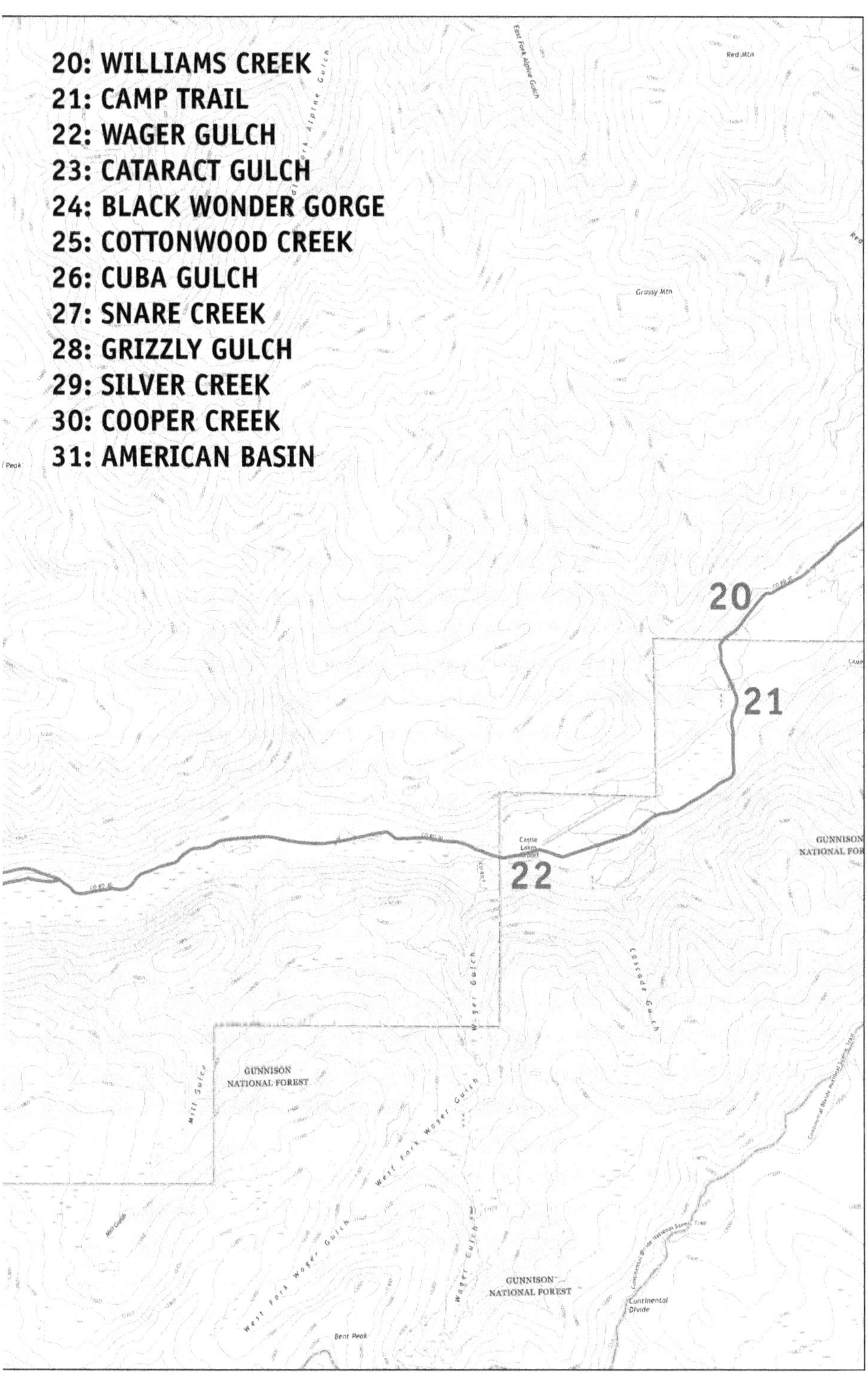

20: WILLIAMS CREEK
21: CAMP TRAIL
22: WAGER GULCH
23: CATARACT GULCH
24: BLACK WONDER GORGE
25: COTTONWOOD CREEK
26: CUBA GULCH
27: SNARE CREEK
28: GRIZZLY GULCH
29: SILVER CREEK
30: COOPER CREEK
31: AMERICAN BASIN

WILLIAMS CREEK

Quad: Lake San Cristobal, Redcloud Peak

DRIVING INSTRUCTIONS: Drive south from Lake City on CO SH 149. Turn right on CR 30 toward Lake San Cristobal. Continue on CR 30 for 6.5 miles and the trailhead is marked on your right. There is parking for several vehicles. Trailhead elevation - 9,200 feet.

THE HIKE: The Williams Creek Trail climbs to the top of the divide separating the Lake Fork of the Gunnison drainage from the Henson Creek drainage and continues down the other side as the Alpine Gulch Trail (east fork). This thru-hike is quite an undertaking; however, the middle section offers some of the most scenic terrain in the area. There are several logical turn-around points short of the top for hikers not wishing to go beyond their capabilities. This section covers the trail to its highest point while the portion on the Henson Creek side of the divide is covered under the Alpine Gulch section. This trail is included in the *Trails Illustrated* map, but only certain portions are included on the quads.

Leaving the trailhead (**20A**), you are heading west and climbing moderately for the first portion of the hike. You will pass through a large open meadow before entering a lightly wooded area. There are two stream crossings during the first mile which should not require stream crossing shoes during the latter portion of the season. Early in the season these may be impassable. The second of these stream crossings is Williams Creek. After the stream crossings, the trail gains elevation as it cuts a narrow path above the creek. At the 1.5 mile point you top out at a beaver pond, which is the first turn-around point, if you want a nice short hike (**20D**).

The trail descends slightly after reaching the beaver pond, crosses a rocky area, then gains elevation following the remnants of the stream which was dammed by the beavers. As you continue to climb adjacent to the stream you will continue to see evidence of the beavers' labors, to little avail, as there is little water in the stream at this point. There is a trail sign (downed at this writing) designating nothing in particular. You then cross the remnants of the stream and climb above it a bit, but thereafter the trail is relatively flat until it again reaches stream elevation. This portion of the trail has a northern exposure, and this area holds snow late into the spring.

Soon afterward, the trail veers to the right and crosses a small open area. There is a second trail sign indicating your trail continues to the right (**20B**). Should you take a left turn at this point, an old mining trail leads to the Castle Lakes Campground. This trail is easy to follow, descends 800 feet over heavily switch-backed terrain, and passes through the Castle Lakes Campground before reaching CR 30, across from the Alpine Vista subdivision entrance 2 miles after leaving the main trail. You are now 1.5 miles from the Williams Creek trailhead. As this route crosses private property for much of its later stages, it is not a recommended route.

Continuing to the right from the trail sign (**20B**), you begin climbing and soon see a third trail sign indicating your trail goes to the left. Continuing to the right will lead you across a large rockslide to nowhere in particular over an old mining road. Following the trail to the left, you climb along the edges of the rockslide for over .25 miles before the trail levels somewhat and turns left toward the west. This flatter spot will lead you through a wooded area until it emerges into one of several open areas, each larger than the previous one. There are fine views of Sunshine Peak and the mountains to the south of the Lake Fork from the last of these meadows. This would be the second logical turn-around point (**20C**).

Leaving the meadow, you turn right toward the north, and after a couple of switchbacks, begin a long climb lasting over a mile. Midway through the ascent the trail crosses a small stream and enters a small meadow, which is used as a hunting camp during autumn. After passing this meadow, the trail begins to climb once again. This long ascent is through an aspen grove, so while it offers little in the way of views of the surrounding mountains, there are rewards in hiking this trail during the autumn.

After hiking 1.5 miles above the lower meadow, the trail turns to the left (north), and the trees turn from aspen to spruce, most of which

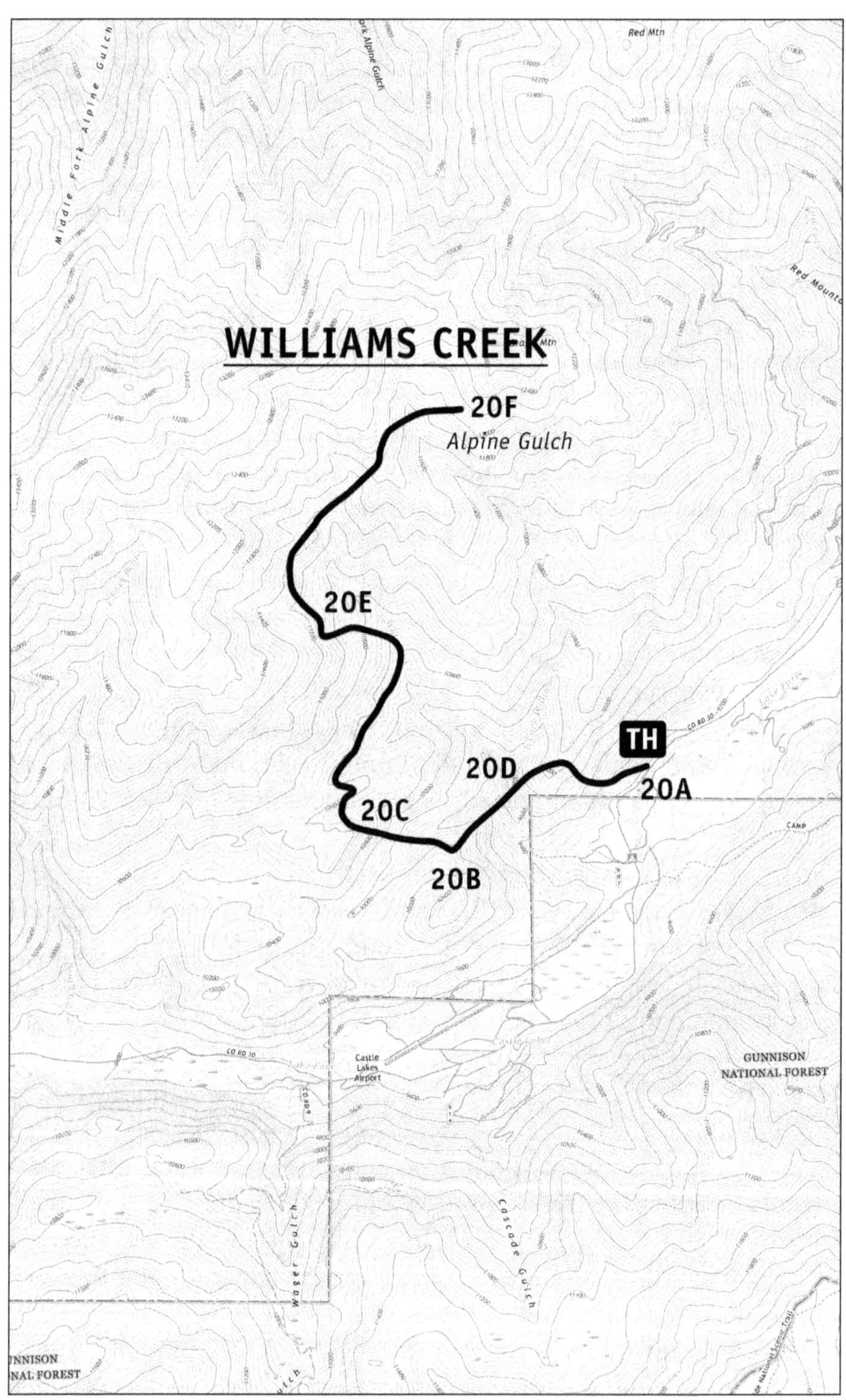

Red Mtn
Red Mount
Middle Fork Alpine Gulch
Alpine Gulch
WILLIAMS CREEK
20F
Alpine Gulch
20E
TH
20D
20A
20C
20B
CAMP
CO RD 30
Castle
Lakes
Airport
CO RD 30
GUNNISON
NATIONAL FOREST
Wager Gulch
Cascade Gulch
GUNNISON
NAL FOREST

are dead. The trail steepens during this next section, and after climbing the steepest part, turns toward the right, continuing through the dead spruce forest and climbing again after a short respite. After one more switchback, you reach the top of the Williams Creek Trail (**20E**) before it enters the transition zone connecting the Williams Creek Trail to the Alpine Gulch Trail. At this point, there are no more trees, and you can see great distances in almost all directions. This would be the next logical turn-around point. I'm calling this point the top of the Williams Creek Trail for purposes of this narrative.

Between this point and the top of the Alpine Gulch Trail there is a transition zone of 4 miles, all above timberline. The views from this zone are among the best in the county. There is only a 600-foot net elevation gain from the top of the Williams Creek Trail to the highest point of the transition zone, but you will gain and lose elevation throughout this zone climbing nearly 800 feet.

Entering the transition zone, you descend, then begin a moderate ascent as you head north. Ahead of you is a range of mountains. From left to right you see Sunshine Peak, Redcloud Peak, two unnamed mountains reaching 13,800 in elevation, and Grassy Mountain. The trail takes you toward the second of the unnamed 13,800 peaks, then turns toward the right as it crosses a stream before climbing along the ridge connecting all of those peaks. After more than a mile in the transition zone, the trail makes a steep descent before crossing a second stream. From there, it climbs toward a high point of the ridge, which is the high point in this trail at over 12,800 feet (**20F**). From there you can see the Henson Creek drainage and the ridge that takes you toward Grassy Mountain. This is roughly the midpoint between the Williams Creek trailhead and the Alpine Gulch trailhead. For those contemplating a thru-hike between those points, Williams Creek is the logical starting point for such a hike for several reasons. The uphill is easier on the Williams Creek side and the trailhead is 200 feet higher in elevation. More importantly, the Alpine Gulch Trail involves numerous water crossings, and it would be best to have wet boots at the end of your trek, rather than for almost the whole trek. The discussion of such a thru-hike beyond the 12,800-foot, high point described above (**20F**) is contained in the section for Alpine Gulch.

RATING: A trip to the beaver pond (**20D**) and back covers 3 miles and 600 feet of elevation gain. It should be accessible to beginning hikers. A trip to the lower clearings **(20C)** and back covers 6 miles and has 1,200 feet of elevation gain. It should be considered an intermediate level hike. A trip to the top of the Williams Creek Trail **(20E)** where it enters the transition zone and back covers 11 miles and has 3,000 feet of elevation gain. This should be limited to experienced hikers. A round trip to the high point of the divide **(20F)** and back is 15 miles in length and has 3,600 feet in elevation gain. It should be limited to the most experienced of hikers. A thru-hike to the Alpine Gulch trailhead is over 14 miles in length and gains 3,600 feet in elevation, before descending 3,800 feet. It too, should not be attempted by any other than experienced hikers.

View from the high point in the transition zone

Glenn Heumann

CAMP TRAIL

Quad: Lake San Cristobal, Finger Mesa

DRIVING INSTRUCTIONS: Drive south from Lake City on CO SH 149. Turn right on CR 30 toward Lake San Cristobal. Continue on CR 30 for 6.8 miles. The trailhead is .3 miles after a bridge over the Lake Fork of the Gunnison River. The trailhead and parking area are well marked on your left. Trailhead elevation - 9,200 feet.

THE HIKE: This trail goes generally northeastward paralleling the Lake Fork, rising above the former Camp Redcloud (hence its name) reaching the Continental Divide where it intersects the La Garita Stock Trail and the Colorado Trail. While the trail goes almost entirely through wooded areas, there are some breakout points offering views of the mountains to the north and west, and the view from the divide is tremendous. Much of the tree cover is aspen, which makes this a fine autumn hike. This is one of the more popular trails in the area. The trail is easy to follow and there are no real terrain issues. The trail appears on the *Trails Illustrated* map but does not appear on the quads.

Once you leave the trailhead (**21A**), you are in the woods and climbing gently for the first .25 miles to where you cross a bridge. After the bridge, the trail turns to the right, although a trail appears to go straight ahead as well. This faux trail disappears quickly. Once you've made the right-hand turn, the trail gains elevation moderately for the next several miles. There are a few switchbacks, but you are generally heading northeast behind the camp. After 2 miles you will cross water (no water crossing shoes needed) and after several more switchbacks you will enter a flat area of sparsely spaced aspen trees which contains several primitive camping shelters. You are halfway to the Continental Divide at this point.

The trail leaves the campsite and heads northeast in the same manner as before. After a bit more than .5 miles, the trees on your left thin sufficiently to have your first good view of the mountains to the north. This is but a preview of the views from the top, but this can be a good turnaround point if you want a shorter hike. Soon, as the tree cover becomes more complete, you turn to your right and gain a bit more elevation before the trail flattens out a bit. This spot offers views of the mountains to the west, but then again, these views fall short of the grandeur available from the top. The trail bears to the left and transverses below several large rocks, gaining little elevation until you emerge from the trees and face a large rockslide. The trail turns right and parallels the rockslide for a bit before it turns right again and reenters the trees. This rockslide is also a logical turnaround point for those wanting a shorter hike (**21C**).

The remainder of the trail is considerably steeper than what you've seen before. It switches back repeatedly while climbing between the rockslide you have just passed and another on the west end of this wooded area. You will hike between these two rockslides, hugging the west end for a while before passing back east where you will emerge from the woods a second time, facing the east rockslide. You will parallel the rockslide once again before turning right into the woods for the final climb. By the time you reach the west rockslide the trail will turn left and emerge from the woods into a large open saddle, which will likely be your destination.

Upon reaching the open saddle, the view behind you is spectacular and it will only get better as you climb toward the top of the saddle. Uncompahgre Peak will emerge from behind the Red Mountain and Grassy Mountain tops which have heretofore been screening it. Make a note of the point you emerge from the woods because the trail disappears in the grassy area of this saddle, and you could have difficulty finding the trail upon your return. The first trail sign that you will see (**21B**) is at the intersection of Camp Trail and the La Garita Stock Trail, although this trail sign only directs you back to the trail head. This is not the same as the Colorado Trail at this point. The Colorado Trail crosses this saddle south and east of the yurt that is to your left as you enter the saddle (**21D**). The yurt was destroyed during the 2018-2019 winter but has since been rebuilt. The Colorado Trail is well marked with its own signature wooden posts. You could go either direction along the Colorado Trail, but that would be more than what most day hikers are willing to undertake. The portion of the Colorado Trail heading east from its intersection with Camp Trail is covered under the section for Jarosa Mesa. The paragraphs below cover the section of the Colorado Trail between the intersection with Camp Trail and the intersection with the Wager Gulch Trail at Carson Saddle.

As you proceed west along the Colorado Trail after its intersection with Camp Trail (**21D**) you pass through a marshy area and enter the woods. Counterintuitively, you are heading in a southeasterly direction. You will climb at a moderate pace through the woods until you reach a clearing after .5 miles and gaining 300 feet. Upon leaving the woods, you are among bushy willows as the trail turns southwest. The Colorado Trail receives quite a bit of traffic and there are carsonite posts placed frequently enough to make this an easy trail to follow. Once out of the woods, you are not gaining or losing significant elevation for the next .5 miles. Ahead of you lies a bump in the ridge and you will climb several switchbacks as you pass to the south of this bump. After passing the bump, the trail is fairly flat for the next mile. You are hiking along the Atlantic side of the Continental Divide and your views to the south and east, while wonderful, fall short of the magnificent views along the Pacific side of the divide, which become apparent on occasion as you progress further. There is a second bump ahead and you will once again pass to the left (south) of the bump after a slight climb. Following this second bump there is a gulch to your right, which gives you views toward the Pacific side of the divide.

Nearly 3 miles after leaving the intersection with Camp Trail, you encounter a steep, rocky incline. This is the first of three climbs you will make before reaching Carson Saddle. Each climb is followed by a flat traverse to the south, then by a descent to a spot where you can see the Pacific drainage. The first of these climbs is the steepest, while the third gains the most elevation. Following the first climb, you reach a point where you can see Lake San Cristobal to your right (north) and a portion of Castle Rock Lake / Continental Reservoir system to your left (south). Following the descent after traversing the first feature, you will have a second view of Lake San Cristobal, although from a further distance since you've hiked nearly a mile since your previous view. This window to the north allows you to see the peaks in the Lake City West group, from Redcloud Peak to Red Mountain and all of the non-red peaks in between. After the second climb, traverse, and descent, you have another window to the Pacific side of the divide, giving you a view of Wager Gulch and the road to Carson Saddle. The ghost town of Carson is not visible from this vantage point. This third climb takes you

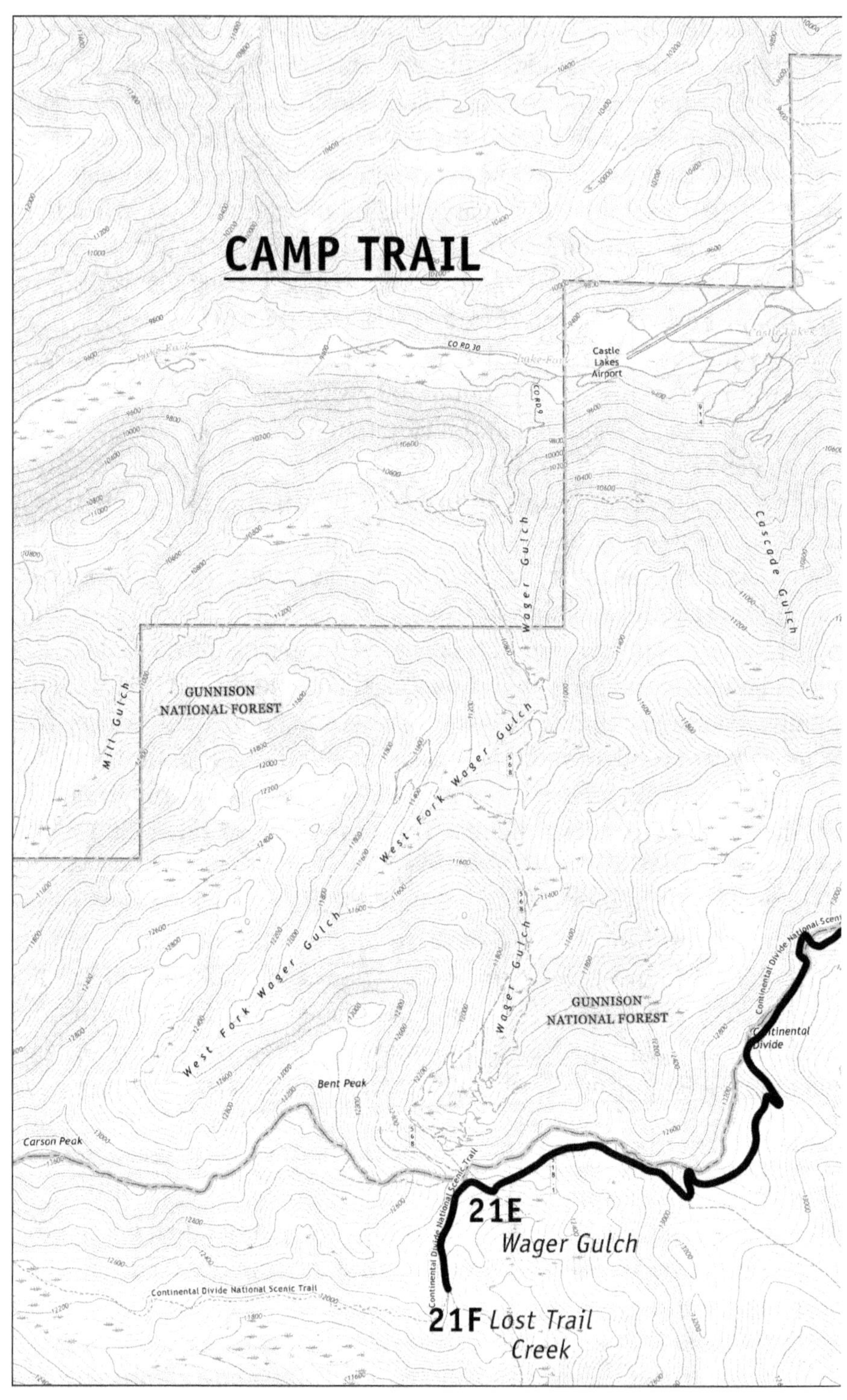
CAMP TRAIL
Castle Lakes Airport
GUNNISON NATIONAL FOREST
GUNNISON NATIONAL FOREST
Mill Gulch
Wager Gulch
Cascade Gulch
West Fork Wager Gulch
West Fork Wager Gulch
Wager Gulch
Continental Divide National Scenic Trail
Continental Divide
Continental Divide National Scenic Trail
Continental Divide National Scenic Trail
Carson Peak
Bent Peak
21E
Wager Gulch
21F Lost Trail Creek

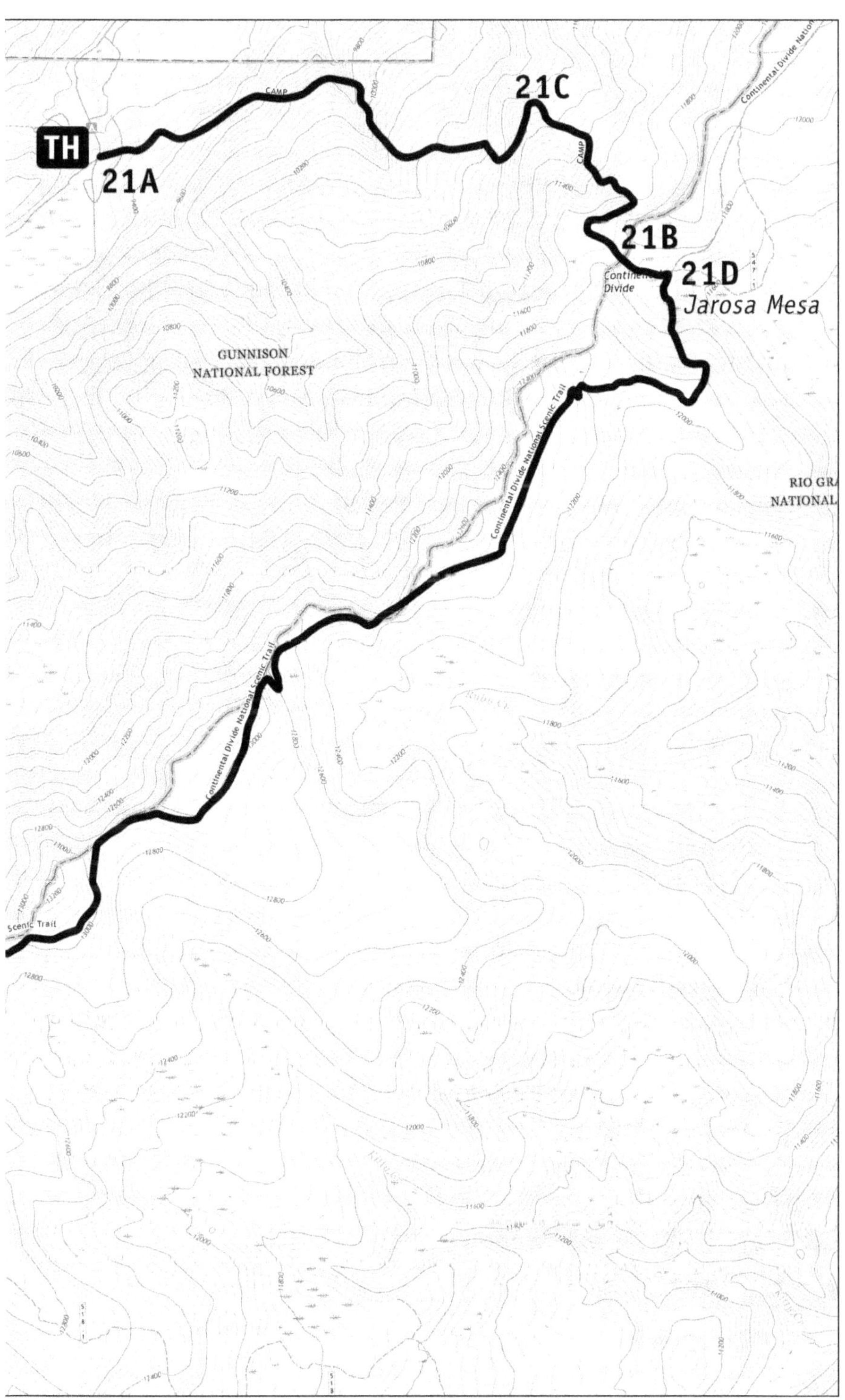
21C
TH
21A
21B
21D
Jarosa Mesa
CAMP
CAMP
Continental
Divide
GUNNISON
NATIONAL FOREST
RIO GR
NATIONAL
Continental Divide National Scenic Trail
Continental Divide National Scenic Trail
Scenic Trail
Continental Divide Natio

to a pass south of Coney Peak where a trail sign indicates that you've reached the highest point on the Colorado Trail at 13,271 feet.

After reaching the highest point on the Colorado Trail, logically you must descend. The next 2 miles take you to Carson Saddle, which is the point on the Continental Divide that separates the Wager Gulch drainage on the Pacific Side from the Lost Trail Creek drainage on the Atlantic side. You will descend 1,000 feet to Carson Saddle. Not long after passing the highest point on the Colorado Trail, the Colorado Trail crosses FSR 518 twice in rapid succession. FSR 518 will lead you to Carson Saddle, and the Colorado Trail joins FSR 518 at a lower elevation, nearer the saddle. You will want to stay on the Colorado Trail. The Colorado Trail takes a more roundabout route and utilizes several switchbacks to create a more gradual descent. FSR 518 is much steeper, and the combination of dirt and loose gravel make a descent by that route more treacherous. FSR 518 also carries significant ATV traffic. Once you have had hiked the lower portion of FSR 518 to Carson Saddle, you'll have had your fill of that road.

As you approach Carson Saddle, there are roads heading in multiple directions. You will first intersect FSR 821 (**21E**), which leads into the Lost Trail Creek drainage. That trail is covered in the section for Lost Trail Creek. At about that point you also reach CR 36 (**21F**) which descends Wager Gulch past the ghost town of Carson, to reach CR 30. The Colorado Trail also continues west toward Durango. The trails descending CR 36, and the continuation of the Colorado Trail as far as the intersection with the Cataract Gulch Trail, are covered under the section for Wager Gulch.

RATING: The distance to the Continental Divide (**21B**) is a 9-mile round trip; this and the elevation gain of 2,500 feet are both significant enough to disqualify this trail for beginners. The terrain is not particularly difficult, and this trail should be suitable for most intermediate hikers. A hike to the first rockslide (**21C**) would be a 6.5 miles round trip gaining 1,800 feet and would also be an intermediate hike. That portion of the Colorado Trail between the intersection with Camp Trail (**21D**) and the intersection with the Wager Gulch Trail (**22A**) covers 8.5 miles and gains 1,600 feet before descending 1,000 feet. Other than distance, there are no navigation issues or terrain issues which would disqualify this section for intermediate hikers. This section of the Colorado Trail is more suited to thru-hikers than day hikers.

WAGER GULCH

Quad: Lake San Cristobal, Finger Mesa, Pole Creek Mountain

DRIVING INSTRUCTIONS: Drive south from Lake City on CO SH 149. Turn right on CR 30 toward Lake San Cristobal. Continue on CR 30 for 8.8 miles (the MP 8 sign is missing as of this writing) and the trailhead is marked on your left, which is also designated as CR 36. This is also FSR 568, but it is not marked as such at the trailhead. There is parking for several vehicles. Trailhead elevation - 9,300 feet.

THE HIKE: Wager Gulch Road is a jeep trail leading to the ghost town of Carson, and beyond to the Continental Divide, where it intersects the Colorado Trail and leads to the east side of the divide via the Lost Trail Creek Trail. This road is accessible by 4WD vehicles as far as the divide, also known as Carson Saddle, but is frequently hiked during the autumn when vehicle traffic is minimal. This is a rough 4WD road with steep and rocky areas. The ghost town of Carson is a well-preserved settlement 4 miles from CR 30. The road above the Carson townsite is a more difficult drive and many hikers may want to park at the Carson townsite for hikes extending beyond Carson Saddle. This trail appears as a road as far as Carson Saddle and as a trail beyond that point on both the *Trails Illustrated* map and the quads. The town of Carson rests upon private land.

Starting from CR 30 **(22A)**, the road gains elevation moderately throughout the entire distance to Carson Saddle. There are several side roads in the first .5 miles leading to private property, but the road to Carson is easy to discern. You will be travelling through a wooded area for the first 2 miles. There is a road heading to the left just before the 2-mile mark. Stay to the right on the more traveled road. At the 3-mile mark there are the ruins of a cabin to your left. The terrain continues to open up as you approach Carson, which is just beyond the 3.5 mile

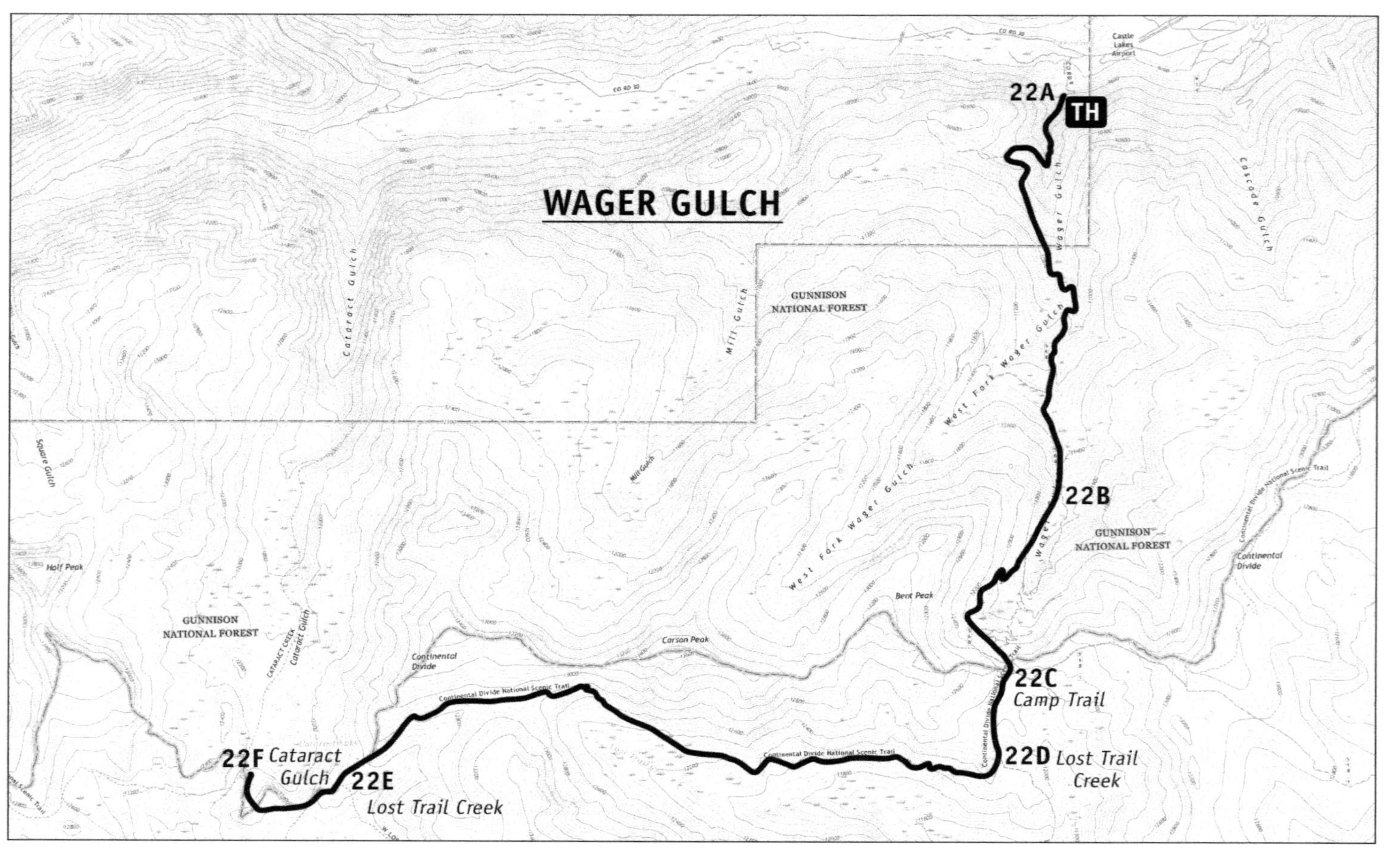

WAGER GULCH
22A
TH
22B
22C
Camp Trail
22D Lost Trail Creek
22E
Lost Trail Creek
22F Cataract Gulch
GUNNISON NATIONAL FOREST
GUNNISON NATIONAL FOREST
GUNNISON NATIONAL FOREST
Cascade Gulch
Cataract Gulch
Mill Gulch
Square Gulch
Carson Peak
Bent Peak
Half Peak
Continental Divide
Continental Divide
West Fork Wager Gulch
Wager Gulch
Castle Lakes Airport
Continental Divide National Scenic Trail
Cataract Creek Cataract Gulch
136

mark across a stream and following a side road leading to your left **(22B)**. You have climbed 2,200 feet to this point.

Continuing up the road for another 1.5 miles and 800 feet you reach Carson Saddle, where you intersect the Colorado Trail. There are several trail intersections at Carson Saddle. The first **(22C)**, heading to the east is the Colorado Trail. There is a carsonite post designating Trail #821, which continues ahead. This is the trail number for the Lost Trail Creek Trail, but you are also on the Colorado Trail for the next .5 miles. At that point **(22D)**, the Lost Trail Creek Trail continues ahead as a double track while the Colorado Trail cuts off to the right as a single track. There are several posts bearing the logos for the Colorado and Continental Divide Trails at that point. The Lost Trail Creek Trail continues ahead and is covered under that section.

Hiking west along the Colorado Trail, you climb for a short distance before beginning a gradual 300-foot descent into the main portion of the Lost Trail Creek drainage. Once into the drainage, the trail begins to climb at a moderate rate, leaving the last few trees, before climbing through tundra and brush toward the head of the drainage. After crossing several small streams, the pass at the head of the drainage becomes visible, still at a distance. As you climb toward the pass, the brush disappears, and the terrain becomes tundra and rocks. At the 3-mile point rock pinnacles appear to your right and the trail steepens, utilizing two switchbacks before you begin your final ascent up the pass. As is the case with many passes, the point that you see ahead is not the high point of the pass. After passing the first of two cairns, you climb a little further up a long and broad saddle before reaching a carsonite post which sits at the top elevation of 13,000 feet. You have gained 900 feet climbing to the top of the pass.

On the west side of the pass, you descend gradually into the West Lost Trail Creek drainage. Watch out for one steep section with loose gravel. After descending .5 miles you reach the first of three trail intersections. The first is the intersection with the West Lost Trail Creek Trail **(22E)** which connects with the Lost Trail Creek Trail after a 7-mile descent. The West Lost Trail Creek Trail is discussed in the section for the Lost Trail Creek Trail. The West Lost Trail Creek Trail heads to the left while the Colorado Trail continues ahead, marked by a wooden sign. A more prominent carsonite post designates FSR 787, which is the Pole Creek Trail. It follows the Colorado Trail for a very short distance.

The second trail intersection, which is shortly after the first, is where the Pole Creek Trail leaves the Colorado Trail. The Pole Creek Trail is not covered in this book. Just above this trail intersection you can see all four lakes in the Cataract Lake system to your right.

After the second trail intersection, you pass to the left of a knoll and Cataract Lake disappears. The trail becomes a steeper descent as you see another small lake that lies above Cataract Lake to the side of the intersection (**22F**) of the Colorado Trail and the Cataract Gulch Trail. Once you've descended to that trail intersection, which is 700 feet below the pass, you'll find that lake to be a nice lunch or camping spot. The trail descending into Cataract Gulch is discussed under the section named Cataract Gulch. The Colorado Trail continues west beyond the lake, but that section of the Colorado Trail, leading to Stony Pass, is not covered in this book.

Rating: The hike to the Carson townsite (**22B**) is a 7-mile round trip, climbing 2,200 feet. It should be considered an intermediate hike. The hike to Carson Saddle (**22D**) is a 10-mile round trip, climbing 3,000 feet. It should also be considered an intermediate hike. A hike from Carson Saddle west along the Colorado Trail to the intersection with the Cataract Gulch Trail (**22F**) is an 11-mile round trip climbing 900 feet on the way out and 1,000 feet on the return trip. While there are no navigation issues and the terrain is good, the distance and the elevation gain should restrict this hike to experienced hikers.

CATARACT GULCH

Quad: Redcloud Peak, Pole Creek Mountain

DRIVING INSTRUCTIONS: Drive south from Lake City on CO SH 149. Turn right on CR 30 toward Lake San Cristobal. Continue on CR 30 to beyond MP 11 where the roads divide. CR 30 continues to the right and becomes the Shelf Road leading to Cinnamon Pass. You will want to go left on CR 35 leading past the mining settlement of Sherman. After 1.1 miles and crossing a bridge over the Lake Fork of the Gunnison River, you will find the parking area for the Cataract Gulch trailhead on your left and an outdoor toilet and picnic area on your right. The trail begins on the east side of the parking area and the trailhead is well marked. Trailhead elevation - 9,600 feet.

THE HIKE: I've described other trails as "dry hikes" where there is an absence of water. This is a wet hike, and it seems there is water everywhere. You cross streams frequently, follow a rushing stream which gives the trail its name, pass below and then above a waterfall, enter into an alpine basin with multiple drainage streamlets and end at four lakes around the Continental Divide. The presence of so much water, the northern exposure of the gulch, and the steep sides to the gulch limiting the sunlight give much of this trail a lush, garden-like quality. Seasonally, there are wildflowers galore at several spots along the trail. The trail has two distinct personalities. The lower portion, below the falls, is intimate, while the upper portion approaching the divide is expansive. This is a very popular trail, for good reason. While the trail has multiple water crossings, water crossing shoes are not a necessity. Late in the season, most of the crossings are manageable. Early in the season, when they are not, you would spend as much time changing shoes as hiking, so you might as well take the plunge and hike with wet boots. This trail appears on both the *Trails Illustrated* map and on the quads.

Upon leaving the parking area (**23A**), you cross a bridge and soon afterward you have two water crossings, which usually have good log crossings. You climb for .5 miles before reaching the registration station. Then the trail climbs gently over a series of eight switchbacks: six together, then a lengthy straight section, then two more. This is the easiest portion of the trail and there are no terrain issues. Following this section of switchbacks, the trail runs parallel to the stream and the climbing becomes more intense. Both the incline and the rocky terrain present challenges during this section. Your rewards are great as this is where the wildflowers begin and there are wonderful views of the rushing stream as it cascades over the rocks. At the 2.5 mile point you cross mine cart railings associated with a mine above you. From there you descend slightly and cross the stream at a fairly wide point. There are usually logs to assist you in this crossing, but if you wish, the stream is not very deep (later in the season) and you might just plow ahead.

After the stream crossing, you climb steeply for a short while as the waterfall comes into view. You will pass near the bottom of the waterfall, then circle around and upward emerging near the top of the falls. There is then a stream crossing above the falls before arriving at a popular spot for camping, picnics, and the like. This is the destination of choice for those not wanting to continue to the divide (**23B**).

For those proceeding to the divide, there is another stream crossing as you leave the picnic / camping area; soon afterward you enter a rocky area. The trail is not difficult to follow as you proceed through the rocks, and there are cairns placed for your assistance as well. This rocky area continues for .5 miles leading you to the lower limits of the alpine basin above, where you will cross water again.

The trail enters the lower portion of the basin and there are multiple streamlets as the drainage paths for the entire basin converge, creating the stream you've been following since the beginning. The presence of so much water allows more vegetation, primarily bushes, than you would ordinarily see in similar basins. The trail curves to the left, climbing out of the bushes into more hospitable vegetation. It continues in a south-easterly direction toward a gap between one rock monolith and the rest of the rocks defining the eastern limits of the basin. You will climb quite a bit during this section, but once you've emerged from the gap you can see the basin and the divide, and you have practically

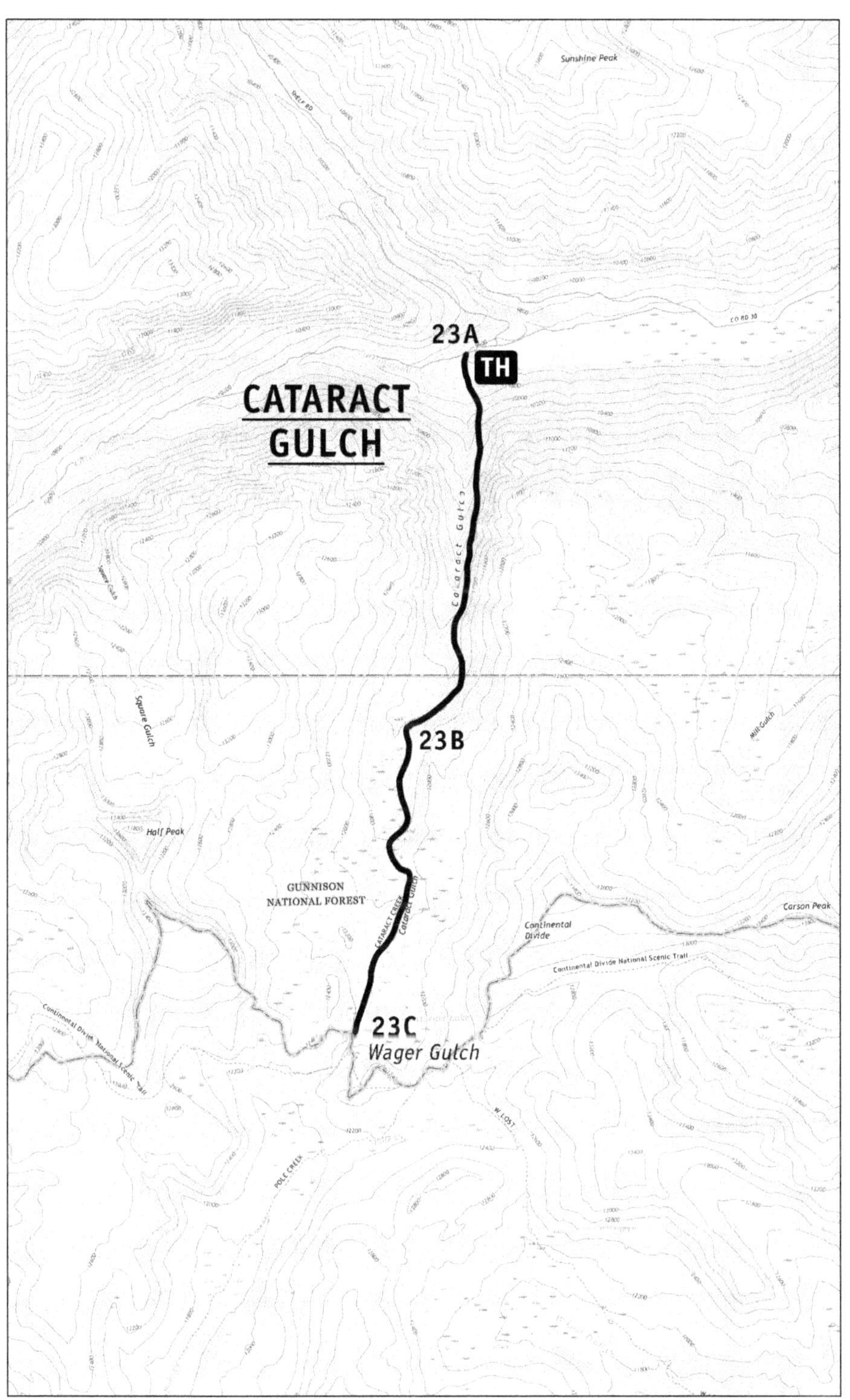
Sunshine Peak
CO RD 30
23A
TH
CATARACT
GULCH
Cataract Gulch
Square Gulch
23B
Mill Gulch
Half Peak
GUNNISON
NATIONAL FOREST
CATARACT CREEK
Cataract Gulch
Continental
Divide
Carson Peak
Continental Divide National Scenic Trail
23C
Wager Gulch
Continental Divide National Scenic Trail
POLE CREEK
W LOST

reached your final elevation. The wildflowers toward the top of the basin are spectacular when in season.

As you hike toward the head of the basin, there are multiple places where you descend a short distance, cross a streamlet, then ascend the next ridge. The trail is not difficult to follow, and there are several posts as you get closer to the divide. Once you've reached the area containing posts, Cataract Lake comes into view. There are three smaller lakes above Cataract Lake. You pass along the west side of Cataract Lake and ascend 200 feet before you reach the Continental Divide. This trail terminates when you reach the Colorado Trail at the top of the divide (**23C**). There is a smaller lake at the top of the divide near the trail intersection. There are two other lakes west of Cataract Lake that are not visible from the trail. The section of the Colorado Trail heading east from this point is covered in the section for Wager Gulch. The portion of the Colorado Trail heading west from this point toward Stony Pass is not covered in this book.

RATING: The trip to the top of the falls (**23B**) is a 6-mile round trip, climbing 1,600 feet. It should be considered an intermediate level hike due to the elevation gain and terrain issues. The trip to the divide (**23C**) is a 12-mile round trip and climbs 2,600 feet. Due to the elevation gain, distance, and terrain issues, this should be limited to experienced hikers.

BLACK WONDER GORGE

Quad: Redcloud Peak

DRIVING INSTRUCTIONS: Drive south from Lake City on CO SH 149. Turn right on CR 30 toward Lake San Cristobal. Continue on CR 30 to beyond MP 11 where the roads divide. CR 30 continues to the right and becomes the Shelf Road leading to Cinnamon Pass. You will want to go left on CR 35 leading past the mining settlement of Sherman. After 1.1 miles and crossing a bridge over the Lake Fork of the Gunnison River you will find the parking area for the Cataract Gulch trailhead on your left and an outdoor toilet and picnic area on your right. The trail begins **(24A)** just north of the picnic table on the right-hand side of the road. The trailhead is unmarked. Trailhead elevation - 9,600 feet.

THE HIKE: This trail follows an old mining road on the opposite side of the Lake Fork from the Shelf Road. The river cuts a gorge which is quite deep in places. Although the hike is generally in wooded (primarily aspen) terrain, clearings emerge from time to time with magnificent views of the gorge and down valley. The road is not usable by vehicles as it is overtaken by aspen trees and a number of downed logs. This trail does not appear on either the *Trails Illustrated* map or the quad.

At its beginning, the trail is a single track that snakes up the side of a hill for a short while until it meets a mining road that serves as the trail for the remainder of the hike. This first section is about as steep as the trail ever becomes, and heads parallel to a fence signifying the boundary with private land. As this portion of the trail is not well developed, you can veer off of it. Remember, if you keep going uphill and stay parallel to the fence you will intersect the mining road.

Once you reach the mining road, turn left and follow the road uphill. Should you turn right you will follow the mining road down

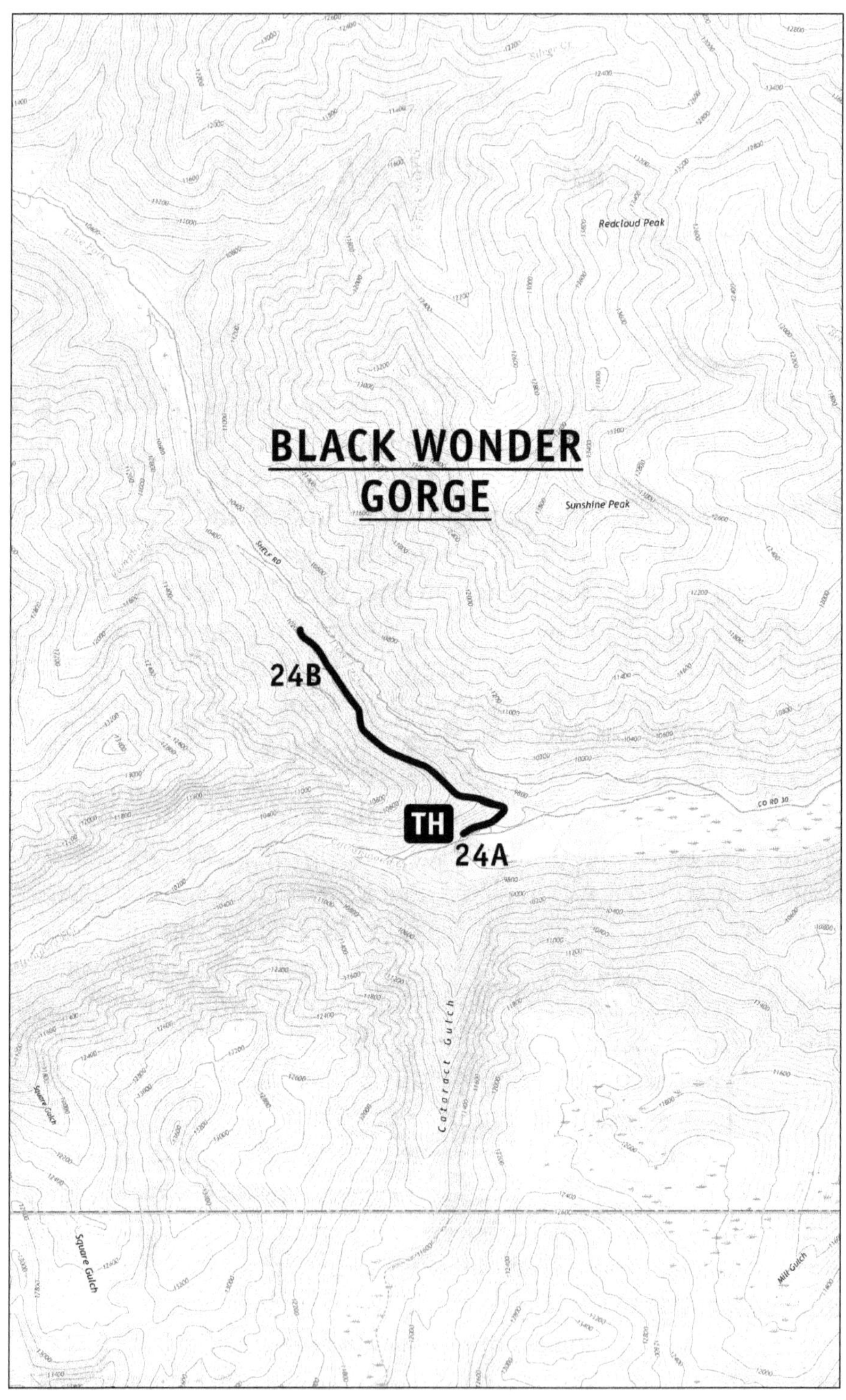

BLACK WONDER
GORGE
Redcloud Peak
Sunshine Peak
SHELF RD
CO RD 30
24B
TH
24A
Cataract Gulch
Square Gulch
Square Gulch
Mill Gulch

to its termination on private land. The intersection of these trails is marked by a sign signifying that the trailhead lies to the right and that you are entering private land. The road switches back several times, breaking into a clearing at each of the two northern switchbacks. There is an interesting side trip originating at each of these switchbacks. North of the first switchback toward the gorge, there is a cave. After the second northern switchback, there is an overlook with a view of a waterfall on the Lake Fork of the Gunnison River. After the last switchback, the road continues to climb further until it levels off for the next mile. You will have gained most of your elevation until you reach the final .5 miles. Not long after a break in the trees where you can get one of the best views down valley, the road forks. The right-hand fork continues for only a couple hundred feet before it ends upon reaching a canyon. The main trail continues to the left marked by a couple of rock cairns then passes the remains of an old mining cabin. Upon reaching a side gulch, the trail turns to the left and becomes steep for a short while. It then switches back in a down valley direction and switches back again until it meets the gulch at a place where you can see a waterfall and the cascading stream coming down the gulch. That is, unless you take this hike in the spring when all the water is still frozen. The road no doubt terminated at a mine when it was first built but the canyon has cut away that portion of the road since then and I have never found the mine. Avalanches occurring during 2019 have blocked the last section of the trail beyond the old mining cabin (**24B**).

Rating: The distance covered (4 miles round trip) and the elevation gain (800 feet) are both modest and the terrain is not particularly challenging. This hike should be suitable for beginners.

COTTONWOOD CREEK

Quad: Redcloud Peak

DRIVING INSTRUCTIONS: Drive south from Lake City on CO SH 149. Turn right on CR 30 toward Lake San Cristobal. Continue on CR 30 to beyond MP 11 where the roads divide. CR 30 continues to the right and becomes the Shelf Road leading to Cinnamon Pass. You will want to go left on CR 35 leading past the mining settlement of Sherman. After 1.1 miles and after crossing a bridge over the Lake Fork of the Gunnison River, you will find the parking area for the Cataract Gulch trailhead on your left and an outdoor toilet and picnic area on your right. The Cottonwood Creek Trail is the continuation of this road. Trailhead elevation - 9,600 feet.

THE HIKE: The "trail" is a road used by vehicles to access the Cuba Gulch and Snare Creek trailheads. This is a four-season trail, although each season presents its own concerns. The road follows Cottonwood Creek to the area where its feeder creeks converge to give Cottonwood Creek its source water. The creek cuts between mountains which rise steeply on either side of the road. Even during a normal winter there is avalanche danger, and debris frequently blocks the trail at places during the spring. That happened in spades during the 2018-2019 winter. While this is a popular trail during the winter for snowshoeing, it should be avoided late in the winter or following a heavy snow due to avalanche danger. During the spring, in addition to avalanche debris, you may be unable to cross Boulder Creek, 2.5 miles in. During the summer you should expect to encounter vehicle traffic. During the fall, this area is popular with hunters. Aside from that, this is a hike that's not particularly difficult and offers some nice views. This road appears both on the *Trails Illustrated* map and on the quad.

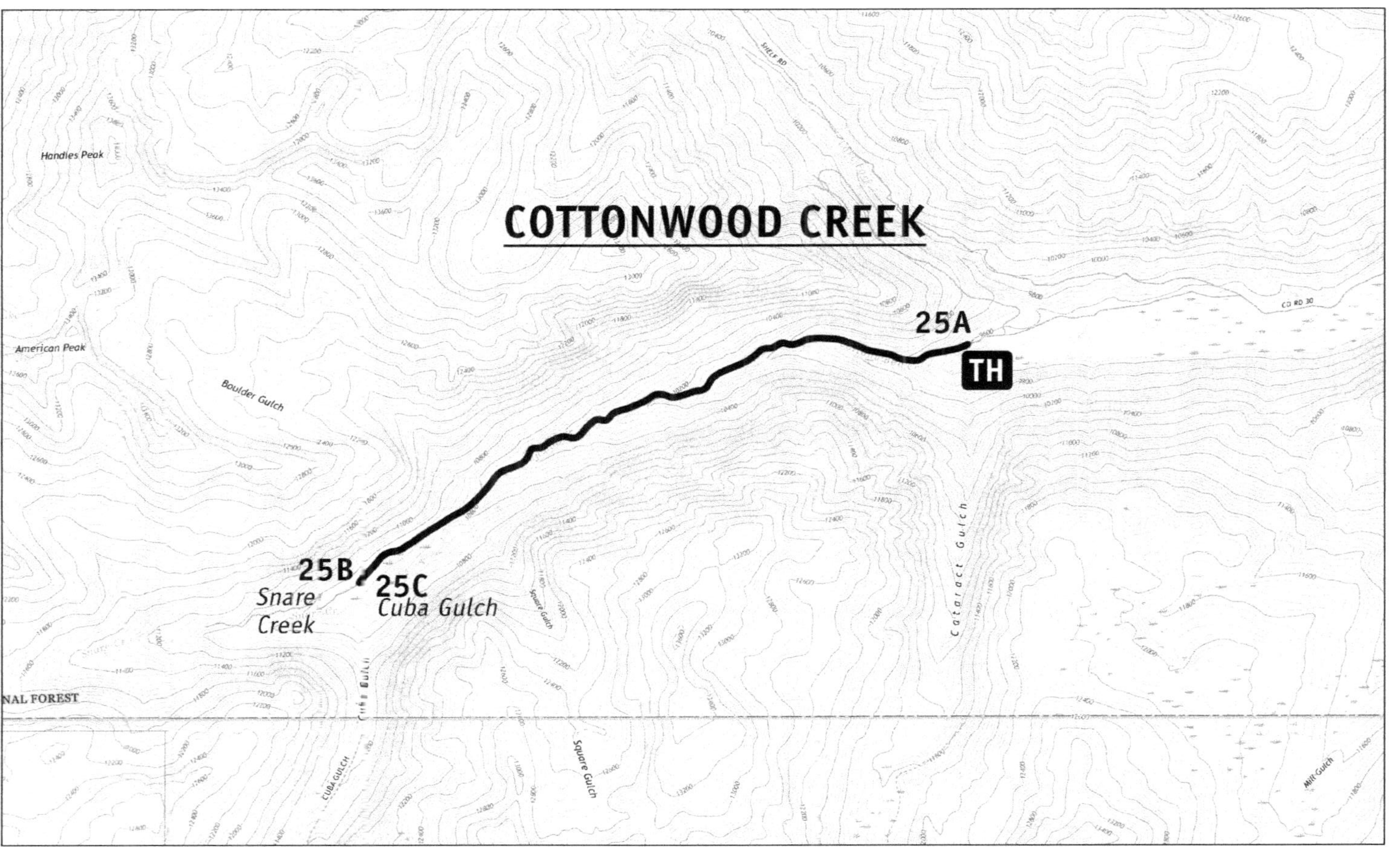
COTTONWOOD CREEK
25A
TH
25B
25C
Snare Creek
Cuba Gulch
Cataract Gulch
Square Gulch
Square Gulch
Boulder Gulch
Handies Peak
American Peak
SHELF RD
CO RD 30
Mill Gulch
NAL FOREST

The beginning of the trail (**25A**) is fairly level, but soon afterward you encounter several moderate inclines, which are about as steep as you will encounter on the trail. The road cuts between wooded areas for much of its distance, although there are several open areas. After .5 miles you encounter an open area and with a waterfall to your left, which is popular with ice climbers during the winter. There are several camping spots on the stream (left) side of the road. At one of these 1 mile in you can see a series of cataracts which are known as Cottonwood Falls. This is the site of the 2008 death of Dr. Leslie Mueller. Her husband was charged with her murder, but two trials ended with juries that were unable to reach a verdict, each resulting in mistrials.

Just beyond the 1-mile point there is a large boulder sitting on the road. From this point on you will see the aftermath of the 2019 avalanches, where thousands of aspen trees were snapped as if they were toothpicks. Other large boulders have fallen into this area from the outcroppings above.

After 2.25 miles the road crosses a small intermittent stream. After another .25 miles you cross Boulder Creek, which may be difficult to cross early in the season but should present little problem later. Immediately after crossing Boulder Creek the quad map indicates a trail going to your right and up Boulder Gulch. I've spoken to an older hiker who spoke well of this trail, but when I attempted to follow it, the trail evaporated after .5 miles. This appears to be one more trail that has been reclaimed by nature. After 3 miles the valley widens and there is a marshy area to your left, in which I've seen moose. To your left there are the remains of a 1940s era pickup truck which is riddled with bullet holes, a la Bonnie and Clyde. From this point on there is little elevation gain and the valley widens into a small park-like area. It then divides with a fainter road, closed to vehicle traffic, leading straight ahead with the main road turning left. This point (**25B**) is the trailhead for the Snare Creek Trail which leads to your right. Continuing left for a few more feet you find the Cuba Gulch trailhead (**25C**) and the parking area for both trails. Both the Snare Creek Trail and the Cuba Gulch Trail are discussed in their own sections.

RATING: The trip to Cuba Gulch and Snare Creek trailheads (**25B,25C**) is a 7-mile round trip and gains 1,100 feet. This should be within the ability of most beginning hikers.

CUBA GULCH

Quad: Redcloud Peak, Pole Creek Mountain

DRIVING INSTRUCTIONS: Drive south from Lake City on CO SH 149. Turn right on CR 30 toward Lake San Cristobal. Continue on CR 30 to beyond MP 11 where the roads divide. CR 30 continues to the right and becomes the Shelf Road leading to Cinnamon Pass. You will want to go left on CR 35 passing the mining settlement of Sherman. After 1.1 miles and crossing a bridge over the Lake Fork of the Gunnison River, you will find the parking area for the Cataract Gulch trailhead on your left and an outdoor toilet and picnic area on your right. The road is 4WD recommended from this point on. Continue up CR 35 for 3.4 miles until you reach the parking area adjacent to the Cuba Gulch trailhead, which is marked. This is just past the Snare Creek trailhead **(27A)**, which is located behind the Road Closed sign. Trailhead elevation -10,700 feet.

THE HIKE: This trail has been rendered nearly impassable by avalanche activity during the 2018-2019 winter. I'm including this section in the hopes that the downed timber is cleared in some future year. As I had not written this section prior to the avalanche, most of what follows in this section comes from memory. This is the only section that was not hiked contemporaneously with the writing of the section. This trail appears on both the *Trails Illustrated* map and on the quads.

The trail crosses water via a log bridge immediately after leaving the trailhead **(26A)**. Most of the hike is a gentle climb through wooded areas, following the creek running through Cuba Gulch. Within the first .25 miles you encounter significant blockage of downed timber which, while possible to bypass, adds to the difficulty of the hike. There is a sturdy bridge less than .5 miles from the trailhead. Most of the blockage is below the bridge, but I am not able to report as to the conditions

Handies Peak
American Basin
American Peak
Boulder Gulch
CUBA GULCH
TH 26A
Snare Creek
Blockage
NISON NATIONAL FOREST
Snare Gulch
Square Gulch
Half Peak
CUBA GULCH
GUNNISON NATIONAL FOREST
CUBA GULCH
Cuba Gulch
SAN JUAN CO
HINSDALE CO
GU
NATION
Continental Divide National Scenic Trail
Continental Divide National Scenic Trail
CUBA GULCH
Continental Divide National Scenic Trail
E. FK. MIDDLE POLE
POLE CREEK
E. FK. MID

above the bridge. This was a popular hike in late July and early August as you would encounter wildflowers. Just before the 2-mile point, the trail crosses a small stream and climbs up into a campground. At this point the trails divide, and neither of these trails is very well traveled. This campground would be the turn-around point for a hiker wanting a shorter hike.

The trail leading to the left climbs steeply through a wooded area gaining 500 feet over .5 miles until it reaches a point where it emerges from the woods and flattens out. From this point the terrain is full of bushes and the trail is overgrown. You can see the obvious destination ahead as you must reach a saddle between two high points. There you would connect with the Colorado Trail, which is well marked at the Continental Divide, a mile from where the Cuba Gulch Trail effectively ends.

The trail leading to the right descends across a grassy and marshy area that is overgrown in this section. The trail emerges as you enter the woods and follows a creek. The trail comes and goes from this point onward. I have not taken this trail and rely on the experience of another hiker.

RATING: This trail should not be attempted in its current condition. Should the logs be cleared, a hike to the campsite is a 4-mile round trip, gaining 700 feet. It would be considered a hike suitable for beginners. Anything beyond the campground should not be attempted by any other than experienced hikers as the conditions are unknown and the covered area is unlikely to be clear even if the lower trail is cleared of debris.

SNARE CREEK

Quad: Redcloud Peak, Handies Peak

DRIVING INSTRUCTIONS: Drive south from Lake City on CO SH 149. Turn right on CR 30 toward Lake San Cristobal. Continue on CR 30 to past MP 11 where the roads divide. CR 30 continues to the right and becomes the Shelf Road leading to Cinnamon Pass. You will want to go left on CR 35 leading past the mining settlement of Sherman. After 1.1 miles and crossing a bridge over the Lake Fork of the Gunnison River, you will find the parking area for the Cataract Gulch trailhead on your left and an outdoor toilet and picnic area on your right. The road is 4WD recommended from this point on. Continue up CR 35 for 3.4 miles until you reach the parking area adjacent to the Cuba Gulch trailhead (**26A**) which is marked. The Snare Creek trailhead is unmarked as such but begins behind the Road Closed sign (**27A**). Trailhead elevation - 10,700 feet.

THE HIKE: This trail follows an old mining road for all but its uppermost portion. The trail climbs significantly but gently, utilizing many switchbacks along a rocky face until it reaches the drainage of a tributary of Snare Creek. It does a double horseshoe before reaching a series of alpine lakes in the upper drainage of Snare Creek proper. While the lower portion of the trail is more work than scenery, the views keep getting better the higher you go. At the end, you are in a basin with up to seven lakes (depending on what you are willing to call a lake) which is infrequently visited and offers a unique mountain experience. This trail is best saved until August or September because of a snowbank that melts late and can't easily be circumvented. This trail appears on both the *Trails Illustrated* map and the quads.

Beginning at the Road Closed sign (**27A**), you will follow an old mining road heading west. Almost immediately after beginning there

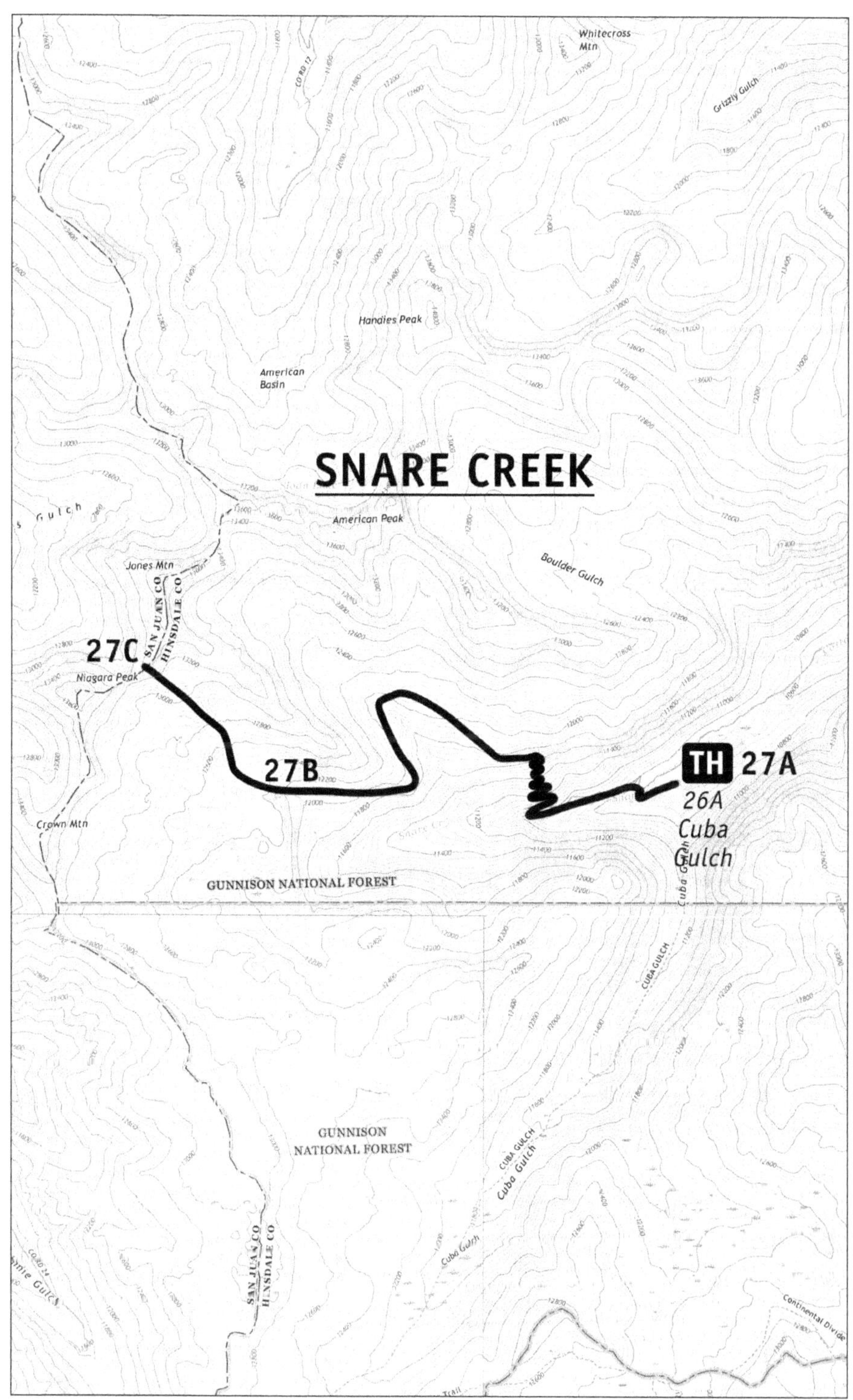
Whitecross
Mtn
Grizzly Gulch
CO RD 17
Handies Peak
American
Basin
SNARE CREEK
American Peak
Boulder Gulch
Jones Mtn
SAN JUAN CO
HINSDALE CO
27C
Niagara Peak
27B
Crown Mtn
TH 27A
26A
Cuba
Gulch
Cuba Gulch
GUNNISON NATIONAL FOREST
GUNNISON
NATIONAL FOREST
SAN JUAN CO
HINSDALE CO
CUBA GULCH
Cuba Gulch
Cuba Gulch
Continental Divide
Trail

is a double-track road veering to your right. You could choose either route because the right-hand trail rejoins the main trail at the second switchback. However, it is steeper and has areas with loose gravel. If you stay to the left, you will have two switchbacks in rapid succession. For the next half .5 miles you can see Snare Creek well below you. There is some downed timber in this section, but this is manageable. There is also a deep trench which can be tricky to cross. You then begin a series of twelve switchbacks that will take you up the face of the unnamed mountain. While the ascent is steady, it is not particularly steep. The road is rocky with sparse vegetation but is wide enough to be safe under most circumstances. You will climb 800 feet before you leave the switchbacks. There is an area near the top of the switchbacks that contains sandy runoff.

Following the final switchback, you continue west through a small, wooded area before breaking into the open along the drainage of a tributary of Snare Creek. There is a partially reconstructed mining cabin on your left at the 3-mile point. After several more switchbacks, you climb very gently toward the head of this drainage and cross the creek after passing a mine. This and any other water crossings on this trail are quite mild by late in the season, and water crossing shoes should not be needed. After crossing the creek, the trail heads back on the opposite side of the creek completing its first horseshoe. It is during this stretch that you will encounter snow early in the season as this is along a steep face with a northern exposure. You will then begin the second horseshoe which takes you around the mountain and into the drainage area of Snare Creek proper. After completing this second horseshoe there will be several small switchbacks taking you into the basin containing the series of lakes. Both horseshoes are covered with rock and scree.

The first lake will be to your left as you enter the basin. This may be as far as you want to go as you've already come 4.5 miles and climbed 1,700 feet. To reach most of the upper lakes would necessitate going off trail at some point and doing some steep climbing. For those willing to do so, the views will make it worth your while. The mining road continues for more than .5 miles past the first lake before ending at a turquoise-colored lake. This is not where the *Trails Illustrated* map indicates that the trail ends as it shows it going over a pass between Niagara Peak and Jones Mountain into the Animas River drainage above Silverton. My quad map shows no trail at this point. I have spotted the semblance of a trail that leaves the mining road several hundred yards below the turquoise lake. This trail comes and goes, being apparent in the rocky areas and disappearing in the tundra. The destination is the pass to the right of Niagara Peak, which is the highest peak you can see from this basin. This will cross a rockslide before reaching the pass to the Silverton side. There is scant evidence of a trail on the Lake City side, and I've seen no evidence of a trail on the Silverton side. Instead of crossing the rockslide to the divide, I recommend stopping at the top of one of the several grassy knolls in the tundra above the lower lakes.

RATING: The distance covered is a 9-mile round trip to the lower lake **(27B)** and an 11-mile round trip to the pass **(27C)**. The elevation gain is 1,700 feet to the lower lake and 2,500 feet to the pass. Both are enough to exclude any beginners. While the trail is easy to follow to the lower lake, from that point on you will have some cross country to make it to the upper lakes or to the divide. Much of the mining road is rocky which will slow you down and will not enhance your experience since you will be watching your step and not the beautiful surroundings. Any intermediate hiker who is comfortable hiking on rock should be able to make it to the lower lake but beyond that should be reserved for experienced hikers.

GRIZZLY GULCH

Quad: Redcloud Peak

DRIVING INSTRUCTIONS: Drive south from Lake City on CO SH 149. Turn right on CR 30 toward Lake San Cristobal. Continue on CR 30 to beyond MP 11 where the roads divide. CR 30 continues to the right and becomes the Shelf Road leading to Cinnamon Pass. While not designated as a 4WD recommended road, that would be my recommendation. Take this right fork and continue 4.0 miles to a parking area that serves both the Grizzly Gulch and Silver Creek trailheads. The trailhead for Grizzly Gulch is behind the two outdoor toilets (**28A**). This trail appears on both the *Trails Illustrated* map and on the quad. Trailhead elevation - 10,400 feet.

THE HIKE: It seems axiomatic that the more difficult the hike, the greater the rewards. This trail would support that proposition. While it is not an easy trail in any respect, the rewards are great. I will describe three variations of the hike which could be described as hard, harder and hardest. The first ends at Grizzly Lake, the second at the head of a beautiful alpine basin, and the third concludes with the climbing of Handies Peak. All begin in the same manner. The trail crosses the Lake Fork of the Gunnison River via a sturdy bridge and begins gaining elevation rapidly. The trail has been improved by the addition of many logs laid across the trail for erosion control purposes, creating a staircase effect. You will enter a wooded area, then alternate between wooded and open areas for 2 miles as you follow the creek flowing down Grizzly Gulch. The views of the creek from the open areas are striking. In two of the last three open areas there are natural drainage ditches that will contain water on a seasonal basis. Early in the season you will want water crossing shoes no matter which variation of this hike you choose. By mid-season the only variation of this hike which crosses any serious

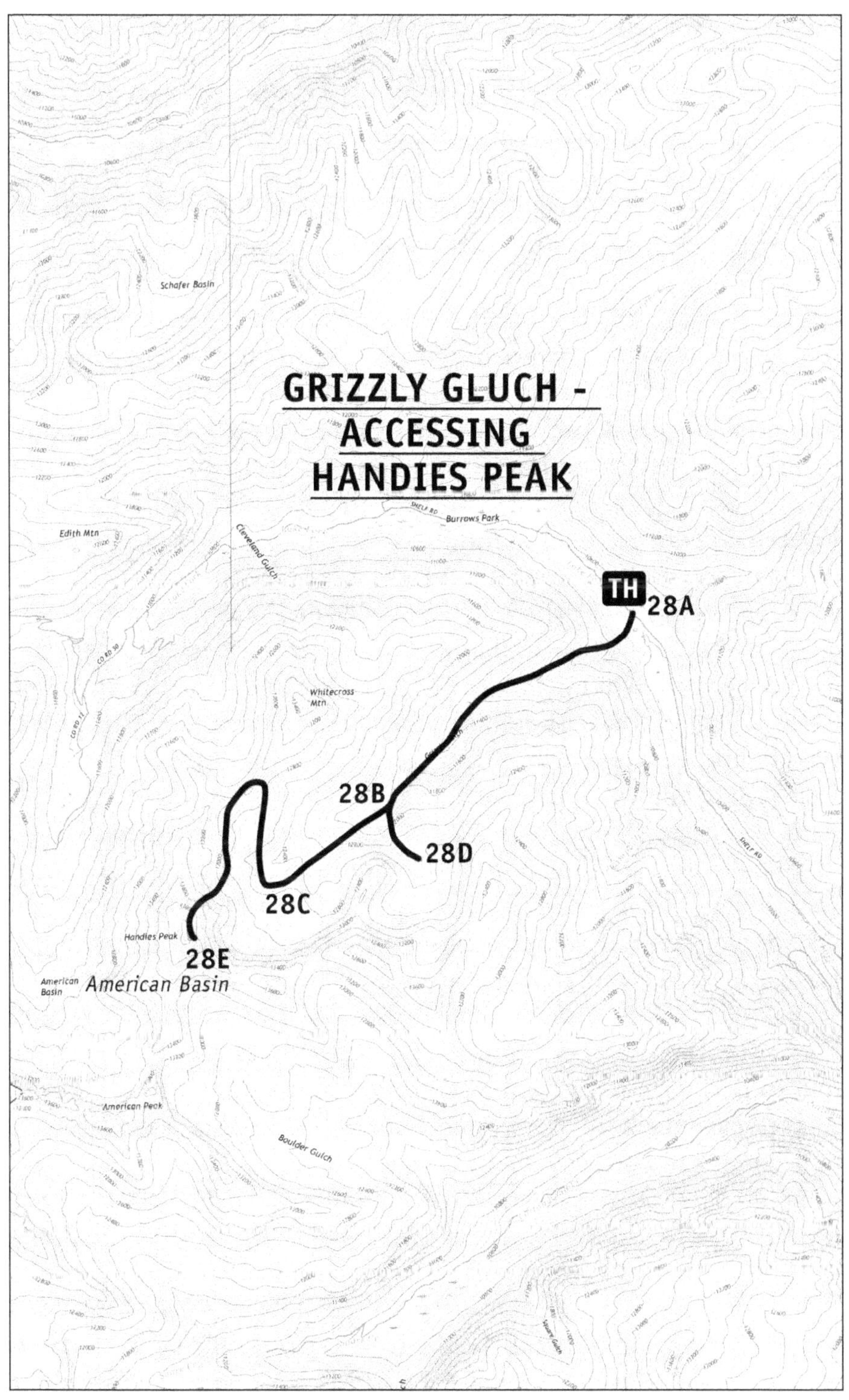

GRIZZLY GLUCH -
ACCESSING
HANDIES PEAK
Schafer Basin
Edith Mtn
Cleveland Gulch
SHELF RD
Burrows Park
Whitecross Mtn
CO RD 30
CO RD 31
TH 28A
28B
28D
28C
Handies Peak
28E
American Basin
American Basin
American Peak
Boulder Gulch
SHELF RD

water is the first one, leading to Grizzly Lake. After passing through the woods following the second drainage ditch, you will enter a beautiful alpine basin. I would describe this basin as American Basin without the cars or the people. If you can, you should try this hike in prime wildflower season (late July and early August).

Once you are in the basin look ahead and to the left. You are looking for the drainage coming out of Grizzly Lake, which is the destination for the first variation of this hike. Leading from the top of this drainage you should see a trail downward and to the right which will pass across or below a snowbank that is present until late in the season most years. You will need to head toward this point eventually so, as the turnoff is unmarked, keep this point in mind. You will want to continue up the basin past the point where the large brush area surrounding the creek ends. From there cross the creek that is to your left (**28B**). This will coincide with a break in the bushes. From that point, move toward the point you spotted earlier at the right side of the snowbank. The trail has been overgrown by short grass but will emerge as you get to rockier ground. The trail is easy to follow through the rockslide but becomes faint once you reach the tundra on the far side of the rocks. However, the location of the lake should be apparent. After passing the rockslide, you climb 200 more feet over the next .25 miles until you reach Grizzly Lake (**28D**). You will top out at 12,300 feet on this first variation of this hike.

Should you be hiking in peak wildflower season, or if you have left behind your water crossing shoes, you may want to take the second variation of this hike, which continues another mile to the head of the basin. This trail is well marked, although it crosses water several times. This should not be an issue later in the season. As you ascend the basin, the trail becomes steeper than what you experienced earlier. If you need to stop periodically you will have magnificent views in all directions. As you reach the head of the basin you will encounter a post with bolts indicating that it once contained a trail sign (**28C**). This would be your stopping point for the second variation of this hike. You are at 12,600 feet.

If you want to continue up Handies Peak, the trail turns to the right and leaves the basin, heading for a saddle between Whitecross Mountain and Handies Peak. Before reaching that saddle, the trail cuts toward Handies Peak, climbing the north face of the peak. The trail is easy to follow up to the peak. That's the only thing easy about it as you have climbed about 1,400 feet since you left the basin. The climb up Handies (**28E**) is far easier from the American Basin side particularly since you start from a point 900 feet higher. Handies Peak has an elevation of 14,048 feet and is the 40th tallest mountain in Colorado.

RATING: The round-trip distance to either the lake (**28D**) or to the head of the basin (**28C**) is 7 miles and the round-trip distance to Handies Peak (**28E**) is 8 miles. You gain 1,900 feet going to the lake, 2,200 feet to the head of the basin, and 3,600 feet to the peak. The only terrain issue on any of these variations, is the rocky final ascent of the peak. The first two variations are within the upper limits of the abilities of intermediate hikers. The third variation should be limited to experienced hikers. For those who are up to the challenge, this is a wonderful trail.

Handies Peak from Grizzly Gulch

Katherine Heidt

SILVER CREEK

Quad: Redcloud Peak

DRIVING INSTRUCTIONS: Drive south from Lake City on CO SH 149. Turn right on CR 30 toward Lake San Cristobal. Continue on CR 30 to beyond MP 11 where the roads divide. CR 30 continues to the right and becomes the Shelf Road leading to Cinnamon Pass. While not designated as a 4WD recommended road, that would be my recommendation. Take this right fork and continue 4.0 miles to a parking area that serves both the Grizzly Gulch and Silver Creek trailheads. The trailhead for Silver Creek is at the north end of the parking area (**29A**). Trailhead elevation - 10,400 feet.

THE HIKE: As this trailhead leads to Redcloud Peak and Sunshine Peak, both fourteeners, it is a popular trail and the number of cars at the trailhead prove this point. While you can't expect solitude, the rewards are many and the views at the upper elevations are among the best in the area. The trail leads first to the summit of Redcloud, then descends 600 feet to a saddle in between Redcloud and Sunshine, before reclaiming most of that elevation during the final ascent to the summit of Sunshine. While this is a long hike, these are not difficult fourteeners. Just watch the weather and get an early start. The trail has five distinct segments, each covering 1 to 1.5 miles, which are discussed in the five following paragraphs. This trail is marked on both the *Trails Illustrated* map and on the quad.

There is a significant amount of elevation to be gained along this trail, and no time is wasted in beginning the climbing. The first segment passes through wooded areas as the trail runs parallel to Silver Creek, but far away and above it enough that you rarely are aware of its presence. The trail has been improved by the addition of many logs placed across the trail for erosion control purposes, creating a staircase effect. The upper portion of this segment shows evidence of the 2019 avalanches, but the trail has been well cleared. This section has been well maintained. After 1.5 miles you emerge from the forest and rarely see a tree beyond this segment.

The second segment is in the open but is best described as crossing one rockslide after another for a mile with few breaks in between. The trail ascends gradually during this segment and is much closer to Silver Creek. While most of the rocks that you cross are of medium size and the gradual ascent is helpful, there are places where the trail steepens and the rocks are pebble sized, creating hazardous conditions on the way down.

Once you have left the last of the rockslides, you are entering the third segment, which is a large bowl area taking you to the upper limits of the Silver Creek drainage, ending at a saddle connecting Redcloud Peak to the unnamed mountain (13,832 elevation) to the northeast. The trail heads east during the lower portion of this segment but turns to the southeast as you gain elevation. The terrain is alpine tundra and the footing on the lower portion of this segment is secure but becomes more troublesome as you enter the upper portion of the segment, and you find loose dirt and pebbles. This area can feature wildflowers, although not as plentifully as basins with a northern exposure. Looking forward from the lower portion of the trail, there appears to be a division of the trails ahead. Once you reach that point, there is a trail sign directing you to the left. I'm not sure if the right-hand trail is only a drainage ditch or if this is an earlier trail closed for erosion control purposes. While the lower portion of this segment ascends at a gradual to moderate pace, the upper portion steepens as you approach the saddle. Once on top of the saddle you have a window to some magnificent views to the east. The third segment covers 1.5 miles. This saddle would be a good turnaround point for hikers not wanting to proceed onward to one or both of the fourteeners ahead. However, those hikers are few and far between as most hikers on this trail want to claim their fourteener.

Leaving the saddle, the trail steepens, and conditions worsen as you begin the ascent of Redcloud Peak. The trail consists of loose rock, dirt, and pebbles for most of this ascent. While this is tough on the way up, it is hazardous on the way down. There are several places where the trail appears to divide. While there are two trail signs directing you, they do

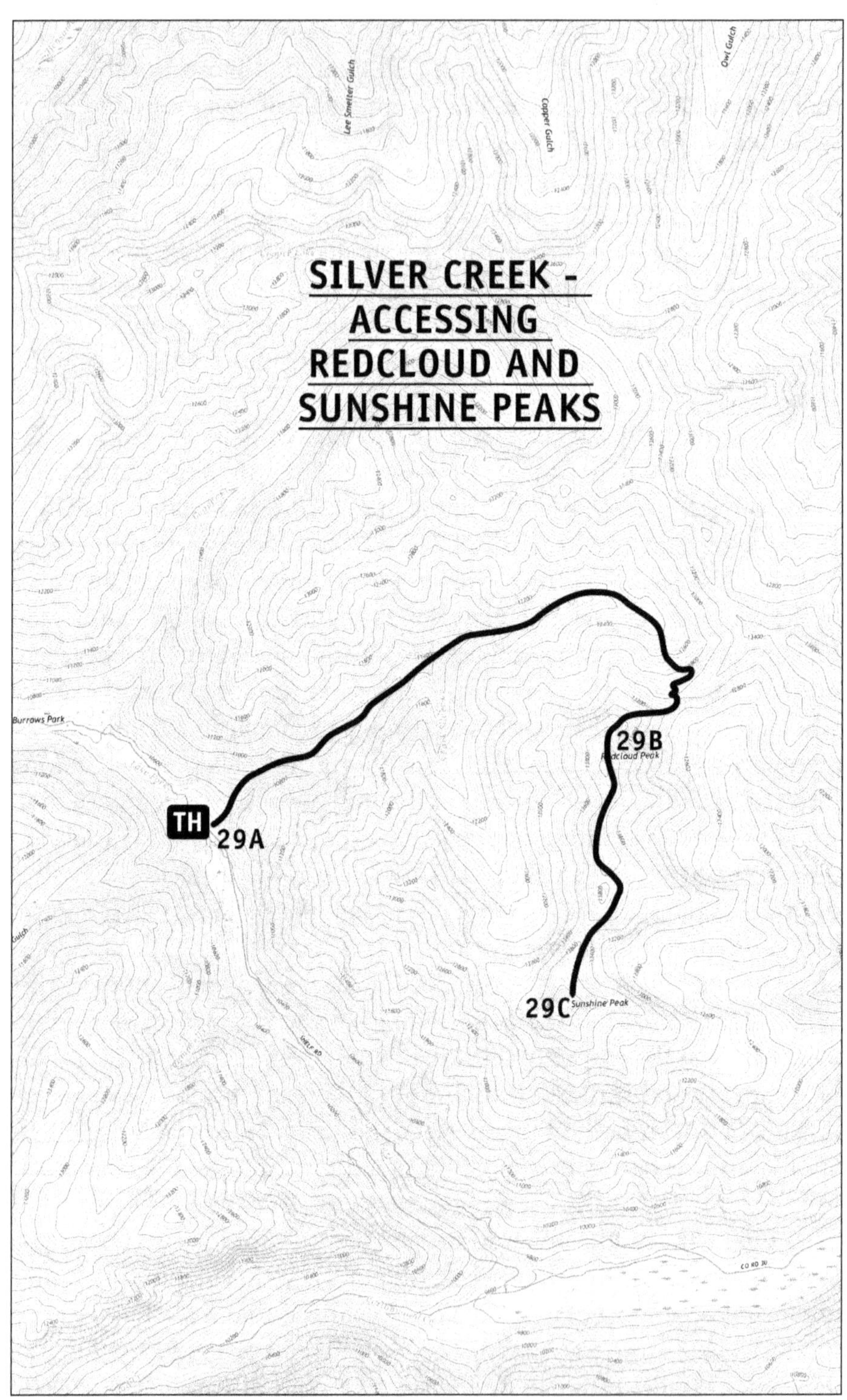
SILVER CREEK -
ACCESSING
REDCLOUD AND
SUNSHINE PEAKS
TH 29A
29B
Redcloud Peak
29C Sunshine Peak
Burrows Park

not cover all of the possibilities. In each case you should take the less steep of the options. As you are climbing, you can see Redcloud Peak above and to your left. What you are climbing is a false peak. When you reach the top of what you can see, you are still a short distance from the actual false peak. After reaching the false peak, you pass along a saddle between the false peak and Redcloud Peak before climbing the final 200 feet to the summit (**29B**). Redcloud Peak is the 45th tallest mountain in Colorado, with a summit elevation of 14,037 feet. The fourth segment covers 1 mile.

For hikers wanting to proceed on to Sunshine Peak, you head to the south, descending moderately for the first half of the 1.5-mile distance between the two peaks. The views during this fifth segment are unparalleled, although 360-degree views can best be had on the two summits. This is because there are two features between the two peaks which can block your views. You pass to the west of the first feature and to the east of the second feature. There is a saddle between the two features and is a sign warning you not to take a short-cut down valley by-passing Redcloud Peak on your return trip from Sunshine Peak. After passing the second feature, you reach a second saddle and begin the final 400-foot climb to the top of Sunshine Peak (**29C**). You are once again on loose rock. Sunshine Peak is the 53rd tallest mountain in Colorado, with a summit elevation of 14,004 feet. The views from the summits of Redcloud and Sunshine are quite special. There is a second approach to Sunshine Peak, which leaves from CR 30 near the Mill Creek Campground. It is exceedingly difficult and will probably take longer to reach Sunshine Peak than the trail we have discussed. I have not included it in this book.

RATING: A round trip to the top of Redcloud Peak (**29B**) is 10 miles, gaining 3,600 feet of elevation. A round trip to Sunshine Peak (**29C**), climbing Redcloud Peak twice in the process, is 13 miles, gaining 4,600 feet gross and 3,600 feet net elevation. Due to the length of the hike, the elevation gain, and the terrain issues, these hikes should be limited to the most experienced of hikers. You will see some beautiful scenery, but this is a brutal hike.

COOPER CREEK

Quad: Redcloud Peak

DRIVING INSTRUCTIONS: Drive south from Lake City on CO SH 149. Turn right on CR 30 toward Lake San Cristobal. Continue on CR 30 to beyond MP 11 where the roads divide. CR 30 continues to the right and becomes the Shelf Road leading to Cinnamon Pass. While not designated as a 4WD recommended road, that would be my recommendation. Take this right fork and continue 4.8 miles. The trailhead is marked on your right (**30A**) and there is a small parking area on your left. Trailhead elevation - 10,600 feet.

THE HIKE: This trail doesn't get nearly as much traffic as Silver Creek Trail or Grizzly Gulch Trail which are in the same area, simply because it doesn't lead to the peak of a fourteener. Yet, the trail is as beautiful as either of those nearby trails. It leads up the Cooper Creek Valley and will take you either to Cooper Lake, the basin at the head of the Cooper Creek drainage, or to the top of the divide between the Lake Fork and Henson Creek drainages. As this is a smaller valley and basin than Grizzly Gulch, American Basin, or Cataract Lakes basin, it leaves the hiker with a more intimate experience. As the basin faces southwest it doesn't get the same quantity of wildflowers as those other basins but still is a fine hike for later in the season. Cooper Lake is nestled in a high rocky area and isn't the most scenic of Hinsdale County's Alpine lakes, but I'm told that it offers fine fishing. The first two versions of this hike are depicted on the *Trails Illustrated* map as well as the quad while the third is depicted only on the quad.

The trail begins on a double track that curves around a couple of low-lying areas before it enters the woods after .25 miles. From this point, it climbs steadily and moderately for the next mile. You will be in the woods well above Cooper Creek, breaking out into three open areas, each area larger than the previous one, before entering the woods for a fourth time. By the time you break into the open for the fourth time, you will be heading down toward your first crossing of Cooper Creek. You should not need stream crossing shoes later in the season for this or any other crossings of Cooper Creek. Early in the season, this trail retains significant amounts of snow, and the stream flow can be heavy and parts of the trail inaccessible.

After the first creek crossing you will climb before reaching the first of several small, wooded areas, the first contains the ruins of a miner's cabin across the creek from a mine and its tailings. You will continue alternating between wooded and open areas for the next .5 miles before breaking into the open for the final time. The ascent is more gradual than it was on the other side of the creek. You will descend slightly to cross Cooper Creek for a second time.

Less than .25 miles from the second creek crossing the trails divide **(30B)**. The main trail is on your left and leads to Cooper Lake. The trail to the head of the Cooper Creek drainage is faint and to your right. This trail divide is marked by a rock cairn to the left of the trail, which will be found shortly after the vegetation changes to a leafy plant suitable for this marshy area. While the trail has been pretty easy to this point, either branch offers challenges of different sorts. This should be your turnaround point if there are any beginners in your group.

If you continue on the main trail to the lake, the trail steepens significantly for quite some time as you climb to above the waterfall formed from draining the lake. By the time you reach the top of the falls and turn left, you will still be climbing, albeit at a lesser rate, as you go through rock-strewn tundra. Looking upward and to your right at this point **(30C)**, you should see the trail taking you to the top of the Lake Fork / Henson Creek divide. Looking ahead, you see the depression where you think the lake should be. No, you've been fooled again. Looking up and to your left, you will see a large rock face 400 feet above you. The lake is behind that face, and you should see the trail to the left of that rock face. The trail comes and goes through this rock scree. This is difficult and sometimes dangerous terrain. After switching back through the scree several times, the trail turns to the right and climbs more gradually along a grassy area for your final ascent to Cooper Lake, which is one of the highest lakes in the county **(30E)**.

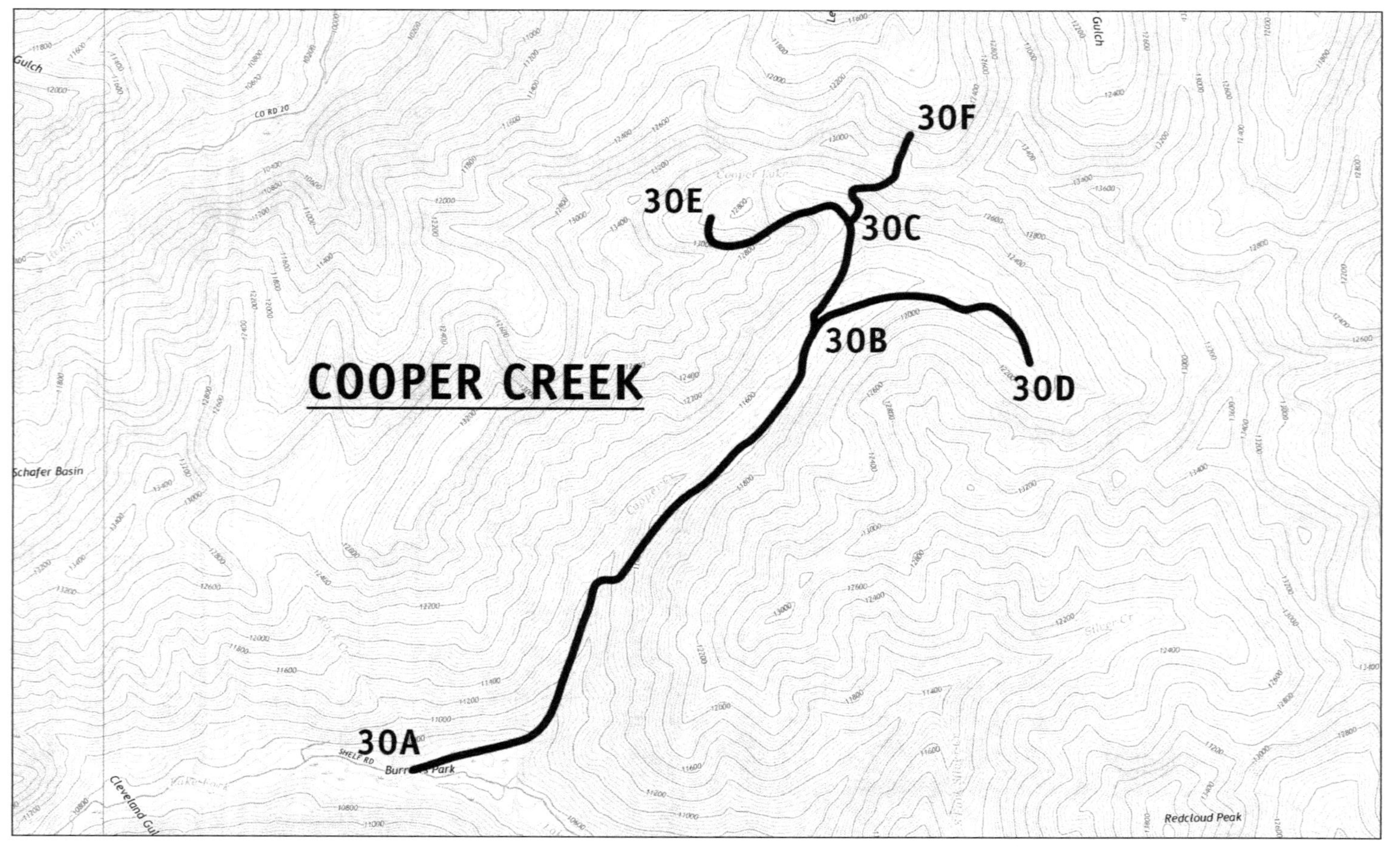
30F
30E
30C
30B
30D
COOPER CREEK
30A
Gulch
Gulch
CO RD 20
Schafer Basin
Cleveland Gulch
SHELF RD
Burrows Park
Redcloud Peak

Returning to the trail divide following the second stream crossing (**30B**), should you want an easier trail, the right-hand trail is more gradual and very scenic. It also receives little use and is difficult to follow. The trail continues on the northwest side of Cooper Creek for .25 miles through marshy vegetation until it passes a rockslide on the other side of the creek. It then descends and crosses the creek. On the southeast side of Cooper Creek, the trail comes and goes through the grass, but is designated by a series of small rock cairns. It matters little if you stay on the trail since you are headed toward the head of the basin, and you will be going cross country at some point anyway. As the trail disappears and the grade increases on the south side of the creek both maps indicate the trail crosses to the north side of the creek where it continues to reach the head of the basin. There is a severe rocky gulch bringing water out of the northern part of the basin that serves as my turnaround point (**30D**). The views from the head of the basin are spectacular.

Should you want the most difficult trail, you can go to the Lake Fork / Henson Creek divide which provides access to Henson Creek and CR 20. This trail does not exactly intersect the main trail to Cooper Lake but is visible climbing the wall above Cooper Lake's drainage waterfall, as described above (**30C**). To reach the visible portion of this trail, you will need to bushwhack through tundra for a bit, keeping the visible portion of the trail in your sights. You will first descend to cross the creek from Cooper Lake and climb across the tundra until you meet the trail. This trail is faint in spots but is not too difficult to follow. It has several switchbacks, and you will cross mine cart railings at two points. Once you have left the tundra, the trail consists of loose gravel much of the way and is quite steep in spots. This can be a dangerous combination, particularly on the way down. You may prefer to walk on the tundra, using the trail as a guide, as the tundra provides surer footing. After a 700-foot climb covering less than a mile, you will reach a saddle which serves as the pass between the Lake Fork and Henson Creek (**30F**). The trail on the Henson Creek side ascends Lee Smelter Gulch from below Capitol City. That trail received significant damage from the avalanches of 2019 and is not easily passible. I have not included that trail in this guidebook.

RATING: A round trip to where the trails divide (**30B**) is 6 miles and a round trip to either Cooper Lake (**30E**), the head of the Cooper Creek Basin (**30D**), or the top of the pass (**30F**) is a 9-mile round trip. You will have gained 1,000 feet to the trail junction, 2,100 feet to Cooper Lake, 1,400 feet to the head of Cooper Creek Basin, and 2,300 feet to the top of the pass. There are no terrain issues to the trail junction, some cross country to the head of the Cooper Creek Basin, and some severe rock scree going to Cooper Lake or to the pass. The hike to the trail junction is suitable for a well acclimated beginner. The hike to the head of the Cooper Creek Basin should not be challenging for an intermediate hiker, but the hike to Cooper Lake or to the divide should be reserved for experienced hikers.

Cooper Lake

Glenn Heumann

AMERICAN BASIN

Quad: Handies Peak

DRIVING INSTRUCTIONS: Drive south from Lake City on CO SH 149. Turn right on CR 30 toward Lake San Cristobal. Continue on CR 30 to beyond MP 11 where the roads divide. CR 30 continues to the right and becomes the Shelf Road leading to Cinnamon Pass. While not designated as a 4WD recommended road, that would be my recommendation. Take this right fork and continue 7.8 miles to where the road again divides. The left fork takes you to American Basin while the right fork continues up Cinnamon Pass. There are two primary parking areas in American Basin. The lower lot is .4 miles from the Cinnamon Pass fork and the upper lot is .7 miles from that fork. A trail leads from the lower lot to the upper lot. All distances and elevation gains are measured from the upper lot. Trailhead elevation - 11,200 feet.

THE HIKE: Aside from being the trailhead for an ascent of Handies Peak, American Basin is a popular destination for non-hikers, especially during the time wildflowers are in bloom, typically late July through early August. The panorama of the rock crags at the head of the basin is one of Hinsdale County's iconic images. Because of this, and because the trailhead services a fourteener, this can be a busy area and parking can be at a premium. In addition to being the trailhead for Handies Peak, you may also hike over the divide between the Lake Fork drainage and the Animas River drainage toward Silverton via the Grouse Gulch Trail. The Grouse Gulch Trail provides an approach to Handies Peak for hikers lacking access to a 4WD vehicle and for those departing from Silverton. A trip to Sloan Lake is a destination for hikers not wanting to climb Handies Peak. All of these trails are marked both on the *Trails Illustrated* map and on the quad.

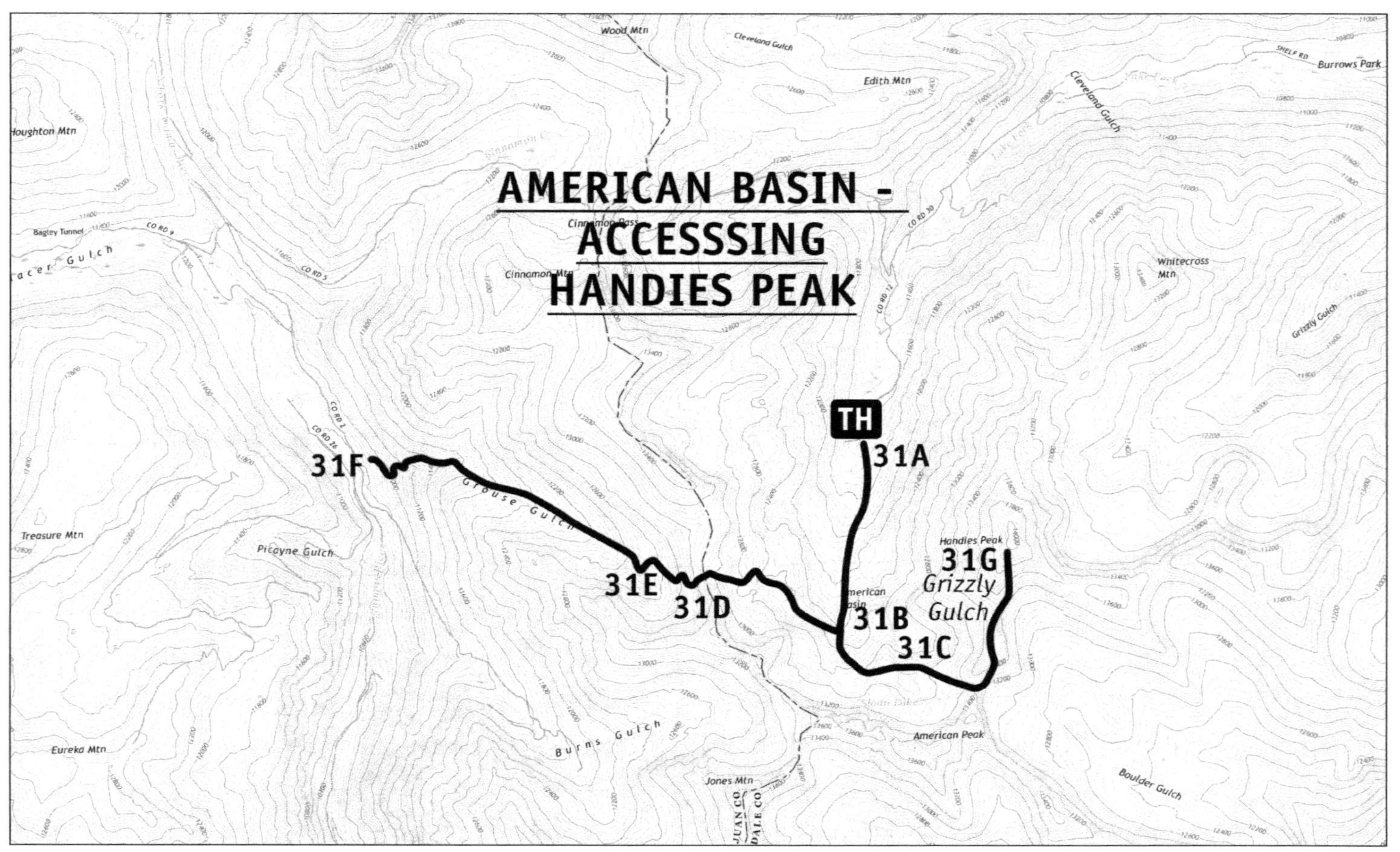
AMERICAN BASIN -
ACCESSSING
HANDIES PEAK
TH
31A
31B
31C
31D
31E
31F
31G
Grizzly
Gulch
Handies Peak
American Peak
Grouse Gulch
Burns Gulch
Picayne Gulch
Treasure Mtn
Eureka Mtn
Houghton Mtn
Bagley Tunnel
Jones Mtn
Boulder Gulch
Grizzly Gulch
Whitecross Mtn
Cleveland Gulch
Edith Mtn
Wood Mtn
Burrows Park
SHELF RD
Cinnamon Pass
Cinnamon Mtn
CO RD 9
CO RD 5
CO RD 2
CO RD 30
CO RD 12

Embarking from the upper parking lot **(31A)**, the trail climbs moderately toward the head of the basin. The trail runs parallel to the Lake Fork of the Gunnison River as it approaches its headwaters. As this trail is well used, there is little difficulty following it. A little over a mile in there is a barely distinguishable, unmarked fork in the trail **(31B)**. The left fork, which is better defined, continues toward Sloan Lake and Handies Peak. The right fork takes you over a pass to Grouse Gulch.

Taking the left fork, the trail turns to the left (east). You've reached the limits of the upper basin and you have several switchbacks as you begin your climb out of American Basin. The trail then flattens as you are passing through tundra. Following a creek crossing there are several more switchbacks, and you reach the turnoff to Sloan Lake **(31C)**, which is marked by a cairn, less than a mile from the Grouse Gulch turnoff **(31B)**. Sloan Lake is less than 100 yards from the turnoff and is a logical turnaround point for any hikers not wishing to proceed to Handies.

After the turnoff to Sloan Lake, the tundra gives way to rock for the next section. There is little net elevation gain as you cross the rockslide, but there is a 50-foot descent that is most unwelcome on the return trip. After you pass through the rockslide, you are hiking in tundra once again and the climb steepens, but still is a moderate climb. There are several switchbacks which lead you to a saddle dividing the Lake Fork drainage from the Cottonwood Creek drainage to the east. Once you've reached the saddle, turn to the left (north); the final ascent of 600 feet to the summit of Handies lies ahead. This is steeper than anything you've done to this point, but the climb is steady over the final .5 miles to the summit. The views from the summit of Handies are unparalleled. In addition to views of the other fourteeners in Hinsdale County, you can see across the divide into the Animas River drainage beyond to the peaks near Ouray and Silverton. The summit **(31G)** can also be reached from the Grizzly Gulch trailhead. Handies Peak is the 39th tallest mountain in Colorado, with a summit elevation of 14,058 feet.

Returning to the turnoff to the Grouse Gulch Trail **(31B)**, taking the right fork, the trail continues to climb moderately as you cross the upper portion of the Lake Fork drainage and begin to climb toward the pass which separates the Lake Fork drainage and the Animas River drainage on the Silverton side of the pass. The trail steepens as you approach the top of the pass, which is less than a mile from the fork in the trail. You will have climbed 500 feet to the trail fork, and another 900 feet as you climb to the top of the pass (**31D**). The views from the top of the pass make it well worth the climb. You will see a small lake below you on the Silverton side.

The descent into Grouse Gulch, on the Silverton side of the pass, is steep for the first 500 feet until you reach the lake, less than a mile away (**31E**). As you approach the lake, the trail appears to divide and there is a cairn. Take the left fork, which passes the lake, before continuing down the gulch. Beyond the lake, the trail takes a more moderate descent for the next mile, and you see evidence of mining activity on both sides of Grouse Gulch. A mile past the lake, the trail steepens as it descends toward San Juan CR 26, where the trail ends (**31F**). There is no signage at the intersection of this trail with CR 26.

RATING: A hike from the American Basin trailhead to the summit of Handies Peak (**31G**) is a 5.5-mile round trip climbing 2,800 feet. While there are no navigation issues and the length of the hike is not excessive, the steepness of the final ascent limits this hike to experienced hikers. A hike from the American Basin trailhead to Sloan Lake (**31C**) is a 4-mile round trip, climbing 1,600 feet. It is suitable for intermediate hikers. A hike from the American Basin trailhead along the Grouse Gulch Trail to its termination at the intersection with San Juan CR 26 (**31F**) is a 9-mile round trip with a 1,400-foot ascent on the way out and a 2,200-foot ascent on the return trip. Due to the distance, elevation gain, and steepness of the trail, this should only be attempted by experienced hikers. A shorter trip to the unnamed lake (**31E**) would be a 5-mile round trip with a 1,400-foot ascent on the way out and a 500-foot ascent on the return trip. Due to the steepness of this trail, this should also only be attempted by experienced hikers. A hike to the top of the pass (**31D**) would be a 4-mile round trip with only the 1,400-foot ascent to the top of the pass. This should be within the capabilities of an intermediate hiker.

Trailheads Located South and East of Lake City via CO SH 149

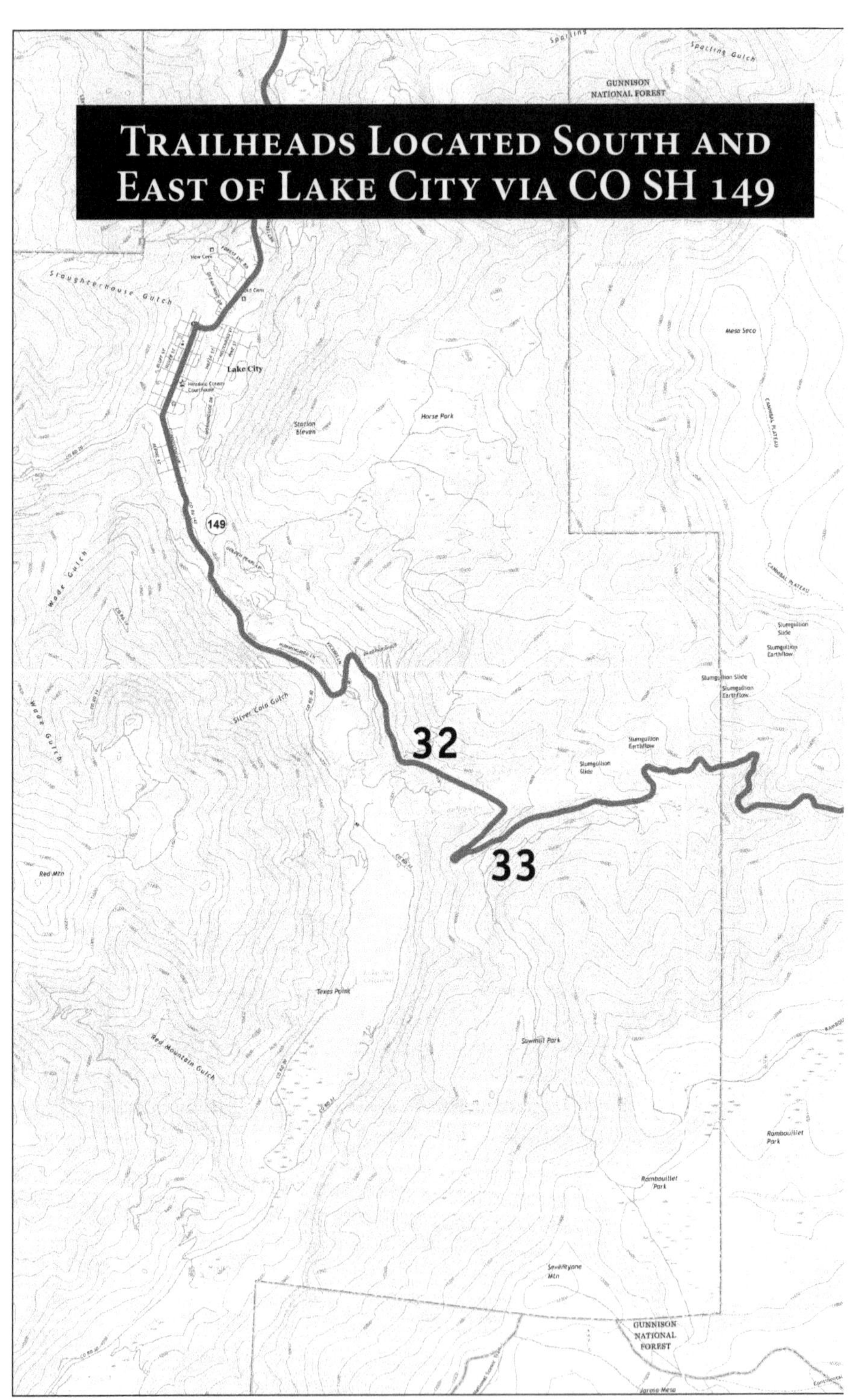

TRAILHEADS LOCATED SOUTH AND EAST OF LAKE CITY VIA CO SH 149
Lake City
149
32
33

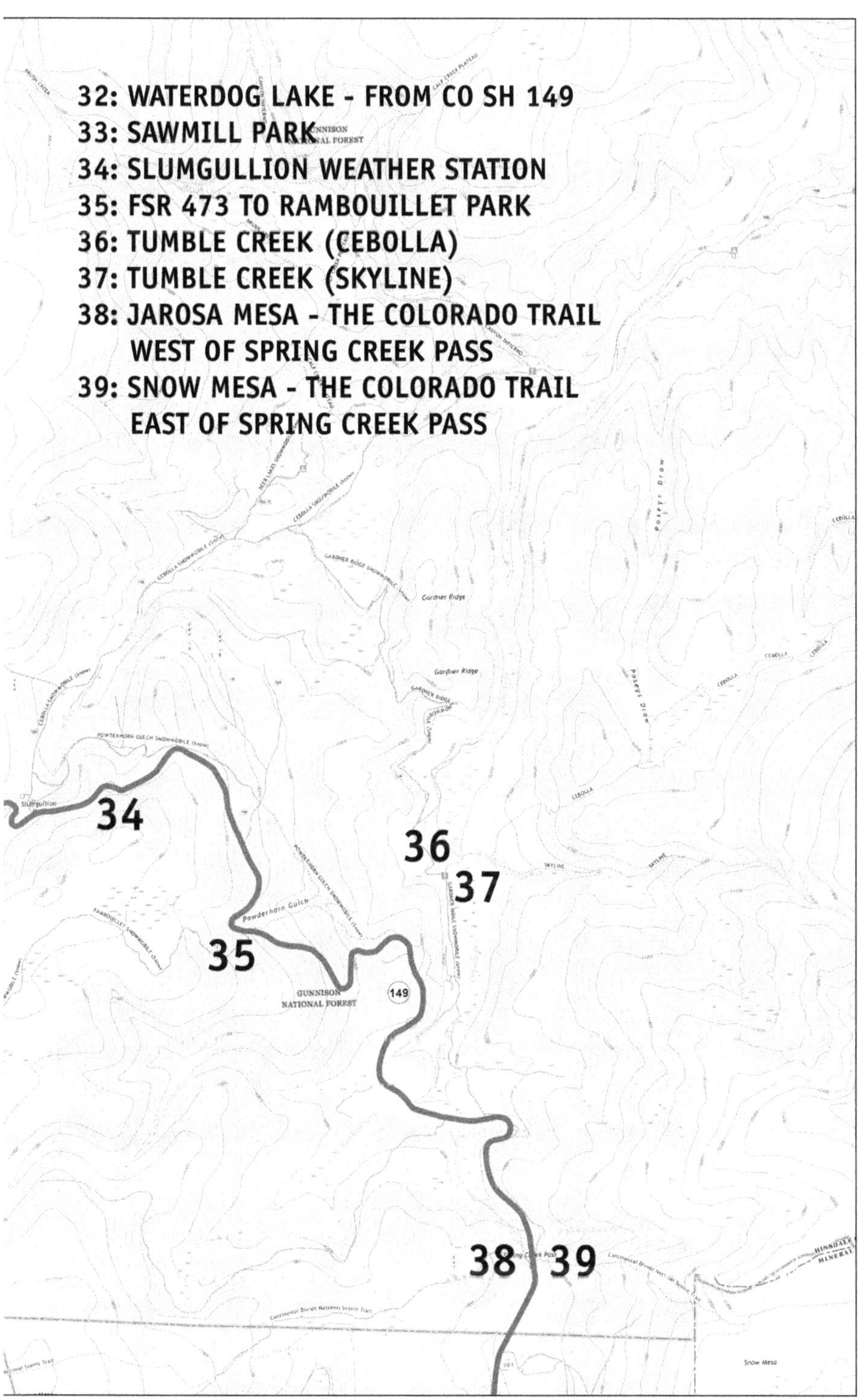

32: WATERDOG LAKE - FROM CO SH 149
33: SAWMILL PARK
34: SLUMGULLION WEATHER STATION
35: FSR 473 TO RAMBOUILLET PARK
36: TUMBLE CREEK (CEBOLLA)
37: TUMBLE CREEK (SKYLINE)
38: JAROSA MESA - THE COLORADO TRAIL
   WEST OF SPRING CREEK PASS
39: SNOW MESA - THE COLORADO TRAIL
   EAST OF SPRING CREEK PASS
34
35
36
37
38
39
149

WATERDOG LAKE – FROM CO SH 149

Quad: Lake City, Lake San Cristobal

DRIVING INSTRUCTIONS: Drive south from Lake City for about 3 miles on CO SH 149. Just past MP 68 there is a turnout to the left. This is the parking area for the trailhead, and ample parking is available. Trailhead elevation - 9,200 feet.

THE HIKE: This trail follows the route used by the San Juan Solstice 50, an ultramarathon running event that occurs annually in late June. The trail is an alternate route to Waterdog Lake, or it can be approached as a thru-hike leading to the trailhead for Waterdog Lake at the wastewater plant in town. The trail is not marked on either the *Trails Illustrated* Map or the quads. Parts of this trail pass through or adjacent to private land.

From the trailhead (**32A**), you climb moderately for the first 2 miles. This initially takes you through an aspen forest and past a beaver pond, running parallel to the highway such that you will hear road noise for the first mile. The trail bends to the north, still climbing through aspen until you break into a small clearing after 1.5 miles. You turn to the right through this clearing and pass through a small patch of forest before emerging in a large park beside a hill. Pay attention to where you enter the park as you will need to reach this spot upon your return. The trail is overgrown through most of the park, so you will be making your own way through the short grass and some bushes. The park is shaped like a fan, and it has a double-track trail along the top of the fan, just below the edge of a forested area. You should head to the left of center as this is the easiest way to access the double track. Once you have reached the double track turn right. After .25 miles the trail will turn to the left and become a single track. Before entering the forest look behind you. You have a wonderful, but fleeting view of Lake San Cristobal.

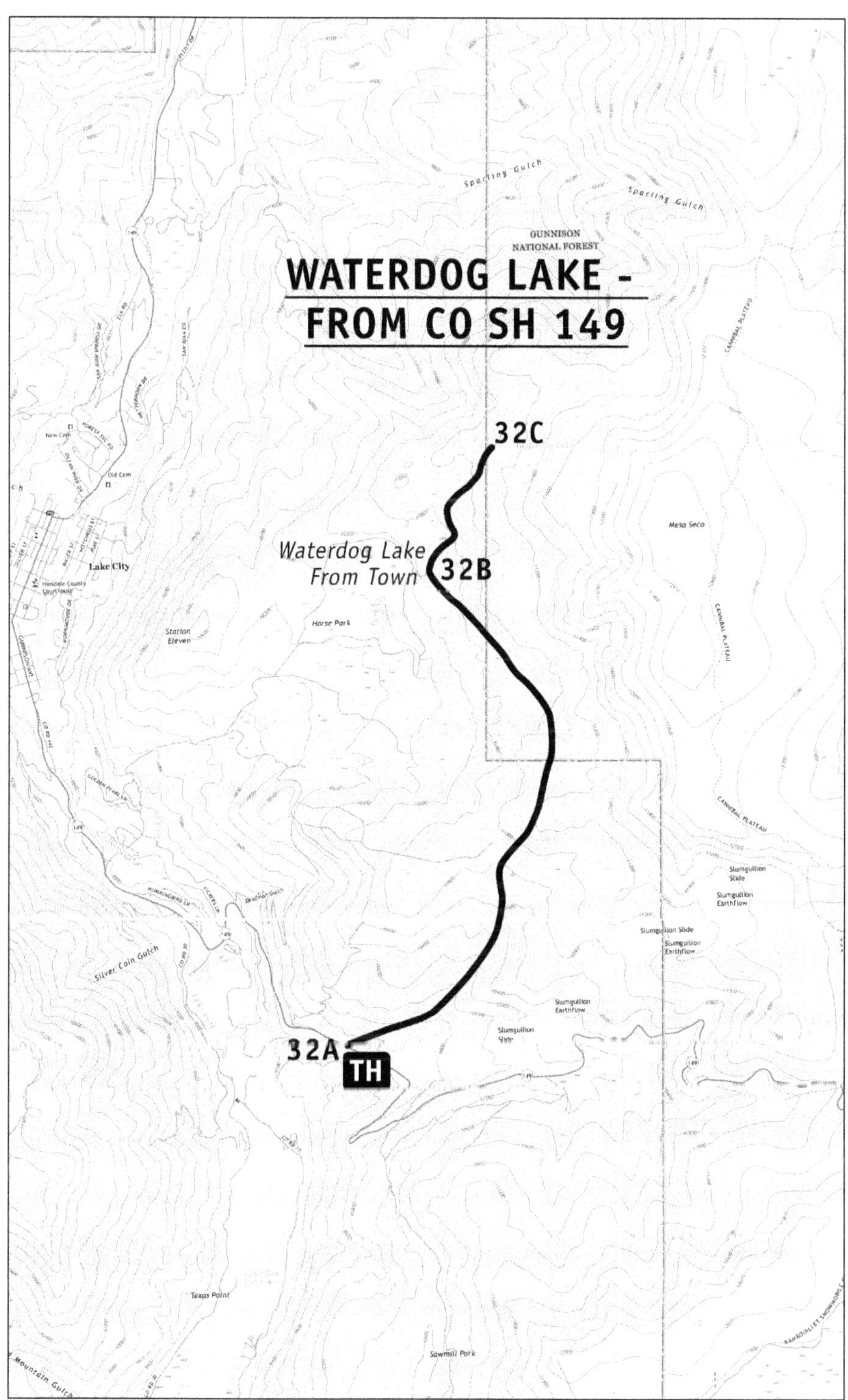
Sparling Gulch
Sparling Gulch
GUNNISON
NATIONAL FOREST
WATERDOG LAKE -
FROM CO SH 149
32C
Mesa Seco
Waterdog Lake
From Town
32B
Lake City
Hinsdale County
Court House
Station
Eleven
Horse Park
CANNIBAL PLATEAU
CANNIBAL PLATEAU
Slumgullion
Slide
Slumgullion
Earthflow
Slumgullion Slide
Slumgullion
Earthflow
Silver Coin Gulch
Deadman Gulch
Slumgullion
Earthflow
Slumgullion
Slide
32A
TH
Texas Point
Sawmill Park

Once you have entered the forest, you will have almost reached your top elevation of 10,700, having climbed 1,500 feet. If you go on to Waterdog Lake, it is at 11,200 feet. Once you have topped out shortly after reaching the forest, you will descend a bit. The trail will flatten out a bit before descending again. Rinse and repeat. There are at least three descents which will be of such magnitude that you will notice them on the return trip. During the next 2 miles the trail alternates between forest and open clearings crossing several small streams. Mesa Seco will be on your right throughout this section while the open areas have occasional views of Crystal Peak, Uncompahgre Peak, Roundtop and Red Mountain. After 2 miles of what I've been describing, you break out into another large park area, known as Horse Park, which gives you a panoramic view of all the aforementioned mountains. When you enter Horse Park, pay particular attention to your surroundings because you will soon intersect with a double track passing through upper Vickers Ranch. The turnoff may not be obvious on the return trip. Once you are on the double track, you will pass through an aspen grove before arriving at the trail sign (**32B**), marked simply "Trail" with an arrow pointing you toward the road to Waterdog Lake, which is still over a mile away. Turning to the left, a single track will lead to town. Both of those trails are discussed in the section named Waterdog Lake – From Town.

RATING: If you go to Waterdog Lake (**32C**), the distance covered (11 miles round trip) and the elevation gain (2,000 feet) are such that this trail is suitable for intermediate hikers. A thru-hike to the Waterdog Lake trailhead in town is 9 miles, gains 1,700 feet, and would also be suitable for intermediate hikers. If you are thru hiking this trail, be advised that the starting point from the highway is 600 feet higher in elevation than the starting point in town. The terrain is not a problem. Much of the trail going through the open areas is prone to being overgrown, as this trail does not get a lot of use, other than by runners on one special Saturday each June.

SAWMILL PARK

Quad: Lake San Cristobal

DRIVING INSTRUCTIONS: Drive south from Lake City on CO SH 149. Just past the Lake San Cristobal Overlook and MP 67 there will be a turnoff to the right, which is designated CR 56 and FSR 3322. Parking for several vehicles is adjacent to this turnoff. Trailhead elevation - 9,900 feet.

THE HIKE: The Sawmill Park Road has some jeep and ATV traffic during the summer and is used by snowshoers and snowmobilers during the winter. It connects with several other trails linking Slumgullion and Spring Creek Passes. While not heavily used by hikers, the interconnections make it a useful trailhead. The trail is wide enough for vehicles for its duration. This trail appears as a road on both the *Trails Illustrated* map and on the quad.

Leaving the trailhead (**33A**), you will gain elevation almost immediately and you will continue through wooded areas for much of the trail. After .5 miles you will see a road veering to your left. This road will connect with the highway near Penniston Park, a mile east of the trailhead. This road is primarily used by snowmobilers as it leaves the highway near a major winter parking and staging area. Continuing straight ahead, your next feature of note will come a little after the 1-mile point. There is a sign designating the turn off to the Jon Wilson Yurt, one of several yurts which are maintained year-round for lodging. The yurt is several hundred yards off the road and overlooks Lake San Cristobal.

Continuing past the turnoff to the yurt, you will soon enter an open area which is much longer than it is wide. This is Sawmill Park. The road passes along the left (east) side of the park and divides near the south end of the park (**33B**). The right fork continues through Sawmill Park and beyond, while the left fork climbs out of Sawmill Park and leads toward Rambouillet Park.

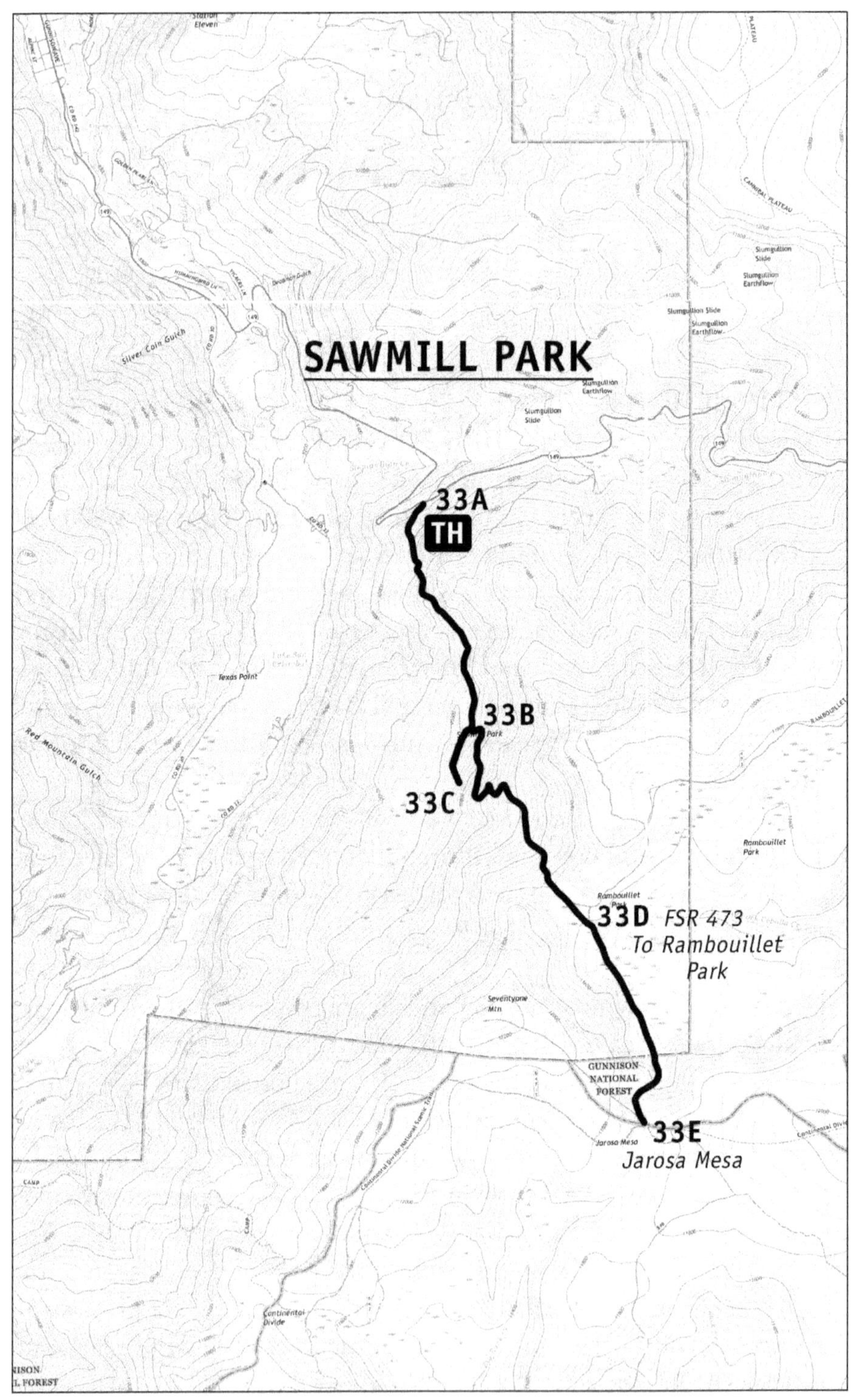
SAWMILL PARK
33A
TH
33B
33C
33D FSR 473
To Rambouillet
Park
33E
Jarosa Mesa
GUNNISON
NATIONAL
FOREST

The road continuing through Sawmill Park is the lesser used of the two forks. It continues north through Sawmill Park past a cabin, before turning west and north and returning to the woods for another mile, where it ends at the top of a steep incline (**33C**).

The road (**33B**) leading to Rambouillet Park climbs through a wooded area and winds its way over the next 2 miles to the west entrance of Rambouillet Park, an enormous open area between two mesas and encompassing both banks of Rambouillet Creek. From there the trail intersects FSR 473. FSR 473 heading north from the intersection is described under the section named FSR 473 to Rambouillet Park. There are two intersections with FSR 473, several hundred yards apart, as that trail forks to accommodate both north bound and south bound traffic on Sawmill Park Road. The first fork (**33D**) is quite faint and can be easily missed. The second fork is better defined and is adjacent to a green underground electric line service unit and a metal post.

Beyond the intersection with FSR 473, Sawmill Park continues to where it meets the Colorado Trail, La Garita Stock Trail, and the road to the top of Hill Seventy-One (**33E**). This is an additional 1.5 miles and, while no net elevation is gained, the road drops 300 feet to cross the main drainage of Rambouillet Park and then gains back that elevation as the road exits Rambouillet Park and enters the saddle between Jarosa Mesa and Hill Seventy-One. Shortly after this elevation gain, you will see the crossing of several trails. Clockwise from where you are standing these are the Colorado Trail (eastbound), the La Garita Stock Trail, the Colorado Trail (westbound), and the road to the summit of Hill Seventy-One. The Sawmill Park Road terminates at this intersection. The La Garita Stock Trail and the Colorado Trail, both eastbound and westbound, are discussed under the section for Jarosa Mesa.

RATING: A hike to the entrance of Rambouillet Park and the junction with FSR 473 (**33D**) is a 7-mile round trip, climbing 1,700 feet. This should be considered an intermediate hike. A hike to Sawmill Park (**33B**) is a 3-mile round trip, climbing 700 feet, and should be accessible to a beginning hiker. The hike via the right fork through Sawmill Park to the end of the road (**33C**) is a 5-mile round trip, climbing 1,100 feet, and is also a hike for beginners. The hike to the intersection of the Colorado Trail (**33E**) is a 10-mile round trip, climbing 1,700 feet net, and should also be considered an intermediate hike.

SLUMGULLION WEATHER STATION

Quad: Slumgullion Pass

DRIVING INSTRUCTIONS: Drive south from Lake City on CO SH 149. Continue about 10 miles passing MP 62. There are two signs designating the Slumgullion Pass Summit, the first for eastbound and the second for westbound traffic. Shortly after passing the second (westbound) sign, .6 miles past MP 62, there is a paved pullout area on your left with room for several cars. The trailhead is unmarked, but it leaves the south side of the road between the parking area and the Slumgullion Pass Summit sign. At this point, you will first see a pole placed to designate snow depth and behind it you will see the Slumgullion Weather Station. The trail begins left (south) of the weather station **(34A)**. Trailhead elevation - 11,500 feet.

THE HIKE: This is an infrequently used trail that leads to a rocky knob at the east end of a ridge separating the Lake Fork of the Gunnison River drainage and the Cebolla Creek drainage. There are 360-degree views from this knob with particularly spectacular views of Red Mountain and the peaks beyond it as well as Uncompahgre Peak and its neighboring peaks. Once on the ridge, the trail is overgrown, but FSR 473 lies to the south, and it is not a difficult off-trail experience to connect with that road. This is a short trail with modest climbing and is well-suited for snowshoeing during the winter. This trail appears on the La Garita, Cochetopa Hills *Trails Illustrated* map but does not appear on the quad.

This trail is difficult to follow. There are orange stringers currently marking some parts of the trail and downed timber has been cut where it crosses the trail. The trail is faint while in the forest and mostly overgrown when in the open. You should expect to find yourself off the trail at some point during your hike.

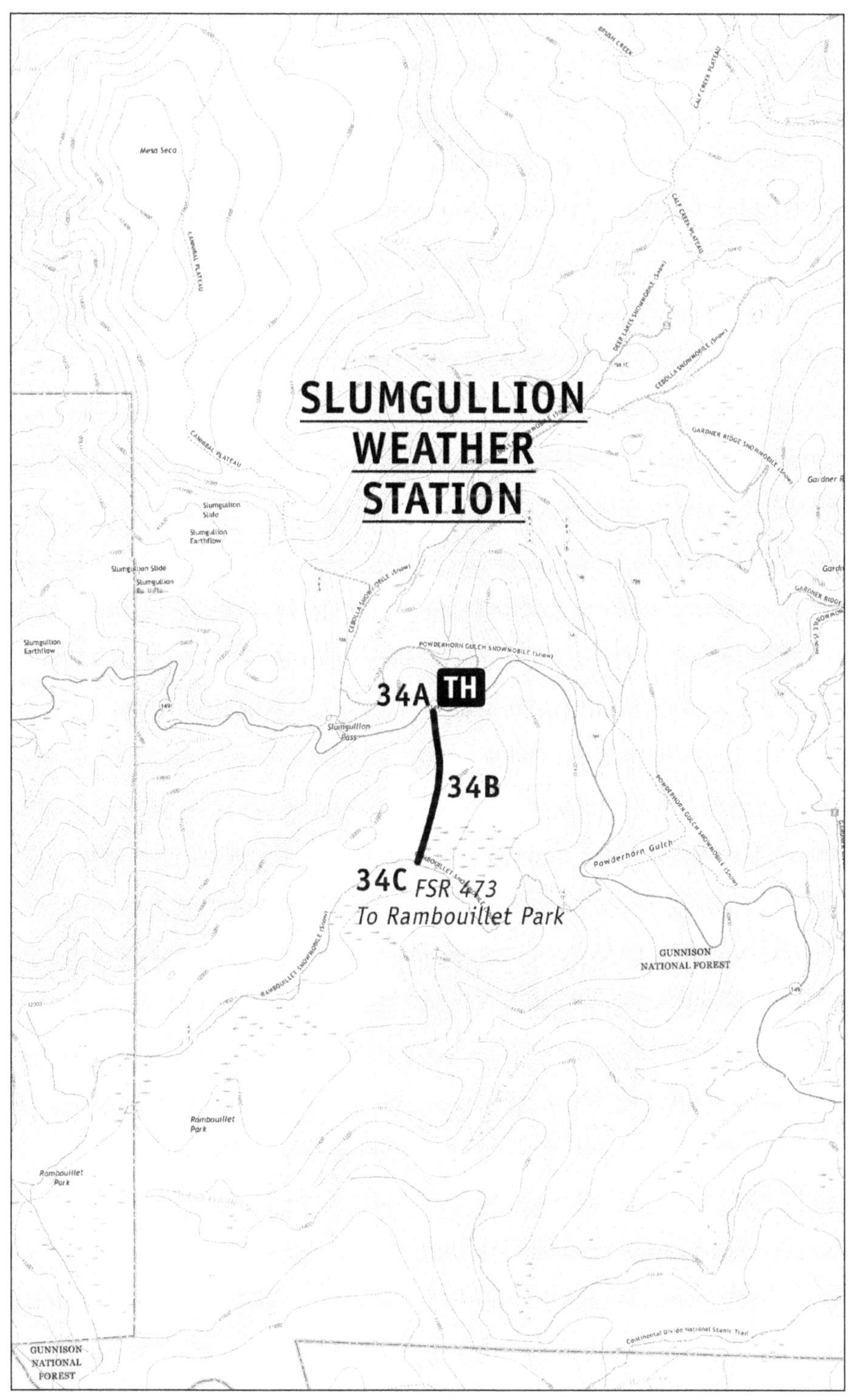

SLUMGULLION WEATHER STATION
34A
TH
34B
34C FSR 473
To Rambouillet Park
Mesa Seca
Slumgullion Slide
Slumgullion Earthflow
Slumgullion Slide
Slumgullion Earthflow
Slumgullion Pass
GUNNISON NATIONAL FOREST
Rambouillet Park
Rambouillet Park
GUNNISON NATIONAL FOREST
Powderhorn Gulch
BRUSH CREEK
Gardner Ridge
Continental Divide National Scenic Trail

From the weather station (34A), the trail climbs gradually to moderately through forest of spruce, most of which are dead. It leaves the forest for a short distance before entering forest once again. You are climbing a ridge and upon reaching the top of the ridge, you leave the trees behind. At the summit, the rocky knob is ahead and to your left **(34B)**. From that knob, you can see ahead (south) to the mesa leading toward Rambouillet Park which is crossed by FSR 473, .5 miles ahead. You may not spot FSR 473, but it is perpendicular to your path to the knob. Look to the south along the horizon to see Rio Grande Pyramid, a mountain shaped, surprisingly, like a pyramid. Keep heading toward Rio Grande Pyramid and you will intersect FSR 473 **(34C)**. Once at FSR 473, you have several thru-hike possibilities. You should refer to the section titled FSR 473 to Rambouillet Park should you wish to pursue following that trail.

RATING: A round trip to the knob described above **(34B)** covers 2.5 miles and gains 500 feet. A round trip to the intersection of FSR 473 **(34C)** covers 3.5 miles and also gains 500 feet before descending 100 feet. While the distance and terrain make this trail suitable for beginners, losing the trail is likely to upset a beginning hiker. The navigation issues dictate that you should have at least one experienced hiker in the group.

FSR 473 TO RAMBOUILLET PARK

Quad: Slumgullion Pass, Lake San Cristobal

DRIVING INSTRUCTIONS: Drive south from Lake City on CO SH 149. Continue about 12 miles, passing MP 60. The highway takes a sharp left turn after this milepost and just before a yellow diagonal warning sign to trucks that a hill lies ahead, FSR 473 intersects the highway. There is a small sign designating this road, and a larger sign behind it indicating road use restrictions. Parking is 100 yards beyond this point on the left side of the highway on a road turnout, often used as a staging area for snowmobiles during the winter. Trailhead elevation - 11,200 feet.

THE HIKE: This trail is a double track used by jeeps, ATVs, and snow-mobiles as well as hikers, cross-country skiers and snowshoe enthusiasts. It is usually groomed during the winter, which is how I came to discover it. As it can easily be missed by passing traffic, it is not used by hikers a great deal. The trail leads through some wonderful scenery and is not particularly difficult. It also connects with the Sawmill Park Trail and the Colorado Trail. Most variations of this trail are marked on both the La Garita, Cochetopa Hills *Trails Illustrated* map and on the quads.

The trail begins as a gentle climb leaving the highway (**35A**) through an area that has been recently cleared of beetle-killed spruce. It enters the woods for a short time, then a small clearing, then re-enters the woods as you continue to climb to the top of an unnamed mesa. After a mile and a 500-foot climb, you reach the top of the mesa, but not its highest point. That is another mile and 200 feet ahead. Once you reach the high point of the mesa, the trail turns left (south) and you descend a bit until you've crossed through the upper drainage of the West Fork Cebolla Creek. You then climb 200 feet to the ridge that separates the West Fork Cebolla Creek drainage from the Rambouillet Creek drainage (**35C**). At this point you enter Rambouillet Park, a huge

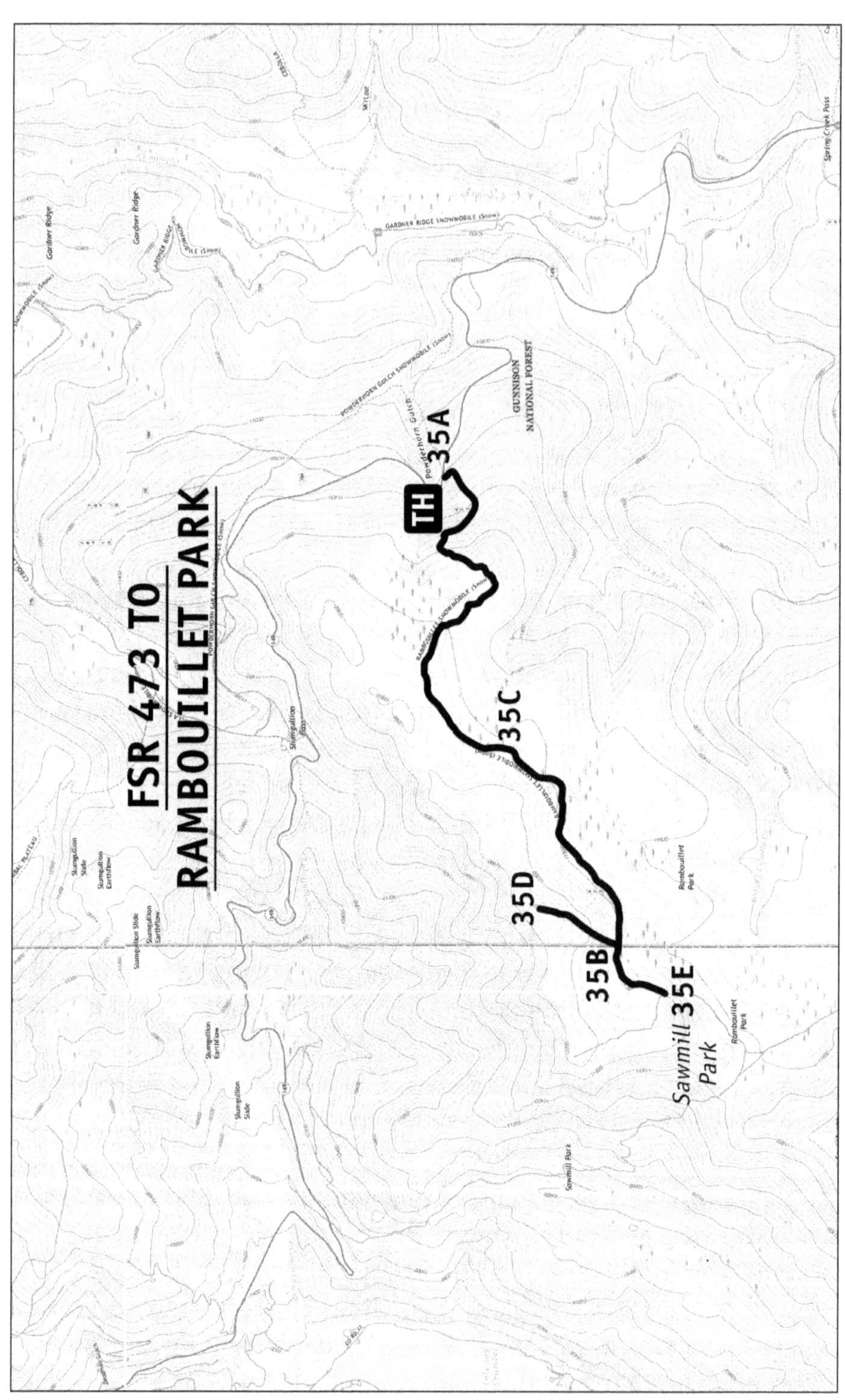

FSR 473 TO
RAMBOUILLET PARK
TH
35A
35C
35D
35B
35E
Sawmill Park
Powderhorn Gulch
Powderhorn Gulch Snowmobile (Snow)
Gardner Ridge Snowmobile (Snow)
GUNNISON NATIONAL FOREST
Rambouillet Snowmobile (Snow)
Gardner Ridge
Rambouillet Park
Sawmill Park
Spring Creek Pass
Slumgullion Pass
Slumgullion Slide
Slumgullion Earthflow

bowl between the mesa you have been on and Jarosa Mesa, to the south. I've seen elk, moose, and coyote in Rambouillet Park at various times, and it is also used for grazing domestic sheep. As the area is quite open and just below 12,000 feet, most of Rambouillet Park offers spectacular views. At this point you've traveled 3 miles, and this would be an appropriate turnaround point for beginning hikers.

As you enter Rambouillet Park, you turn toward the west and travel at the edge of the park for 2 miles through the upper drainage of Rambouillet Creek along the north end of the park without gaining or losing much elevation. At that point, another double-track trail intersects from the right as it comes down a ridge (**35B**). This trail leads to Slumgullion Peak (elevation 12,210) which isn't much of a peak, but rather one of several bumps along a long ridge separating Rambouillet Park from points to the north and west. It's not quite a mile up to Slumgullion Peak (**35D**) with a 400-foot climb. This is a worthy destination as the views from Slumgullion Peak are nothing short of fantastic. Slumgullion Peak is mislabeled Hill Seventy-One on some maps. Hill Seventy-One is actually 3 miles south of Slumgullion Peak and contains much of the communication equipment for Hinsdale County.

Should you not detour to Slumgullion Peak but continue along FSR 473, you will make a short but rather steep descent into the main portion of the Rambouillet Park drainage. On your left will be the timbers which once served as the platform for the Rambouillet yurt, which was dismantled circa 2013. This trail continues, passing through brush and small trees, until you reach a fork in the road. Both forks intersect with the Sawmill Park Road 100 yards from the fork, creating a triangular intersection (**35E**). The right-hand fork leads to Sawmill Park Road heading north, and the left-hand fork leads to Sawmill Park Road heading south. Sawmill Park Road is discussed under that section.

RATING: A hike to the entrance of Rambouillet Park (**35C**) is a 6-mile round trip, gains only 600 feet, is well marked, and can be hiked by beginning hikers. The hike to either Slumgullion Peak (**35D**) or the Sawmill Park intersection (**35B**) and back would be an 11-mile hike, although neither hike adds much elevation gain beyond the entrance to Rambouillet Park. The total elevation gain from the highway to Slumgullion Peak is 1,000 feet and the gain to the Sawmill Park Road intersection is only a net 500 feet, although the gross gain would be 700 feet. These would be suitable hikes for intermediate level hikers.

TUMBLE CREEK (CEBOLLA)

Quad: Slumgullion Pass, Mineral Mountain

DRIVING INSTRUCTIONS: Drive south from Lake City on CO SH 149. Continue about 15 miles to beyond MP 57 and take a left on the road leading to Oleo Ranch (CR 17). Continue 2 miles on the Oleo Ranch Road to the Tumble Creek trailhead, which is well marked on your right with ample parking. The Tumble Creek trailhead serves both the Cebolla Trail and the Skyline Trail. These trails begin together but soon separate, and each is given a separate discussion. Trailhead elevation - 10,300 feet.

THE HIKE: The Cebolla Trail goes from the trailhead at Tumble Creek for over 20 miles terminating in Sagauche County north of Stewart Peak. This discussion includes the trail as far east as Martinez Creek. Further discussion of this trail is included in the discussion of the Rough Creek Trail. This trail appears on both the La Garita, Cochetopa Hills *Trails Illustrated* map and the quads.

Both the Cebolla Trail and the Skyline Trail go east from the Tumble Creek trailhead **(36A)** and connect with other trails further east, allowing for several multi-day loop possibilities. As would be expected, the Skyline trail takes the higher and more scenic route. The Cebolla trail does not receive as much foot traffic as it does horse traffic. The area is used for cattle grazing and there are more than a few cow pies to dodge. The area was badly scarred by the spruce beetle kill (circa 2013), and does not drain well, leaving it muddy or marshy in spots. Despite all that, it does have its moments.

Before you leave your car, put on your stream crossing shoes and carry your boots, as you will have two stream crossings in the first .25 miles. Head east from the trailhead gently downward through pasture. You will pass through a gate and cross Cebolla Creek shortly afterward.

After crossing Cebolla Creek you will pass through another gate and then cross Tumble Creek. You should not need your stream crossing shoes after this point on either the Cebolla Trail or the Skyline Trail, although there is water to cross on both trails. The trail turns south and shortly afterward you will see a trail sign designating that Tumble Creek is straight ahead (**36C**) and Martinez Creek is to your left (**36B**). The Skyline Trail follows Tumble Creek and the Cebolla Trail leads to Martinez Creek.

Turning left from the trail sign, you will climb through a draw into a pasture where the trail comes and goes. There is a series of posts to guide you through the pasture. Pay attention to these posts as on the way back or you may find yourself on a horse trail leading to Oleo Ranch, a mile from where you parked. The posts will lead you to a wooded area where the woods bulge out in front of you and to the left, leaving a fold in between. The trail leads to the bulge, in front and follows the edge of the trees to the fold where it enters the forest and becomes better defined. The trail gains elevation gently through the forest and tops out at a point 300 feet above where you entered the forest and 700 feet above the trailhead. Shortly before reaching this high point, you will pass a rock cairn on your right, before the trail takes a left turn. Pay attention to that point since you will need to find it upon your return because the trail continues downward and to the right at this point. There are several routes that horses have taken through the woods, and not all are equal.

At the top, the forest parts and you are in a small corridor of pasture with trees on either side. Continue through this corridor following the posts, which will lead you back into a small, wooded area before you descend into a large open drainage before crossing a waterway called Posey's Draw. This is a bowl-shaped area that allows drainage to the northwest but accumulates water from all other directions. The trail will take you across Posey's Draw and keep you high enough on the other side to avoid the soup at the bottom of the bowl. As you continue following the posts, you are now heading east and gaining elevation slightly. There is a swampy drainage area that you will want to climb above before crossing, but you won't avoid the water entirely. The trail continues east, following the posts north of Posey's Draw until it reaches the end of the open area. You will enter a forest containing dead spruce trees and live aspen for only a short while before emerging to the open once again.

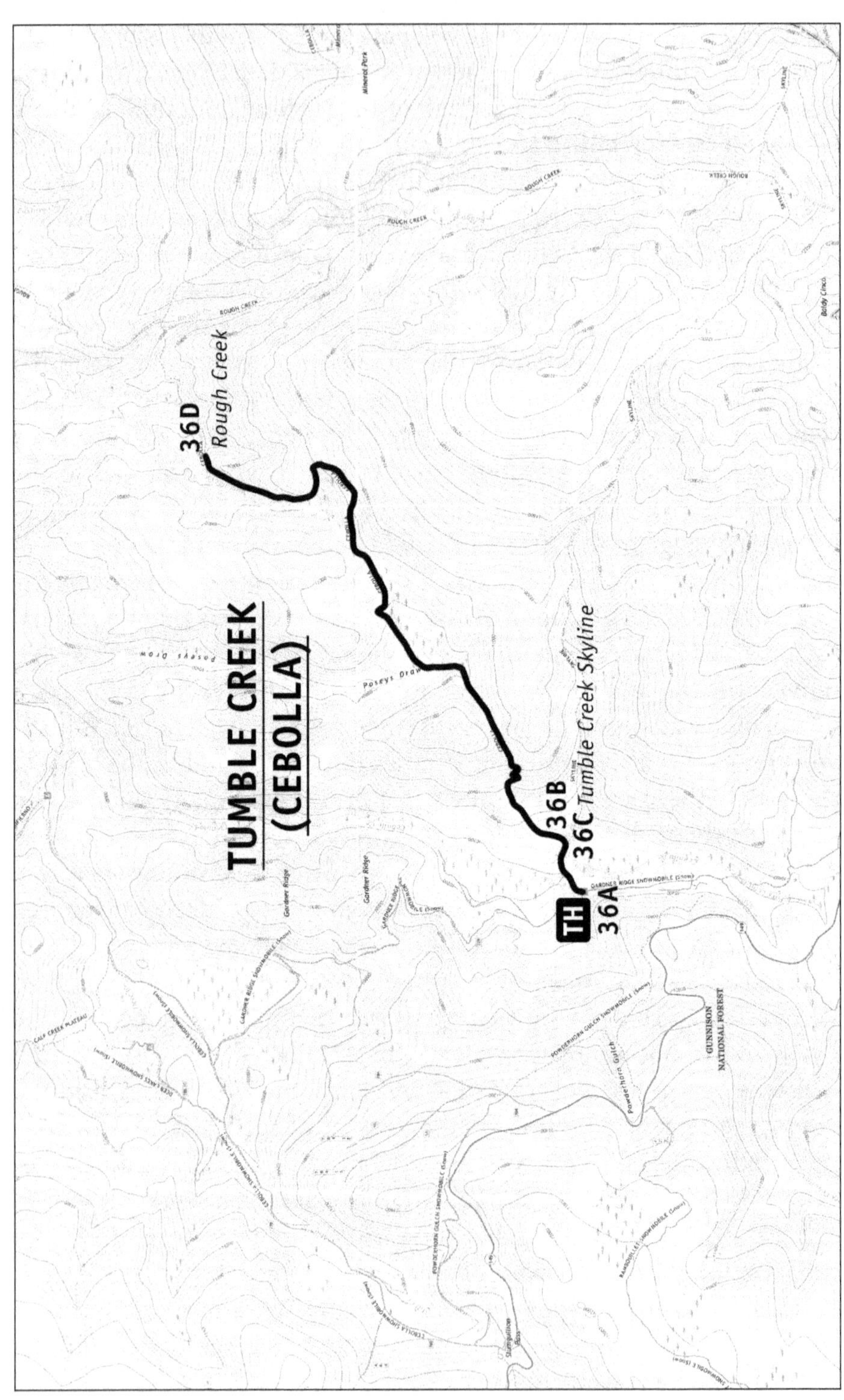

36D
Rough Creek
TUMBLE CREEK
(CEBOLLA)
Poseys Draw
Tumble Creek Skyline
36B
36C
36A
TH
GUNNISON
NATIONAL FOREST

At this point you are at the top of the drainage of Martinez Creek and the *Trails Illustrated* map shows a gap in the trail, emerging east of Martinez Creek and then crossing back west of the creek, before descending the creek further. I've seen no evidence of any of this. The Martinez Creek drainage is like a deep V through an open corridor with trees on either side. The trees come closer to the creek as it loses elevation. The trail is no longer designated by posts at this point but is pretty well defined as it descends 600 feet before crossing Martinez Creek, which is designated by a broken trail sign **(36D)**. If you wish to go further, the discussion is continued in the Rough Creek section. At this point you have covered 4.5 miles and are at about the same elevation as what you started, having climbed 700 feet, descended 300 feet, reclimbed those 300 feet and descended 700 feet.

RATING: The distance covered to the intersection with Martinez Creek **(36D)** is a 9-mile round trip and the elevation gain is 1,000 feet each direction. Both are beyond modest and there are navigation challenges. Beginners should avoid this trail. It is suitable for intermediate hikers.

The author and Ziggy

Glenn Heumann

TUMBLE CREEK (SKYLINE)

Quad: Slumgullion Pass, Baldy Cinco

DRIVING INSTRUCTIONS: Drive south from Lake City on CO SH 149. Continue about 15 miles to beyond milepost 57 and take a left on the road leading to Oleo Ranch (CR 17). Continue 2 miles on the Oleo Ranch Road to the Tumble Creek trailhead, which is well marked on your right with ample parking. The Tumble Creek trailhead serves both the Cebolla Trail and the Skyline Trail. These trails begin together but soon separate and each is given a separate discussion. Trailhead elevation - 10,300 feet.

THE HIKE: The Skyline Trail goes from the trailhead at Tumble Creek (**37A**) for 8 miles to where it intersects the Colorado Trail. A mile before that point, it intersects the Rough Creek Trail at its termination point. This leads to several multi-day hiking possibilities. The first several miles of the Skyline Trail follow Tumble Creek, and there are spots where the creek overflows into the trail. The brush is heavy, and the trail has few spots which could be described as memorable. However, once it climbs to the headwaters of Tumble Creek, the trail opens up significantly and the views from which the trail received its name become apparent. If you plan on a short hike, you will return disappointed. If you're up for a longer hike, the rewards are there. This trail appears on both the La Garita, Cochetopa Hills *Trails Illustrated* map and on the quads.

Before leaving your car, put on your stream crossing shoes and carry your boots, as you will have two stream crossings in the first .25 miles. Head east from the trailhead (**37A**) gently downward through pasture. You will pass through a gate and cross Cebolla Creek shortly afterward. After crossing Cebolla Creek you will pass through another gate and then cross Tumble Creek. You should not need your stream crossing shoes after this point on either the Cebolla Trail or the Skyline Trail, although there is water to cross on both trails. The trail turns south and shortly afterward you will see a trail sign designating that Tumble Creek is straight ahead (**37B**) and Martinez Creek is to your left (**37D**). The Skyline Trail follows Tumble Creek and the Cebolla Trail leads to Martinez Creek.

Turning right from the trail sign (**37B**), the trail ascends gently, following Tumble Creek which remains on your right until the 2-mile mark. Tumble Creek widens at several points as it heads east, with swampy willows providing good habitat for moose, which I've seen several times in this area. The trail is not difficult to follow and is marked by posts regularly. On the return trip, there is a trail intersection leading to your right up a small incline. This is not the main trail, which follows the creek.

At the 2-mile point, the trail crosses to the south side of Tumble Creek and climbs through a wooded area for .25 miles before crossing back to the north side. This detour avoids several rockslides on the north side of the creek. On your return trip, when you approach this last stream crossing there is a trail heading to the right, gaining elevation to go above the rockslides. This trail is faintly visible at the earlier stream crossing. I've been on this north side trail only far enough to determine that it is not the preferred route.

Once you are back on the north side of Tumble Creek, the elevation gain increases as you begin the long climb out of the Tumble Creek drainage. The terrain changes from forest (dead spruce) to tall grass containing bushes, to shorter grass as you near the head of the Tumble Creek drainage. Looking behind you will see Mesa Seco, Uncompahgre and the nearby peaks, or the Red Mountain to Sunshine Peak panorama depending on where you are.

As you reach the upper portion of the Tumble Creek drainage, the surrounding area widens, and the trees disappear. Views of the backside of Baldy Cinco, and the ridges on either side of the Rough Creek drainage prevail. You think you have reached the upper limits of the Tumble Creek drainage at the 4.5-mile point but there is still a little elevation to be gained before you enter the Rough Creek drainage. Here the trail may be overgrown in places, but there are posts placed such that you shouldn't have trouble finding your way. Hiking through the upper Tumble Creek drainage, the trail passes by a tiny pond, around

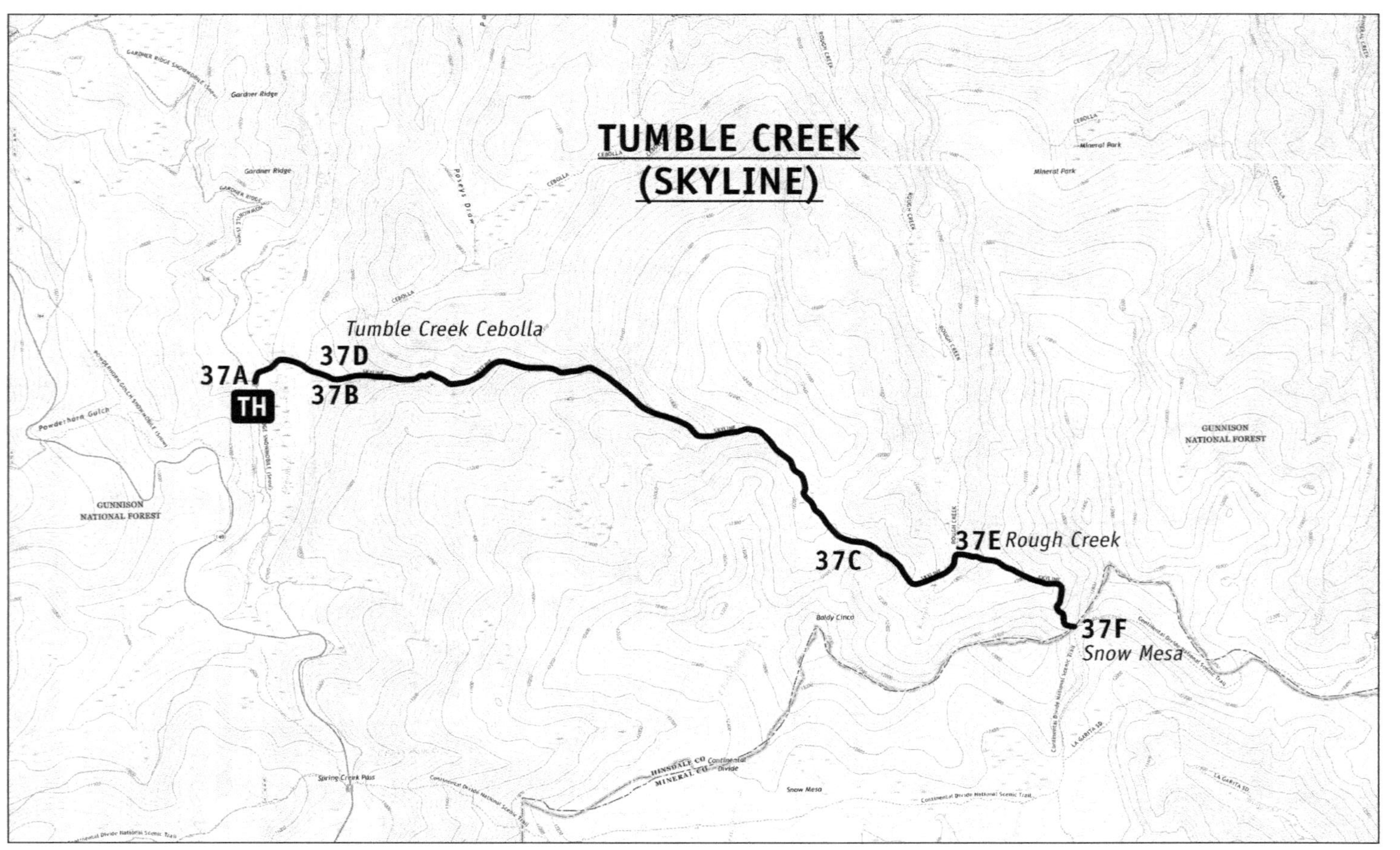

TUMBLE CREEK (SKYLINE)

or through marshy areas, and over a stream before climbing to a mixed vegetation area below a rockslide behind Baldy Cinco. Most of the trees in this area are dead. During this mixed vegetation area, which you enter at the 5.5-mile point, the trail is much easier to follow. During this mixed vegetation area, the trail divides **(37C)**. The right fork of the trail climbs for a short distance where it ends. This point has fine views of the Rough Creek area and is an appropriate turnaround point for a day hike. Any continuation along the Skyline Trail on the left fork is best left to a multi-day expedition.

The Skyline Trail descends from the fork **(37C)** through the mixed vegetation area for .5 mile, then enters a short grass bowl for the rest of the descent to Rough Creek. The trail is overgrown for the remainder of the distance to the Rough Creek Trail intersection, but there are posts guiding your way. The posts will be particularly useful on the return trip, as the place where the trail exits the mixed vegetation area is not apparent. After descending 500 feet over the next .5 mile, and crossing water several times, you should see the trail sign indicating the junction with the Rough Creek Trail **(37E)**. The Rough Creek Trail is discussed under that section.

The Skyline Trail continues beyond the Rough Creek Trail junction for 1 mile climbing rather steeply to where it intersects the Colorado Trail, 6½ miles east of Spring Creek Pass **(37F)**. The Skyline Trail from the Rough Creek Trail intersection to the Colorado Trail intersection is seldom used and can be confusing to follow. There are cairns in places, but from the lower portion of the trail, you cannot see the destination. Only later can you see the window that will offer views of the Atlantic side of the divide. The portion of the Colorado Trail from the top of the pass westward is discussed in the Snow Mesa section.

RATING: The distance covered to the trail fork in the mixed vegetation area **(37C)**, is 11 miles round trip, and the elevation gain (2,000 feet) make it suitable for intermediate hikers. Extending the hike to the Rough Creek Trail junction **(37E)** is a 500-foot decline over the next mile and extending the hike to the Colorado Trail junction **(37F)** regains 900 feet over an additional mile. Both should be reserved for experienced hikers.

JAROSA MESA

Quad: Slumgullion Pass, Lake San Cristobal

DRIVING INSTRUCTIONS: Drive south from Lake City on CO SH 149. Continue about 16 miles to Spring Creek Pass at MP 55. There is ample parking in a lot to the right. A second parking area is adjacent to the outdoor toilets. The trailhead is to the west of the outdoor toilets. Trailhead elevation - 10,900 feet.

THE HIKE: This hike goes west from Spring Creek Pass along the Colorado Trail and Continental Divide Trail. As such it gets a fair amount of use from thru-hikers on those trails. Those thru hiking the Continental Divide Trail typically pass from west to east during late June. Those thru hiking the Colorado Trail will typically pass from east to west beginning in mid-July. While this trail will lead to Durango, this book has only included that portion between its intersections with the Skyline Trail and the Cataract Gulch Trail. The portion of the Colorado Trail leading east from Spring Creek Pass to the intersection with the Skyline Trail is discussed under the section for Snow Mesa. I'm covering the section that leads west from Spring Creek Pass to the intersection with Camp Trail here. The Colorado Trail heading west from the Camp Trail intersection is discussed under the sections for Camp Trail and Wager Gulch. There are two variations to the trail heading west from Spring Creek Pass, as the Colorado Trail and Continental Divide trail were re-routed circa 2008. The old version of the trail follows the La Garita Stock Trail, also designated FSR 547. A bit beyond the 2-mile point, the re-routed Colorado Trail leaves the La Garita Stock Trail, only to intersect again at the point where both trails meet the Sawmill Park Road. This is a dry hike and most of the time you are exposed, so take extra water and sunscreen. This trail appears on the La Garita, Cochetopa Hills *Trails Illustrated* map while the Slumgullion Pass quad contains the La Garita Stock Trail but not the rerouted Colorado Trail.

The trailhead is on the west side of the parking area (**38A**). The trail is a double track and vehicles are allowed, although infrequently encountered (except for snowmobiles during the winter). The trail immediately begins a moderate ascent mostly through open areas, but partly in trees. After .5 miles the trail enters a forest for .25 miles and stops gaining elevation for a while. After emerging from the forest, the trail continues west along the Continental Divide, with far reaching views to the south. The trail is in an open area for more than a mile without gaining much elevation. It then enters another wooded area, and a moderate ascent begins as the trail begins to climb Jarosa Mesa. After emerging from the woods, you will cross a small intermittent stream. This is the only water to be found along the trail and it cannot be relied upon. Shortly after crossing this water, the trails divide; the new Colorado Trail is to your right. It is a single track well marked by posts (**38B**). The La Garita Stock Trail continues to the left and remains a double track.

As both of these trails meet later at the same point (**38E**), a hiker can go out on one trail and back on the other or go out and back on the same trail. The new Colorado Trail is 1 mile shorter, has a greater elevation gain, and wonderful views of the Pacific side of the Continental Divide. The views from the La Garita Stock Trail, while not insignificant, pale by comparison. If going out one trail and back the other, take the new Colorado Trail out, otherwise the great views will be behind you.

The new Colorado Trail climbs Jarosa Mesa gradually at first through an open area. The trail steepens a bit as it goes alongside a forest of spruces, most of which are dead, and steepens even more when climbing to the top of the mesa. Once at the top, the view of all the mountains west of Lake City is spectacular. The top of Jarosa Mesa is a reasonable turnaround point (**38C**). If you continue to where the new Colorado Trail meets the La Garita Stock Trail and the Sawmill Park Road (**38E**), you have 1.5 miles to go and you lose the views as you descend from the mesa. This intersection of trails deserves a name. I thought of Grand Junction, but that name is already taken. Petite Junction anyone? This junction of trails, while easy to identify, is only marked as a hunting unit boundary and can be a bit confusing. Clockwise from where you stand on the new Colorado Tail you see the La Garita Stock Trail to your left, the continuation of the Colorado Trail, a short trail leading to

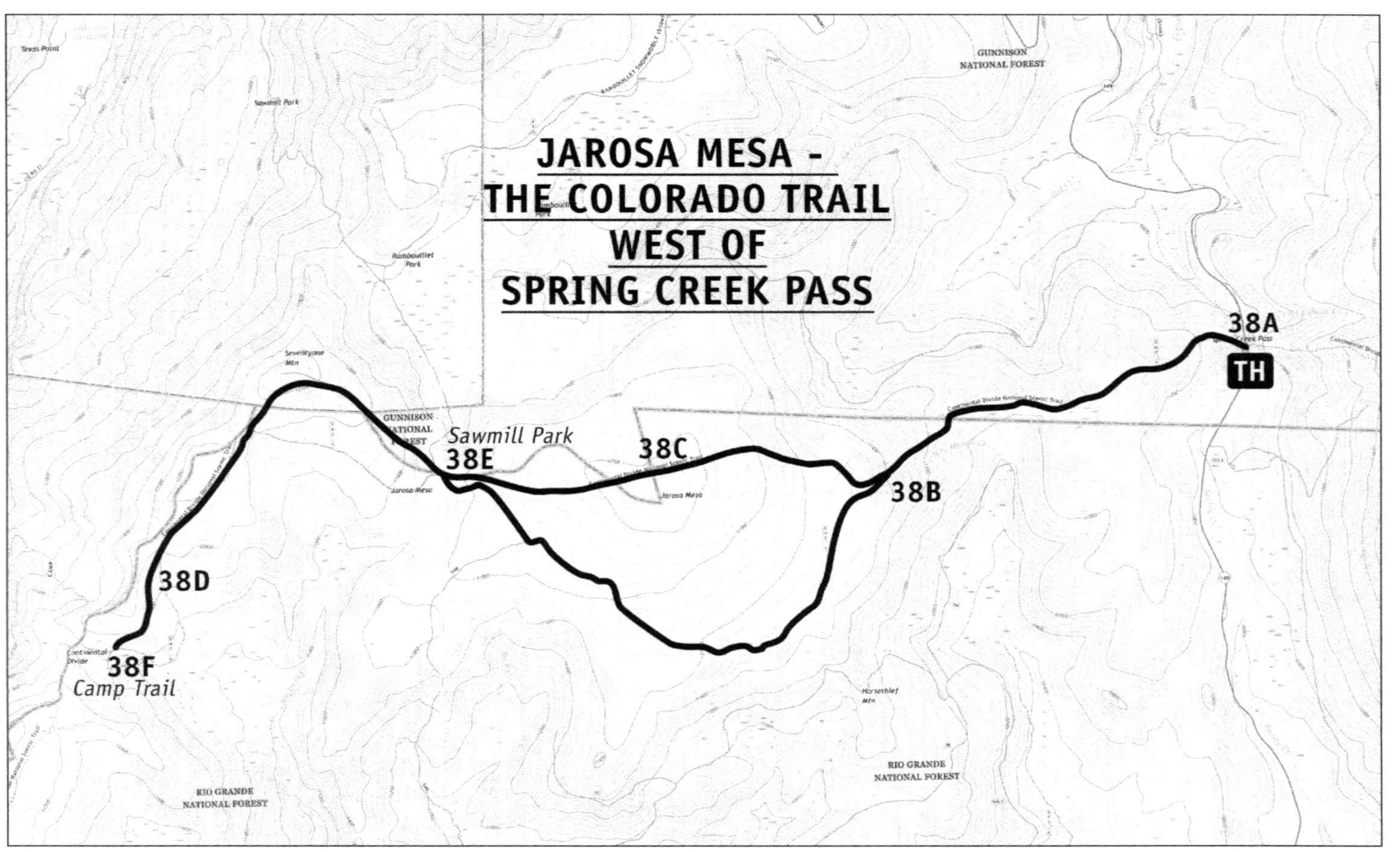
JAROSA MESA -
THE COLORADO TRAIL
WEST OF
SPRING CREEK PASS
38A
TH
38E
Sawmill Park
38C
38B
38D
38F
Camp Trail
GUNNISON NATIONAL FOREST
RIO GRANDE NATIONAL FOREST
Texas Point
Sawmill Park
Rambouillet Park
Seventyone Mtn
Jarosa Mesa
Horsethief Mtn
Continental Divide National Scenic Trail

the summit of Hill Seventy-One upon which sits much of the County's communication equipment, and the Sawmill Park Road. The trail along the Sawmill Park Road is covered under that section.

Returning to the point where the new Colorado Trail separates from the La Garita Stock Trail (**38B**), the La Garita Stock trail passes along the Atlantic side of the Continental Divide. It offers views of the mountains to the south of the divide as well as views of the lakes above Continental Reservoir. It works its way around Jarosa Mesa, while the new Colorado Trail goes over the top. Having said that, the La Garita Stock Trail tops out at only 300 feet below the high point of the new Colorado Trail. This trail climbs several hundred feet and enters a brushy area. After hiking 1 mile from the point where the trails divide, there is a primitive gravesite to the north. After emerging from the brush, the trail passes through tundra for the remainder of the hike and descends to the saddle between Jarosa Mesa and Hill Seventy-One, where it rejoins the Colorado Trail.

Should you wish to continue along the Colorado Trail beyond Petite Junction (**38E**), there are two carsonite posts ahead. One bears the Colorado Trail emblem, and the other designates the trail as FSR 547. The Colorado Trail continues west through an open area, gaining elevation gradually. There is one short descent before regaining the gradual climb. You can see that the trail leads to a saddle between Hill Seventy-One, hosting the communication equipment, and a hill to the south. Once you reach the saddle, you can once again view the mountains west of Lake City. From the top of the saddle, the trail takes a left turn and climbs the hill south of Hill Seventy-One. This is a 500-foot elevation gain from Petite Junction. From the top of this hill, you see the ridge that will parallel the Colorado Trail for the next portion of the journey.

You will descend this hill at a gentle pace, but after .5 miles the descent steepens as you approach the saddle that connects to the next hill. Near the saddle, the trail divides (**38C**). The La Garita Stock Trail proceeds on a double track to your left while the Colorado Trail proceeds on a single track to the right. These two trails will intersect again after a mile. The La Garita Stock Trail takes the longer route through an open area, while the Colorado Trail takes a more direct route through a lightly wooded area of spruce, most of which are dead. Taking the Colorado Trail through this forest, you descend gently for .5 miles before you emerge in a large meadow, nearly surrounded by trees. Upon reaching the meadow you will see three posts ahead, and to one to your right. The post to your right leads to a yurt, which was destroyed during the 2018-2019 winter, but has since been rebuilt. The three posts ahead of you lead to the intersection with the La Garita Stock Trail (**38D**). The two trails go in different directions after this intersection. The Colorado Trail continues straight ahead. The portion of the Colorado Trail between this point and Carson Saddle is covered under the section for Camp Trail.

Should you take a right at the intersection (**38D**), the La Garita Stock Trail continues for several hundred yards to the point where it intersects with Camp Trail, which is marked by a trail sign (**38F**). As this trail sign is in short grass, there is little evidence of a trail in the direction the sign designates; it is fully overgrown. Should you wish to proceed down to the Camp Trail trailhead, you should look at the range of mountains on the horizon. Cast your eyes on Red Mountain and walk toward that peak. I shouldn't have to tell you which peak is Red Mountain, but to avoid any doubt, it is the peak furthest to the right. Walking toward Red Mountain, stay to the right of the brush and you will spot the trail shortly before it descends into the trees. The rest of this trail is covered under the section for Camp Trail.

RATING: There is nothing difficult about either of these trails other than their length. A trip to the first junction of the trails (**38B**) and back would cover 4.5 miles and gain 500 feet in elevation. A trip to the top of Jarosa Mesa via the new Colorado Trail (**38C**) would cover 8 miles and gain 800 feet in elevation. Both of these hikes would be suitable for beginners. A round trip to the Sawmill Park Road junction (aka Petite Junction) via the new Colorado Trail (**38E**) would cover 11 miles and have the same 800-foot gain plus, an additional 300 feet on the return trip up the mesa. A round trip to the Sawmill Park Road junction (**38E**) via the La Garita Stock Trail would cover 13 miles and have a 600-foot elevation gain. Due to the distances involved, the latter two trails should be considered appropriate for intermediate hikers. Continuing from the Sawmill Park Road junction (**38E**) along the Colorado Trail to where it intersects Camp Trail (**38F**) would add 3 miles (6 miles round trip), with a 500-foot gross and 0 net elevation gain. This too, would be an intermediate level hike, but adding this portion of the Colorado Trail would be more suitable for a multi-day thru-hike than for a day hike.

TRAILHEAD 39

SNOW MESA

Quad: Slumgullion Pass, Baldy Cinco

DRIVING INSTRUCTIONS: Drive south from Lake City on CO SH 149. Continue about 16 miles to Spring Creek Pass at MP 55. There is ample parking in a lot to the right. Trailhead elevation - 10,900 feet.

THE HIKE: This hike goes east from Spring Creek Pass along the Colorado Trail and Continental Divide Trail. As such it gets a fair amount of use from thru-hikers on those trails. Those thru hiking the Continental Divide Trail will typically pass from west to east during late June. Those thru hiking the Colorado Trail will typically pass from east to west beginning in mid-July. While this trail will lead to Denver, I'm only going to cover the section that will lead to the intersection with the Skyline Trail, discussed under the section called Tumble Creek (Skyline). This hike can be taken to the rim of Snow Mesa, to the summit of Baldy Cinco or to the Skyline Trail intersection. This is a dry hike, so take extra water. It can get quite windy on Snow Mesa and climbing Baldy Cinco, so dress appropriately. While the trail parallels the Continental Divide, you are on the Atlantic side of the divide for the duration of the hike. This trail appears on both the La Garita, Cochetopa *Trails Illustrated* map and the quads.

The trailhead is on the east side of the highway, which you must cross after leaving the parking area and crossing a creek **(39A)**. It immediately begins a moderate ascent and enters a forest. After almost a mile, it breaks into an open area dotted with cairns, and the trail flattens out a bit. The trail begins ascending again as it re-enters the forest. After the second forest, it enters a rocky area, and you climb through a rock trough to reach the rim of Snow Mesa beyond the 2-mile point. Look back from time to time as you ascend; the views are not to be missed. Once you've reached the rim of Snow Mesa **(39D)**, you may

201

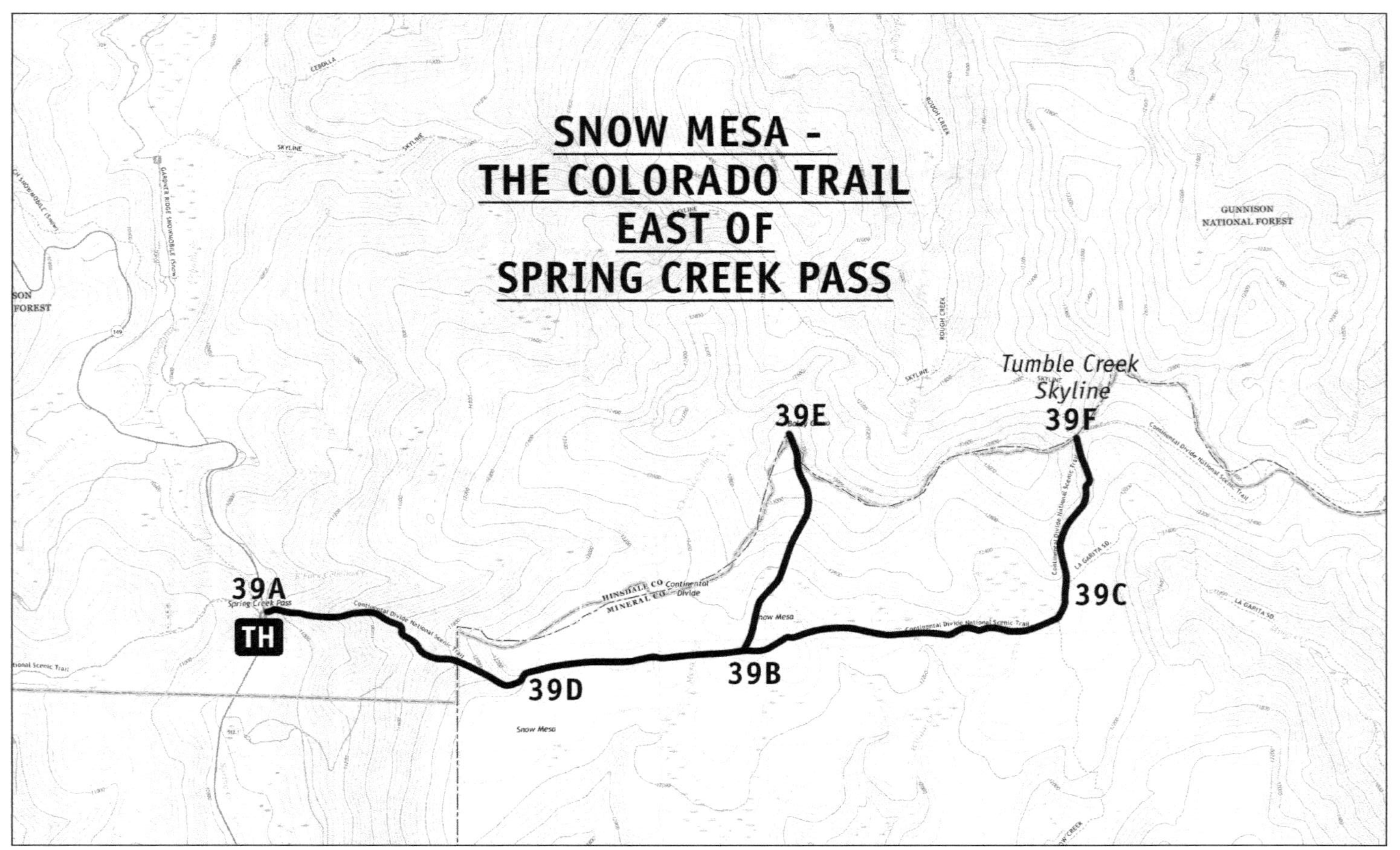
SNOW MESA -
THE COLORADO TRAIL
EAST OF
SPRING CREEK PASS
Tumble Creek
Skyline
39E
39F
39A
Spring Creek Pass
TH
39C
39D
39B
GUNNISON
NATIONAL FOREST

want to venture off the trail to the left and follow the rim to an overlook area where the views are even better.

To continue to the summit of Baldy Cinco, hike east along the Colorado Trail for 1 mile. The trail along the top of the mesa is about as flat as you will find in the area. After descending to cross a draw and ascending the other side, look for a trail marker, which is the sixth marker on the top of the mesa **(39B)**. From there you will veer off to the left. The climb up Baldy Cinco has no established trail. You will see two peaks with a saddle between them. Baldy Cinco is the peak to your right. The summit of the other peak, Baldy No Se, is 70 feet shorter than the summit of Baldy Cinco.

As you head toward Baldy Cinco, choose whatever route makes most sense — but stay between the draw you just crossed and another draw to the east. There is a cairn on the east side of what appears to be the summit. Aim for this point and stay to the east of it to avoid rocky areas. This portion of the ascent is quite steep, but you are in short grass, so the terrain is tolerable. Once you have reached the cairn you have reached a false summit. The actual summit is almost .5 miles to the north, and you have another 300 feet to climb. Upon reaching the summit **(39E)** you have views to the north into the Cebolla Creek area, to the south back across Snow Mesa, and toward Creede. The water you see to the west is Continental Reservoir.

While Snow Mesa has been fairly flat up to the point of the Baldy Cinco turnoff **(39B)**, the Colorado Trail becomes more rolling from this point eastward. You cross three draws in succession: the first slight, the second deep, and the third wide, and there are several smaller draws thereafter. Each of these forms the upper drainage of Willow Creek. There is water in the second and third draw and one of the later smaller draws late in the season.

After 3.5 miles along the top of Snow Mesa (5.5 miles from the trailhead), you see a pond to your left and the trail turns from eastbound to northbound passing the pond. The *Trails Illustrated* map and the Baldy Cinco quad both show intersections with two trails near the pond. There is no trail marker indicating an intersection with the Willow Creek Trail, and the trail is apparently overgrown in this area. There is a trail marker indicating the intersection with Trail #803, which is the Miners Creek Trail **(39C)** and there is a cairn a short distance from the trail sign. From the cairn you can see the faint outlines of a trail heading southeast toward Creede. As the Miners Creek Trail is totally within Mineral County, it is not covered in this book.

The trail changes character as it heads north from the pond. You are passing along the uppermost portion of the Miners Creek Basin, which is large, deep, and beautiful. To the left there are rock outcroppings shortly above you, and to the right you look down into the Miners Creek Basin. There are seasonal wildflowers. You travel 1 mile after leaving the pond, gaining elevation gradually, until you see the pass ahead of you leading to the Pacific side of the Continental Divide, where the trail steepens. The pass is a small window where the Colorado Trail intersects with the Skyline Trail (**39F**). The trail sign indicates the trails on the Pacific side of the divide which lead to the Tumble Creek and Rough Creek trailheads. The trail on the Pacific side of the divide is covered under the section named Tumble Creek (Skyline).

RATING: The shorter hike to rim of Snow Mesa (**39D**) is a 4-mile round trip climbing 1,300 feet. It can be done by any intermediate hiker. The hike to the summit of Baldy Cinco (**39E**) is a 10-mile round trip that climbs over 2,400 feet. It may be taxing for an intermediate hiker due to the distance and the steepness of the ascent to the false summit. A hike to the intersection with the Skyline Trail (**39F**) is a 13-mile round trip that gains a net 1,400 feet. Despite the distance, this should also be considered an intermediate level hike.

Trailheads Located South and East of Lake City via CR 50 (FSR 788)

Trailheads Located South and East of Lake City via CR 50 (FSR 788)

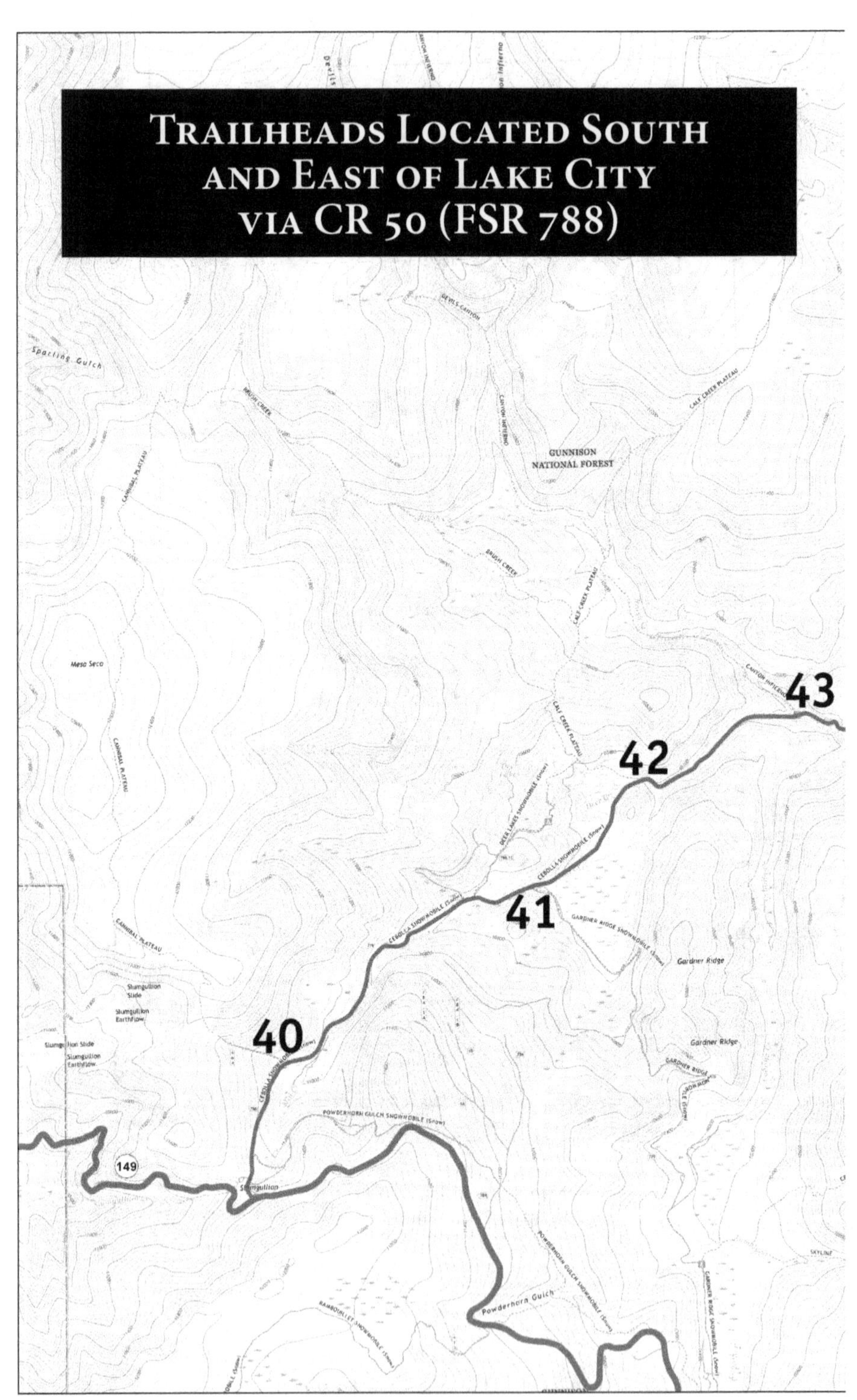

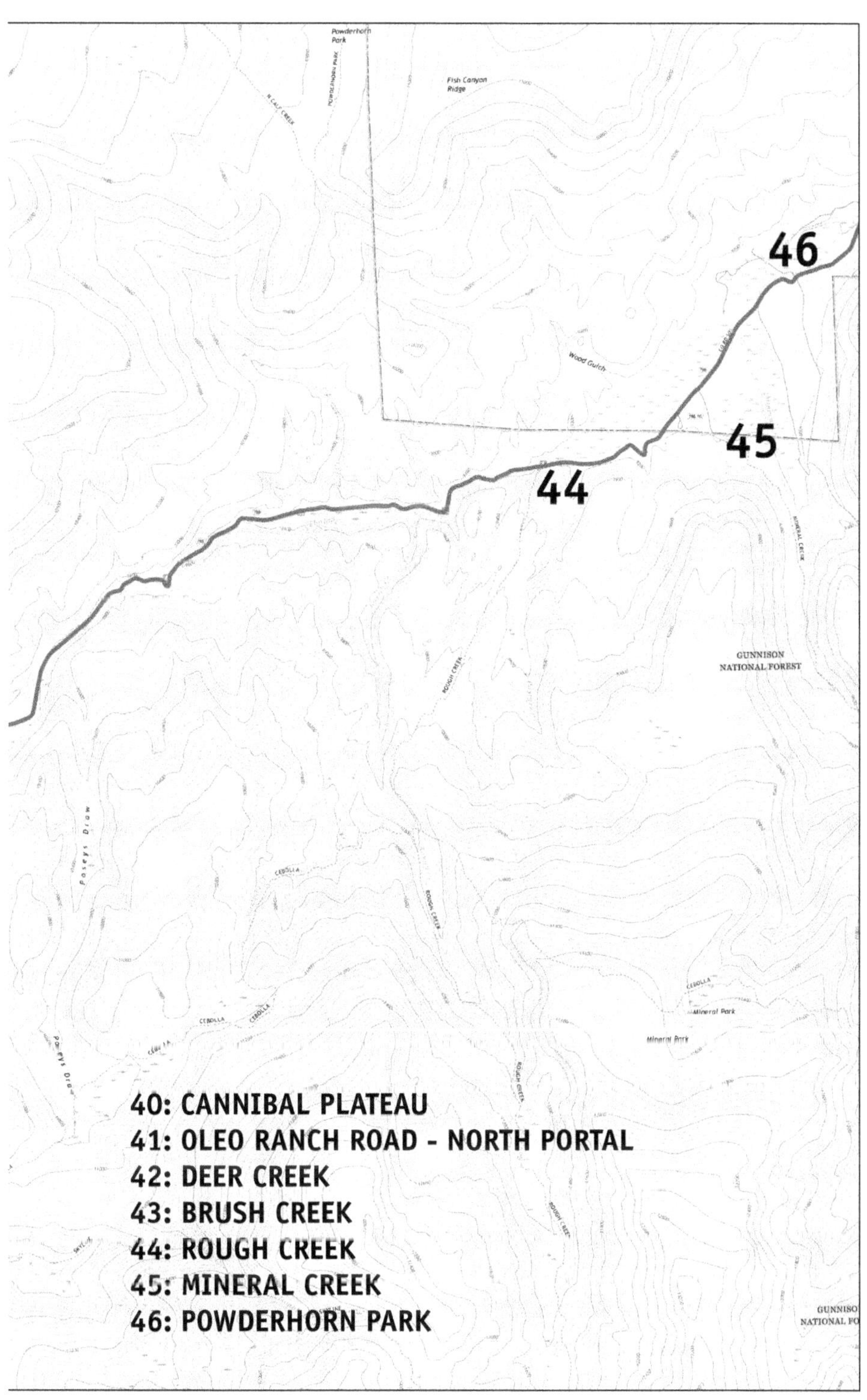

40: CANNIBAL PLATEAU
41: OLEO RANCH ROAD - NORTH PORTAL
42: DEER CREEK
43: BRUSH CREEK
44: ROUGH CREEK
45: MINERAL CREEK
46: POWDERHORN PARK

CANNIBAL PLATEAU

Quad: Slumgullion Pass, Cannibal Plateau

DRIVING INSTRUCTIONS: Drive south from Lake City on CO SH 149. Continue about 10 miles to the Cebolla Creek Rd (also known as the Deer Lakes Rd, CR 50, and FSR 788), past MP 63. Take a left on this road and continue 1.0 mile to the Cannibal Plateau trailhead, which is marked by a sign on the left side of the road. Limited parking is available at the trailhead. Trailhead elevation - 11,100 feet.

THE HIKE: This hike takes you to the top of Mesa Seco, which is a significant geologic feature for the area. About 1300 AD the mesa broke apart which set the Slumgullion Earthflow in motion, which upon reaching the Lake Fork of the Gunnison River, created a natural dam. The water behind the dam is Lake San Cristobal, the second largest natural lake in Colorado. From the top of Mesa Seco, you can look down upon the earthflow and see this wonder of nature from an unmatched perspective. The trail continues across Mesa Seco and down to a saddle connecting Mesa Seco and Cannibal Plateau. Here, the Cannibal Plateau Trail connects with the trail originating at the Deer Creek trailhead. The Cannibal Plateau Trail is open to ATV use from July 1 through September 30 and gets a fair amount of use by ATVs during that period. A shorter hike will take you to the Slumgullion overlook, and just beyond it to a point to the west overlooking upper Vickers Ranch. A longer hike will cross Mesa Seco and connect you with the trail originating at the Deer Creek trailhead and on to Cannibal Plateau. This trail appears on both the La Garita, Cochetopa Hills *Trails Illustrated* map and the quads. This is a dry hike, so you should take extra water with you.

From the trailhead (**40A**), the trail rises steadily over the first 2 miles until you reach the lip of Mesa Seco. This is a double track and is

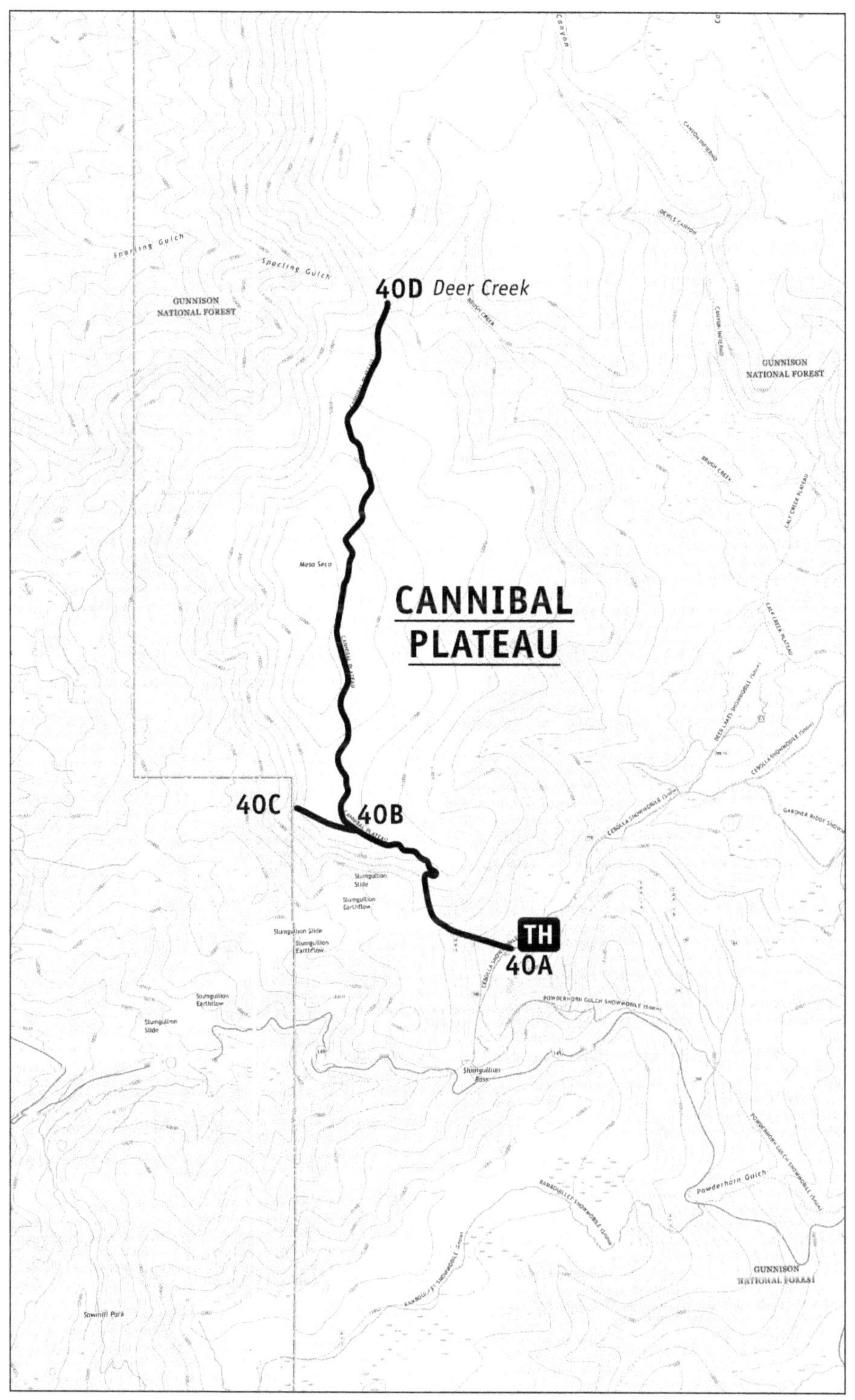
40D Deer Creek
GUNNISON
NATIONAL FOREST
GUNNISON
NATIONAL FOREST
CANNIBAL
PLATEAU
40C
40B
TH
40A
GUNNISON
NATIONAL FOREST

mostly in the open, although it passes through a short section of forest at the 1-mile point. There are several switchbacks and, while the rise is not steep, it never really lets up. The views of the jagged broken section of Mesa Seco, as well as to the south and west are spectacular. As you reach the lip of Mesa Seco, there is a white tipped metal post designating that vehicle traffic is prohibited on the branch of the fainter trail heading to the left **(40B)**. This trail will take you to the Slumgullion overlook, from where you can see where the rest of Mesa Seco has gone. Continuing west from that point for less than .5 miles you will reach the west edge of Mesa Seco and have an overlook of the upper Vickers Ranch and the mountains to the west. A good vantage point is marked by two posts, in close proximity. This will be the turnaround point for the shorter of the two hikes **(40C)**.

Should you wish to take the longer hike, at the white tipped metal post **(40B)** continue to the right, over the more clearly defined trail. You will continue to climb, but at a lesser pace as you cross Mesa Seco. There are two high points, or bumps, on the mesa to your left which obliterate your views to the west. The views to the east, overlooking other mesas, are far less spectacular. Either of the two high points on Mesa Seco offers views to the west, but neither one exceeds the view described in the previous paragraph. You will continue to climb until you reach a point to the east of the second bump on the mesa. The trail to the point to the east of the second bump is fairly flat. After that point, you begin your descent from Mesa Seco to the saddle below connecting Mesa Seco and Cannibal Plateau. You have gained 1,600 feet, to this point and you will give back 800 feet as you descend to the saddle. This is a tough 800 feet to regain on your return trip.

The terrain along Mesa Seco is short grass, and that will continue as you descend to the saddle, although you begin passing through bushes on your way down. As you approach the saddle, you enter a forest comprised of spruce trees which show signs of beetle kill. There is a small open area .5 miles into the forest. To your right in this open area is the trail **(40D)** which leaves from the Deer Creek trailhead. It is not evident in spots within the grassy open area, but it becomes more evident as you enter the trees. If you are planning a thru-hike between the Deer Creek trailhead and the Cannibal Plateau trailhead, you may wish to leave from the Deer Creek trailhead, as this point could be missed coming from the Cannibal Plateau trailhead. One hundred yards beyond the trail intersection there is a carsonite post indicating that you are on Trail #464. If you reach this post, you have gone too far - unless you are planning to continue up Cannibal Plateau, which also offers spectacular views. The portion of the Cannibal Plateau Trail beyond the Deer Creek Trail intersection (**40D**) is discussed in the Deer Creek section.

RATING: The shorter hike to the Slumgullion overlook and the upper Vickers Ranch overlook (**40C**) and back covers 5 miles and climbs 1,100 feet. This is within the capabilities of any intermediate hiker. The trail to the Deer Creek Trail intersection (**40D**) is a 12-mile round trip and climbs 2,400 feet gross, 1,600 on the way out and 800 on the return trip. This trail should only be undertaken by experienced hikers.

South and west from Mesa Seco

Katherine Heidt

OLEO RANCH ROAD – NORTH PORTAL

Quad: Cannibal Plateau, Slumgullion Pass

DRIVING INSTRUCTIONS: Drive south from Lake City on CO SH 149. Continue about 10 miles to the Cebolla Creek Rd (also known as the Deer Lakes Rd, CR 50, and FSR 788), past MP 63. Take a left on this road and continue 3.1 miles to where a road turns to the right. This is also .4 miles past the turnoff to Deer Lakes Campground. Very limited parking is available at the trailhead. Trailhead elevation - 10,400 feet.

THE HIKE: This trail follows the old stagecoach road which led from Del Norte to Lake City. It is road quality the entire distance but closed to vehicular traffic for all but the southernmost three miles. The trail goes over a low elevation pass between the Mill Creek drainage on the north and the Cebolla Creek drainage on the south. As the trail is groomed for snowmobile usage during the winter and has very gentle elevation gains, it is an excellent trail for cross-country skiing or snowshoeing. It gets little usage other than during the winter. This trail appears on the quads but not on the La Garita, Cochetopa Hills *Trails Illustrated* map. A portion of this trail passes through or adjacent to private property.

There is no marked trailhead. The junction of the Cebolla Creek (Deer Lakes) Road and a well-developed road to the right is your starting point **(41A)**. Less than .25 miles from the Cebolla Creek Road, you will encounter a fence with a gate that is unlocked only in the winter. After crossing the fence, continue south with an open area to your left, which is private land. After less than a mile, you enter forest and the trail begins climbing, ever so gradually. There is one switchback before you reach the top of the unnamed pass at the 2-mile point. Shortly before reaching the top of the pass, a road junction occurs. The fork to the right heads downhill toward no place in particular. The fork to the

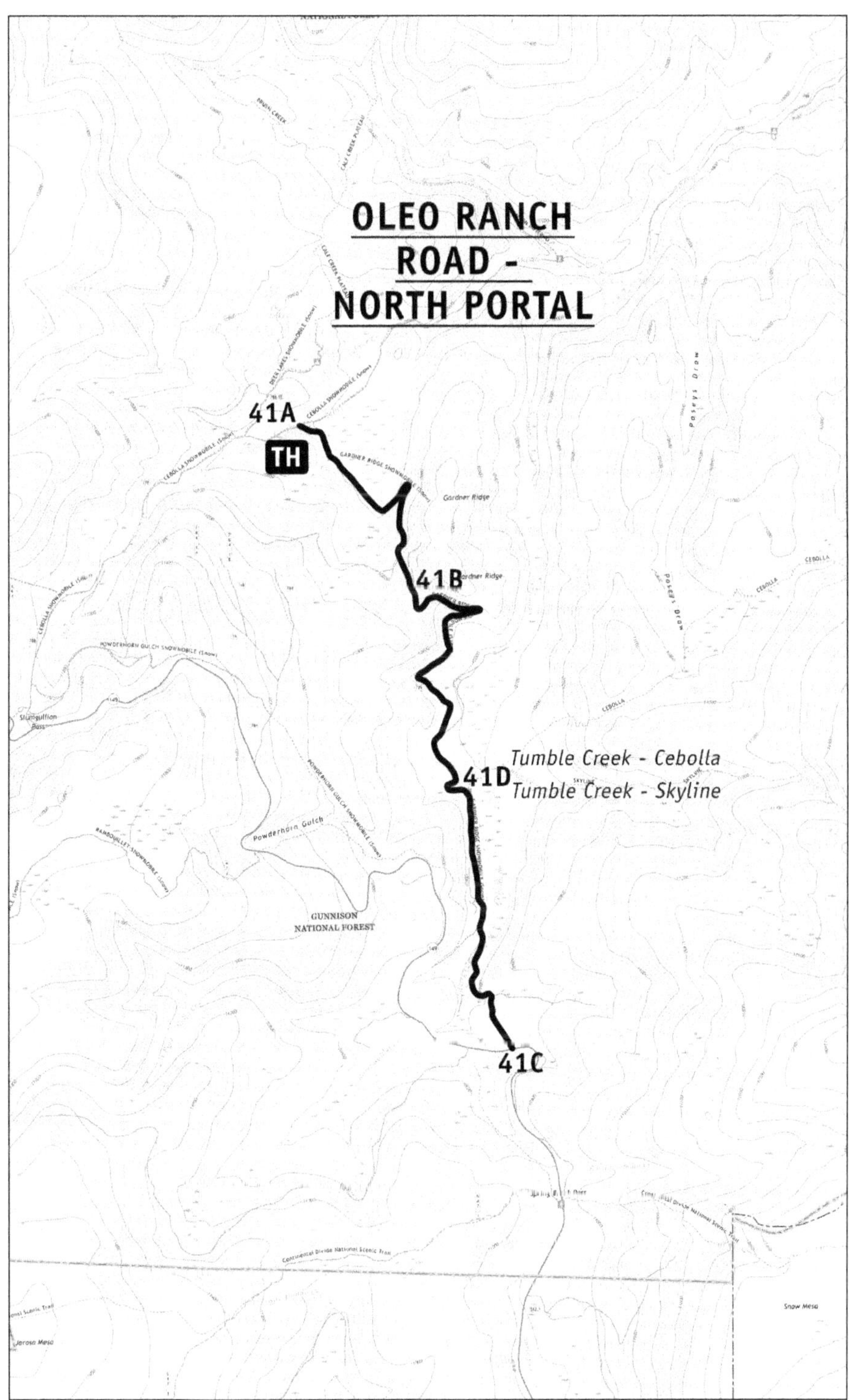
OLEO RANCH
ROAD -
NORTH PORTAL
41A
TH
41B
41D
41C
Tumble Creek - Cebolla
Tumble Creek - Skyline
GUNNISON
NATIONAL FOREST

left continues to climb until you reach the top of the pass. As the top of the pass (**41B**) is still in forest, there is little in the way of scenery from the top.

As you descend into the Cebolla Creek drainage, the landscape opens up a bit; after the first switchback you have a nice view of Cebolla Creek and Tumble Creek below you. You are adjacent to private land for much of this section of the hike. The trail hugs the ridge as it heads downward into the Cebolla Valley. There are ranch buildings and a residence as you reach the valley floor and the trail snakes around a bit more before you reach the Tumble Creek trailhead to your left (**41D**). This trailhead serves the Cebolla Trail and the Skyline Trail, which are discussed under the sections named Tumble Creek (Cebolla) and Tumble Creek (Skyline). The Tumble Creek trailhead is two miles from CO SH 149, and you pass Oleo Ranch, a guest ranch, a mile before reaching the highway (**41C**), near MP 56. There is minimal elevation gain or loss between the Tumble Creek trailhead and the highway.

RATING: A hike to the top of the pass (**41B**) and returning covers 4 miles and has a 400-foot elevation gain. It is a hike easily within a beginner's ability. A hike to the Tumble Creek trailhead (**41D**) and returning covers 8 miles and has a 400-foot elevation gain in each direction. It too should be considered a trail for beginners, with the only caveat being the distance. A thru-hike to CO SH 149 (**41C**) covers 6 miles with a 400-foot elevation gain, followed by a 400-foot elevation drop. It can be undertaken by beginners as well.

DEER CREEK

Quad: Cannibal Plateau

DRIVING INSTRUCTIONS: Drive south from Lake City on CO SH 149. Continue about 10 miles to the Cebolla Creek Rd (also known as the Deer Lakes Rd, CR 50, and FSR 788), beyond MP 63. Take a left on this road and continue 4.1 miles to the Deer Creek trailhead, which is marked by a sign on the left side of the road. Very limited parking is available at the trailhead. Trailhead elevation - 10,200 feet.

THE HIKE: I'm at a bit of a loss as to what to call this trail. The trailhead is where the Cebolla Creek Road crosses Deer Creek so I'm comfortable calling this the Deer Creek trailhead. However, the trail leaves the creek immediately. The trailhead signage indicates you are following the Calf Creek Plateau Trail, but that trail separates from our trail after a couple of miles. The trail follows the upper portion of Brush Creek, but we have a Brush Creek trailhead, and that trail is commonly called the Brush Creek Trail. This trail leads to Cannibal Plateau but alas, that trail name is taken as well. I'll call this the trail leaving from the Deer Creek trailhead. Only the portion of the trail that is part of the Calf Creek Plateau Trail appears on the quad map. Much of the remainder of the trail appears on the La Garita, Cochetopa Hills *Trails Illustrated* map, but several miles of a loop are absent from that map. Having said that, this trail is not difficult to follow. The trail is open to ATV usage from July 1 through September 30, and much of the trail is a double track. Although open to ATV usage, I haven't seen too much evidence of current usage. There are swampy areas, downed timber and other obstacles which would send many an ATV owner back to the trailhead, provided he values his vehicle. I've seen use by hunters, but I have never seen another hiker on this trail and hoofprints outnumber boot prints by a wide margin. As is the case with most of

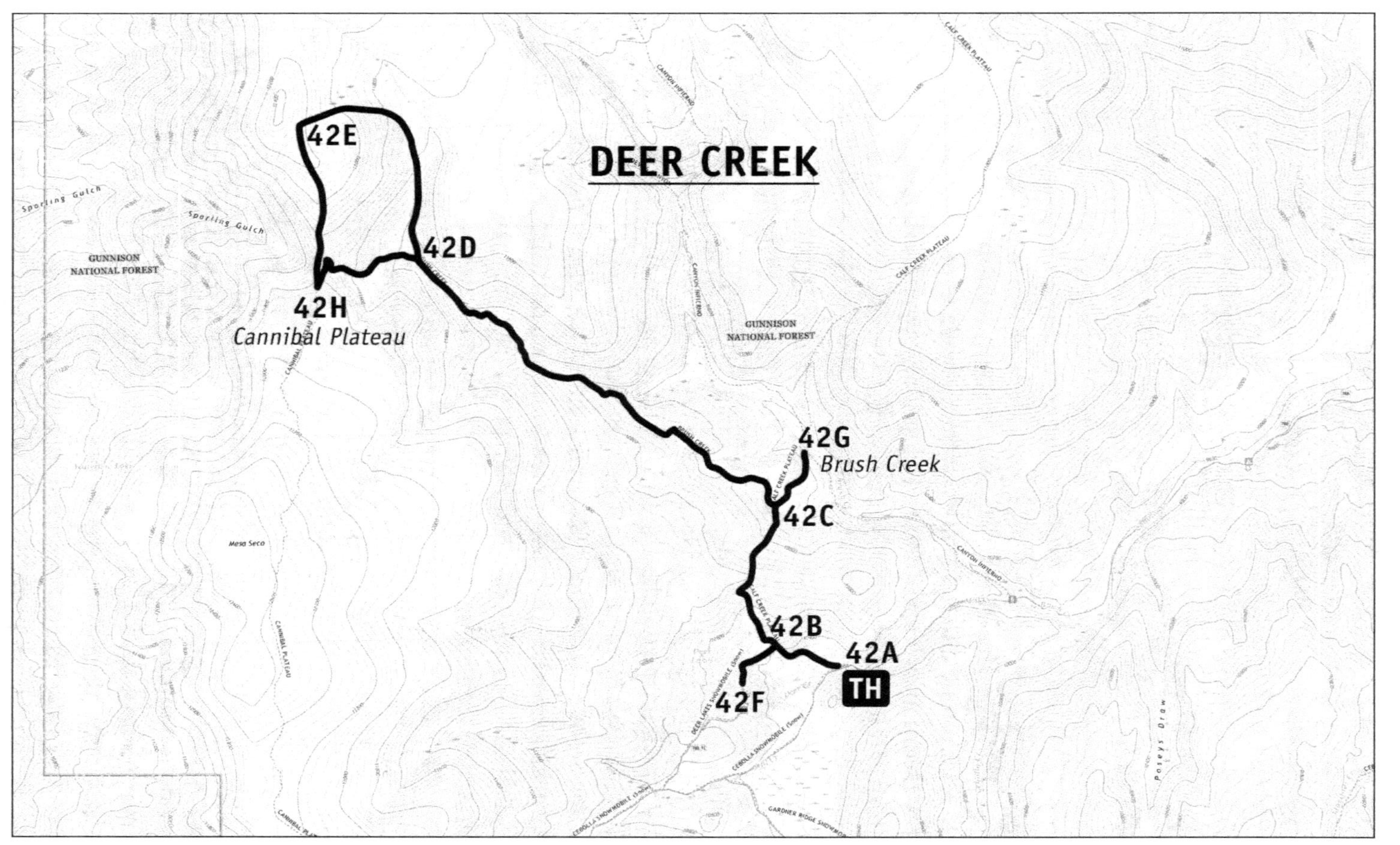
DEER CREEK
Brush Creek
Cannibal Plateau
Sporting Gulch
GUNNISON NATIONAL FOREST
Mesa Seco
Poseys Draw
CALF CREEK PLATEAU
CANYON INFERNO
42A
42B
42C
42D
42E
42F
42G
42H
TH

the trails in the Powderhorn district, this trail connects with several others.

Leaving the trailhead (**42A**), you are in a large park area for the first mile at the edge of a forest. After 1 mile there is a trail sign (**42B**) indicating that you should go to the right for the Calf Creek Plateau Trail or to intersect the Brush Creek Trail, which is what you will likely want to do. Although there is no designation on the trail sign, a trail to the left leads to the Deer Lakes area, .5 miles away. That option is discussed later. Continuing to the right, you climb at a modest rate as you enter the forest, and you top out for the early part of the hike after you have gained 600 feet. You will promptly descend 400 feet going through a small open area before re-entering the forest. After you leave the forest for a second time, you will enter a large open area where the trail is marked by posts leading to your right (**42C**). This is the Calf Creek Plateau Trail that will join the Brush Creek Trail after .5 miles, just before a major stream crossing (**42G**). Your hiking options from that point are many and described in the section for Brush Creek. For a beginning hiker, or a hiker seeking a shorter hike, a loop can be taken starting at the Deer Creek trailhead, following the Calf Creek Plateau Trail to its intersection with the Brush Creek Trail (**42G**), taking that trail 2 miles to its trailhead, and following the Cebolla Creek Road for 1.2 miles back to your starting point (**42A**).

Should you wish to continue on the Deer Creek Trail, take a left at the post (**42C**) which appears as you enter the large open area, following the double track. This will be a gradual climb over the next several miles, starting out in this open area and working into woods to the left of upper Brush Creek. There are several stream crossings and a couple of muddy or marshy areas to navigate around. None of the stream crossings are severe enough to require water crossing shoes. At the 4.5 mile point the canyon narrows and there is a rockslide on the right. The trail will enter a grassy area and cross the stream several times before emerging on the left bank. The trail becomes a double track once again as it climbs out of this area. Just after this, the double track cuts to the right and a faint trail continues to the left (**42D**). Both of these trails will intersect the Cannibal Plateau Trail at different points, and you may loop back to this point. The trail to the left is depicted on the *Trails Illustrated* map and if you are attempting to hike the Deer Creek Trail as a loop, you should go left, because the intersection of this trail and the

Cannibal Plateau Trail can be difficult to find from the other direction. The trail to the left is not well defined and may seem to disappear at one point. If you have difficulty following it, bear to the left and you will see the trail emerge below a rockslide at the top of the open area toward the left. The trail will then enter the trees, and the climb is steeper than what you have seen to this point. The trail flattens out as it enters an open area, then intersects the Cannibal Plateau Trail (**42H**). Take a right on the Cannibal Plateau Trail if you wish to continue the loop or take a left if you wish to hike to the trailhead of the Cannibal Plateau Trail. That trail is described under the section named Cannibal Plateau.

If you have taken a right turn to continue the loop, you will soon pass a carsonite post indicating that you are on Trail #464. The trail is fairly flat for .25 miles, then it becomes a steep incline as you ascend Cannibal Plateau. Once you have gained sufficient elevation, the views to the west are spectacular. You have more climbing to do before reaching a post where the trails divide (**42E**). The left fork heads to the top of Cannibal Plateau and you can continue on, through short grass, toward Devils Lake. The right fork continues the loop, and you soon begin descending Cannibal Plateau on its southeast flank and begin to follow the Brush Creek headwaters down to where the loop concludes (**42D**). This last mile before reaching the intersection point is in the open, with forest to your right with a meadow and Brush Creek to your left.

Returning to the trail sign 1 mile from the trailhead (**42B**), turn left if you want to go to the Deer Lakes area. This trail is easy to follow and it neither gains nor loses much elevation as it stays in the open area, just below the trees. There is a guidepost without a trail sign, then another post bearing a trail sign indicating that this trail intersects the Calf Creek Plateau Trail in .25 miles. After the trail sign, the trail crosses a creek before descending and crossing a dam at the uppermost lake. By this point you are within the Deer Lakes Campground, and a road takes you uphill to the pay station near the center of the campground (**42F**). From this point you can either return to your starting point (**42A**), 1.5 miles away or you can continue along the road until it connects with the Cebolla Creek Road, 1.5 miles from the Deer Creek trailhead (**42A**).

RATING: A round trip to the intersection with the Brush Creek Trail (**42G**) covers 4.5 miles and gains 600 feet before descending a like amount on the way out, and the same on the return trip. It is suitable for beginning hikers. The loop taking the Calf Creek Plateau Trail to Brush Creek, back to the Brush Creek trailhead, and back to the Deer Creek trailhead via the Cebolla Creek Road covers 5 miles. The elevation gain is 600 feet gross (0 net, as it's a loop), and this hike could also be made by a beginning hiker. The loop taking the main trail up Cannibal Plateau **(42E)** covers 12 miles with a 2,100-foot net elevation gain, with the 400-foot drop in the second mile needing to be made up on the return trip. Save energy and water for this climb. The Cannibal Plateau loop should only be undertaken by experienced hikers. A hike to the Deer Lakes Campground **(42F)** is a 3-mile round trip, gaining 400 feet. It is suitable for beginning hikers. A loop hike through the Deer Lakes Campground following the Deer Lakes Cutoff Road to the Cebolla Creek Road and returning to the Deer Creek Trailhead covers 4 miles and also gains 400 feet. It too, is suitable for beginning hikers.

Autumn in Hinsdale County

Glenn Heumann

BRUSH CREEK

Quad: Cannibal Plateau

DRIVING INSTRUCTIONS: Drive south from Lake City on CO SH 149. Continue about 10 miles to the Cebolla Creek Rd (also known as the Deer Lakes Rd, CR 50, and FSR 788), past MP 63. Take a left on this road and continue 5.3 miles to the Brush Creek trailhead, which is marked by a sign on the left side of the road. Limited parking is available at the trailhead. Trailhead elevation - 9,900 feet.

THE HIKE: The Brush Creek Trail, also known as the Canyon Inferno Trail, is an easy hike to the extent that the trail follows the creek. It intersects the Calf Creek Plateau Trail at the 2-mile point, and at the 3.5 mile point the trail divides with one trail leading toward Cannibal Plateau and the other to Devil's Lake. Most of the trails in the Powderhorn district connect, and this trail offers several possibilities for multi-day trips. The basic Brush Creek Trail is quite popular and supports deer, moose, and other wildlife. This trail appears both on the La Garita, Cochetopa Hills *Trails Illustrated* map and on the quad.

From the trailhead (**43A**), the trail rises gently as it follows the creek. The trail is primarily in forest for the first 1.5 miles. After you break into the open, the trail appears to divide with the left fork rising up a hill and the right fork continuing along the stream before crossing a side stream. Take the right fork. The trail on the left fork phases out before going much further, but it would take you in the direction of the Deer Creek Trail, which can be better accessed from the Calf Creek Plateau Trail (which you will reach in another .5 miles). You will be in the open for the next section of the hike, and 2 miles from the trailhead you will cross Brush Creek, shortly after passing the trail sign showing the intersection with the Calf Creek Plateau Trail (**43H**) which leads back to the Deer Creek trailhead and to Deer Lakes. That section of

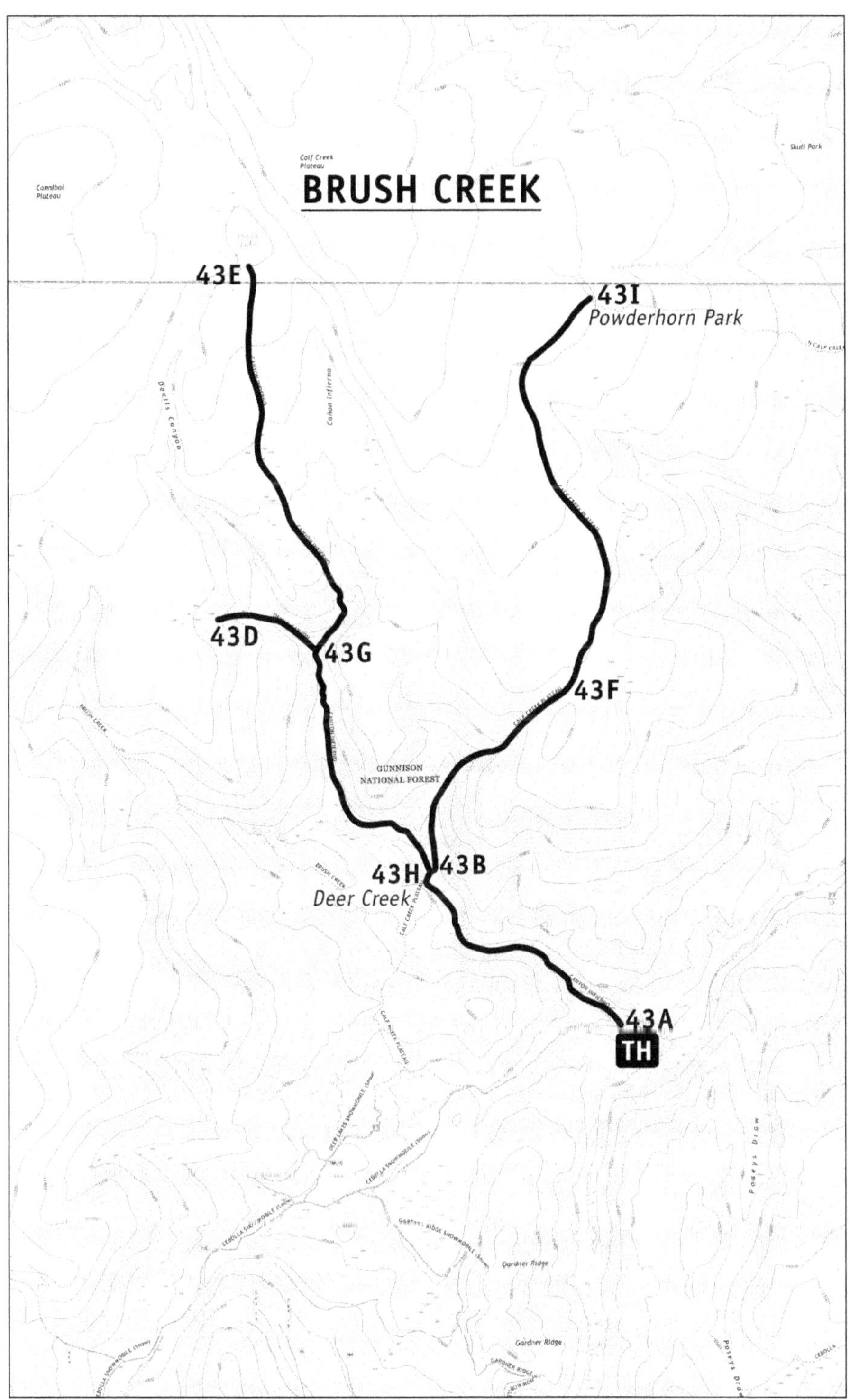

Calf Creek Plateau
Cannibal Plateau
Skull Park
BRUSH CREEK
43E
43I
Powderhorn Park
43D
43G
43F
GUNNISON NATIONAL FOREST
43H
43B
Deer Creek
43A
TH

the Calf Creek Plateau Trail is discussed under the section for the Deer Creek trailhead.

The crossing of Brush Creek will require water crossing shoes early in the season. Shortly after crossing the stream, you will see a second trail sign (**43B**). To the right is the continuation of the Calf Creek Plateau Trail, leading you to Calf Creek Plateau. That trail will be discussed later in this section. The continuation of the Brush Creek Trail will take you to the left. You will now be following Brush Creek on the east side of the creek. After .5 miles from the water crossing, the creek divides. Brush Creek continues to the left, while the trail follows the right branch along Canyon Inferno. After 1 mile of mostly wooded hiking, the trail again divides. The trail sign (**43G**), missing at this writing, indicates the left fork follows Devil's Canyon and the right fork leads to Devil's Lake.

The Devil's Canyon Trail crosses a stream shortly after the fork and continues along Devil's Canyon for less than .5 miles before crossing a stream and heading toward Cannibal Plateau. The Devil's Canyon Trail gets limited hiker use, but there is plenty of evidence of use by hunting parties. The trail is not difficult to follow along the stream and there are two posts to assist you. After the second stream crossing the trail climbs toward the top of Cannibal Plateau. The maps indicate that the trail leads to the top of Cannibal Plateau, but in practice the trail has been obliterated by tall brush and there is limited evidence of the trail after you leave a hunter's camp (**43D**) several hundred yards after the second stream crossing.

The trail to Devil's Lake takes the right fork at the trail fork (**43G**). Shortly beyond the trail fork there is a sign indicating that it is 3 miles to Devil's Lake, although it's nearly a mile more than that. The trail continues on the east side of the Canyon Inferno waterway for .25 miles, and you pass two trail signs indicating that you are entering the Powderhorn Wilderness before the trail turns to the left and crosses the stream. The trail is not difficult to identify on the other side of the stream and continues to follow the stream for a short distance before turning left. Ahead of you is an open area which is a moderate to steep climb up the side of Cannibal Plateau. The trail crosses another stream and has several switchbacks before it levels out a bit. You are still in the open but heading toward trees. There are several cairns to guide you in this area, but any assistance in navigation is suddenly going to end.

Pay attention to your surroundings as you will need to reach this point on your return trip. There is faint evidence of the trail as you enter the trees, but you will want to go ahead and to the left as it is the shortest distance through the trees. You should emerge in an open area that has trees on three sides. Once again, pay particular attention to your surroundings as you will need to enter the forest at this point on your return trip.

Once you are in the open, look toward the north. There are two plateaus close to one another as you look toward the horizon. You are hiking along Cannibal Plateau which is the plateau on the left. Calf Creek Plateau is on the right, and at the point of contact, it is the higher of the two in elevation. The spot along the horizon where they meet is your destination. Devil's Lake lies in a fold between the two plateaus. You will have little guidance from this point on as there are few cairns, and the trail is overgrown for much of the remaining distance to Devil's Lake. As you head toward Devil's Lake you will have a brushy open area on your right and some trees on your left. Go between the brush and the trees as you climb further up Cannibal Plateau. You will want to both gain elevation and stay out of the brush as long as you can. Once you have gained elevation, you will need to head toward the right and enter the brush. Fortunately, there are passageways through the brush, not unlike a maze. Keep your sights on the point where the plateaus meet, and once you emerge from the brush there is a faint trail which takes you the rest of the way to Devil's Lake (**43E**). Devil's Lake is quite large, perhaps forty acres, and there are sites suitable for camping. As there are no trees, but many rocks, there is an other-worldly feeling when at this lake. There are other trails leading to Devil's Lake which are covered in the Devil's Creek, Powderhorn Lakes, and Powderhorn Park sections. There are opportunities for multi-day hikes and thru-hikes which would feature a stop at Devil's Lake.

Returning to the stream crossing at the 2-mile point, the trail leading to Calf Creek Plateau separates from the Brush Creek Trail immediately after crossing the stream and is marked by a trail sign (**43B**). The Calf Creek Plateau Trail climbs a ridge and there is a post at the top of the ridge. From there the trail follows a drainage gulch until it reaches the top of the plateau. For nearly the first mile, the trail is on the north side of the gulch, ascending gently to moderately, passing a Powderhorn Wilderness boundary sign and going through mostly open areas. This trail does not get much use, but it is not difficult to follow as it ascends the gulch to the north side of the waterway, which is dry for most of the season. After nearly 1 mile, the trail crosses the waterway and enters the woods. The trail steepens and is a moderate to steep climb for the rest of the distance to the top of the plateau. While you are in the woods, the trail is easy to follow, but after entering a lightly wooded area it is overgrown by grass in places. Just keep within sight of the gulch waterway and continue climbing. Near the top of the lightly wooded area, you will pass a pair of water troughs. It isn't much further to the top of the plateau from this point. As you emerge from the trees, you will stop climbing as you enter the vast expanse of Calf Creek Plateau (**43F**). This is a logical turnaround point for most hikers, unless you are intending to connect with one of the other trails crossing the Powderhorn Wilderness. The view back down the gulch is of Mesa Seco.

Should you continue further on the Calf Creek Plateau Trail, the trail is overgrown for much of the top of the plateau. There is a series of twelve posts which will guide you over the next 2 miles. These are placed such that once you have reached a post you can usually see the next post. The first section of the Calf Creek Plateau Trail atop of the plateau is in short grass, with brush to your left and trees to the right. The posts lead you between the brush and the trees heading northeast, before turning north as you enter the brush after the fifth post. You remain in brush for over .5 miles, but there are passageways between clumps of brush and the bushes are not too tall. You emerge from the brush before reaching the eleventh post and from where you see the final post atop a ridge. The posts end, but there are a few cairns as you continue north, descending slightly through another brushy area. There is another ridge ahead and above you which contains a post. Once you've reached this post there are no more navigation aids. Don't despair, because your destination is the intersection with the North Calf Creek Trail which is perpendicular to the Calf Creek Plateau Trail. The North Calf Creek Trail leads from Powderhorn Park to Devil's Lake but has only a few posts to help you find your way. Some years ago, there was an old, poorly maintained trail sign marking the intersection of the Calf Creek Plateau Trail and the North Calf Creek Trail (**43I**). I did not locate this trail sign on my last two visits to the area. The intersection of the two trails is 3 miles from the point you first entered Calf Creek Plateau, but you have only gained 400 feet of elevation over that distance. The North Calf Creek Trail is discussed under the section for Powderhorn Park.

RATING: A hike to the point where the trails divide departing to Devil's Canyon and Devil's Lake **(43G)** is a 7-mile round trip and gains 1,000 feet. This is a good hike for beginners. Extending the hike up Devil's Canyon to the hunters' camp **(43D)** will add another 1.5 miles and 200 feet of elevation gain. This is still suitable for beginners. A hike to Devil's Lake **(43E)** is a 14-mile round trip gaining 2,100 feet. Due to the distance and navigation issues, this hike should only be undertaken by experienced hikers. A hike to the entry point of Calf Creek Plateau **(43F)** is an 8-mile round trip and gains 1,700 feet. It is suitable for intermediate hikers. A hike to the intersection of the Calf Creek Plateau Trail and the North Calf Creek Trail **(43I)** is a 14-mile round trip gaining 2,100 feet. It should be limited to experienced hikers due to the distance and navigation issues.

Summer In Hinsdale County
Katherine Heidt

ROUGH CREEK

Quad: Mineral Mountain, Baldy Cinco

DRIVING INSTRUCTIONS: Drive south from Lake City on CO SH 149. Continue about 10 miles to the Cebolla Creek Rd (also known as the Deer Lakes Rd, CR 50, and FSR 788), past MP 63. Take a left on this road and continue 10.0 miles to the Rough Creek trailhead, which has signs on both sides of the road. Parking is available just to the west of the trailhead, which is on the south side of the road, passing through a gate **(44A)**. Trailhead elevation - 9,200 feet.

THE HIKE: The Rough Creek Trail goes for 8 miles where it terminates at the intersection with the Skyline Trail. It intersects the Cebolla Trail at the 3-mile point. This section discusses the full 8 miles of the Rough Creek Trail, and that section of the Cebolla Trail west to Martinez Creek and east to the intersection with the Mineral Creek Trail. Other discussion of the Cebolla Trail can be found in the Tumble Creek (Cebolla) section. All discussion of the Skyline trail can be found in the Tumble Creek (Skyline) section. Because of the connectivity of these trails, there are several multi-day loop possibilities. None of these trails get a great deal of use, but all are fairly easy to follow as each gets a fair amount of horse traffic. All of this trail system appears both on the La Garita, Cochetopa Hills *Trails Illustrated* map and on the quads.

The Rough Creek Trail **(44A)** begins with several switchbacks climbing from the road. Once you pass the boundary sign for the La Garita Wilderness, keep your eyes open for a trail intersection 200 yards beyond the sign. This is soon after you have reached a fairly level area and have come into an open area. The main trail continues to your right, but there is a pack trail that goes to the left. You will want to note this spot for the return trip since your most natural course would be to

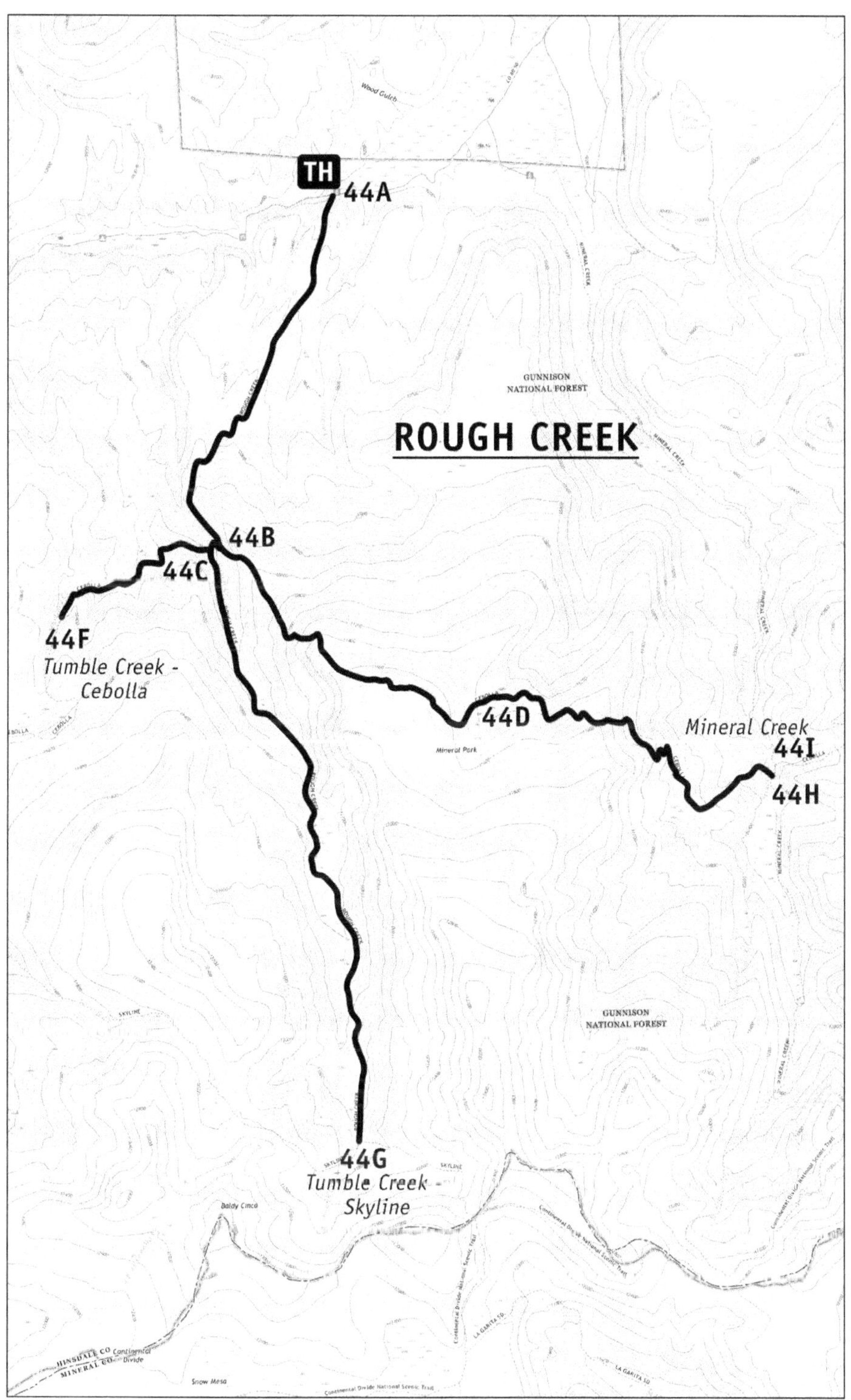

TH
44A
ROUGH CREEK
GUNNISON NATIONAL FOREST
44B
44C
44F
Tumble Creek - Cebolla
44D
Mineral Creek
44I
44H
44G
Tumble Creek - Skyline
GUNNISON NATIONAL FOREST

continue straight down the pack trail which will take you to the Cebolla Creek Road .25 miles east of where you parked.

Once you have passed this point, the trail rises moderately over the next 2 miles going through lightly wooded areas that allow for views behind you of the Cebolla Creek drainage and the Powderhorn Park area. While you are heading toward Rough Creek, you will have no indication of being near the creek or any other water source until you have gone 2.5 miles. At that point, you will begin to hear the creek well below you. The trail flattens out a bit and the sounds of the creek are more distinct. You can finally see the creek shortly before the crossing.

On your left will be a trail sign indicating the trail to Mineral Creek (**44B**). This is the Cebolla Trail heading east. The trail sign for the Cebolla Trail heading west (**44C**) is on the other side of the creek. Rough Creek carries quite a bit of water, and the preferred crossing strategy will depend on where you are during the season. Early in the season the flow is such that you may not wish to cross it without boots and poles. Even late in the season you may need stream crossing shoes. The most obvious crossing points will leave you upstream from where the trail hits the opposite bank, so bear right after crossing. You will see a wide exposed (and often muddy) trail leading you up from the creek, and you will see the trail sign for the Cebolla Trail (**44C**) at the top of this incline. To go west on the Cebolla Trail you should turn right and follow the trail directing you to Martinez Creek. While the trail sign does not indicate it, to continue up Rough Creek to the Skyline Trail intersection continue straight ahead.

The next section of the Rough Creek Trail leads you through a grove of aspen trees lasting for 1.5 miles. During the fall, the colors of the aspen combined with the sounds of the stream flow offer a feast for the senses. The trail is climbing moderately during this section and, even though the trail does not carry as much traffic as it did below, the trail is not difficult to follow. At the 4.5 mile point the foliage turns from aspen to evergreen, and the trail steepens as you begin your ascent into the upper Rough Creek drainage. From this point on, there are multiple streams feeding into Rough Creek from several directions. One of these streams commandeers the trail for a while during one of the steeper climbs.

At the 5-mile point, the trail opens up and you are in a valley containing the upper Rough Creek drainage for the remainder of the hike. The terrain consists of bushes and tall grass near the creek, with shorter grass further away, with forest on each side of the valley. The trail enters the valley on the west side of the creek, staying in the short grass section below the trees but well above the creek. The trail is not very well-defined, but there are several cairns and posts to assist you. However, after less than a mile in the valley the trail appears to go nowhere from a post that was supposed to show you the way. The trail, undefined at this point, descends and crosses the creek at a point where the creek is making several sharp curved turns. Above the creek on the east side, posts and a better-defined trail emerge. This is the most confusing portion of the hike.

Once you have found the trail on the east side of Rough Creek, the trail climbs gently through short grass for the next mile. The trail is fairly well-defined through this section, and there are cairns and posts to guide you as well. At the 7-mile point, the trail enters a small grove of trees in a marshy area which appears to be fire scarred. The trail disappears through this section but reappears once you have crossed a water-bearing ditch which can be stepped over in spots. The trail becomes steeper for the final mile. While it passes through short grass, it is not very well defined during this section. There are cairns and posts placed to guide you. In any event, you are passing into the uppermost portion of the Rough Creek drainage and there is little doubt as to which direction you must go. You will then see the back side of a trail sign ahead of you (**44G**). Once you can see the front of the trail sign, looking down valley, it indicates that the Rough Creek trailhead is in front of you, the trail leading to the Tumble Creek trailhead is to your left, and the trail leading you to a junction with the Colorado Trail is to your right. These are two portions of the Skyline Trail and are discussed under the section named Tumble Creek (Skyline).

Back at the first creek crossing (**44C**), the trail to Martinez Creek climbs several hundred feet through a wooded area before it descends the same elevation and emerges in an open area. This area is used as a hunters' camp in season, and the trail remains recognizable as it crosses this grassy area. After entering the woods, the trail climbs 500 feet parallel to Martinez Creek, crossing several small tributaries. After you have gone 1.5 miles from the Rough Creek crossing, you will cross Martinez Creek which is indicated by a (broken at this writing) trail sign (**44F**). Martinez Creek carries far less water than Rough Creek, and you should not need stream crossing shoes. For a description of the Cebolla Trail west of this point, refer to the Tumble Creek (Cebolla) section.

The Cebolla Trail heading toward Mineral Creek **(44B)** rises moderately to steeply as you leave the Rough Creek drainage and ascend to the divide leading to the Mineral Creek drainage. The trail has one point of possible confusion. At the point of the second switchback, which is not far from the first switchback, you enter a break between two groves of aspen trees and your natural inclination would be to go straight ahead, and indeed there is a trail continuing in that direction. Instead, you should turn to the right as indicated by a rock cairn and a post to go though the passage created by the removal of trees which may have been a mining or logging road. I call this passage the fairway. You will continue along the fairway for .75 miles, ascending moderately, before turning left at the first of seven remaining switchbacks. The climbing becomes more severe, despite the switchbacks, as you are climbing up the side of the Rough Creek / Mineral Creek divide. At the last switchback, you turn right into a wooded area comprised of spruce trees, most of which are dead, and the ascent becomes much more gradual. You continue east through this dead forest for .75 miles, until you reach a flat, lightly wooded area. There is a large cairn to guide you back into the forest upon your return. The trail is lightly defined along the top of this ridge at first and then disappears as you reach the first of a series of posts along the gradual descent. The first three posts are well placed, but the fourth post cannot be seen from the third as you enter a more heavily wooded area for a short distance. You then emerge into a large, open expanse known as Mineral Park **(44D)**. The posts lead along the north side of the park, near the edge of the woods as you descend toward a small creek which eventually joins Mineral Creek several miles below. By the time you have reached the eighth post, you can see the trail as it gains definition on the other side of the creek. Posts nine and ten are on the west side of the creek, while the eleventh and final post is on the east side of the creek, shortly before the trail enters the woods.

After crossing the creek, you ascend slightly through the woods. The trail had a great deal of recent stock traffic when I passed this way and the trail was quite muddy, even though there had not been recent rainfall. Between the mud and the dung, this was not a pleasant portion of the hike. However, this did not last long; the mud disappeared as I reached the top of the ridge separating the drainage of the stream that I recently crossed from the remainder of the Mineral Creek drainage. The trail continues through the woods and descends moderately to steeply for the next 2.5 miles toward Mineral Creek. There are two sections of this descent that contain switchbacks during the steeper portion of the decline. After the second set of switchbacks, the descent moderates and .75 miles later you reach Mineral Creek. Upon reaching Mineral Creek, you encounter the remnants of a bridge. As the bridge over Mineral Creek is unusable, you will need to cross the creek, which is several feet below each bank. The stream carries quite a bit of water well into the season. It is not recommended that you attempt to cross the creek early in the season, and you should plan on keeping your boots on as you cross later in the season, as the water may still be knee deep. On the opposite side of the creek there is a meadow with two trail signs. The sign on your right indicates that the East Mineral Creek Trail continues upstream along Mineral Creek, the Mineral Creek trailhead lies to your left, and the route to Rough Creek is from whence you came (**44H**). The trail sign on your left indicates that the East Mineral Creek Trail continues upstream along Mineral Creek, the Mineral Creek trailhead lies to your left, and the route to Spring Creek, continuing along the Cebolla Trail, is straight ahead (**44I**). That portion of the Cebolla Trail is not covered in this book. The Mineral Creek Trail is discussed in the section under that name.

RATING: If you use the Rough Creek crossing (**44B**) as your turn-around point, your round-trip distance is 6 miles, and your elevation gain is 800 feet. This section is suitable for well acclimated beginners. Should you continue up Rough Creek to its intersection with the Skyline Trail (**44G**), the round-trip distance is 16 miles, and the elevation gain is 2,500 feet. Due to the distance and the navigation issues discussed above, this should only be undertaken by experienced hikers. Should your destination be Martinez Creek (**44F**), your round-trip distance is 9 miles, and your elevation gain is 1,300 feet. This would be suitable for any intermediate hiker. Should you travel to Mineral Park (**44D**), your round-trip distance is 13 miles and your elevation gain is 2,400 feet. This should only be undertaken by experienced hikers. A trip beyond Mineral Park would be beyond the limits of a day hike, unless it were taken as part of a multi-day hike, or as a thru-hike beginning at the Rough Creek trailhead and ending at the Mineral Creek trailhead. Such a thru-hike would cover 15 miles and gain 2,400 feet before descending 2,500 feet. This should be reserved for experienced hikers.

MINERAL CREEK

Quad: Mineral Mountain, Baldy Cinco

DRIVING INSTRUCTIONS: Drive south from Lake City on CO SH 149. Continue about 10 miles to the Cebolla Creek Rd (also known as the Deer Lakes Rd, CR 50, and FSR 788), past MP 63. Take a left on this road and continue 11.2 miles where a sign indicates the road to the Mineral Creek trailhead. Turn right, and you will pass through the first of two gates which are generally closed. The trailhead is .5 miles from the point you have left the Cebolla Creek Road. There is ample parking at the trailhead, which is well marked. Trailhead elevation - 9,100 feet.

THE HIKE: The Mineral Creek Trail follows Mineral Creek southward for 5 miles, to where it intersects the Cebolla Trail. It continues southward an additional mile, where the trail divides. Both the East Mineral Creek Trail and Mineral Creek Trail intersect the Colorado Trail after an additional hike of 2.5 miles. That portion of the Mineral Creek Trail north of the intersection with the Cebolla Trail is not covered in this book. The Mineral Creek Trail receives a fair amount of horse traffic, but little foot traffic. This is a shame because it is a lovely hike, and not a particularly difficult one. This trail appears on both the La Garita, Cochetopa Hills *Trails Illustrated* map and on the quads.

Leaving the trailhead (**45A**), you intersect a cross trail almost immediately. Turn left and proceed east. There are several exits off of the main trail, some leading to places where horses are unloaded. On your way back, the second off-ramp will lead you to the trailhead and back to your car.

After .25 miles ascending gently through a wooded area, you encounter a gate leading you onto private land. A map of the La Garita Wilderness stands next to the gate. After passing through the gate, you descend gently over the next .5 miles where you find a second gate.

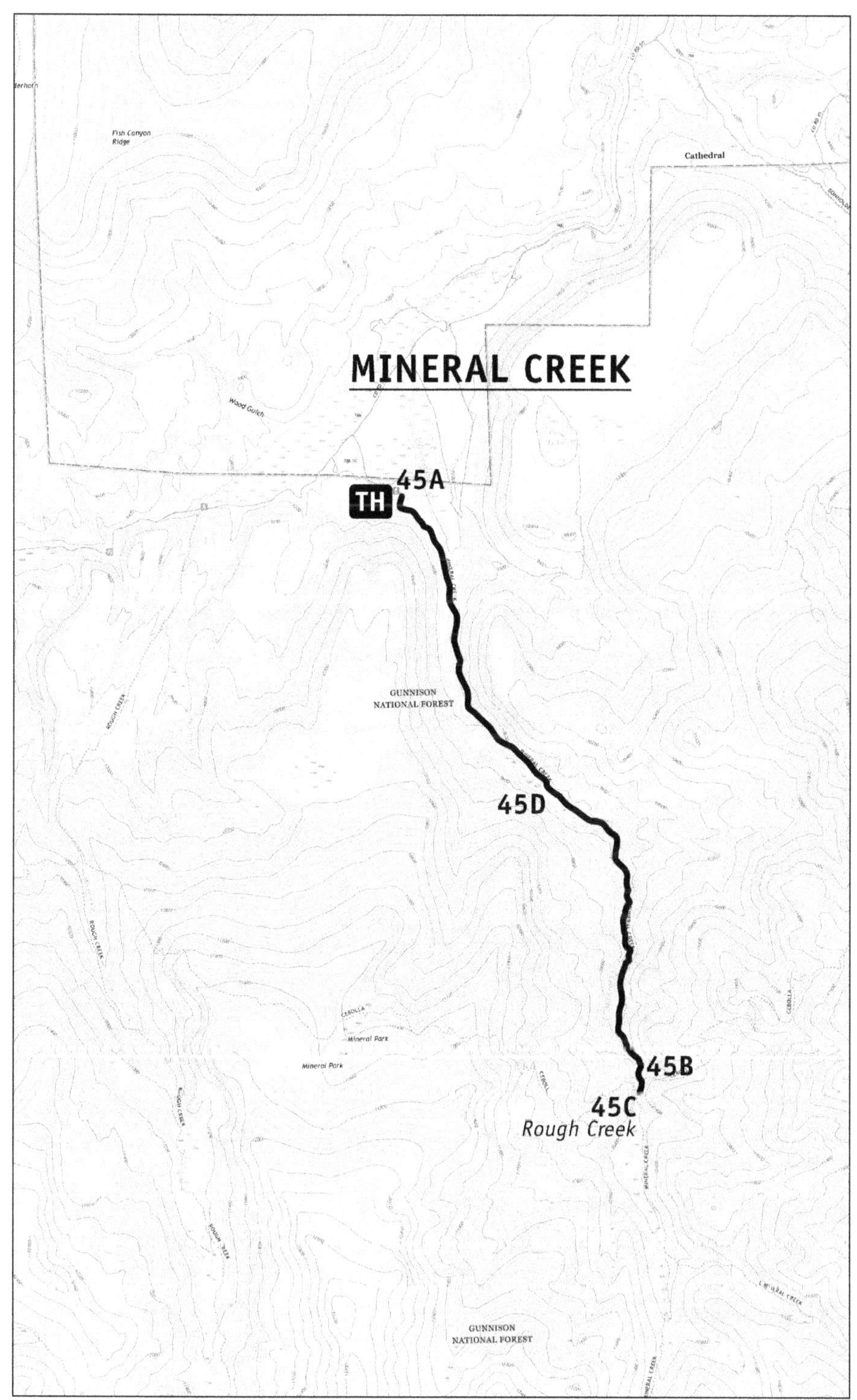

MINERAL CREEK
TH
45A
45D
45B
45C
Rough Creek
GUNNISON NATIONAL FOREST
GUNNISON NATIONAL FOREST
Fish Canyon Ridge
Wood Gulch
Cathedral
Mineral Park

This marks the end of your journey through private land with a sign indicating the boundary of the La Garita Wilderness. The next portion of the trail is a gentle ascent, near Mineral Creek in spots, primarily in open area. There are several places over the next several miles where the trail divides. In a couple of instances, the lesser traveled trail leads to a campsite, and in another the two trails merge after a short distance. Your rule of thumb in these situations should be to follow the more heavily traveled trail. If you find yourself in a campsite with no obvious way out, go back and try the other fork.

At the 2-mile point you reach the first two of several stream crossings. These two are side streams flowing into Mineral Creek and you encounter them back-to-back. Neither requires stream crossing shoes later in the season. At the 2.5 mile point you reach Mineral Creek (**45D**), where stream crossing shoes are usually helpful. While you cross water several times after crossing Mineral Creek, you should not need stream crossing shoes again. This would be a logical turnaround point for any beginners in the group.

After crossing to the east side of Mineral Creek, the ascent remains gradual as you pass through an open area of short grass, sage, and bushes. This continues for .5 miles where you enter forested areas for the duration of the trail until you reach the Cebolla Trail intersection. While in the forest, you remain near Mineral Creek and there are several campsites nearby. The trail steepens, but never becomes more than a moderate climb.

At the 4.5 mile point there is a series of large rock monoliths to your left, several of which are close to the trail. I call these the pinnacles. At the 5-mile point you enter an open area. At the lower end of the open area there is a trail sign (**45B**) indicating the first intersection with the Cebolla Trail, leading to the east. The sign indicates this is the trail toward Spring Creek. This trail is seldom used, although the beginning portion is clear enough to see where you enter the trees. That portion of the Cebolla Trail heading east from the Mineral Creek Trail into Saguache County is not covered in this book.

Several hundred yards from the first junction with the Cebolla Trail, you encounter a second trail sign (**45C**). This is the junction with the Cebolla Trail heading west. The sign indicates the direction to take to Rough Creek. As this trail junction is in a grassy area, the Cebolla Trail is overgrown. Heading back to the northwest, there are the remnants of a bridge crossing Mineral Creek several feet above the creek. The Cebolla Trail is on the other side of the bridge, leading up a ridge, but it is not visible from the east side of Mineral Creek. I was unable to find the trail leading to Rough Creek on my first several visits to this point, and anyone wanting to take the Cebolla Trail should approach it from the Rough Creek side, heading east. As the bridge over Mineral Creek is unusable, you will need to cross the creek, which is several feet below each bank. The stream carries quite a bit of water well into the season. It is not recommended that you attempt to cross the creek early in the season, and you should plan on keeping your boots on as you cross later in the season, as the water may still be knee deep. That portion of the Cebolla Trail heading west from the Mineral Creek Trail (**45C**) is covered in the section for Rough Creek.

RATING: A hike to the first crossing of Mineral Creek is a 5-mile round trip and gains 300 feet. It is suitable for beginning hikers. A round trip to the junction with the Cebolla Trail covers 10 miles and gains 1,200 feet. This is suitable for intermediate hikers.

Winter in Hinsdale County

Katherine Heidt

POWDERHORN PARK

Quad: Mineral Mountain, Cannibal Plateau

DRIVING INSTRUCTIONS: Drive south from Lake City on CO SH 149. Continue about 10 miles to the Cebolla Creek Rd (also known as the Deer Lakes Rd, CR 50, and FSR 788), past MP 63. Take a left on this road and continue 11.7 miles to the Powderhorn Park trailhead (**46A**), which is marked by a sign on the left side of the road. Ample parking is available in a lot on the right-hand side of the road, just after you cross Mineral Creek. Trailhead elevation - 9,100 feet.

THE HIKE: This trail travels through some pretty country on the way up the east side of Calf Creek Plateau. As much of the area is open, the views are such that this is a journey hike rather than a destination hike. Powderhorn Park is a large open area surrounded on all sides by forest. The Powderhorn Park Trail connects with both the East Fork of the Powderhorn Creek Trail and the North Calf Creek Trail. It is essentially a dry hike, and you should take extra water. The trail doesn't get much foot traffic but gets a fair amount of horse traffic. This trail appears both on the La Garita, Cochetopa Hills *Trails Illustrated* map and on the quads.

You begin this trail on private land and follow a double track passing through a gate which is usually kept closed, then crossing Cebolla Creek over a vehicle bridge. After several hundred yards, the double track turns right through another closed gate, while the trail veers to the left. A trail sign indicates the single track as the trail you should follow. You begin a moderate climb, passing through an open spot in a fence to continue until you pass through another gate, which is also usually kept closed. At this point you pass from private land into the Powderhorn Wilderness. The trail continues climbing moderately through the open area and after nearly a mile you turn left sharply and begin climbing a ridge. Once on the top of the ridge, you leave all vestiges of private land and ranching behind. The trail cuts to the right and maintains elevation for several hundred yards until a trail sign indicates that your trail turns to the left. For the next mile, you have a gradual to moderate ascent through mostly open areas with views to the left of the Rough Creek drainage and the range that includes Baldy Cinco. At the 2-mile point, you enter an aspen forest, and the ascent becomes more gradual. While in the aspen forest, you will cross a small stream, which will be your last source of water on this trail. This stream is small and not a problem to cross.

After a mile in the aspen forest, you emerge into an open area and continue a gentle climb, alternating between open and wooded areas until you reach a point where the trail begins to get rockier, and you pass through a fence. The trail passes next to a large rock monolith and curves around to the right, then you begin a short, steep climb to the rim of the plateau and the southeast entrance to Powderhorn Park. This is the most common turnaround point, but two trails lead onward from this point. The trail sign **(46B)** at the entrance to Powderhorn Park indicates that to the right is the trail to the East Fork of the Powderhorn River and that it leads to Robbers Roost. The trail sign indicates the way you just came from Cebolla Creek and the trailhead. It does not indicate that if you continue straight ahead, you will be on the North Calf Creek Trail.

Should you wish to continue through Powderhorn Park to Robbers Roost, the trail will take you north. The trail through Powderhorn Park consists of short grass and some bushes which have largely overtaken the trail. This is no real cause of concern, as hiking over the short grass is in some ways preferable to hiking in a rutted trail. Occasionally the trail tries to appear, but it is difficult at times to tell what is trail, and what is erosion. Never mind, just continue north through Powderhorn Park, staying on the left side of the fairway. Powderhorn Park is fairly flat, but you will be gaining elevation to a slight degree until you reach the north end of the park. At the high point, you have a small window to view the West Elk Range, many miles to the north.

At the north end of the park, bear to the left and follow the drainage leaving the park which is the East Fork of Powderhorn Creek. The trail will emerge as you leave the park, and as you descend into an open area there is also a post marking your way. The trail begins to fade as you

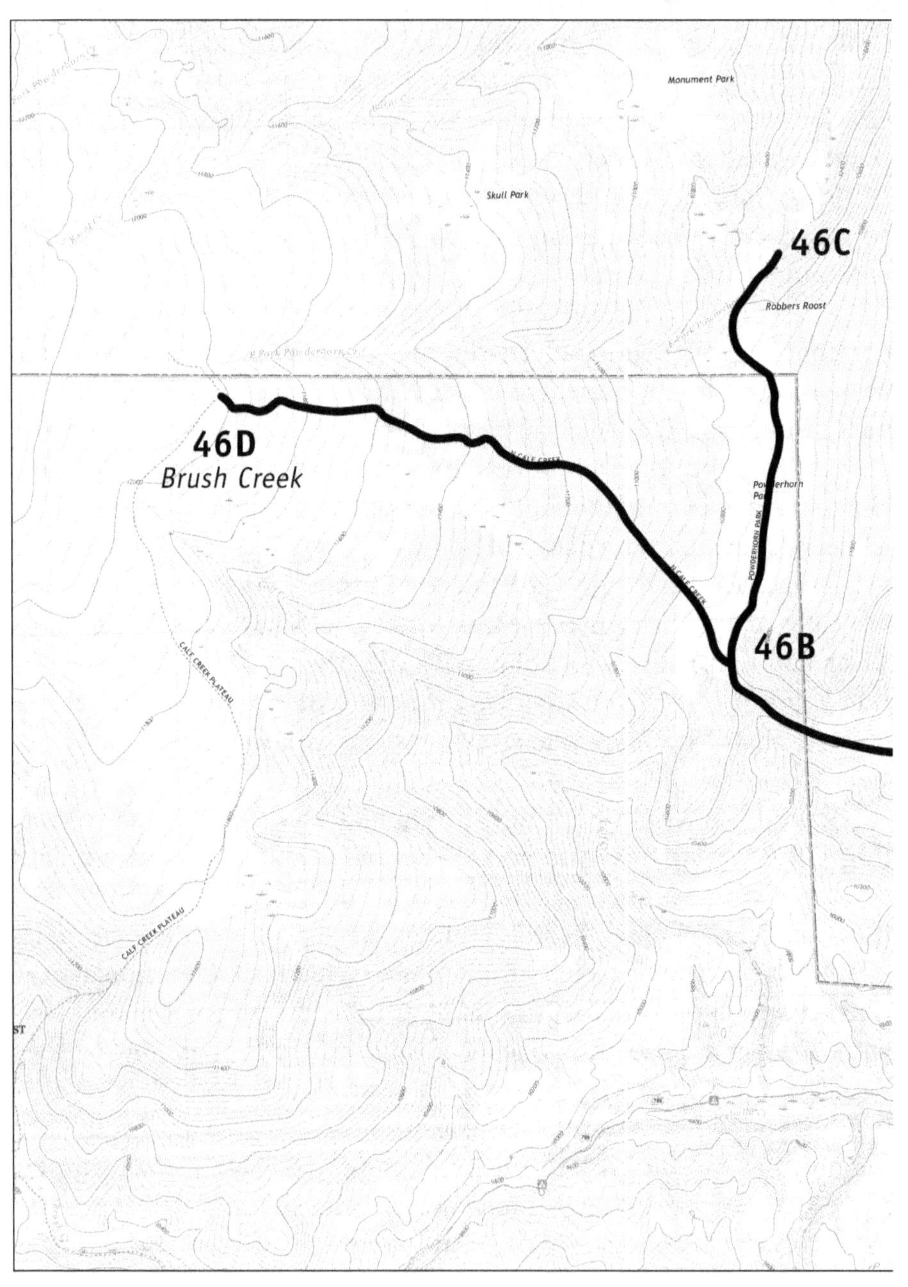
Monument Park
Skull Park
46C
Robbers Roost
46D
Brush Creek
Powderhorn Park
POWDERHORN PARK
46B
CALF CREEK PLATEAU
CALF CREEK PLATEAU

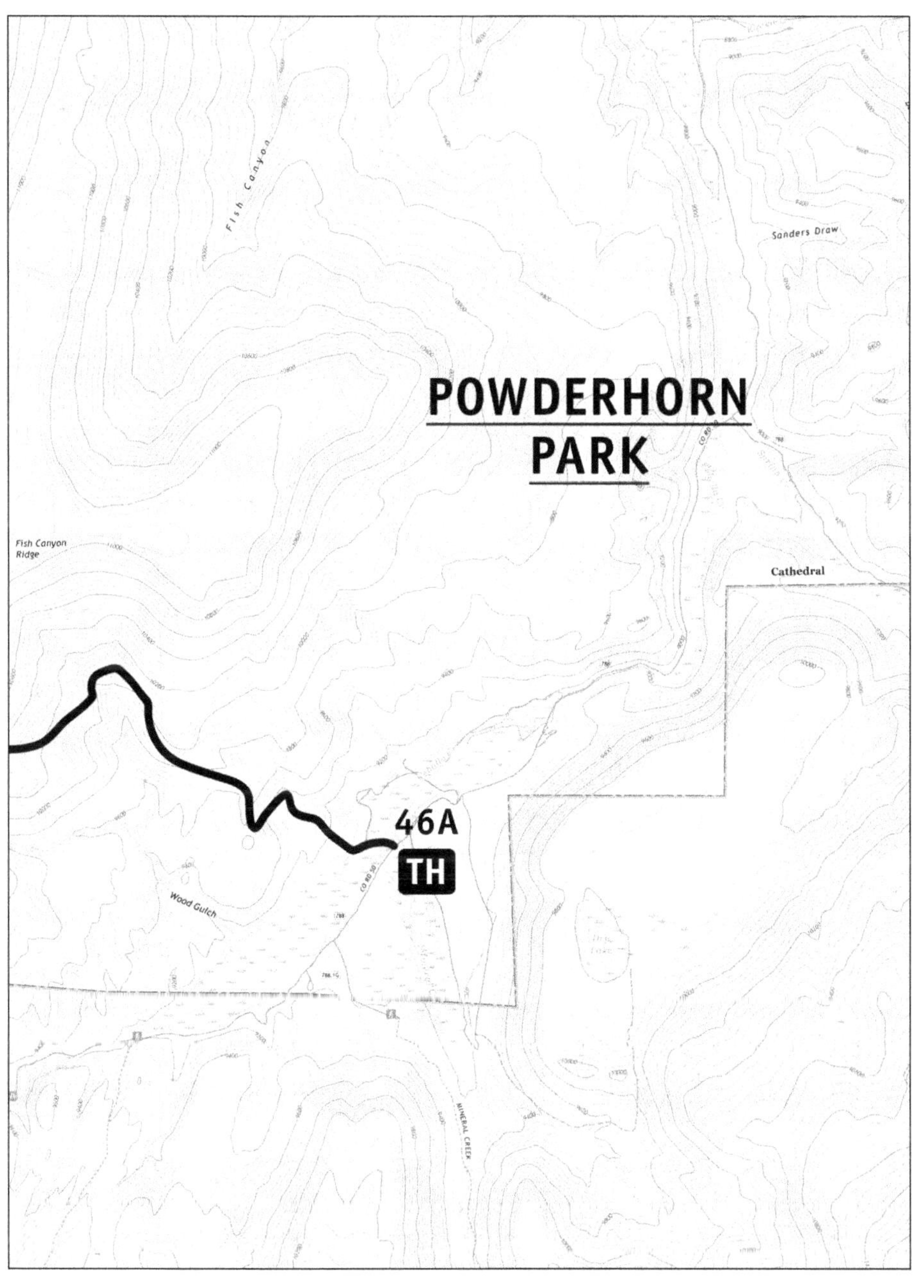

Fish Canyon
Sanders Draw
POWDERHORN
PARK
Fish Canyon
Ridge
Cathedral
Wood Gulch
46A
TH
MINERAL CREEK

approach the river and is completely obliterated by the time you enter the forest. While both the *Trails Illustrated* map and the quad indicate that this trail continues along the East Fork to its trailhead at the end of Ten Mile Springs Road, there are several miles where you would be hard pressed to find a trail. This is also true should you begin this trail from the East Fork trailhead at Ten Mile Springs. Just over 2 miles from that trailhead, the trail disappears. To navigate the entire East Fork trail, you should be prepared for some serious bushwhacking and your trail mates won't let you plan any more hikes.

At about the time you last see the trail after leaving the Powderhorn Park, you can see a small cabin across the stream which was once used in ranching operations. To reach this cabin, which isn't particularly noteworthy, you need to cross the stream which is overgrown by bushes on both sides. Sight of the cabin is enough to claim you've covered this trail to its logical conclusion (**46C**). Looking back up toward Powderhorn Park, you see some rock outcroppings with a flat lookout area on top. This is what I believe is called Robber's Roost, and I don't know the significance behind the name.

Returning to the trail sign at the southeast entrance to Powderhorn Park (**46B**), the North Calf Creek Trail leads to the northwest and is visible throughout the park amid the tall grass. The lower portion of the North Calf Creek Trail receives a fair amount of horse traffic, so the trail is not difficult to follow for the next 2 miles until you reach a hunting campsite. Beyond that it is quite difficult to follow, but more on that later. Beginning at the trail sign, the trail remains in Powderhorn Park for .5 miles before entering a corridor containing baby aspen with mature aspen forest on either side. The trail ascends gradually through this area, and the corridor gives way to a more traditional trail through a forest. You remain in the forest for over a mile, and the forest leads to several small clearings prior to emerging in a large bushy open area as you continue to ascend Calf Creek Plateau. Hiking this trail several years earlier, I found a series of posts guiding me across Calf Creek Plateau to the point where a trail sign marked the intersection with the Calf Creek Plateau Trail (**46D**), which is discussed under the section for Brush Creek. At my last two visits to this area, I found only two standing posts and I was unable to find the trail sign marking the junction of these two trails. The trail is not evident as you cross Calf Creek Plateau. Finding your way back to the trailhead can be a challenge, unless you mark the spot where you have emerged from the woods. I was unable to do so on my most recent trip and I'll describe an alternate return route.

As you emerge from the woods onto the upper portion of Calf Creek Plateau, there is a ditch to your right. This marks the headwaters of the East Fork Powderhorn Creek. While the North Calf Creek Trail passes to the south of this creek, there is a cairn and a trail on the north side of the creek. By descending this ditch, which is only lightly wooded, you can reach the point below Robber's Roost where you intersect the East Fork Trail, just north of Powderhorn Park. Alternatively, you can follow the ditch for a mile and turn to the right, making your way through the woods until you reach Powderhorn Park (which is big enough to be difficult to miss). In any event, the North Calf Creek Trail is difficult to follow, and any hiker should be prepared to find himself off-trail at some point. I've hiked this trail twice and have had difficulty both times.

From the intersection of the Calf Creek Plateau Trail and the North Calf Creek Trail (**46D**), the maps indicate that the North Calf Creek Trail continues to the northwest for another 3 miles before turning to the southwest as it makes a descent to Devil's Lake. There is no current evidence of this trail nor are there any posts to guide you. A determined hiker with compass skills or a GPS device should be able to find the lake as the terrain across Calf Creek Plateau is not difficult. The trail to Devil's Lake is evident in a rocky area northeast of the lake. However, a trip to Devil's Lake from Powderhorn Park would be a multi-day hike and won't be further discussed in this book. For hikers wishing to visit Devil's Lake, better routes exist and are discussed in the sections for Brush Creek, Devil's Creek and Powderhorn Lakes.

RATING: The trail to the entrance of Powderhorn Park (**46B**) and back covers 8 miles and gains 1,900 feet. It is suitable for any intermediate hiker. To continue to the cabin below Robbers Roost (**46C**) adds another 5 miles to this hike with little net change in elevation. The length of that trail could tax an intermediate hiker, but the additional miles are over mostly easy terrain. A hike to the intersection of the North Calf Creek Trail and the Calf Creek Plateau Trail (**46D**) is a 16-mile round trip gaining 2,900 feet. It should be attempted only by experienced hikers who are fully aware of the navigational challenges.

South from Handies Peak

Katherine Heidt

Trailheads Located South of Spring Creek Pass via CO SH 149

TRAILHEADS LOCATED SOUTH OF
SPRING CREEK PASS VIA CO SH 149

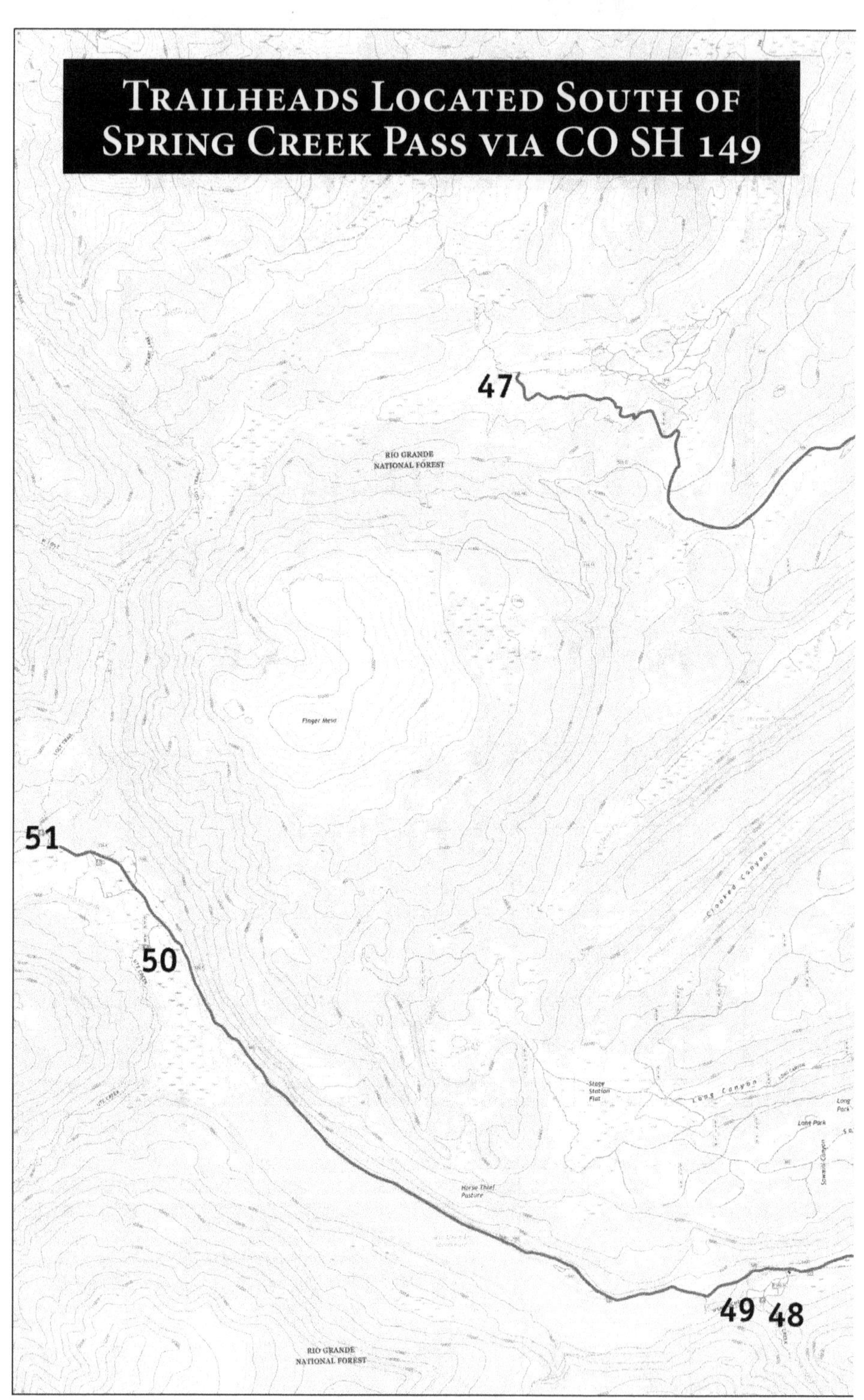

47
RIO GRANDE
NATIONAL FOREST
Finger Mesa
51
50
Horse Thief
Pasture
Stage
Station
Flat
RIO GRANDE
NATIONAL FOREST
49 48

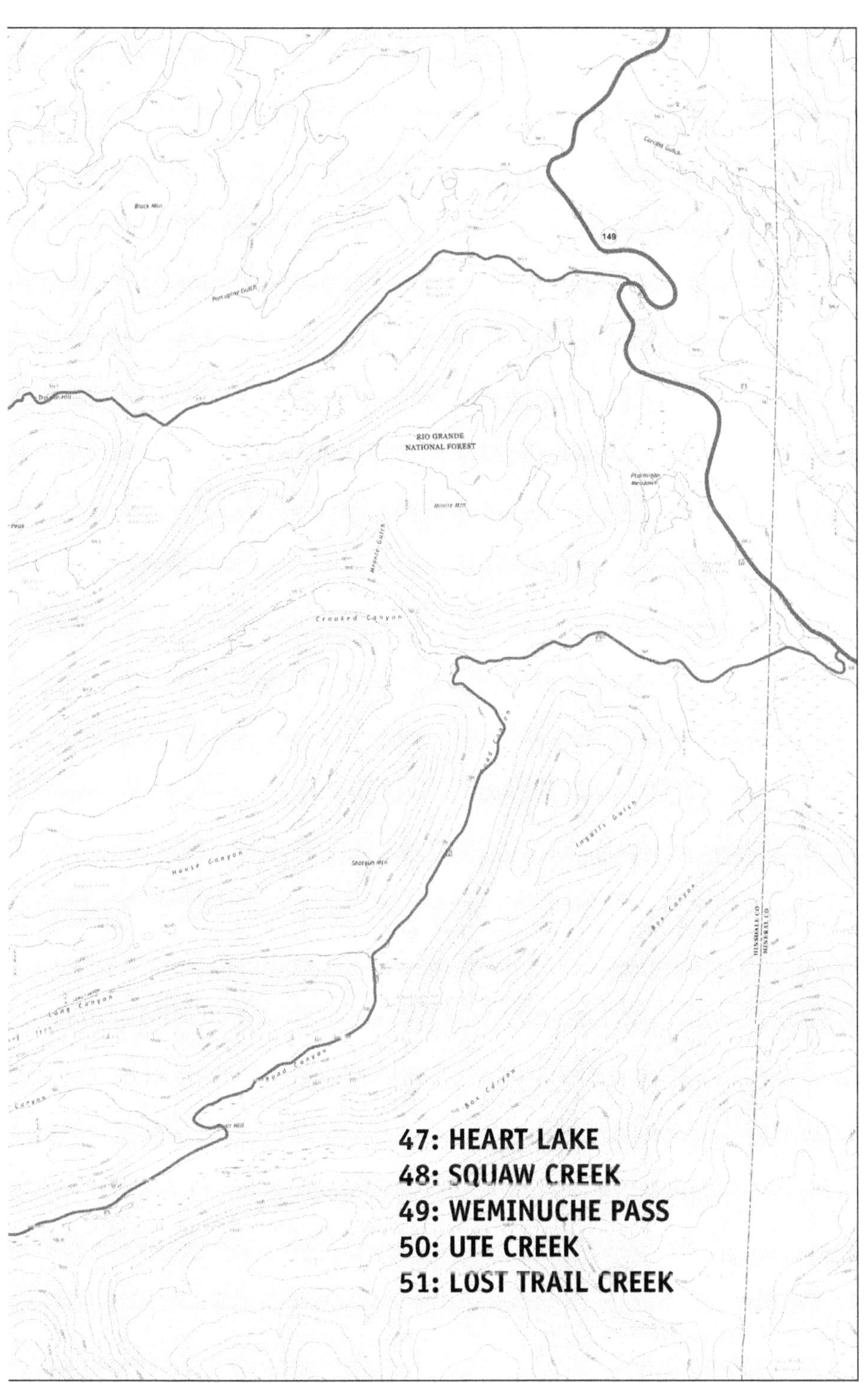

47: HEART LAKE
48: SQUAW CREEK
49: WEMINUCHE PASS
50: UTE CREEK
51: LOST TRAIL CREEK

HEART LAKE

Quad: Finger Mesa

DRIVING INSTRUCTIONS: Drive south from Lake City on CO SH 149. Continue 25 miles to the South Clear Creek Road (FSR 515), which is past MP 46. Turn right and go 4.1 miles to where FSR 515 ends and take a right turn onto FSR 516. Take FSR 516 for 3.9 miles to where it intersects with a 4WD road leading to your left (FSR 518). Take this road for 1.7 miles to where it intersects with another 4WD road (unmarked). Take a left and this road ends 300 yards later. The trailhead is behind a "Road Closed" sign **(47A)**. There is parking for several vehicles at the trailhead. Except for the last turn, there is signage at each intersection indicating the direction to Heart Lake or the Heart Lake Road. Arriving at the trailhead is the most complicated part of this hike. Trailhead elevation - 10,500 feet.

THE HIKE: The Heart Lake Trail travels its first 3 miles through a wide, flat valley. The first half of the trip through the valley is littered with rocks and boulders, while the second half is virtually rock free. There is a 300-foot elevation gain over the first 3 miles of this trail as it passes through the valley. Once it leaves the valley, the trail gains elevation quite rapidly, gaining 900 feet over the 1.5 miles from the valley to Heart Lake. This trail appears on both the *Trails Illustrated* map and on the quad.

The trail follows a double track for much of its distance through the valley, although with the number of boulders present in the lower half of the valley, it is easy to see why the Forest Service closed this trail to vehicular traffic. There are several single-track trails running parallel to the double-track trail. Some of these trails rejoin the double-track trail and some disappear. While the trail isn't hard to follow, staying on it isn't imperative as the grass on the floor of the valley isn't tall and the

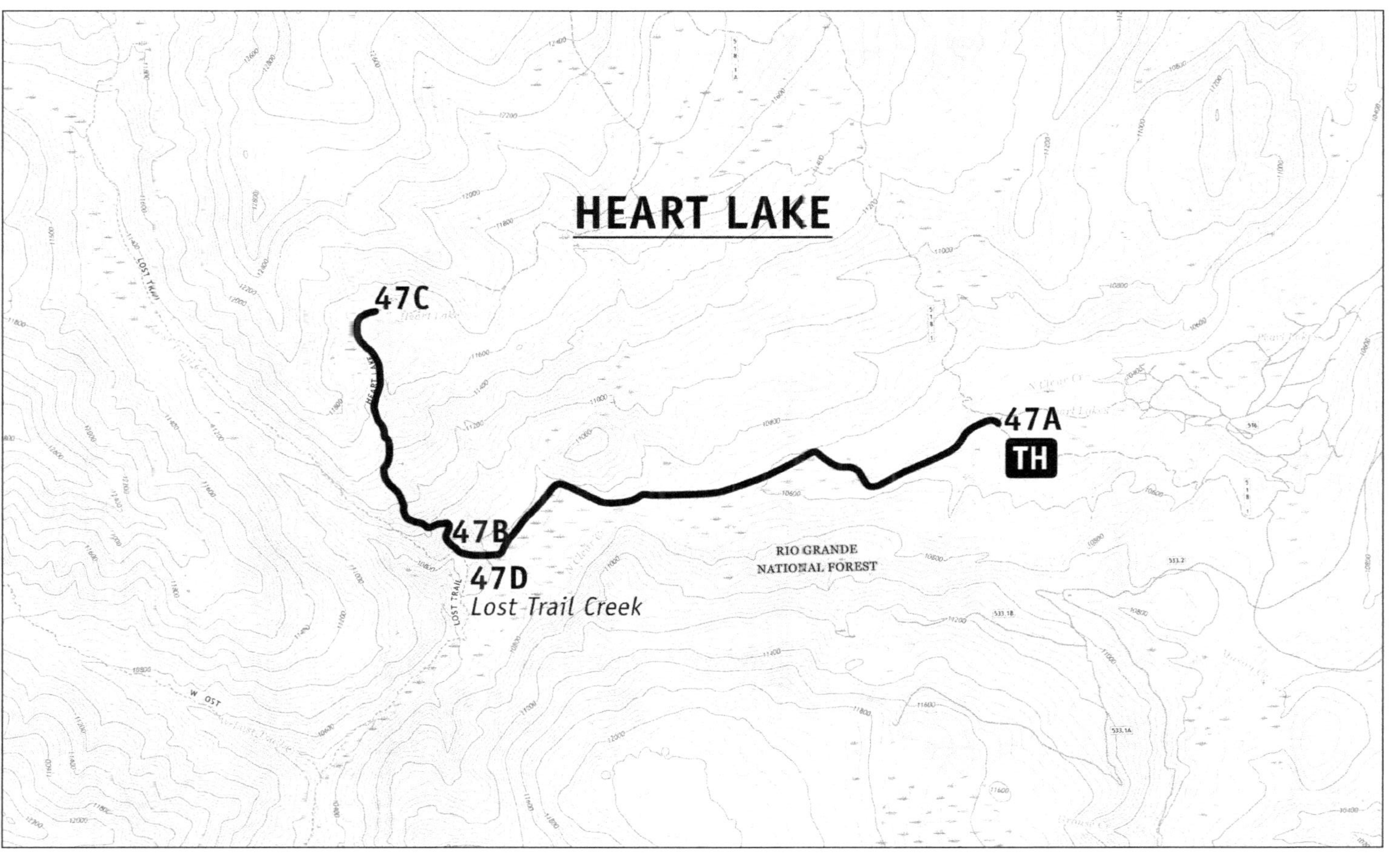
HEART LAKE
47C
47A
TH
47B
47D
Lost Trail Creek
RIO GRANDE
NATIONAL FOREST
LOST TRAIL
W OST

exit from the valley at the west end is obvious. There are several water crossings which should not be an issue late in the season but might require water crossing shoes early in the season. The trail stays to the north side of the valley throughout, and at the 2-mile point it nearly touches the valley wall.

As you approach the 3-mile point, you will see fencing ahead. There is both a rail fence and a barbed wire fence behind it. Follow the fencing, staying to the right and after passing a post, you will encounter a road (**47D**). This is the Lost Trail Creek Trail, which leads to Carson Saddle on the Continental Divide. The Lost Trail Creek Trail is covered in the section under that name. Take a right turn on the Lost Trail Creek Trail, which doubles as the Heart Lake Trail for .25 miles; after climbing through some trees, you will enter an open area containing two trail signs. The left-hand trail (FSR 821) will take you to Carson Saddle via the Lost Trail Creek Trail. The right-hand trail (FSR 823) takes you to Heart Lake (**47B**).

The trail begins to climb moderately to steeply over the next 1.5 miles through mostly wooded areas as you climb toward Heart Lake. Several places along the way you see breaks in the trees where you think a lake should be. Alas, it's just a clearing. Each time you think you've reached your top elevation and you level out for a short while you start to climb again. Finally, you reach Heart Lake (**47C**), which has good campsites, and is one of the prettier lakes in the area. It would have been even prettier before the spruce trees succumbed to the pine mountain beetles' appetite. To state the obvious, it is heart shaped. There is a ridge above it and trees on two sides.

RATING: The round trip to Heart Lake (**47C**) covers 9 miles and climbs 1,200 feet. The first portion, through the valley, is suitable for beginners. The second section, climbing up to Heart Lake, is a bit challenging, but should be achievable by intermediate hikers as the trail is easy to follow and there are no terrain issues.

SQUAW CREEK

Quad: Little Squaw Creek, Weminuche Pass

DRIVING INSTRUCTIONS: Drive south from Lake City on CO SH 149. Continue 30 miles to the Rio Grande Reservoir Road (FSR 520), which is past MP 42. Turn right and go 11.5 miles into the Thirty Mile Campground. Parking for backpackers is marked within the campground and the trailheads for both the Squaw Creek Trail and the Weminuche Pass Trail are south of the parking area (**48A**). Trailhead elevation - 9,400 feet.

THE HIKE: The Squaw Creek Trail follows Squaw Creek for over 8 miles to the Continental Divide and connects with several trails on the west side. Unless you are embarking on a multi-day backpacking trip, a day hike along Squaw Creek has no particular destination, but the pleasures of the journey are many. Squaw Creek ascends gently toward the divide and passes through an open valley with aspen trees on either side, making this an ideal fall hike. This would be a good hike to take a visitor on during the fall as the foliage can be seen without substantial elevation gains. This trail appears on both the Weminuche Wilderness *Trails Illustrated* map and on the quads.

From the trailhead (**48A**), the trail ascends gently to moderately for .25 miles then descends a similar amount until you reach Squaw Creek which you cross over a sturdy bridge. To your left during this first .5 miles, you can see the remnants of the Papoose Creek fire (2013) which consumed over 100,000 acres. Although the Squaw Creek Trail is adjacent to the burned area, the area through which you will hike was untouched by the Papoose Creek fire.

After crossing the bridge at the .5-miles mark, you enter the Weminuche Wilderness, and the trail ascends gently to moderately over the next half mile as Squaw Creek passes through a rocky canyon. At

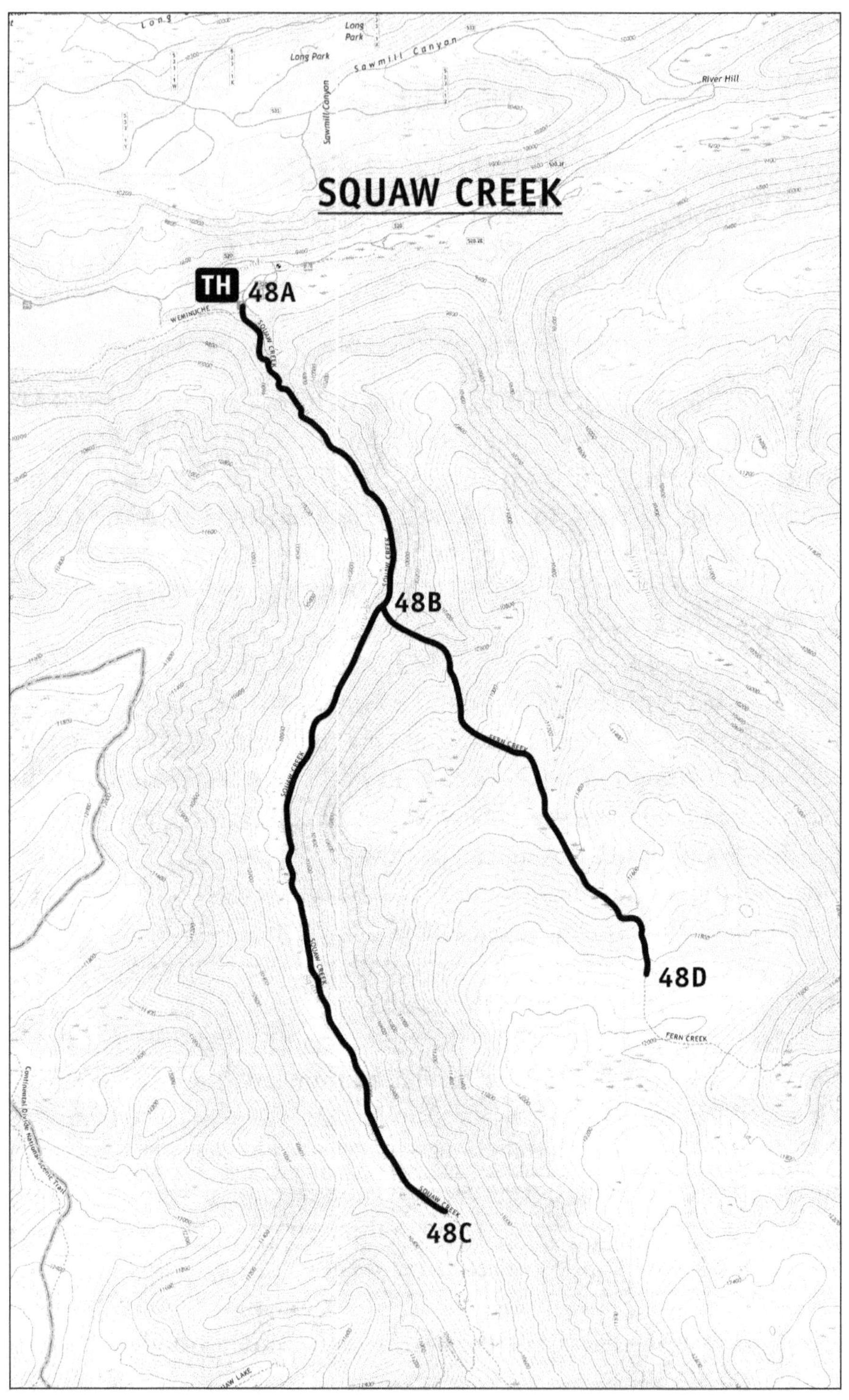

SQUAW CREEK
TH 48A
48B
48C
48D
Long Park
Long Park
Sawmill Canyon
River Hill
WEMINUCHE
SQUAW CREEK
FERN CREEK
FERN CREEK
Continental Divide National Scenic Trail
SQUAW LAKE

the 1-mile mark the canyon widens and the climb becomes much gentler. For the next several miles, you will not be gaining much elevation as you follow the creek through an ever-widening drainage area. A bit past the 2-mile point there is a side trail to your left **(48B)**. This is not well marked and is just past the point where you cross over a side creek which goes under the trail through a culvert. More on this connecting trail, called the Fern Creek Trail later. As the canyon widens, there are several small ponds throughout the area, and moose can occasionally be found. From the 1-mile point onward you are in the open, passing below the trees, which are predominantly aspen from mile 1 to mile 4, and beetle killed spruce thereafter. As stated earlier, there is no logical turnaround point. I have gone 5 miles along the creek before returning **(48C)**.

The trail leading to your left at the 2-mile point is called the Fern Creek Trail **(48B)** and it follows a side stream for only a short while before turning to the right and climbing up the ridge that follows the eastern side of the Squaw Creek Valley. This trail climbs through lightly wooded areas over the next 2 miles with a moderate to steep elevation gain. This trail gets a fair amount of use during hunting season, but little use otherwise. In any case, it is not difficult to follow for several miles. At the 2-mile point (after leaving the main trail), this trail emerges from the woods and descends a few feet onto a small flat, open area. The trail climbs more gradually from this point forward, as you are approaching the top of the ridge. As you continue to climb, you pass through lightly wooded areas until you reach a large open area at the top of the ridge. The trail continues through this open area, crosses water once, and .25 miles later the trail divides **(48D)**. You are 2.5 miles from the original trail intersection at this point. The quad indicates that the right fork, called the Fern Creek Cutoff, leads back to the Squaw Creek trail 4 miles from the trailhead, however this trail does not appear on the Weminuche Wilderness *Trails Illustrated* map. The trail is very faint and, although I followed it for a while, I can't vouch that it is used enough to be visible as it returns to the Squaw Creek Trail. I found the point where the Fern Creek Cutoff intersects the Squaw Creek Trail shortly after crossing a creek at the 4-mile point on the Squaw Creek Trail. There is a small cairn to the left of the trail and the Fern Creek Cutoff can be seen faintly as it climbs a hill to the left. Returning to the trail fork of the Fern Creek Trail and the Fern Creek

Cutoff (**48D**), the quad indicates that the left fork, constituting the Fern Creek Trail continues across the top of the ridge, past several lakes and over the Continental Divide. Again, the trail is not well defined beyond the fork, and I did not continue very far beyond that point. The fork in the trails is a logical turnaround point as you've reached the top of the ridge. The return trip back to Squaw Creek offers views of the other side of the Squaw Creek Valley as well as the mountains on the north side of Rio Grande Reservoir.

RATING: The first 5 miles of the Squaw Creek Trail (**48C**) only gains 800 feet, is well marked, and can be hiked by beginning hikers. A trip up the Squaw Creek Trail, up the Fern Creek Trail to the intersection with the Fern Creek Cutoff (**48D**) is a 9-mile round trip, gaining 2,400 feet, and should be considered an intermediate hike.

Spring in Hinsdale County

Katherine Heidt

WEMINUCHE PASS

Quad: Little Squaw Creek, Weminuche Pass

DRIVING INSTRUCTIONS: Drive south from Lake City on CO SH 149. Continue about 30 miles to the Rio Grande Reservoir Road (FSR 520), which is past MP 42. Turn right and go 11.5 miles into the Thirty Mile Campground. Parking for backpackers is marked within the campground and the trailhead for both the Squaw Creek Trail and the Weminuche Pass Trail is south of the parking area (**49A**). Trailhead elevation - 9,400 feet.

THE HIKE: The Weminuche Pass Trail parallels the south shore of the Rio Grande Reservoir before turning south along Weminuche Creek, following the creek to the top of Weminuche Pass, which is a low elevation crossing of the Continental Divide. From there it connects with several trails on the west side of the divide, which can be utilized for a multi-day trip. The hike to the top of Weminuche Pass, a 11 mile round trip, is more than adequate for a day hike. This is a popular trail for hunters, and you will likely have company if you hike this trail during hunting season. This trail appears on both the Weminuche Wilderness *Trails Illustrated* map and on the quads.

Leaving the trailhead (**49A**), you will gain little net elevation for the first mile as you pass the dam and service buildings for the Rio Grande Reservoir and hike underneath a powerline. This is hardly a wilderness experience, but after a mile you enter the Weminuche Wilderness. You continue alongside the reservoir and cross a small stream to begin a gradual ascent for the next mile until you turn south away from the reservoir. Shortly after turning south, you descend and cross Weminuche Creek over a sturdy bridge. You then continue along the west side of Weminuche Creek climbing moderately. After a couple of switchbacks, the ascent becomes more gradual as you leave the canyon formed by

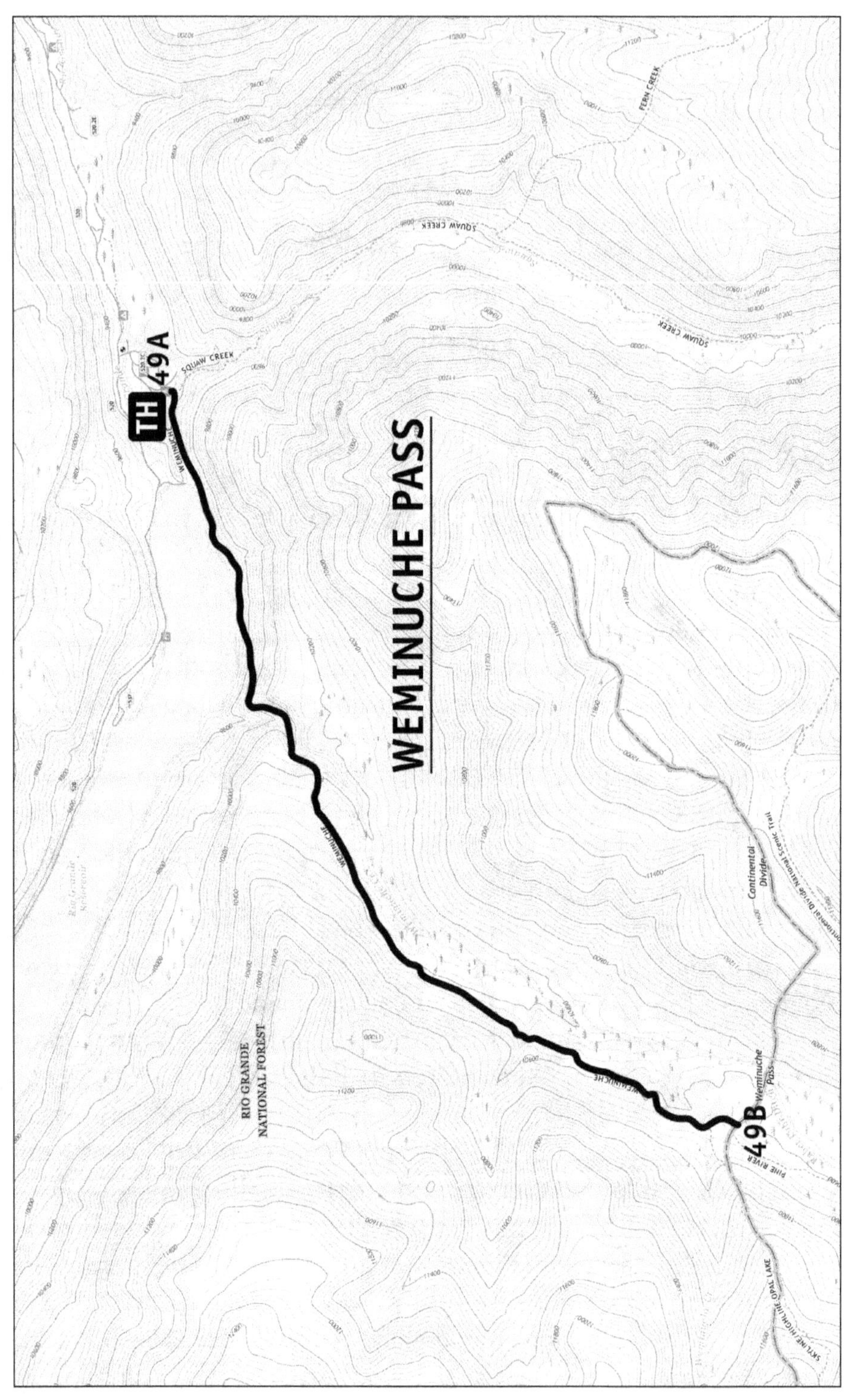

WEMINUCHE PASS
TH
49A
49B
SQUAW CREEK
FERN CREEK
SQUAW CREEK
RIO GRANDE
NATIONAL FOREST
Continental Divide
Weminuche Pass
PINE RIVER

Weminuche Creek and gain some distance from the creek. The terrain is mostly open from this point on, with a few forested areas from time to time. The Weminuche Creek drainage is wide and bowl-like, but it may not seem like it because the climb is so gradual. There are several stream crossings along the way, but only two could present a problem early in the season. Both have log crossings. The first is 4.5 miles from the trailhead and the second is immediately before you reach the Continental Divide at Weminuche Pass. The ascent is so gradual during the upper portion of the trail that it hardly seems appropriate to call the high point a pass. You reach it after passing through a forest, where you realize that there is no more elevation to gain. The pass **(49B)** is not marked as such, although there are several cairns with posts indicating the trail for your way back should you go further along one or more of the unmarked hunting trails leading various directions from the top of the pass. When you reach the pass, you are one mile from intersecting the Continental Divide Trail.

RATING: The trail only gains 1,200 feet over its 11-mile round trip and is suitable for intermediate hikers. Beginning hikers should enjoy this trail if they turn around midway.

UTE CREEK

Quad: Finger Mesa, Weminuche Pass, Rio Grande Pyramid

DRIVING INSTRUCTIONS: Drive south from Lake City on CO SH 149. Continue about 30 miles to the Rio Grande Reservoir Road (FSR 520), which is past MP 42. Turn right and go 16.9 miles where you reach the turnoff to the trailhead. Turn left and continue .3 miles to the trailhead, which is well marked (**50A**). Trailhead elevation - 9,500 feet.

THE HIKE: The Ute Creek trailhead is several miles west of the Rio Grande Reservoir. Due to the distance from town, getting to the trailhead is time consuming and the trail is used more during hunting season than for hiking. The trail heads south into the Weminuche Wilderness and follows Ute Creek, branching off to several other trails a significant distance ahead. Black Lake is seven miles from the trailhead and within the upper limits as a destination for a day hike. This trail appears on both the Weminuche Wilderness *Trails Illustrated* map and on the quads.

Within the first .25 miles the trail crosses the Rio Grande River. This is wider than your typical creek crossing but not too deep, unless it is early in the season when it can be impassable. You will want stream crossing shoes in any event. While you have multiple water crossings later in the hike, you will not need your stream crossing shoes after crossing the Rio Grande.

After crossing the river, the trail climbs moderately through a grassy meadow until you reach the sign designating the Weminuche Wilderness boundary when you enter a mixed aspen and spruce forest, where you will remain for the next 2 miles. The trail is easy to follow throughout this hike. You are heading south for the first mile until you reach Ute Creek. Thereafter, the trail turns to the southwest. The trail parallels Ute Creek from this point, but for the next mile it is well above

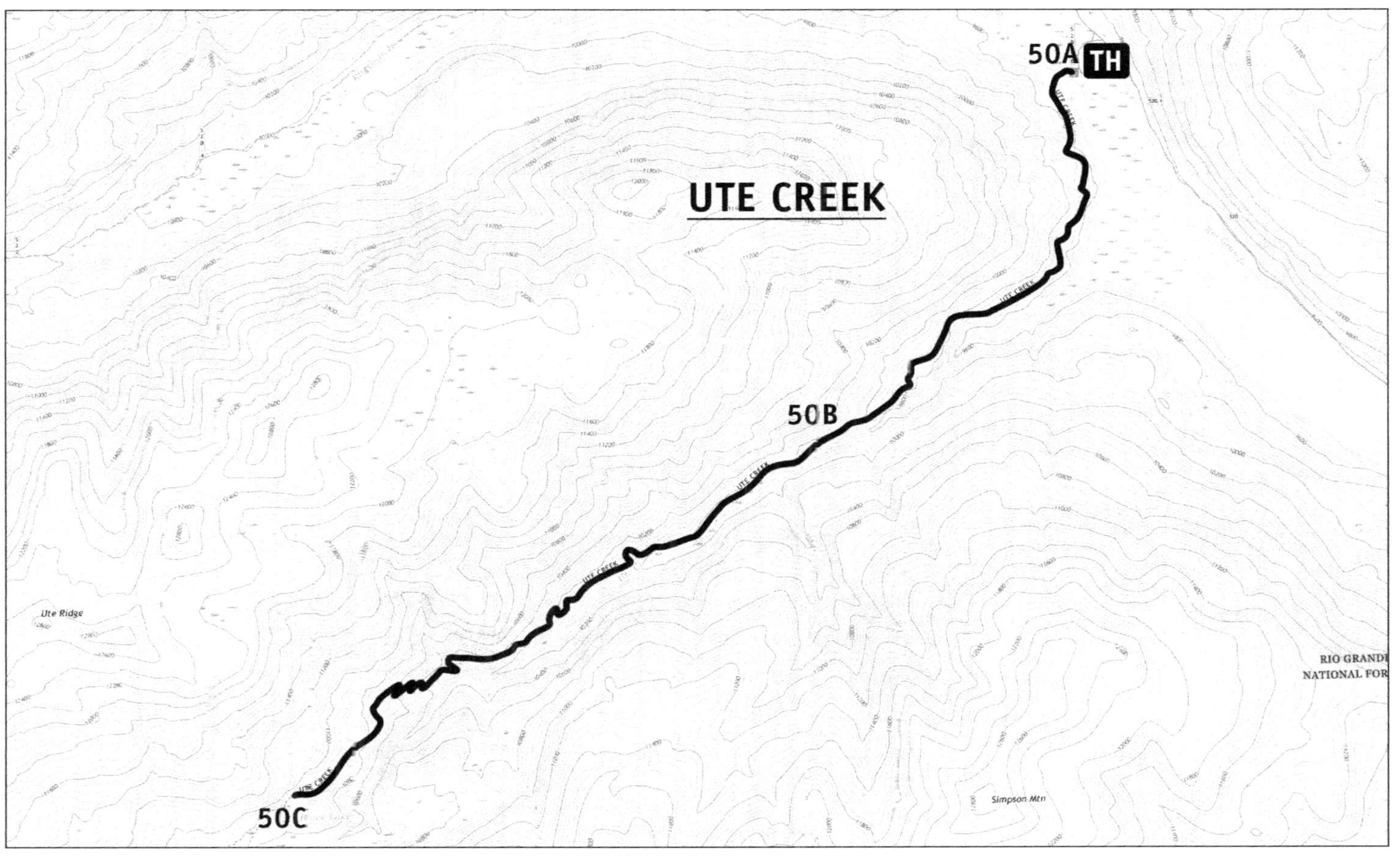

50A TH
UTE CREEK
50B
50C
Ute Ridge
Simpson Mtn
RIO GRANDE
NATIONAL FOR

the creek and some distance away. You will regularly hear the creek but rarely see it. The trail is ascending gently as it follows Ute Creek.

At the 2-mile mark the trail opens up. There are trees to your right, but it is open to your left down to Ute Creek, which is much closer. There are several ledges along this part of the trail where you can peer down to the cascading water. At the 3-mile mark the trail descends quickly to stream level and the valley widens. There are willows on either side of the stream, and after passing through some of them, you emerge into a meadow of tall grasses. During the fourth mile the trail gains very little elevation, and the stream has stopped cascading. Beavers have been at work in this area and at the 4-mile point there is a dark, ugly pond below you, parallel to Ute Creek. This is not Black Lake. You have another 3 miles to go and 800 feet to climb. The beaver ponds would be a suitable turnaround point for hikers wanting a shorter hike (**50B**). I have seen moose in this area.

Leaving the beaver ponds, the trail continues to parallel Ute Creek though the woods, gaining elevation at a gentle rate. After .5 miles you reach two switchbacks as the trail begins to climb at a gentle to moderate rate. Following these two switchbacks, the trail crosses a rockslide before reaching a second pair of switchbacks .5 miles past the first set. After this the trail is no longer close to Ute Creek but is still taking you in the same southwesterly direction. After another .5 miles you reach a set of six switchbacks and the trail steepens somewhat, but never beyond a moderate climb. After this set of switchbacks, you are 1 mile from Black Lake (**50C**), which is small mountain lake, surrounded by trees on three sides with a view of the mountains some distance south of the lake through an open portal. There is ample camping near the lake, and this is used as a hunters' campsite during the autumn. And yes, the lake is black.

RATING: A round trip to Black Lake (**50C**) covers 14 miles and gains 1,400 feet. Other than the length, it would be suitable for beginners. Because of the distance, it taxes the capabilities of an intermediate hiker. A shorter hike to the beaver ponds (**50B**) would be an excellent introduction to the area for a beginning hiker. Such a hike covers 8 miles and gains 500 feet of elevation.

LOST TRAIL CREEK

Quad: Finger Mesa, Pole Creek Mountain

DRIVING INSTRUCTIONS: Drive south from Lake City on CO SH 149. Continue 30 miles to the Rio Grande Reservoir Road (FSR 520), which is past MP 42. Turn right and go 18.4 miles, where the trailhead is well marked (**51A**). Trailhead elevation - 9,800 feet. Parking is available for several cars at the trailhead.

THE HIKE: The Lost Trail Creek trailhead is several miles west of the Rio Grande Reservoir. Due to the distance from town, getting to the trailhead is the most difficult part of your day. The trail heads north toward the Continental Divide. The trail branches off at the 2-mile mark, the branches reaching the divide opposite the head of the Wager Gulch Trail and the Cataract Gulch Trail. Lost Trail Creek Trail is wider than a single track, but narrower than a jeep trail. It is open for ATV usage, but not for side-by-side vehicles. West Lost Trail Creek Trail is a single track and does not allow ATVs. While awkwardly named, Lost Trail Creek Trail is not difficult to follow. Both the lower portions and the uppermost portions of Lost Trail Creek Trail are very scenic. The middle portion, not so much. West Lost Trail Creek Trail is scenic throughout. This trail appears both on the *Trails Illustrated* map and on the quads.

The trail climbs gently over the first 2 miles, going alternatively through wooded and open areas. To your left in the open areas is a battleship-shaped feature, complete with ship's prow and smokestacks. Okay, that might be a bit much, but it is a scenic view of an interesting geologic feature. Looking down valley you can see the west end of Rio Grande Reservoir. After 1 mile, you pass through a gate and continue to climb gradually through alternating wooded and open areas. During the second mile you begin to hear Lost Trail Creek, and you cross West

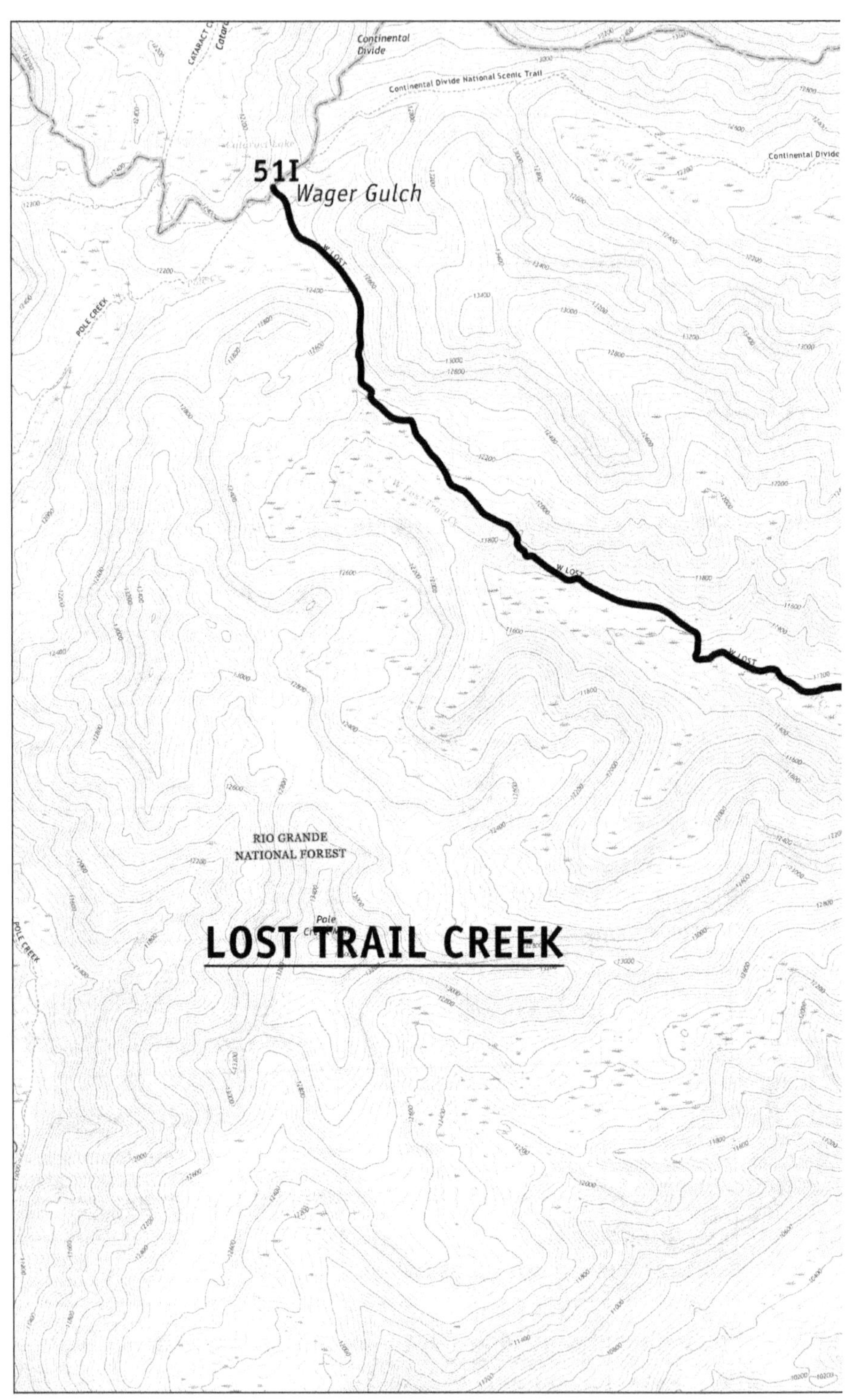
Continental
Divide
Continental Divide National Scenic Trail
Continental Divide
511
Wager Gulch
W LOST
W Lost Trail
W LOST
W LOST
POLE CREEK
POLE CREEK
RIO GRANDE
NATIONAL FOREST
Pole
Creek
LOST TRAIL CREEK

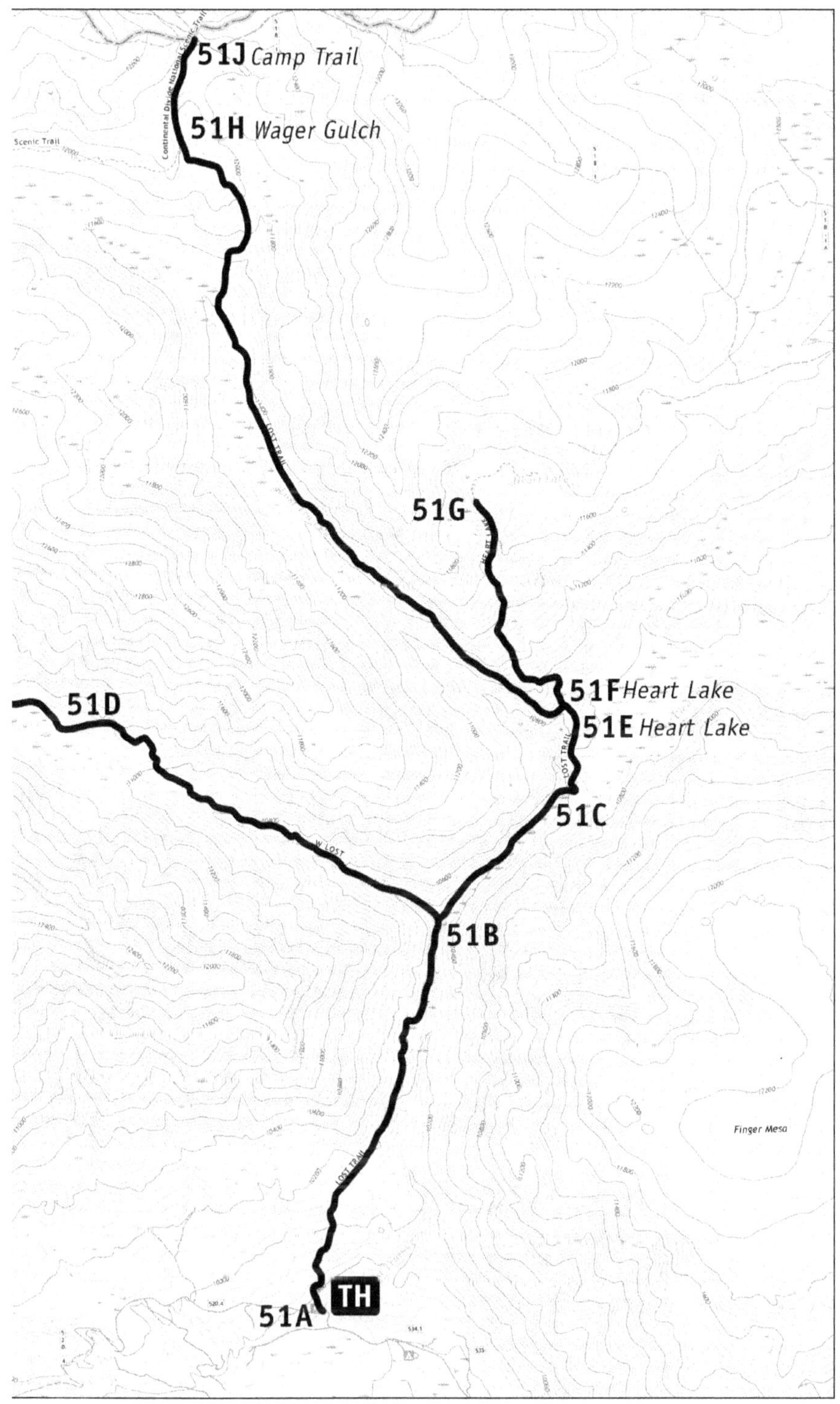

51J Camp Trail
51H Wager Gulch
Scenic Trail
Continental Divide National Scenic Trail
LOST TRAIL
51G
51D
51F Heart Lake
51E Heart Lake
LOST TRAIL
51C
W LOST
51B
Finger Mesa
LOST TRAIL
TH
51A

Lost Trail Creek at the 2-mile mark just before it joins Lost Trail Creek. The creek carries too much water early in the season to safely cross, but there is a four-log wide makeshift bridge just above the trail, which is passable. Just after the creek crossing the trails divide (**51B**). The left fork is West Lost Creek Trail which will connect with the Colorado Trail at the Continental Divide opposite the Cataract Gulch Trail. The right fork is Lost Trail Creek Trail which will connect with the Colorado Trail opposite the Wager Gulch Trail. These trails are only given their numerical designations on the trail signs. West Lost Trail Creek Trail is Trail #822 and Lost Trail Creek Trail is Trail #821.

Continuing on Lost Trail Creek Trail, you are climbing gradually through an open area over the next .5 miles. At that point you reach a rather perplexing stream crossing. The trail appears to follow the stream and there is no indication of it leaving the stream on either side. There is heavy vegetation around the stream at this point. Actually, Lost Trail Creek is to your right and the stream you are seeing ahead of you is the trail, which contains quite a bit of water for the 50 yards you must wade through until you see the trail turning to the right, crossing Lost Trail Creek, and emerging on the east side of the creek. You may want stream crossing shoes for this crossing. This is a logical turnaround point (**51C**) for beginners, or hikers wanting a shorter hike.

Once you have crossed Lost Trail Creek, the trail climbs steeply up an embankment which serves as the east bank of the creek. From this point on the trail follows the creek but is well above it. After .25 miles you pass through a gate, and immediately afterward there is a sign to your right indicating that the area is closed. This is the first (**51E**) of two such signs that you will encounter which signal the intersection with the Heart Lake Trail, which will overlay the Lost Trail Creek Trail for the next .25 miles. The combined trails climb steeply through woods before flattening out as you reach a small meadow. Here there are two trail signs bearing only trail numbers. Trail #823 is Heart Lake Trail and is to your right (**51F**). The better worn trail is Trail #821, which is Lost Trail Creek Trail to your left. The Heart Lake Trail is covered under the section bearing that name.

Lost Trail Creek Trail continues to climb moderately to steeply as you leave the meadow. For the next section you are in forest but can see down and to your left at regular intervals. You continue to be able to hear Lost Trail Creek well below you, but you cannot see it. There are views of the Rio Grande Pyramid to your left. You will climb steadily for over a mile from the Heart Lake Trail intersection through forest before the trail flattens out. Shortly afterward, you emerge from the trees into the upper Lost Trail Creek drainage, which is a massive open area offering spectacular views. The next mile is a gradual climb running parallel to Lost Trail Creek, crossing water near the end of the mile. Then the trail becomes much steeper, and you see ahead where the trail appears to divide. The left side appears to be the easier climb, while the right side is much more severe. The trails don't actually divide, and the right-hand side is where the trail leads as the trail continues as it leaves Lost Trail Creek and begins the climb to Carson Saddle. Here you climb 800 feet over a short distance. After this climb, which is the toughest part of the hike, you can see ahead to Carson Saddle, and you pass through a gate with metal posts designed to keep the larger ATVs off of the lower portions of Lost Trail Creek Trail. To the left of this intersection are signs indicating that two trails below are closed to vehicles. Shortly after passing through the gate, the westbound junction with the Colorado Trail is to your left (**51H**). The sections ahead, including the westbound portion of the Colorado Trail nearest to the Carson Saddle, as well as the uppermost portion of Lost Trail Creek Trail reaching the Carson Saddle, are discussed under the section for Wager Gulch. The eastbound section of the Colorado Trail (**51G**) is covered under the section for Camp Trail.

Returning to the intersection of Lost Trail Creek Trail and West Lost Trail Creek Trail (**51B**), you pass through a gate to take the west trail. This gate is narrow enough to prevent ATVs to pass. The trail follows West Lost Trail Creek, climbing moderately for the first portion. The first mile after the trail intersection is in the open, passing into wooded areas for the next 2 miles, before entering an open alpine basin prior to the 3-mile mark. At the 2-mile mark there is a sign, warning hikers to stay off a dangerous rockslide. There aren't that many rocks near the sign, and you've already passed a more impressive rockslide. Shortly after that sign the trail reaches an intermittent stream and there is no obvious trail on the other side. The trail follows the stream bed as you head upstream for 100 feet before the trail emerges from the stream bed on your left.

Once you have reached the open area just before the 3-mile mark (**51D**) you can see the Continental Divide at the head of the basin. This is a logical turnaround point for hikers not wishing to proceed to the Continental Divide. There is a pond to your left for those who want to fish.

Continuing along West Lost Trail Creek Trail, the elevation gain is gentle for the first portion of the ascent toward the head of the basin. Your first landmark is another sign warning of rockslide danger, at a spot with very few rocks. Next, you will see a faint trail heading to the right. This leads to a hunters' camp, and a similar trail rejoins the main trail a mile ahead. Following that, there is a fork in the trail. You should take the right fork, as there is a sign along the left fork indicating that the area is closed. All of the lower half of the basin passes through grass and bushes. Even though this trail does not get a great deal of use, and there are no significant trail markers, the trail is well defined and easy to follow. While you are parallel to West Lost Trail Creek throughout the ascent of the basin, you cross quite a few feeder streams. None of these should pose a problem.

As you reach a point 7 miles from the trailhead, you enter a forest comprised of spruce, most of which are dead, and the trail steepens to a moderate ascent for most of the upper half of the basin, with a few steep spots thrown in for good measure. You are in the forest for less than a mile, and as you emerge you are in grass and bushes for the next mile heading toward a gap between two unnamed mountains. This gap may look like your destination, but it is not. Once you've reached the gap you will have gained most of your elevation. The intersection with the Colorado Trail along the Continental Divide is less than a mile away. The terrain turns to tundra, and you descend a bit before the final ascent to the Continental Divide. There is ample signage at the intersection with the Colorado Trail (**51I**). If this is your turnaround spot, you may wish to hike a few more feet on the north side of the Colorado Trail where there is a grassy ridge offering a view of all four lakes in the Cataract Lakes system.

RATING: A round trip hike to the crossing of Lost Trail Creek (**51C**), which is the second major stream crossing, covers 5 miles and gains 800 feet. This would be suitable for beginning hikers. A round trip hike to Heart Lake (see the section for Heart Lake) from this trailhead covers 10 miles and gains 1,900 feet (**51G**). This would be pushing the upper limits for intermediate hikers. A round trip hike along Lost Trail Creek Trail to Carson Saddle (**51J**) covers 16 miles and gains 2,500 feet. This should be limited to experienced hikers up for a long hike. A round trip hike along West Lost Trail Creek Trail to the intersection of the Colorado Trail **(51I)** covers 19 miles and gains 2,600 feet. This too, should be limited to experienced hikers due to the distance. A round trip hike along West Lost Trail Creek Trail to the opening of the upper West Lost Trail Creek Basin **(51D)** is a 10-mile hike gaining 1,400 feet. This is an intermediate level hike.

The author and Ziggy.

Katherine Heidt

Postscript

Having concluded the narrative portion of the book I wanted to offer some of my opinions and insights. The front section of a daily newspaper is to give the news (supposedly) free of bias while the opinions of the editorial staff appear in a separate section. I want to do the same here, although I'm not sure I've succeeded in keeping my biases out of the narrative.

It has been said that there are no bad dogs, only bad dog owners. Similarly, there are no bad hikes, only bad hikers. The same cannot be said as to trips to the trailhead. One must deal with bad roads, distance, and multiple vehicles. On a recent hike returning from my parking place at the Carson townsite, down Wager Gulch (a difficult 4WD road), I encountered thirteen vehicles. That was after passing seventeen vehicles on the final leg of my hike from Carson Saddle to the Carson townsite. While the trailheads you approach from Henson Creek (Nellie Creek, Matterhorn Creek etc.) are some of the most spectacular in the area, I find myself hiking these less often because of road conditions leading to the trailhead.

There are hikes that are more popular than others. Certainly, any of the trailheads which service the area fourteeners fit into that category. Difficulties finding parking places at the trailhead and passing dozens of other hikers en route may lessen the appeal of a given hike. I've listed later several hikes which fit in the categories of, "Popular and with good reason," "Hidden gems," and "Was that really worth the effort?"

Sometimes you don't have all day for a hike. I'm listing shorter hikes I like below. Correspondingly, some of the longer hikes and thru-hikes can be highlights of a hiker's season, albeit with challenges commensurate with a longer hike and certain logistical issues.

Not all short hikes are easy hikes. Even an experienced hiker should have a few hikes in mind for when he will be taking guests or children who want to see what this area is all about. I've listed several "Hikes for beginners" below.

While most hikes start and end at the same trailhead, using the same route going out and returning, there are opportunities for "loop hikes," which start and end at the same place using different routes out and back. There are also "thru-hikes," which start and end at different trailheads. I've listed several of each of these possibilities below.

I've been occasionally asked what my favorite hike is. I've responded with the question, "Which season?" There are hikes especially suited to each season and I'm including a listing of hikes which have both pleasures and concerns corresponding to the four seasons of Hinsdale County.

SPRING – This is also known as mud season. Between mud and residual snow, many trails are either impassible or downright unpleasant. There are also issues gaining access to trailheads as many of our access roads are closed well into May. The Cebolla Creek Rd (also known as the Deer Lakes Rd, CR 50, and FSR 788) doesn't usually open until Memorial Day. The Henson Creek Road (CR 20) opens in stages from the gate at MP 5 leading to Engineer Pass during May. The Upper Lake Fork Road (CR 30) is closed from where the Shelf Road begins until sometime in May, although the remainder of CR 30, as well as CR 35 leading from the Shelf Road intersection to the Cataract Gulch trailhead, is open throughout the winter. In the spring, I find myself hiking in areas that have a southern exposure with few trees as these areas benefit from more sunlight and snow should disappear more quickly. A trail that is rocky or has some elevation gain is less likely to be muddy. Several of the hikes that I list below are hikes that I didn't list in the narrative previously. Consider the following for spring hiking:

Shelf Road (CR 30) – The Shelf Road, while closed to vehicles during much of the spring, is a decent spring hike. It has a southern exposure, and its surface is not likely to be muddy. The 4-mile distance (one way) between the beginning of the Shelf Road to the Silver Creek – Grizzly Gulch parking lot makes a nice outing.

Cottonwood Creek – This gets plenty of sun, has a surface unlikely to be muddy, and has enough elevation gain to drain well. You are unlikely to get beyond the stream crossing at the 2.5 mile point due to high water flow.

Alpine Road (FSR 868) – This has a southern exposure, and the sections with trees typically lose their snow early, but this trail can get muddy at the 2.5-mile point before you reach the trailhead for the Little Elk Trail.

Independence Gulch – As much of this trail is in the open, it loses its snow early, and has the terrain and elevation gain to avoid mud. There can be residual snow in the wooded area beyond the 2-mile point.

Henson Creek Road (CR 20) – This is kept open during the winter up to a gate beyond MP 5, and the snow crews will be working toward opening Engineer Pass during the spring, having cleared the snow in the areas below. The distance from the winter gate to Capitol City is 3.5 miles (one way) and is likely to be clear with minimal mud.

SUMMER – While summer is prime hiking season and all of the area trails are good summer trails, there are two factors to consider in the summer, wildflowers and mosquitos. Wildflowers of various sorts populate the area trails from June through August, but late July to early August is prime wildflower season. There are trails to avoid while mosquitos are most prevalent, typically June to early July. While I always carry a high-grade insect repellant, that doesn't keep the mosquitos from swarming. I've been driven off a mountain more than once by those pests. Some trails should be avoided early in the season because stream flow may be high, and you may not be able to reach your intended destination. By the same token, trails featuring waterfalls will be at their best early in the season. The following hikes have particular relevance during the summer:

Cataract Gulch – This trail is well suited for the growth of wildflowers because of its northern exposure and proximity to water. There are two areas which feature wildflowers along this hike, the stretch beyond the opening switchbacks, featuring Columbine, and the upper basin featuring the various types of Indian Paintbrush. The waterfall is splendid throughout the season, but the stream crossing below the waterfall may be difficult to cross before mid-July. This is a wonderful trail at any time, but particularly during wildflower season.

Grizzly Gulch – This is also a splendid trail during wildflower season. I've described this trail as "American Basin without the people and the cars." If going to Grizzly Lake, the stream crossing is manageable by mid-July.

Modoc Falls – This short hike leads to a waterfall, which should be seen early in the season.

Crystal Lake and Larson Lakes – For some reason this area is prone to mosquitos early in the season. Both are wonderful hikes and should be taken after mid-July to be able to enjoy them fully.

Snow Mesa – I get a kick out of meeting some of the Colorado Trail thru-hikers who pass through the area from mid-July through mid-August. Many hikers wait at Spring Creek Pass to catch a ride into Lake City for supplies and a good meal. I break my "no hitchhikers" rule to give these intrepid hikers a ride.

AUTUMN – Autumn means fall colors and hunters. The aspen generally begin turning their colors by September 15, and most of the leaves are down by October 1. The cottonwoods start their changes a bit later but retain their leaves until mid-October. The exact dates of the hunting seasons vary from year to year, but generally no hunting begins before September 1. Bowhunting and muzzle loading (black powder) season continues through September, and rifle season begins in October and continues into November. I've listed the locations of various hunting camps I've encountered in the general narrative. Wear orange. The hikes listed below have special considerations for autumn:

Camp Trail – This is the quintessential fall hike. Aspen dominates the lower and middle portion of the trail and the various breaks in the trees offer views of other places in the upper Lake Fork Valley which feature aspen.

Rough Creek – From the creek crossing to just below where the trail enters the open area of the upper Rough Creek drainage, aspen are the prevailing species. There are more of the red and orange aspen here than most other places, and the best views of the trees are those across the stream. With the vivid colors and the sound of a rushing stream, this is as close to sensory overload as I've experienced while hiking.

Devil's Creek – You are hiking among the aspen from the point you enter the wilderness area to the point where you turn south for the final several miles to Devil's Lake. The best spot for viewing is when you enter the open area several miles after passing the cow camp.

Waterdog Lake – From Town – The portion of this trail just below Horse Park is aspen heaven.

Weminuche Pass – This is a popular trail for hunting parties. During an October trip, on my way up I only passed two hunters hiking near the bridge. When reaching Weminuche Pass a found a tent which could have housed a small circus with outlying tents to spare. Coming down

I was passed by nine parties of horses carrying hunters and equipment. I'm not sure how many animals were bagged, but I'll bet they had a great party each evening. As I hike with a dog, I'd have to yield the trail on multiple occasions.

Ute Creek – Hunters like this trail as well. Coming down this trail from Black Lake during September, I encountered a bowhunter who was using two llamas as his pack animals. Later I passed a party of twelve horses carrying hunters and equipment. My dog, Ziggy didn't know what to think of the llamas.

WINTER – Hinsdale County is a winter wonderland, and those who engage in the winter sports can take full advantage of what the area has to offer. Most hikers can adapt to snowshoeing rather easily. While cross-country skiing takes a while to achieve a level of proficiency that allows full enjoyment, I've found it well worth the effort. I enjoy cross-country skiing more than downhill skiing at this point in my life. While snowshoers can go on almost any trail, cross-country skiing is best done on groomed trails, and Hinsdale County has a trail system of over 100 miles of groomed multi-use trails. Grooming usually begins in late December and continues through early March. You should expect to encounter snowmobiles on these trails. Cross-country skiers prefer to stay on trails where the elevation gain or loss is minimal. I need to say a word about avalanche danger. Avalanche danger is greatest in the steeper areas west of town, after heavy snowfalls and late in the season. Accordingly, most of the trails I list are east of town:

Nellie Creek (CR 23) – While west of town, this trail has had less avalanche activity than other areas. The first 2 miles of the Nellie Creek Road, leading up to the first stream crossing are very popular with snowshoers. The road is too steep to be popular with cross-country skiers. This is best for earlier in the season while avalanche danger is less.

Sawmill Park Road (CR 56) – This is a groomed trail that is also popular with snowshoers. Popular destinations are the Jon Wilson Yurt, Sawmill Park, and Penniston Park, via the connecting trail. Again, this is too steep to be attractive to cross-country skiers. Avalanche danger is minimal.

Jarosa Mesa – This groomed trail is popular with both snowshoers and cross-country skiers. The only place where a skier might find it too steep is near the beginning of the trail, but this is for only a short distance. A popular destination is the point where the Colorado Trail and the La Garita Stock Trail divide, a bit over 2 miles in. As you are on top of the Continental Divide, there is no avalanche danger.

Oleo Ranch Road (CR17) – This is the road which leads to the Tumble Creek trailhead, then over a low pass until it reaches the Cebolla Creek Rd (also known as the Deer Lakes Rd, FSR 788 and CR 50) less than a mile beyond the Deer Lakes turnoff. This is a groomed trail, and the first 2 miles are fairly flat making it a good place for a beginning cross-country skier to practice. Beyond that point the road gains elevation gently until it reaches the top of the pass, 3.5 miles from the highway. There is no avalanche danger.

Cebolla Creek Rd (also known as the Deer Lakes Rd, FSR 788, and CR 50) – This groomed trail leads to both the Deer Lakes campground and to the Oleo Ranch Road – North Portal. The descent is gentle enough to be a fun ski run on the way down but a workout on the way up, as the grade never really levels for long. Deer Lakes Campground at 3.5 miles in is a popular destination. As it connects with the Oleo Ranch Road, this makes for a nice thru-hike. You should start at the Cebolla Creek Road side, as it is 700 feet higher in elevation. There is minimal avalanche danger.

POPULAR AND WITH GOOD REASON – Trails can gain popularity for a number of reasons; the view, the moderateness of the hike, and proximity to town come to mind. Popularity grows by word-of-mouth and internet posting, so the good trails only get more popular. By far the most popular, and busy, trails service Hinsdale County's fourteeners. If you're looking for solitude, look somewhere other than the hikes listed below:

Nellie Creek (Uncompahgre) – As the sixth highest peak in Colorado, and as Hinsdale County's signature mountain, this is probably the most hiked trail in the area. It is not a particularly difficult climb as fourteeners go. A number of hikers climb Uncompahgre on a significant birthday. Weddings take place at the summit. This is for good reason as the views from the summit do not disappoint.

American Basin (Handies) – This hike offers the splendor of American Basin combined with the ascent of a fourteener. Handies Peak, approached from American Basin, is the easiest climb of the area fourteeners. This helps to overcome the fact that it is quite a drive to the trailhead. The views from the summit are among the best in the area.

Alpine Gulch – There is an intimacy to the lower portion of this trail as the canyon arises above you on both sides. The sound of rushing water only adds to the experience. As long as stream crossings offer a pleasant challenge and not an obstacle to a hiker, this trail offers a lot. And did I mention that the trailhead is close to town and easy to reach.

Cataract Gulch – This trail offers so much, from the sound of the stream, the waterfall, the wildflowers, and the grandeur of the upper basin that it is no surprise that it has become many people's favorite hike. Count me among the admirers.

Camp Trail – With its moderate climb, grand views of the upper Lake Fork Valley, and magnificent fall colors, this is a favorite trail of many local residents. It's easy to reach the trailhead and a hike can be fashioned for hikers of any ability.

HIDDEN GEMS – These are hikes where you aren't likely to encounter any other hikers. Most are hikes along streams and offer a full complement of great views. They also offer the solitude that should come with hiking in the mountains. If you like the trails listed below, share your recommendations judiciously:

Mineral Creek – This is a lovely hike along a stream that gains elevation gently. The lower portion of the trail is open with views up valley, while the upper portion is in trees passing rock pinnacles. The trailhead is a bit out of the way.

Snare Creek – Leaving from the same parking area as the Cuba Gulch trailhead, the Snare Creek Trail receives little use. After the tedious climb up switchbacks for the first hour, the trail opens up into an alpine basin, loops across that basin then loops around again to an area of tundra and small lakes overlooked by three thirteeners and offering views of the lakes and drainage below.

Cooper Creek – Although the Cooper Creek trailhead is less than a mile from the Silver Creek / Grizzly Gulch trailheads it doesn't get a tenth of the traffic of the other two trails. That's fine because this is a lovely hike which offers an intimate view of the upper Cooper Creek Valley. Other hikers might spoil that intimacy. You can go to Cooper Lake, but my preference is to continue toward the headwaters of Cooper Creek.

El Paso Creek – Once you are out of the woods, you are in an upper alpine environment southwest of Uncompahgre Peak. The lack of a parking lot and signage along the road designating the beginning of the trail have kept this hidden from many hikers.

FSR 473 to Rambouillet Park – Although this road is open to ATVs, you aren't likely to see any, or anyone else for that matter. Once you have passed through the lower woods, you are on a mesa with views in all directions at various points along the way. Finding a herd of elk in Rambouillet Park can be a thrilling experience.

WAS THAT REALLY WORTH THE EFFORT? – Some trailheads are so hard to reach that it spoils the hike that follows. On top of that, having reached the trailhead, the hike that follows may be short or uninspiring. The following trails are ones that having hiked them once, you may not care for a repeat engagement:

Cuba Gulch – Even before this trail was closed by an avalanche, this trail had lost its luster for me. The trip to the trailhead requires 4WD for the last 3.5 miles and the trail ends (for most hikers) 2 miles after leaving the trailhead. Besides, there is a section where you hike through brush, and I was usually wet afterward.

East Fork Powderhorn Creek – It is a long trip to the trailhead with the last 8 miles over a rough road. There is an ugly stream crossing soon after leaving the trailhead. The main trail is overgrown soon after you've reached the 2-mile point. The side trip to Powderhorn Swamp, while a unique place, is steep.

Weminuche Pass – The first section of the trail follows a powerline and passes the plant at the dam of Rio Grande Reservoir. The next section hikes along the side of the reservoir, which after experiencing mountain lakes, is decidedly uninspiring. Things pick up a bit as you climb toward Weminuche Pass along side of, but some distance from, a creek. The arrival at the pass is anticlimactic, as it is so flat that you can't really tell when you reached the top. Oh yeah, and it's a long way to get to the trailhead.

Cebolla Trail – After two stream crossings, you enter the woods and only emerge once at a large meadow that has swampy areas before entering the woods again for good. It's not a very memorable hike. At least it's not difficult to reach the trailhead.

Silver Creek – It may be blasphemous to trash a trail leading to two of our fourteeners, but this trail has terrain issues for much of the way. This detracts from the wonderful views that you don't see because you're constantly having to look at your feet.

SHORT HIKES – Believe it or not, often I have other things to do during the day other than hike. While I hike faster than most hikers,

I can complete each of these hikes in less than 3.5 hours. As a bonus, all of the trailheads are close to Lake City. If you don't have the time or inclination for a longer hike the following hikes are rated from quickest to longest:

Fannie Fern – This trailhead is just outside the town limits, and I can reach the Fannie Fern Mill and return in 1.75 hours. While there are several variations of this hike, it is a good alternative if you are on a tight schedule.

Waterdog from CO SH 149 to the Lake San Cristobal overlook – This trailhead is less than 5 miles from town, and I have made it to the Lake San Cristobal overlook at Upper Vickers Ranch and returned in 2.25 hours. That destination is remarkable for its views to the west and to the south.

Independence Gulch – This trailhead is also less than 5 miles from town. I have hiked both the Independence Gulch loop and the hike to the intersection of the Little Elk Trail in 3 hours. The open nature of the terrain and the wide views available make this a personal favorite.

Waterdog Lake from town to Station Eleven – This trailhead is within the town limits, leaving more time for hiking. I've made it to Station Eleven and returned in 3 hours. This is the destination of choice for views overlooking the town and lake.

Devil's Creek to the overlook past the cow camp – The trailhead is 8 miles from town. I've made it to the overlook and returned in 3.25 hours. This would be the view of choice of Uncompahgre Peak and the points north from the east side of the highway.

HIKES FOR BEGINNERS- Whether you are looking for an easy hike, or if you have guests visiting, these hikes are ideal for beginners, including children:

Big Blue – While it takes a while to get to the trailhead, the resulting hike is as gentle as you will find in the area. This trail can be taken to the first stream crossing, or anywhere short of that point without finding a climb or terrain that would be a problem. There is very little elevation gain.

Brush Creek – The stream crossing is your likely destination, although there's nothing beyond it that's problematic, so long as your guests don't get spooked by crossing a stream. This trail has a gentle climb, passes along a stream, and offers the chance to see moose. What's not to like?

Mineral Creek – While it takes a while to get to the trailhead, this is a lovely hike along a stream with very little elevation gain. The stream crossing is your likely destination.

Jarosa Mesa – After the initial climb, there isn't a lot of elevation gain and much of the hike is in the open, offering views to the south and east. This is an easy introduction to the Colorado Trail. The point where the Colorado Trail breaks off from the La Garita Stock Trail is your likely destination.

Black Wonder Gorge – As most of the easier trails are east of town, I wanted to include a hike west of town into the mountains. After the initial climb, you are on a mining road and the elevation gain is modest. Make sure your guests see the cave and the waterfall. You are opposite the Shelf Road so expect some road noise.

LOOP HIKES – All of these offer some new territory on the return trip, while allowing you to return to where you parked. Two of these involve hiking from one trailhead to another along a road for a short distance. Two others return you to a spot you have passed on the trip out, creating more of a lollipop or lasso shaped hike rather than a true loop. The Crystal Lake to Larson Lakes hike is a true loop.

Deer Creek to Brush Creek loop – This loop is a bit more than 5 miles and can be taken equally well from either direction. There is a 1.25-mile hike along the Cebolla Creek Rd (also known as the Deer Lakes Rd, CR 50, and FSR 788) to complete the loop.

Independence Gulch loop – This is a lollipop whereby the first 1.5 miles is common to both the trip out and the return trip. This loop is generally hiked with the right fork taken on the way out, connecting it to the Little Elk Trail shortly after you've stopped climbing then descending back along a water line until you rejoin the main trail. This is a 6-mile hike.

Powderhorn Lakes loop – This trail is also a lollipop whereby the first 1.5 miles is common to both the trip out and the return trip. Once you reach the first meadow, bear right around the trees then begin climbing Calf Creek Plateau. Once on the top of the plateau, you will see the rocks which surround the upper lake off in the distance. Cross the plateau in the direction of the rocks until you see the lakes. The trail crosses a rockslide before reaching the upper lake and returning by the traditional route. This has enough navigation issues that you should be familiar with the area before attempting this hike. This is a longer hike at 9 miles.

Mary Alice Creek to Matterhorn Creek loop – This is the other hike which completes the loop by hiking along a road, in this case the North Henson Creek Road for the .7 miles between the turnoff to the Matterhorn Creek trailhead and the Mary Alice Creek trailhead. You should park along the North Henson Creek Road near the Mary Alice Creek trailhead, enter along the trail along Mary Alice Creek, and work your way over to Matterhorn Creek and down. This has more scenery packed into it than any of the other loops. This is a 7-mile hike.

Crystal Lake to Larson Lakes loop – While both Crystal Lake and Larson Lakes are wonderful destinations, the country between them is pretty special as well. While a long hike at 14 miles, this is the type of hike that can be the highlight of a hiker's year.

THRU-HIKES – While having the challenge of placing vehicles at two spots, thru-hikes can be exhilarating. There is something special about not retracing your steps and entering at one place and exiting at another. While there are a multitude of possibilities, the following can be pretty special:

Big Blue Creek from Nellie Creek to Big Blue Creek trailhead – This thru-hike should be taken with Nellie Creek as your starting point as you'll get your climbing out of the way early, and you finish your hike 1,700 feet lower than where you start. You will have four major stream crossings over the 12 miles of this hike.

Waterdog Lake trails from CO SH 149 to town – Start from the highway as it is 1,200 feet higher in elevation than the trailhead in town. This trail offers plenty of scenery packed into its 9 miles.

The Ridge Stock Driveway from Matterhorn Creek to Nellie Creek – I'm a fan of the Ridge Stock Driveway as it, in my opinion, offers the best views per mile of any trail in the area. Starting at the Matterhorn Creek trailhead you can pass below Wetterhorn, Matterhorn, and Uncompahgre Peaks before arriving at the Nellie Creek trailhead 9 miles later. This is a more difficult hike than the previous two hikes listed. I recommend taking it from this direction, despite the similarity of trailhead elevations, because the section of the trail north of the El Paso Creek Trail junction has loose gravel and is safer to climb than to descend.

Handies Peak thru-hike from American Basin to Grizzly Gulch – This hike passes through beautiful country throughout the journey. Handies is easier to climb from the American Basin side, and the descent down Grizzly Gulch does not present any particular issues. It will seem like more, but this is a 7-mile hike.

The "up and over" hike from the Williams Creek to the Alpine Gulch trailheads – This is another hike that would be the highlight of a hiker's year. The 4 miles above timberline during the transition zone between the Williams Creek and Alpine Gulch Trails offer views which are my personal favorites. You should start on the Williams Creek side, so if the stream crossings leave you with wet boots, you'll be near the end of your hike. This is a long hike at 14 miles, and you will climb 3,600 feet before descending 3,800 feet, but if you're up for the challenge, you won't be disappointed.

The author and Ziggy

Glenn Heumann

Acknowledgements

All maps depicted are reprints of maps created by the U.S. Geological Survey.

I want to thank Harvey DuChene for helping me write those portions of the "Hinsdale County" and "Crystal Peak / Clay Pots" sections that deal with geological matters.

I want to thank Glenn Heumann for his contributions which include providing me with updates on more recent conditions for trails for which I had previously written the narrative and assisting me with the editing of this narrative. Glenn accompanied me on several of these hikes.

I want to thank Katherine Heidt for her assistance in editing the narrative, and for her many helpful suggestions made during the course of writing the narrative.

The cover photo is by Michael Underwood. The remaining photographs are courtesy of Glenn Heumann and Katherine Heidt, with the exception of the photograph below which is courtesy of Burton Gregg.

Finally, I want to acknowledge the many contributions to this narrative made by Ziggy, my companion on the vast majority of these hikes. Ziggy was a German Shepherd / Husky mix that was in a rescue program when I first met him in 2012. He progressed from not understanding the purpose of a switchback, to being able to find where little used trails reemerged after disappearing in overgrown areas. Ziggy had a contagious enthusiasm at the beginning of each day and liked nothing better than hiking. I'm told that German Shepherds are happiest when working and Ziggy saw his job as that of a trail guide. After over 700 hikes, Ziggy retired from hiking in 2021 as he developed hip issues. Given the places he's been and the things that he's seen, I find it one of nature's great tragedies that dogs are partially colorblind.

Ziggy 2010-2021

Burton Gregg

Appendix

Trailhead Number	Trailhead Name	Beginning Point	Turnaround Point	Destination Description	Rating	Beginning Elevation	Elevation Gain - Net	Round Trip Milage
1	Larson Lakes	1A	1D	Thompson Lake	Beginner	9,400	1,000	2
1	Larson Lakes	1A	1E	Larson Lakes	Intermediate	9,400	1,700	10
1	Larson Lakes	1A	1G	Intersect Independence Gulch Trail	Experienced	9,400	1,800	15
2	Crystal Lake	2A	2E	Crystal Lake	Intermediate	9,400	2,400	8
2	Crystal Lake	2E	2F	Sidehike to ridge overlooking Henson Creek	Experienced	11,800	200	2
2	Crystal Lake	2A	2G	Crystal Peak	Experienced	9,400	3,500	15
2	Crystal Lake	2A	2A	Crystal / Larson loop	Experienced	9,400	2,800	14
3	Waterdog Lake - From Town	3A	3C	Waterdog Lake	Intermediate	8,700	2,500	9
3	Waterdog Lake From Town	3A	3D	Station Eleven	Intermediate	8,700	2,100	6
4	Fannie Fern	4A	4F	Fannie Fern Mill	Beginner	8,800	900	4
4	Fannie Fern	4A	4G	Mining Cabin	Experienced	8,800	2,200	8
4	Fannie Fern	4A	4H	Ski Hill thru hike	Intermediate	8,800	900	4.5
5	Independence Gulch	5A	5C	Little Elk Trail intersection	Intermediate	8,400	1,800	5
5	Independence Gulch	5A	5A	Independence Gulch Loop	Intermediate	8,400	1,800	6
5	Independence Gulch	5A	5D	Bill Hare / High Bridge divide	Intermediate	8,400	2,100	8
5	Independence Gulch	5A	5F	Ridge above Little Elk Creek Drainage	Experienced	8,400	2,100	18
6	Devil's Creek	6A	6B	Overlook beyond cow camp	Intermediate	8,400	1,600	7
6	Devil's Creek	6A	6C	Head of Devil's Creek	Intermediate	8,400	2,600	9
6	Devil's Creek	6A	6D	Devil's Lake	Experienced	8,400	3,400	14
7	Little Elk	7A	7B	Ridge above Little Elk Creek Drainage	Experienced	9,300	800	7.5
8	Ridge Stock Driveway - North Portal	8A	8B	Northernmost knob	Experienced	10,000	1,900	8

8	Ridge Stock Driveway - North Portal	8A	8C	Crystal / Larson cutoff	Experienced	10,000	2,200	13
9	Big Blue Creek	9A	9B	Creek crossing	Beginner	9,700	500	9
9	Big Blue Creek	9A	9C	Slide Lake	Intermediate	9,700	700	11
10	Powderhorn Lakes	10A	10E	Upper Powderhorn Lake	Intermediate	11,000	700	11
10	Powderhorn Lakes	10A	10A	Powderhorn Lakes Loop	Experienced	11,000	1,300	10
10	Powderhorn Lakes	10A	10F	Devil's Lake	Experienced	11,000	1,600	14
10	Powderhorn Lakes	10A	10G	Hidden Lake	Experienced	11,000	1,000	11
11	East Fork Powderhorn Creek	11A	11C	Campsite where trail disappears	Beginner	9,500	300	4.5
11	East Fork Powderhorn Creek	11A	11D	Powderhorn Swamp	Intermediate	9,500	800	6
12	Alpine Gulch	12A	12H	Top of East Fork Alpine Gulch	Experienced	9,000	2,800	10
12	Alpine Gulch	12A	12I	Junction with Williams Creek Trail	Experienced	9,000	3,800	14
12	Alpine Gulch	12A	12E	End of trail along West Fork Alpine Gulch	Beginner	9,000	1,200	7
12	Alpine Gulch	12A	12F	Mine shaft on top of knoll	Experienced	9,000	2,100	10
12	Alpine Gulch	12A	12G	Grassy Mountain	Experienced	9,000	3,800	13
13	Modoc Falls	13A	13B	Modoc Falls	Beginner	9,200	200	1
14	Crystal Peak / Clay Pots	14A	14C	Crystal Peak	Experienced	10,500	2,300	9
14	Crystal Peak / Clay Pots	14A	14D	Clay Pots	Experienced	10,500	2,100	9
15	El Paso Creek	15A	15C	Lunch Mountain	Intermediate	11,000	1,300	6
15	El Paso Creek	15A	15D	Junction with Ridge Stock Driveway	Experienced	11,000	1,400	10
16	Nellie Creek	16A	16F	Uncompahgre Peak	Experienced	11,400	2,900	7.5
16	Nellie Creek	16A	16I	Junction with El Paso Creek Trail	Experienced	11,400	1,500	9
16	Nellie Creek	16A	16G	Top of Ridge Stock Driveway	Intermediate	11,400	1,400	7
16	Nellie Creek	16A	16J	Junction with Crystal / Larson cutoff	Experienced	11,400	1,400	14
16	Nellie Creek	16A	16H	Bottom of basin	Intermediate	11,400	1,000	5
16	Nellie Creek	16A	16K	Slide Lake	Experienced	11,400	2,000	13
17	Matterhorn Creek	17A	17J	Saddle below Wetterhorn Peak	Intermediate	10,800	2,300	6.5

Trailhead Number	Trailhead Name	Beginning Point	Turnaround Point	Destination Description	Rating	Beginning Elevation	Elevation Gain - Net	Round Trip Milage
17	Matterhorn Creek	17A	17F	Matterhorn / East Fork Junction via Matterhorn	Experienced	10,800	1,700	11
17	Matterhorn Creek	17A	17F	Matterhorn / East Fork Junction via East Fork	Experienced	10,800	1,700	9
17	Matterhorn Creek	17A	17A	Matterhorn / East Fork loop	Experienced	10,800	1,700	10
17	Matterhorn Creek	17A	17L	Junction with El Paso Creek Trail	Intermediate	10,800	1,400	8.5
18	Mary Alice Creek	18A	18B	Saddle between Mary Alice Cr / Matterhorn Ck	Intermediate	11,000	1,400	4.5
18	Mary Alice Creek	18A	18A	Mary Alice Ck / Matterhorn Ck loop	Experienced	11,000	1,400	7
18	Mary Alice Creek	18A	18G	Creek crossing along Ridge Stock Driveway West	Experienced	11,000	1,500	7
18	Mary Alice Creek	18A	18E	Pass between Mary Alice Cr / Wetterhorn Ck	Experienced	11,000	2,000	9
18	Mary Alice Creek	18A	18D	Junction of Middle Fork Creek / Wetterhorn Ck Trails	Experienced	11,000	1,600	11
19	Horsethief Trail	19A	19C	American Lake	Intermediate	12,600	(300)	7
19	Horsethief Trail	19A	19E	Creek crossing along Ridge Stock Driveway West	Experienced	12,600	800	15
20	Williams Creek	20A	20D	Beaver pond	Beginner	9,200	600	3
20	Williams Creek	20A	20C	Lower Clearings	Intermediate	9,200	1,200	6
20	Williams Creek	20A	20E	Top of Williams Creek Trail	Experienced	9,200	3,000	11
20	Williams Creek	20A	20F	High point of the Williams / Alpine transition zone	Experienced	9,200	3,600	15
20	Williams Creek	20A	12A	Williams / Alpine thru hike	Experienced	9,200	3,600	14
21	Camp Trail	21A	21C	First rockslide	Intermediate	9,200	1,800	6.5
21	Camp Trail	21A	21B	Junction with La Garita Stock Trail	Intermediate	9,200	2,500	9

21	Camp Trail	21D	21F	Colorado Trail - Camp Trail Intersection to Carson Saddle	Intermediate	11,700	1,600	8.5
22	Wager Gulch	22A	22B	Carson townsite	Intermediate	9,300	2,200	7
22	Wager Gulch	22A	22C	Carson Saddle	Intermediate	9,300	3,000	10
22	Wager Gulch	22C	22F	Colorado Trail - Carson Saddle to Cataract Lakes	Experienced	12,300	900	11
23	Cataract Gulch	23A	23B	Top of waterfall	Intermediate	9,600	1,600	6
23	Cataract Gulch	23A	23C	Junction with Colorado Trail	Experienced	9,600	2,600	12
24	Black Wonder Gorge	24A	24C	Trail blockage	Beginner	9,600	800	4
25	Cottonwood Creek	25A	25B	Cuba Gulch trailhead	Beginner	9,600	1,100	7
26	Cuba Gulch	26A	Blocked	Blocked trail	Blocked	10,700	Blocked	Blocked
27	Snare Creek	27A	27B	Lower lake	Intermediate	10,700	1,700	9
27	Snare Creek	27A	27C	Pass between Snare Creek / Animas River drainages	Experienced	10,700	2,500	11
28	Grizzly Gulch	28A	28D	Grizzly Lake	Intermediate	10,400	1,900	7
28	Grizzly Gulch	28A	28C	Head of Grizzly Gulch	Intermediate	10,400	2,200	7
28	Grizzly Gulch	28A	28E	Handies Peak	Experienced	10,400	3,600	8
29	Silver Creek	29A	29B	Redcloud Peak	Experienced	10,400	3,600	10
29	Silver Creek	29A	29C	Sunshine Peak	Experienced	10,400	3,600	13
30	Cooper Creek	30A	30B	Trail fork past second water crossing	Beginner	10,600	1,000	6
30	Cooper Creek	30A	30D	Head of Cooper Creek Basin	Intermediate	10,600	1,400	9
30	Cooper Creek	30A	30E	Cooper Lake	Experienced	10,600	2,100	9
30	Cooper Creek	30A	30F	Divide overlooking Henson Creek drainage	Experienced	10,600	2,300	9
31	American Basin	31A	31C	Sloan Lake	Intermediate	11,200	1,600	4
31	American Basin	31A	31G	Handies Peak	Experienced	11,200	2,800	5.5
31	American Basin	31A	31D	Pass between Lake Fork / Animas River drainages	Intermediate	11,200	1,400	4
31	American Basin	31A	31E	Unnamed lake	Experienced	11,200	1,400	5
31	American Basin	31A	31F	Grouse Gulch trailhead at San Juan CR 26	Experienced	11,200	1,400	9

Trailhead Number	Trailhead Name	Beginning Point	Turnaround Point	Destination Description	Rating	Beginning Elevation	Elevation Gain - Net	Round Trip Milage
32	Waterdog Lake - From CO SH 149	32A	32C	Waterdog Lake	Intermediate	9,200	2,000	11
32	Waterdog Lake - From CO SH 149	32A	3A	Waterdog thru hike to Lake City	Intermediate	9,200	1,700	9
33	Sawmill Park	33A	33B	Sawmill Park trail fork	Beginner	9,900	700	3
33	Sawmill Park	33A	33C	Sawmill Park right fork to end	Beginner	9,900	1,100	5
33	Sawmill Park	33A	33D	Junction with FSR 473	Intermediate	9,900	1,700	7
33	Sawmill Park	33A	33E	Junction with Colorado Trail	Intermediate	9,900	1,700	10
34	Slumgullion Weather Station	34A	34B	Knob atop ridge	Experienced	11,500	500	2.5
34	Slumgullion Weather Station	34A	34C	Junction with FSR 473	Experienced	11,500	500	3.5
35	FSR 473 to Rambouillet Park	35A	35C	Entrance to Rambouillet Park	Beginner	11,200	600	6
35	FSR 473 to Rambouillet Park	35A	35D	Slumgullion Peak	Intermediate	11,200	600	11
35	FSR 473 to Rambouillet Park	35A	35E	Junction with Sawmill Park Road	Intermediate	11,200	500	11
36	Tumble Creek (Cebolla)	36A	36D	Martinez Creek	Intermediate	10,300	1,000	9
37	Tumble Creek (Skyline)	37A	37C	Trail fork	Intermediate	10,300	2,000	11
37	Tumble Creek (Skyline)	37A	37E	Junction with Rough Creek Trail	Experienced	10,300	2,000	13
37	Tumble Creek (Skyline)	37A	37F	Junction with Colorado Trail	Experienced	10,300	2,400	15
38	Jarosa Mesa	38A	38B	Colorado Trail and La Garita Stock Trail separate	Beginner	10,900	500	4.5
38	Jarosa Mesa	38A	38C	Top of Jarosa Mesa	Beginner	10,900	800	8
38	Jarosa Mesa	38A	38E	Sawmill Park Trail junction via Colorado Trail	Intermediate	10,900	800	11
38	Jarosa Mesa	38A	38E	Sawmill Park Trail junction via La Garita Stock Trail	Intermediate	10,900	600	13

38	Jerosa Mesa	38E	38F	Colorado Trail from Sawmill Park junction to Camp Trail junction	Intermediate	11,700	500	3
39	Srow Mesa	39A	39D	Rim of Snow Mesa	Intermediate	10,900	1,300	4
39	Srow Mesa	39A	39E	Baldy Cinco	Intermediate	10,900	2,400	10
39	Snow Mesa	39A	39F	Junction with Skyline Trail	Intermediate	10,900	1,400	13
40	Cannabal Plateau	40A	40C	Snow Mesa - Vickers Ranch overlook	Intermediate	11,100	1,100	5
40	Cannabal Plateau	40A	40D	Junction with Deer Creek Trail	Experienced	11,100	1,600	12
41	Oleo Ranch Road - North Portal	41A	41B	Top of pass	Beginner	10,400	400	4
41	Oleo Ranch Road - North Portal	41A	41D	Tumble Creek trailhead	Beginner	10,400	400	8
41	Oleo Ranch Road - North Portal	41A	41C	Thru hike to CO SH 149	Beginner	10,400	400	6
42	Deer Creek	42A	42G	Junction with Brush Creek Trail	Beginner	10,200	600	4.5
42	Deer Creek	42A	42A	Deer Creek / Brush Creek loop	Beginner	10,200	600	5
42	Deer Creek	42A	42E	Cannibal Plateau loop	Experienced	10,200	2,100	12
42	Deer Creek	42A	42F	Deer Lakes Campground	Beginner	10,200	400	3
42	Deer Creek	42A	42A	Deer Lakes Campground loop	Beginner	10,200	400	4
43	Brush Creek	43A	43G	Trail fork between Devil's Canyon and Devil's Lake Trails	Beginner	9,900	1,000	7
43	Brush Creek	43A	43D	Devil's Canyon	Beginner	9,900	1,200	8.5
43	Brush Creek	43A	43E	Devil's Lake	Experienced	9,900	2,100	14
43	Brush Creek	43A	43F	Southwest rim of Ca.f Creek Plateau	Intermediate	9,900	1,700	8
43	Brush Creek	43A	43I	Junction with North Calf Creek Trail	Experienced	9,900	2,100	14
44	Rough Creek	44A	44B	Junction with Cebolla Trail	Beginner	9,200	800	6
44	Rough Creek	44A	44G	Junction with Skyline Trail	Experienced	9,200	2,500	16
44	Rough Creek	44A	44F	Martinez Creek	Intermediate	9,200	1,300	9
44	Rough Creek	44A	44D	Mineral Park	Experienced	9,200	2,400	13

Trailhead Number	Trailhead Name	Beginning Point	Turnaround Point	Destination Description	Rating	Beginning Elevation	Elevation Gain - Net	Round Trip Milage
44	Rough Creek	44A	44A	Rough Creek / Mineral Creek / Cebolla Creek Road loop	Experienced	9,200	2,400	15
45	Mineral Creek	45A	45D	Mineral Creek	Beginner	9,100	300	5
45	Mineral Creek	45A	45C	Junction with Cebolla Trail	Intermediate	9,100	1,200	10
46	Powderhorn Park	46A	46B	Southeast entrance to Powderhorn Park	Intermediate	9,100	1,900	8
46	Powderhorn Park	46A	46C	Cabin below Robbers Roost	Intermediate	9,100	1,900	13
46	Powderhorn Park	46A	46D	Junction with Calf Creek Plateau Trail	Experienced	9,100	2,900	16
47	Heart Lake	47A	47C	Heart Lake	Intermediate	10,500	1,200	9
48	Squaw Creek	48A	48C	Five miles from Trailhead along Squaw Creek Trail	Beginner	9,400	800	10
48	Squaw Creek	48A	48D	Junction with Fern Creek Cutoff Trail along Fern Creek Trail	Intermediate	9,400	2,400	9
49	Weminuche Pass	49A	49B	Weminuche Pass	Intermediate	9,400	1,200	11
50	Ute Creek	50A	50B	Beaver pond	Beginner	9,500	500	8
50	Ute Creek	50A	50C	Black Lake	Intermediate	9,500	1,400	14
51	Lost Trail Creek	51A	51C	Lost Trail Creek Crossing	Beginner	9,800	800	5
51	Lost Trail Creek	51A	51G	Heart Lake	Intermediate	9,800	1,900	10
51	Lost Trail Creek	51A	51J	Carson Saddle	Experienced	9,800	2,500	16
51	Lost Trail Creek	51A	51I	Colorado Trail via West Lost Trail Creek Trail	Experienced	9,800	2,600	19
51	Lost Trail Creek	51A	51D	Pond at lower West Lost Trail Creek Basin	Intermediate	9,800	1,400	10

INDEX